Perspectives in Interactional Psychology

Perspectives in Interactional Psychology

Edited by
Lawrence A. Pervin
Rutgers University
New Brunswick, New Jersey

and

Michael Lewis
Institute for the Study of Exceptional Children
Educational Testing Service
Princeton, New Jersey

Plenum Press · New York and London

Library of Congress Cataloging in Publication Data

Main entry under title:

Perspectives in interactional psychology.

Includes bibliographies and index.
1. Psychology – Philosophy. 2. Personality and situation. 3. Personality and culture. 4. Genetic psychology. I. Pervin, Lawrence A. II. Lewis, Michael, 1937 (Jan. 10)-
[DNLM: 1. Behavior. 2. Internal–external control. 3. Psychology. BF121 P464]
BF38.P42 150'.19'2 78-13514
ISBN 0-306-31146-1

Acknowledgment

Parts of the chapter by Paul L. Wachtel were excerpted from *Psychoanalysis and Behavior Therapy: Toward an Integration,* © 1977, by Paul L. Wachtel, Basic Books, Inc., Publishers, New York, New York.

A Division of Plenum Publishing Corporation
227 West 17th Street, New York, N.Y. 10011

Printed in the United States of America

This volume is dedicated to the memory of

Professor Klaus Riegel

who died during the preparation of this book, leaving the chapter found herein as one of his last works. This dedication is particularly fitting given his commitment to the integration of human potential with human culture as one of the most important aspects of psychological inquiry.

Contributors

C. Daniel Batson, *Department of Psychology, University of Kansas, Lawrence, Kansas*

Louise Carter-Saltzman, *Department of Psychology, University of Washington, Seattle, Washington*

Jay S. Coke, *Department of Psychology, University of Kansas, Lawrence, Kansas*

John M. Darley, *Department of Psychology, Princeton University, Princeton, New Jersey*

Jean Edwards, *Department of Psychology, York University, Toronto, Ontario, Canada*

Norman S. Endler, *Department of Psychology, York University, Toronto, Ontario, Canada*

Raymond Launier, *Department of Psychology, University of California, Berkeley, California*

Richard S. Lazarus, *Department of Psychology, University of California, Berkeley, California*

Michael Lewis, *The Infant Laboratory, Institute for Research in Human Development, Educational Testing Service, Princeton, New Jersey*

John A. Meacham, *Department of Psychology, State University of New York at Buffalo, Buffalo, New York*

Lawrence A. Pervin, *Department of Psychology, Rutgers University, Livingston College, New Brunswick, New Jersey*

Klaus F. Riegel, *Late of the Department of Psychology, University of Michigan, Ann Arbor, Michigan*

Jay S. Rosenblatt, *Institute of Animal Behavior, Rutgers-The State University of New Jersey, Newark, New Jersey*

Richard E. Snow, *School of Education, Stanford University, Stanford, California*

Ervin Staub, *Department of Psychology, University of Massachusetts, Amherst, Massachusetts*

Paul L. Wachtel, *Department of Psychology, City College of the City University of New York, New York, New York*

Preface

An old woman walks slowly up the hill from the store to her house. The hill is quite steep and the packages she carries, heavy. The two ten-year-olds watching her feel sorry for her and, moving toward her, ask if they might help carry the packages. They easily lift them and with almost no effort bring the shopping bags to the top of the hill.

After receiving all A's in his first term in college, F. finds that this term is much harder, especially his physics courses, in which he is failing. He has talked to his professor twice, but finds he cannot understand what she is teaching. "Somehow," he thinks, "if she could only present the material in a different way, I could understand it better!"

A month ago, as B. lay playing quietly in his crib, a toy key slipped out of his hand onto the floor. Almost immediately he turned his attention to another toy, close by, which he took up and put into his mouth. Yesterday, very nearly the same thing happened, except this time as soon as the toy key fell, he began to cry loudly, forcing me to stop what I was doing and retrieve it for him. It seemed in the first case that he forgot it, while yesterday, even though it was gone, out of his sight, he still remembered it and wished it back.

These three examples of diverse human behavior point to the central theme of this volume, namely, the causes of behavior. For some, behavior is primarily determined by the biological–maturational process. Altruism, scholastic performance, and developmental stages are all primarily controlled by some internal process, having some biological–genetic explanation. For others, human behavior is controlled almost solely by the culture in which the behavior is emitted. Such a view of behavior control utilizes such principles as cultural relativity, age standards, and learned behavior. Both positions, and the view of humankind that they underlie, find strong adherents, and the models that are produced in their behalf strongly influence our lives. Yet, there are other views that need articulation so that the debate remains fluid and even.

For us, the model of humankind that both fits our personal view and the data is that of the interaction between the two: the interaction between human potential and human culture. The purpose of this volume is to present to the reader that view. We have chosen a set of scholars who represent diverse interests within the field of psychology. Each presents the interactional viewpoint; thus, although the content differs from chapter to chapter within the volume, the theme remains the same: to wit, the resolution of the internal–external conflict through the interactional approach.

The diversity of themes within this viewpoint, each by an expert, gives the reader the opportunity to examine the problem as it affects the entire psychology inquiry. Thus, there are chapters on development, personality, education, biosocial and social psychology, and psychopathology. The integration of such diversity cannot rest within the content that each contributor offers. Rather, it must rest with the central viewpoint of this volume. Simply stated, it remains that human behavior is the interaction between the biological and cultural forces that from birth to death shape our lives.

LAWRENCE A. PERVIN
MICHAEL LEWIS

Contents

Overview of the Internal–External Issue

Lawrence A. Pervin and Michael Lewis

This chapter begins with a discussion of the internal-external issue in psychology—the tendency to emphasize characteristics that are part of the organism and thereby internal to it, or characteristics that are part of the environment and thereby external to the organism, in explaining behavior. While virtually all psychologists recognize the importance of both organism and environment, the tendency within virtually all fields of psychology—perception, learning, cognition, personality, social psychology, developmental psychology—has been to emphasize and focus virtual exclusive attention on one or the other set of determinants. Thus, it is that an outstanding psychologist such as Jenkins (1974) can describe a virtual conversion experience, suggesting that we throw out the old, mechanistic, associationism theory of memory and recognize that experience is the result of the interaction between the experiencer and the world.

Not only do psychologists tend to emphasize one or the other set of determinants, but such emphases tend to be associated with different views of the person (i.e., Locke-Kant, passive-active), and with different views about how and where research should be conducted (Broadbent, 1973; Cronbach, 1957; Harré and Secord, 1973). Finally, one may note that at times differing emphases on the determinants of behavior appear to be associated with differing political and social ideologies. Broadbent (1973), after contrasting "active" and "passive" theories of perception (i.e., those that emphasize perception in terms of hypotheses or models within the organism as opposed to those that emphasize perception in terms of stimulation by the outside world),

Lawrence A. Pervin • Department of Psychology, Rutgers University, Livingston College, New Brunswick, New Jersey 08903. Michael Lewis • The Infant Laboratory, Institute for Research in Human Development, Educational Testing Service, Princeton, New Jersey 08540.

goes on to suggest the following:

> I sometimes toy with the idea that belief in the various theories of perception might be associated with belief in the corresponding theories of scientific method, and also of politics. Just possibly, all believers in pure positivism might also support the passive theory of perception, and also support a political theory in which control by the environment was dominant. Just possibly, belief in a single strong political ideology might encourage a belief in rationalism rather than empiricism in science, and in the active organization of perception by the man himself. (1973, p. 38)

There is evidence that an interactional view is becoming the zeitgeist in personality research and theory (Endler and Magnusson, 1976; Magnusson and Endler, 1977), and also is becoming an increasingly important emphasis in other parts of psychology: social psychology (Argyle and Little, 1972; Harré and Secord, 1973; Schachter, 1964); organizational psychology (Frederiksen, Jensen, and Beaton, 1972; Kohn and Schooler, 1973; Vroom, 1964); psychotherapy (Bandura, 1969; Goldstein and Stein, 1976; Sloane, Staples, Cristol, Yorkston, and Whipple, 1975); and perception (Broadbent, 1973). There appears to be increasing recognition that behavior is almost always a complex interaction between organism and environment and that as one moves up the scale phylogenetically, the complexity of organism—environment or internal–external interactions increases dramatically (David and Snyder, 1951; Hinde, 1974; Wilson, 1975). In man there is enormous, though not unlimited, ability to adapt to and affect a broad range of environments.

Within the context of the current zeitgeist, however, there remain a number of problems. Most significantly, there is a danger that it may become so fashionable to be an interactionist that we never bother to examine the meaning of the term and the requirements of a truly interactionist theoretical position. Clearly, it is not enough to say that organisms interact with environments, or that internal determinants interact with external determinants, since, as we have seen, virtually all theorists take such a position. Rather, what is needed is a definition of the relevant organism and environment variables and a delineation of the processes of exchange between the two. The question of process, or how, remains critical to the interactionist perspective and one wonders whether any position can be truly interactionist without addressing this question.

In sum, throughout the history of psychology as a whole, and within many of its subdivisions, one can find evidence of competing emphases on internal and external determinants of behavior, emphases that reflect different philosophies of the person and get translated into different research strategies. There is evidence within many parts of psychology of a growing interest in conceptual approaches that stress the interaction between internal and external determinants. While representing a promising advance, the interaction perspective remains in need of considerable conceptual clarification, and its translation into promising research results remains to be demonstrated. It is to these issues that the chapters in this book are addressed.

1. *Developmental Psychology*

Developmental psychology has a focus and interest in change: first, a description of the change, usually as a function of age, and second, the processes underlying the change itself. In the first instance, the description of change, there has been much success with each succeeding generation focusing on both new ways of characterizing the change as well as considerations of the various domains of behavior. Thus, for example, the 1960s were characterized by interest in cognitive problems of thinking and reasoning whereas the 1950s were interested more in personality problems such as dependency and achievement.

The processes undergoing change are more central to the theme of this volume, namely, the internal and external determinants of behavior. This is so since the major theoretical positions concerning the process of development itself revolve around the two issues of internal and external controls of development and the resolution of this conflict by the utilization of theories of interaction and transaction. The models of human development that accompany these three views comprise the major themes underlying the study of change. Within developmental theory the view that internal determinants are preeminent in the cause of change is championed by the maturationalists who would argue, at least in the strong form of the argument, that change is produced by biological predetermination. Change can be characterized as an unfolding of this predetermined pattern, the pattern itself most likely being under genetic control. The influences of experience, learning, or reinforcement are minimal. Examples representing this point of view are often given that involve motor development; thus, the body turning, sitting, crawling, and finally walking sequence is seen as a sequence unaffected by experience and under biological control.

Models involving external influences as determinants of behavior likewise tend to stress a unitary notion as to cause of developmental growth. Models that rely on the proposition that development is a function of external influences usually center around traditional learning theory (Bijou and Baer, 1961, for example) or social-learning theory (Walters and Parke, 1965). These theories stress that behavioral change comes about through the reinforcement contingencies of the environment, the environment being either other social agents or nonsocial outcomes. For example, the acquisition of social roles, in particular sex-role behavior, has been argued to be a function of the differential reinforcement contingencies parents use toward sons and daughters (Maccoby and Jacklin, 1974).

The third view of development, the one developed by Piaget (1952) is the interactive model in which development is a function of both biological and environmental determinants. Within this broad view, namely, that development cannot be viewed from the limited perspectives of either internal or external determinants but rather some combination, there emerges a variety of models. Interactional models (Lewis and Lee-Painter, 1974) usually refer to models where individual elements are possible to discern and that interrelate so as to produce some outcome. Transactional models (Sameroff and Chandler, 1975; Lewis and Cherry, 1977) refer to models in which the individual elements making up the transaction are relatively unimportant and the focus of the study is on the transaction itself. While there exist important differences between them, these various models share a common belief, the importance of studying the relationship between the various elements or causes.

2. *Personality—Social Psychology*

As in much of the rest of psychology, the dichotomy between internal and external causes of behavior has a history within personality and social psychology. Indeed, the relationship (or lack of it) between personality and social psychology is interesting in this regard. Whereas the former has tended to be primarily interested in internal characteristics as dispositions of individuals, the latter has tended to be primarily interested in external characteristics or environmental characteristics affecting groups of people or people generally. Thus, back in 1951 Newcomb criticized the existence of two social psychologies, one emphasizing the organism and tending to ignore the environment, with the other treating the human organism as an empty receptacle and a passive recipient of environmental events: "My basic dissatisfaction in the psychological social psychology is that it has never really faced the implications of the psychologist's claim to study the 'organism in environment' " (Newcomb, 1951, p. 32). Whereas in 1943 Ichheiser suggested that the emphasis on interpreting individual behavior "in the light of personal factors (traits) rather than in the light of situation factors" was one of the fundamental sources of misunderstanding personality at the time, in 1971 Carlson was asking: "Where is the person in personality research?" Sandwiched in between was Murphy's (1947) emphasis on an interactionist, biosocial view that avoided an exclusive emphasis on the organism ("organism error") or an exclusive emphasis on the environment ("environment error").

While the issue of internal versus external determinants of behavior has a long history in the field, controversy reached a peak in the late 1960s in terms of the person–situation issue. Mischel's 1968 book, *Personality Assessment*, focused attention on issues that were brewing in the field and that needed both articulation and presentation of relevant data. Basically, Mischel was critical of traditional personality theories (i.e., trait theory and psychodynamic theory) for their emphasis on internal properties of the organism and the associated assumption of longitudinal and cross-situational stability of behavior. The trait theory and dynamic theory models of hierarchically arranged internal entitities were rejected in favor of an emphasis on changes in stimulus (external) conditions that modify how people behave in a situation and that result in relatively situation-specific behavior. Since behavior was assumed to depend on stimulus conditions, regularities in behavior were to be explained in terms of regularities in external events rather than in terms of internal characteristics. Personality consistency is dependent on stable environmental supports rather than on stable response predispositions in persons.

Mischel's critique of traits and dynamic theory was not entirely accurate or fair. Trait theorists such as Allport and Cattell did emphasize the importance of situations but held that traits were useful concepts for describing and predicting behavior when it is broadly sampled over a range of situations. Traits, then, were aggregate measures that could be more or less useful in predicting behavior in specific situations. Analytic theorists recognize the importance of environmental events and the difficulty of making either long-term, longitudinal predictions or predictions of overt behavior from an understanding of internal structures alone. Internal structures give a certain character or style to behavior while the multidetermined aspects of complex human behavior provide for variability in behavior and for occasional "out of character" functioning. At the same time, it is true that such positions failed to give systematic attention to external, situational factors and suggested a degree of stability and consistency in behavior that could not be supported by the data at hand.

Like so many similar issues in the field, the person–situation issue saw a period of vigorous debate of opposing points of view followed by efforts to bring the alternative positions together in some conceptually meaningful fashion. Block's (1977) critique of the situationist point of view is noteworthy in its suggestion that little can be concluded regarding the usefulness of traits and psychodynamic approaches from studies using poor designs and weak conceptual measures. His own contention is that results concerning evidence of consistency and stability depend on the research methods used and the data acquired. Thus, he suggests that well-done studies using observer ratings and self-descriptions or self-reports show indisputable and appreciable personality coherence and stability while studies using test data derived from artificial tests or laboratory situations have resulted in erratic evidence of personality consistency. It would seem clear that people are consistent in some ways some of the time (Bem and Allen, 1974) and that research conditions can lead to an emphasis on person effects or situation effects depending on the behaviors investigated, situations used, and the subjects involved (Epstein, 1977; Olweus, 1977). In this sense, the issue is clearly similar to the old nature–nurture controversy.

At this point, most investigators appear to be moving toward an emphasis on interactions between persons and situations (Magnusson and Endler, 1977), so much so that one recent reviewer of the field called interactionism the zeitgeist of the times (Ekehammar, 1974). But there have been interactionist positions in the past and perhaps for no other reason than this we must be careful in our evaluation of the significance of this recent development. For example, one problem that immediately arises, and that shall be considered in further detail later in the chapter, is that various personality and social psychologists mean very different things by the term "interaction." Thus, there is the danger of assuming a common conceptual or methodological base that in fact is nonexistent. Second, there is the question of units to be employed. Are we to use separate person and situation units, and if so, of what kind, or are we to use units that themselves reflect the relationship between persons and situations? Finally, there remains the question of processes or how. Some time ago Anastasi (1958) noted how in developmental psychology attention shifted from the issue of individual or environment (nature or nurture) to how much of each or proportions of the variance that could be accounted for by each. She then suggested that attention needed to be given to the question of how—how genetic predispositions interact with environmental influences. The analogy would suggest that the issue is not whether behavior is consistent or situation-specific, or whether persons or situations are more important, or how much of the variance is accounted for by person factors and how much by situation factors, but rather the issue is how characteristics of the organism interact with characteristics of the situation to produce the observed regularities in behavior.

3. *Genetic Psychology*

The term "genetic psychology" conveys little clear meaning since it has been taken to mean many diverse things. In its simplest form it makes reference to the genotype as the source for all behavioral activity and states that there is a perfect or near perfect relationship between the phenotype and the genotype. The variations between this relationship then become the grounds for the debate.

The strongest statement then would hold to the view that the causes of behavior X can be found in some genetic structure whose expression is likewise X. A middle position would argue that behavior X can be found in some disposition of a genetic structure to interact with the environment. Thus, behavior X is a function of genetic structure A and environment B. The discussion of the interaction between A and B in its general form becomes the more specific in the discussion of the amount or influence of genetic dispositions and environmental influence. This issue has made itself most recently felt in the discussion of the causes of IQ scores with exponents of the genetic view arguing for a genetic heritability coefficient of .80 (Jensen, 1969). This coefficient has, of late, come under some question (Kamin, 1974). Regardless of whether the value of it becomes fixed upon following the disclosure of Burt's errors, the notion of a fixed heritability quotient as a factor, independent of the nature of the environment, argues against this model of causality.

A more interactive model of genetic determinism has been proposed by Waddington (1962). In Waddington's view of developmental canalization the genotype provides a setting for development; however, any number of outcomes are possible, depending on the individual's experience. For some outcomes, only one pathway is possible while for others it may be multiply determined. Thus, a highly canalized aspect of development has only a very limited outcome whereas in a weakly canalized aspect there are multiple possibilities.

Of course, a still more interactive model would argue for a genetic environment transaction in which the elements themselves, environment and genes, were not divisible, but in fact so interrelated that the effects of each could not be measured. Such a model would have to argue that the genotype has no expression except as it relates to experience. Thus, for this model the distinction between genes and experience is without foundation.

4. Perception and Cognition

The domains of perception and cognition, having similar themes can, for the sake of our discussion, be treated as one. The study of perception and cognition, like other aspects of psychological enquiry, is prescribed by the particular model of the nature of man. In the two prevailing views man is to be viewed either as a passive recipient, being acted upon or alternatively, one who models his world and who by his actions affects his perceptions and cognitions. The former passive model is compatible with the position that there exists a real world and the function of man's perceptions and cognitions is to uncover that world while in the active model the world of experience and knowledge is the result of the interaction between the external world, however defined, and man himself.

The more passive view of perception is that the information within the external world is more important than the act of reconstructing the information according to the organism's plans or needs. The structure of perception, in this model, is thought to reside in the stimulus and not in the person, and while the organism may possess structures for uncovering the stimulus's properties, the properties themselves reside in the stimulus itself (E.J. Gibson, 1969; J.J. Gibson, 1963; Lorenz, 1965).

In the noninteractive view, while the organism very actively seeks and attends to information, he does not structure it himself. Gibson (1969) expresses this view as follows: "I assume with J.J. Gibson (1960) that there is a structure in the world and structure in the stimulus and that it is the structure in the stimulus . . . that constitutes information about the world" (pp. 13–14). Learning about the environment does not occur through an active process but through the organism's ability to extract information, for example, by recognizing distinctive features. Interestingly, representations of these features are stored and although the information is not reconstructed before processing, cognitions, occur.

Alternative views that also concentrate on the compelling power of the environment have been put forth by such theorists as Lorenz, 1966. The innate releasing mechanism (IRM) notion, much prevalent in ethological work, provides the mechanism whereby a stimulus, through some as yet undefined neural system, predisposes the organism to act.

The active model of man has been referred to as the constructivist position and holds to the view that perception and cognition are the consequence of the interaction between the organism and its environment. Bartlett (1932), for example, defined a schema as an organized internal structure that is formed by the active process of reconstructing stimulus information. The structures themselves are reorganized because of the interpretation of the incoming information, much the same view as that held by others, for example, Piaget (1952). Moreover, structure is defined as originating within the organism, not within the stimulus (Neisser, 1967). The active model of perception and cognition rejects the notion of a passive copy theory. Perceptual as well as cognitive structures are created through the interaction of the organism's internal structures and the external world. Processes such as assimilation and accommodation, disequilibrium/equilibrium account for the process of creating, the active construction of percepts and knowledge through the use of information from the external involvement that is then reordered, directed, and developed on the bases of past experiences, preferences, and expectations.

5. *Educational Psychology*

The internal-external dichotomy in educational psychology has focused on the role played in the learning process of learner characteristics, such as aptitude, and teacher or learning environment characteristics. While historically there has been an emphasis on the student or the teacher, the student or the mode of presentation, the student or the learning environment, during the 1960s there was an increased emphasis on the relationships between students, curricula, and schools (Pervin, 1968). This emphasis was well captured by Stern's observation, "An environment must be suited to the species; if it isn't, the organisms die or go elsewhere" (1962, p. 727). Researchers studying the educational process increasingly emphasized the interaction between internal person characteristics (e.g., cognitive style, needs, values) and external learning environment characteristics (e.g., degree of structure in the environment, organization of material, teacher personality characteristics).

Undoubtedly the most influential publication in this area was Cronbach's (1957) call for an integration of the two disciplines of scientific psychology, for consideration of the interactions between individual variations and treatment variations. Suggesting the development of laws of the behavior of organism-in-situation, Cronbach specifically focused on the practical problem of finding the best means of designing treatments to fit groups of students with particular aptitude patterns and of allocating students with particular characteristics to alternative treatment environments. Indeed, there was a libertarian emphasis to Cronbach's remarks such that the greatest social benefit was seen as being derived from an applied psychology that could find for each individual an optimum treatment environment.

While Cronbach's call for an interactionist approach met an enthusiastic response, the payoff in terms of research findings was not nearly as impressive. Berliner and Cahen (1973), reviewing the research concerning trait-treatment interactions in learning, concluded that "there is little experimental evidence that the area is as rich in factual information as anecdotal reports lead us to believe. Second, the studies that can be classified as trait-treatment investigations yield little reliable data" (p. 83). These authors expressed particular concern about the numerous cases where interactions observed in one study were not confirmed in another study. A similar point was made by Cronbach (1975) in his return to the question of the two disciplines of scientific psychology. Commenting on the attempts by him and Snow to generalize from the literature, Cronbach emphasized the inconsistent findings that came from roughly similar inquiries. His conclusion was not that true aptitude-treatment interactions do not exist, but that such interactions may be more complex and of a higher order than previously anticipated. A similar conclusion was reached by Hunt (1975), who cautioned against rejecting the person–environment interaction approach to education before it had actually been tried.

In sum, educational psychologists have attempted to go beyond Watson's exclusive emphasis on treatments and Thurstone's exclusive emphasis on individuals to an emphasis on person–environment or aptitude-treatment interactions. However, theory has not been able to progress so rapidly as had been anticipated due to uncertainty concerning the major variables to be investigated and to the posibility that, as Cronbach described it, "once we attend to interactions we enter a hall of mirrors that extends to infinity."

6. *Clinical Psychology*

Among other things, clinical psychologists concern themselves with the causes and treatment of psychopathology. Within both areas of concern the Freudian psychodynamic and Skinnerian behavioral orientations have served as competing internal–external models respectively. Thus, the Freudian has typically enphasized the interplay among various internal forces in the development of psychopathology (i.e., anxiety and the mechanisms of defense) and structural reorganization as the goal of therapy (i.e., where Id was Ego shall be). In contrast to such an internal view is the behavioral emphasis on behavioral deficits due to lack of environmental reinforcement and inappropriate behaviors regulated by maintaining conditions in the environment as basic to behavioral pathology. In conjunction with this, then, behavior modificationists seek to facilitate the acquisition of new responses and extinguish old responses through the manipulation of reinforcement conditions in the environment. Self-control, currently so much a part of behavior modification, does not refer to the control of forces inside the self but rather to the ability of the individual to affect those conditions in the environment that are involved in the regulation of his or her behavior. The "medical model" controversy to a large extent involves this fundamental difference in views concerning the relationship between internal and external determinants of pathology and behavior change.

What is interesting in this field of psychology is the movement of proponents of each point of view toward consideration of variables emphasized by the other point of view and the extent to which the importance of internal-external interactions continues to be ignored or given minimal emphasis. Within the analytic framework there has been an increased emphasis on cognitive controls as efforts to bring about an equilibrium between inner strivings and the demands of reality (Klein, 1970). The ability of the individual to regulate the balance between internal and external factors is now seen by some analysts as critical in determining the psychological well-being of the individual (Menninger, Mayman, and Pruyser, 1963). Furthermore, it is increasingly recognized that environmental, external factors must be taken into account in order to understand why and when an illness occurs and why and when it disappears (Voth and Orth, 1973). At the same time that some analysts are becoming interested in external factors, some behavior modificationists are becoming interested in what people say to themselves and in such internal phenomena as affect, imagery, and sensations (Lazarus, 1976; Meichenbaum, 1973). While important fundamental differences remain, the point is that there is increasing recognition of the importnce of both internal and external variables.

At the same time, it remains true that neither approach has tended to give much attention to the interaction between internal and external phenoemena. For example, there is the question addressed by Lazarus and Launier in this volume of how stress can be understood as involving an interaction or transaction between individual and environment. Or, on a broader scale, there is the issue of understanding how various pocesses of exchange between individual and environment lead to the development of psychopathology. The closest current approximation to such thinking would appear to be that of researchers of family processes who look at breakdown in one or more members as expressive of ongoing processes of exchange among members of the family system (Lennard and Bernstein, 1969; Spiegel, 1971). Concerning treatment and behavior change, it is surprising to note the extent to which interactions have been ignored as a basic, fundamental element of research in the area. If much of therapy is a learning process, then following Cronbach's (1957) suggestion, wouldn't it make sense that different treatment aproaches would be appropriate for different patients with different psychological problems? Obviously, the investigation of the interactions between external, treatment approaches and internal, personality characteristics represents an extremely complex matter. Yet, it is striking how little effort has been put in this direction of research, and one suspects that the cause of this has more to do with ideological splits between internal and external points of view than with the inherent complexity of the model of research.

7. Issues within an Interactional Perspective

In not asking ourselves to choose between internal and external, between person and situation or nature and nurture, we may appear to have made significant progress. However, one may ask whether such a perception is based on genuine achievement or on a shared platform of rhetoric. Unless we are prepared to confront the conceptual and methodological issues relevant to an interactionist position, our perception of progress may prove to be illusory. At least three issues appear to be critical. First, there is the issue of defining what is meant by interactionism. Related to this is the question of useful statistical techniques of analysis. Second, there is the question of the internal and external units to be employed in our research. Third, there is the question of the processes that are involved in the multifaceted interactions or transactions that occur between the organism and its environment.

7.1. Meaning of the Term "Interaction"

In reviewing the literature one may be struck by the many different ways in which the term "interaction" is used. A similar observation has been made by Olweus (1977) and by Overton and Reese (1973). The following distinctions among ways in which the term has been used are based on, though they are not identical with, the observations of these authors.

7.1.1. Descriptive Interaction. At times the study of two or more persons interacting with one another is taken as an illustration of interaction research. The confusion here is between a description of the phenomenon, social interaction, and a conceptual effort to understand that phenomenon. An illustration of the former would be an investigation of how schizophrenic disorders manifest themselves in interpersonal processes. An example of the latter would be how the nature of the social interaction that occurs reflects the characteristics of the participants and the context within which the social interaction is occurring (Lennard and Bernstein, 1969). Another example of the latter would be an effort to understand the process of interpersonal communication in terms of context, personality characteristics, feedback loops, and processes of reciprocal influence (Rausch, 1965). The point is that it is important to distinguish between descriptive interaction and other meanings of interaction to be discussed. One may or may not analyze social interactions in such terms.

7.1.2. Statistical Interaction. This meaning of interaction is the one used in analysis of variance studies. In the analysis of variance components technique used by Endler, the conclusion is drawn that "the interaction of subjects with situations contributes more of the variance than does either by itself" (Endler and Hunt, 1966, p. 341). This meaning of the term "interaction" is rejected by Olweus. He challenges the appropriateness of this statistical technique for addressing questions of how persons and situations interact with one another and suggests that the technique cannot be used as a test between predictions from person models, situation models, and interaction models. In addition, this meaning of the term "interaction" is rejected by both Olweus and by Overton and Reese because it suggests a relationship between two independent variables that can be combined or connected in relation to a dependent variable. According to Overton and Reese, the model assumes a plurality of causes that operate in a unidirectional way. Such a model is rejected as consistent with a mechanistic position and inconsistent with the organismic position espoused by these authors.

It is easy to confuse the conceptual approach of interactionism with a particular statistical technique, such as analysis of variance, because of the interaction term used in the analysis of variance procedure and because of the paucity of other techniques directly reflective of complex interactions. However, such a confusion is to be avoided for two main reasons. First, as noted, the presence of a significant statistical interaction may say little about the underlying relationships between the variables. Second, the absence of a statistically significant interaction effect does not mean that complex interactive relationships are not present among the variables. As Cronbach (1975) has noted, enormous volumes of data may be required to pin down interactions where one is not guided by strong prior knowledge. He further points to the need for systematic observation and exorcism of the null hypothesis, a point to which we shall return in the next section.

7.1.3. Additive Interaction. Here the term interaction is used in a general sense to refer to a relationship between variables that combine with or add to one another to produce an effect. As in the statistical sense, interaction here refers to two or more independent variables that are connected in their relationship to a dependent variable. The effect of each independent variable could be observed independently of the other, either in relation to the dependent variable under consideration or in relation to another dependent variable. However, in contrast with the statistical sense of the term, one need not be able to demonstrate this relationship through an analysis of variance procedure. Furthermore, the suggestion is that the two independent variables have a linear relationship to one another. Thus, for example, F. H. Allport (1955) refers to the view of some perceptual theorists that various factors interact to produce a single summated effect: interaction means summation.

7.1.4. Interdependent Interaction. Here interaction refers to two or more variables that can be independently measured but whose effects can only be understood in relation to one another. Since each variable never exists in isolation its effect is dependent upon its relationship to other variables. The relationships between variables may be linear but they may also be nonlinear. When a phenomenon is conceived of in terms of the effect of many interdependent variables, we are faced with the problem of a system, a complex network of interdependent variables such that a change in the status of one variable may have varying consequences for all other related variables. This kind of interaction would appear to be the essence of the view that we can never understand persons in isolation from situations or situations in isolation from persons, and of the view that the effects of heredity and environment can only be understood in relation to one another. It would also appear to be this meaning of the term interaction that calls attention to the question of "How?" or the nature of the processes relating the variables of interest. Instead of focusing on proportons of variance to be accounted for, as in the second model, or on the independent though perhaps additive features of the variables, as in the third model, attention here focuses on questions such as "How do persons and situations interact with one another?" and "How do genetic and environmental differences interact with one another?" (Anastasi, 1958;

Endler, 1973; Olweus, 1976; Overton and Reese, 1973; Pervin, 1968). While assuming the potential for independent measurement of the relevant variables, this model suggests the variables themselves never operate in isolation from one another.

7.1.5. Reciprocal Action–Transaction. The last model to be discussed would appear to be an extension of the fourth model in terms of the process emphasis but at times it is also taken to suggest new and different relationships. The essence of this model, apparently the one favored by Overton and Reese, is the view that the variables of interest are constantly influencing one another, the action of one affecting another variable that in turn affects the nature of the first variable. The position is stated as follows:

> external condition can never in itself be the sole determinant of an effect. Rather, cause and effect or environmental event and organism stand in a relationship of *reciprocal action* in which each member affects and changes the other. Here, then, we have reciprocal causation, or *interaction*, and this accounts, in part, for the organismic rejection of mechanistic analytic procedures which maintain that a complete efficient causality is possible. (Overton and Reese, 1973, p. 78)

This view is contrasted with the mechanistic concept of interaction presented as follows: "An interaction between behavior and environment means simply that a given response may be expected to occur or not depending on the stimulation the environment provides" (Bijou and Baer, 1961, p. 1). The organismic orientation of Overton and Reese places emphasis on the interaction (i.e., reciprocal action) between parts of the organism and between the organism and its environment.

There appear to be many components to the Overton and Reese rejection of the mechanistic model and emphasis on reciprocal action. For example, they appear to be rejecting all of the following: the effects of a single variable; a restrictive model of additivity–linearity; a model of unidirectional causality; and, a static as opposed to a process model. The essence of their emphasis, however, appears to be on the process conception; that is, what appears to make this model of interaction distinctive from the fourth (i.e., interdependent) model is that it requires consideration of a time orientation. The fourth model allows for reciprocal action, but since it does not specify a time or process orientation it does not require such action to occur. In fact, however, where a process of interpersonal action is relevant the fourth model would automatically lead to a reciprocal action view; person and situation are interdependent. What the fourth model leaves room for that is not permitted by the reciprocal action view is that one of the variables continues to affect the other variables without being changed by them. One could conceive, for example, of aspects of the person and the physical environment being interdependent in influencing behavior without the physical environment being changed by the process. In fact, however, it would seem likely that most processes of interest to psychologists are of the reciprocal-action type.

The models of interaction discussed above can be related to the analysis by Dewey and Bentley (1949) of differing interpretations of the causes of phenomena (Pervin, 1968; Spiegel, 1971). Here a distinction is made between interpretations of *self-action*, *interaction*, and *transaction*. Interpretations based on a self-action view regard objects as behaving under their own power. Interpretations based on an interaction view regard one object as acting upon another object in a causal way. Each such causal relationship may be seen as leading to the establishment of a fact. The view is relatively static since the relationship presumably ends when one has established the effect of one variable upon another, much as we do in our independent variable-dependent variable experimental design. Finally, interpretations based on a transactional view regard objects as being in a continuous state of influencing and being influenced by other objects. Essentially, then, transactionalism has three properties: (a) Each part of the system has no independence outside of the other parts of the system or the system as a whole. In other words, no one constituent of a relationship can be adequately specified without specification of the other constituents. (b) One part of the system is not acted upon by another part, but instead there is a constant reciprocal relationship. There are not cause–*effect* relationships but transactions that occur over time. (c) Action in any part of the system has consequences for other parts of the system. With regard to organism and environment, a distinction is drawn as follows:

> If interaction assumes the organism and its environmental objects to be present as substantially separate existences or forms of existence, prior to their entry into joint investigation, then transaction assumes no preknowledge of either organism or environment alone as adequate, not even as respects the basic nature of the current conventional distinctions between them, but requires their primary acceptance in common system, with full freedom reserved for their developing examination. (Dewey and Bentley, 1949, pp. 122–123)

7.2. *Units of Analysis and Analysis of Relationships*

While this description of transactional relationships appears to follow the emphasis given in the reciprocal action model indicated before, it also appears to leave room for consideration of a new concept, that a relationship defines the phenomenon itself rather than expressing the interdependent action of independently defined variables. In other words, there is no organism or environment, there is only an organism–environment relationship; there is no mother or child, there is only a mother–child relationship; there is no heredity or environment, there is only a heredity–environment relationship. It is not just that it is possible to consider such relationships, but that there is nothing but such relationships! Not only are they interdependent, but they owe their very existence and definition to one another. F. H. Allport (1955), who was very concerned with the issue of internal and external determinants of perception, gave serious consideration to the transactionalist view. However, he rejected it as an answer to the "inside-outside problem," suggesting that with everything participation there is no one to participate; perceived and object of perception must exist separately as well as being interconnected parts of the perceptual process.

Another aspect of this question concerns whether having defined a phenomenon in relationship terms (e.g., mother–child relationship) it is not possible to again consider it in terms of the interaction between internal and external determinants. Thus, for example, change in the mother or the child can be a source of internal stimulation and pressures from other members of the family or the surrounding environment a source of external stimulation. Lennard and Bernstein (1969) are concerned with exactly these types of questions in their study of family processes where one member of the family is considered psychologically disturbed. They consider the family as a unit and then ask how familial processes are affected by the behavior of an individual member as well as by the context or setting within which the members interact. The question they specifically address is how behavior within the family unit is a function of (i.e., interaction between) enduring individual attributes and specific social contexts.

Thus, whatever the commonalities among proponents of the interactionist viewpoint, we are left with differences concerning the kinds of units to be used in our research and the relationships among the units to be emphasized. F. H. Allport's inside-outside problem remains a very live issue.

7.3. *Nature of the Observations and a Time-Process Perspective*

We appear to be becoming increasingly cognizant of the restrictions that have been placed upon us by the exclusive emphasis on physics and logical positivism as models of science and research. Many investigators are questioning whether the emphasis on prediction and control, and on the manipulation of independent-dependent variable relationships, are the most productive directions for our research efforts. We increasingly hear calls for a spirit of inquiry and an emphasis on observation rather than an emphasis on proof. Perhaps the attention paid in parts of biology to description and taxonomy will provide a needed correcive influence in this area. Indeed, it is interesting to note here the increasing mutual interest between biology and psychology and the importance of biologists on biological thought in psychology today (e.g., Piaget, ethology, general systems theory).

The work of the ethologists would appear to be of particular significance in regard to the issues under consideration. First, in terms of conceptualization, ethologists such as Hinde (1974) continually emphasize the interaction between internal and external determinants in accounting for behavior. Complex social behavior is always seen as reflecting the interactions among variables such as hormone level, prior learning experience, eliciting stimuli in the environment and surrounding context cues. Second, in terms of locus of research, there is an emphasis on naturalistic observation and what Jenkins (1974) has called ecological validity. Such an orientation does not preclude laboratory experimentation. Rather, however, it suggests that the phenomenon studied in the laboratory should be relevant to behavior in the natural environment and that findings established in the laboratory must be checked against data based on *in vivo* observation (Bronfenbrenner, 1975; Lockard, 1971; Willems, 1973).

A third relevant point concerns the proper time perspective for our observations. The interactionist perspective, and the work of the ethologists, suggests the need for a broader temporal context than the single act (Rausch, 1977). If we take the process question seriously, then we must be prepared for long-term observations and appreciation of complex relationships. Much of our research to date has involved a freezing of behavior rather than a witnessing of the unfolding of behavior. Observations of the flow or stream of behavior give evidence to both the stability and the plasticity of behavior. In attempting to adapt to the environment, the organism expresses both efforts to preserve its structure and to respond to environmental contingencies. The behaving organism is constantly striving to preserve order in the face of changes in the quality and quantity of internal and external stimuli. Processes such as regulation, adaptation, and exchange seem to be at the core of organismic behavior and an understanding of such processes would appear to require long-term observations and a longer time perspective than is often the case in psychology today. Observation of behavior as process suggests that variables often indeed have a reciprocal effect upon one another and that the determinants of action at one point in the process can be very different from and understood only in the light of determinants of action at another point in the process (Ryan, 1972).

8. Summary

The above discussion can be seen to have a number of different issues associated with it. Some of these issues are inherent in the distinctions drawn by the various models while others appear to be byproducts of essential distinctions. At the heart of the various models of interaction are fundamental issues concerning the kinds of variables we consider, how we study them, where we study them, and the time span of our investigations. Among the questions raised are the following: Should we focus our considerations on the study of main ffects and leave the study of interactive effects for later or should we immediately jump to the consideration of interactive effects? Should we study phenomena in the laboratory where experimental control may be possible or should we seek to study phenomena as they occur naturalistically? Can we limit our consideration to additive, linear relationships or must we also consider nonlinear relationships? Can there be interactions in terms of kind as well as amount (e.g., interactions between coping strategy and kind of stress as well as between coping strategy and amount of stress)? What are the limitations of static investigations limited to a particular point in time as opposed to process investigations that consider relationships over a period of time? Is it best to focus attention at a molecular level or at a more molar level of analysis? Can all phenomena be understood in terms of multiple cause–effect relationships or are there relationships other than of a cause–effect nature? Of the models suggested, it would appear that the interdependent model of interaction provides the soundest basis for inquiry into these types of questions. Such a model allows for the independent definition of the variables of interest and consideration of various kinds of relationships among them. As noted, this model focuses attention on the critical question of "How?" or the process of interaction. While emphasizing cause–effect relationships, such a model recognizes that these relationships may be complex and involve multiple, interconnected cause–effect relationships. While allowing for investigations of reciprocal action or circular cause–effect relationships, the model does not insist that all interactions involve such reciprocal relationships of mutual influence. Ideally, the interdependent model provides the framework for statements concerning the complex processes occurring in relation to independently defined but interdependent phenomena. The task becomes one, then, of defining the units of the person and the situation, or the critical variables internal to the organism and those external to it, and then studying the processes through which the effects of one are tied to the operations of the other.

References

Allport, F.H. *Theories of perception and the concept of structure*. New York: Wiley, 1955.

Anastasi, A. Heredity, environment, and the question "How?". *Psychological Review*, 1958, *65*, 197–208.

Argyle, M., and Little, B.R. Do personality traits apply to social behavior? *Journal for the Theory of Social Behavior*, 1972, *2*, 1–35.

Bandura, A. *Principles of behavior modification*. New York: Holt, Rinehart, & Winston, 1969.

Bartlett, F. *Remembering: A study in experimental and social psychology*. London: Cambridge University Press, 1932.

Bem, D.J., and Allen, A. On predicting some of the people some of the time: The search for cross-situational consistencies in behavior. *Psychological Review*, 1974, *81*, 506–520.

Berliner, D., and Cahen, L. Trait-treatment interaction and learning. In F. Kerlinger (Ed.), *Review of research in education*. Itasca, Ill.: F. Peacock, 1973.

Bijou, S. and Baer, D., *Child development: A systematic and empirical theory, Vol. 1*. New York: Appleton-Century-Crofts, 1961.

Block, J. Advancing the psychology of personality: Paradigmatic shift or improving the quality of research. In D. Magnusson and N.S. Endler (Eds.), *Personality at the crossroads: Current issues in interactional psychology*. Hillsdale, N.J.: Erlbaum, 1977, pp. 37–63.

Broadbent, D.E. *In defence of empirical psychology*. London: Methuen, 1973.

Bronfenbrenner, U. Developmental research, public policy, and the ecology of childhood. *Child Development*. 1974, 45, 1–5.

Carlson, R. Where is the person in personality research? *Psychological Bulletin*, 1971, *75*, 203–219.

Cronbach, L.J. The two disciplines of scientific psychology. *American Psychologist*, 1957, *12*, 671–684.

Cronbach, L.J. Beyond the two disciplines of scientific psychology. *American Psychologist*, 1975, *30*, 116–127.

Cronbach, L.J., and Snow, R. *Aptitudes and instructional methods*. New York: Irvington, 1977.

David, P.R., and Synder, L.H. Genetic variability and human behavior. In J.H. Rohrer and M. Sherif (Eds.), *Social psychology at the crossroads*. New York: Harper, 1951, pp. 53–82.

Dewey, J., and Bentley, A.F. *Knowing and the known*. Boston: Beacon, 1949.

Ekehammar, B. Interactionism in personality from a historical perspective. *Psychological Bulletin*, 1974, *81*, 1026–1048.

Endler, N.S. The person versus the situation—a pseudo issue? A response to Alker. *Journal of Personality*, 1973, *41*, 287–303.

Endler, N., and Hunt, J.McV. Sources of behavioral variance as measured by the S-R Inventory of Anxiousness. *Psychological Bulletin*, 1966, *65*, 336–346.

Endler, N., and Magnusson, D. (Eds.), *Interactional psychology and personality*. Washington, D.C.: Hemisphere, 1976.

Epstein, S. Traits are alive and well. In D. Magnusson and N.S. Endler (Eds.), *Personality at the crossroads: Current issues in interactional psychology*. Hillsdale, N.J.: Erlbaum, 1977, pp. 83–98.

Frederiksen, N., Jensen, O., and Beaton, A. *Prediction of organizational behavior*. Elmsford, N.J.: Pergamon, 1972.

Gibson, E.J. *Principles of perceptual learning and development*. New York: Appleton-Century-Crofts, 1969.

Gibson, J.J. The concept of the stimulus in psychology. *American Psychologist*. 1960, *15*, 694–703.

Gibson, J.J. *The senses considered as perceptual systems*. Boston: Houghton Mifflin, 1966.

Goldstein, A.P., and Stein, N. *Prescriptive psychotherapies*. New York: Pergamon, 1976.

Harré, R., and Secord, P.F. *The explanation of social behavior*. Totowa, N.J.: Littlefield, 1973.

Hinde, R.A. *Biological bases of human behavior*. New York: McGraw-Hill, 1974.

Hunt, D.E. Person–environment interaction: A challenge found wanting before it was tried. *Review of Educational Research*, 1975, *45*, 209–230.

Ichheiser, G. Misinterpretation of personality in everyday life and the psychologist's frame of reference. *Character and Personality*, 1943, *12*, 145–152.

Jenkins, J.J. Remember that old theory of memory? Well, forget it. *American Psychologist*, 1974, *29*, 785–795.

Jensen, A. How much can we boost IQ and scholastic achievement? *Harvard Educational Review*, 1969, *39*(1).

Kamin, L.J. *The science and politics of I.Q.* Hillsdale, N.J.: Erlbaum, 1974.

Klein, G.S. *Perception, motives and personality*. New York: Knopf, 1970.

Kohn, M.L., and Schooler, C. Occupational experience and psychological functioning: an assessment of reciprocal effects. *American Sociological Review*, 1973, *38*, 97–118.

Lazarus, A.A. (Ed.), *Multimodal behavior therapy*. New York: Springer, 1976.

Lennard, H.L., and Bernstein, A. *Patterns in human interaction*. San Francisco: Jossey-Bass, 1969.

Lewis, M., and Cherry, L. Social behavior and language acquisition. In M. Lewis and L. Rosenblum (Eds.), *Interaction, conversation and the development of language: The origins of behavior* (Vol. 5). New York: Wiley, 1977.

Lewis, M., and Lee-Painter, S. An interactional approach to the mother-infant dyad. In M. Lewis and L. Rosenblum (Eds.), *The effect of the infant on its caregiver: The origins of behavior*, Vol. 1. New York: Wiley, 1974.

Lockard, R.B. Reflections on the fall of comparative psychology: Is there a message for us all? *American Psychologist*, 1971, *26*, 168–179.

Lorenz, K. *On aggression*. New York: Harcourt Brace, 1966.

Maccoby, E.E., and Jacklin, C.N. *The psychology of sex differences*. Stanford: Stanford University Press, 1974.

Magnusson, D., and Endler, N.S. (Eds.), *Personality at the crossroads: Current issues in interactional psychology*. Hillsdale, N.J.: Erlbaum, 1977.

Meichenbaum, D.H. Cognitive factors in behavior modification: Modifying what clients say to themselves. In C. Franks and G.T. Wilson (Eds.), *Annual Review of Behavior Therapy*. New York: Brunner/Mazel, 1973, pp. 416–431.

Menninger, K., Mayman, M., and Pruyser, P. *The vital balance*. New York: Viking, 1963.

Mischel, W. *Personality assessment*. New York: Wiley, 1968.

Murphy, G. *Personality: A biosocial approach to origins and structure*. New York: Harper, 1947.

Neisser, U. *Cognitive psychology*. New York: Appleton-Century-Crofts, 1967.

Newcomb, T.M. Social psychological theory: Integrating individual and social approaches. In J.H. Rohrer and M. Sherif (Eds.), *Social psychology at the crossroads.* New York: Harper, 1951, pp. 31–52.

Olweus, D. Personality and aggression. In J.K. Cole and D.D. Jensen (Eds.), *Nebraska symposium on motivation.* Lincoln: University of Nebraska Press, 1973, pp. 261–321.

Olweus, D. Personality factors and aggression—with special reference to violence within the peer group. In J. de Wit and W.W. Hartup (Eds.), *Determinants and origins of aggressive behavior.* The Hague: Mouton, 1974, pp. 1–36.

Olweus, D. A critical analysis of the "modern" interactionist position. In D. Magnusson and N.S. Endler (Eds.), *Personality at the crossroads: Current issues in interactional psychology.* Hillsdale, N.J.: Erlbaum, 1977, pp. 221–234.

Overton, W.F., and Reese, H.W. Models of development: Methodological implications. In J.R. Nesselroade and H.W. Reese (Eds.), *Life span developmental psychology.* New York: Academic, 1973, pp. 65–86.

Pervin, L.A. Performance and satisfaction as a function of individual–environment fit. *Psychological Bulletin,* 1968, 69, 56–68.

Piaget, J. (1936) *The origins of intelligence in the child.* New York: International Universities Press, 1952.

Piaget J. (1937) *The construction of reality in the child.* New York: Basic Books, 1952.

Rausch, H.L. Interaction sequences. *Journal of Personality and Social Psychology,* 1965, *2,* 487–499.

Rausch, H.L. Paradox levels and junctures in person–situation systems. In D. Magnusson and N.S. Endler (Eds.), *Personality at the crossroads: Current issues in interactional psychology.* Hillsdale, N.J.: Erlbaum, 1977, pp. 287–304.

Ryan, J. IQ—the illusion of objectivity. In K. Richardson, D. Spears and M. Richards (Eds.), *Race and intelligence: The fallacies behind the race-IQ controversy.* Baltimore: Penguin Books, 1972.

Sameroff, A. and Chandler, M. Reproductive risk and the continuum of caretaking casualty. In F. Horowitz (Ed.), *Review of child development research,* Vol. 4. Chicago: University of Chicago Press, 1975.

Schachter, S. The interactions of cognitive and physiological determinants of emotional state. In L. Berkowitz (Ed.), *Advances in experimental social psychology.* New York: Academic, 1964, pp. 49–80.

Sloane, R.B., Staples, F.R., Cristol, A.H., Yorkston, N.J., and Whipple, K. *Psychotherapy versus behavior therapy.* Cambridge, Mass.: Harvard University Press, 1975.

Spiegel, J.P. *Transactions.* New York: Science, 1971.

Stern, G.G. Environments for learning. In N. Sanford (Ed.), *The American college.* New York: Wiley, 1962, pp. 690–730.

Voth, H.M., and Orth, M.H. *Psychotherapy and the role of the environment.* New York: Behavioral, 1973.

Vroom, V.H. *Work and motivation.* New York: Wiley, 1964.

Waddington, C. *New patterns in genetics and development.* New York: Columbia, 1962.

Walters, R., and Parke R. The role of distance receptors in the development of social responsiveness. In L. Lipsitt and C. Spiker (Eds.), *Advances in child development and behavior,* Vol. 2. New York: Academic Press, 1965.

Willems, E.P. Behavioral ecology and experimental analysis: Courtship is not enough. In J.R. Nesselroade and H.W. Reese (Eds.), *Life span developmental psychology.* New York: Academic, 1973, pp. 195–217.

Wilson, E.O. *Sociobiology.* Cambridge, Mass.: Harvard University Press, 1975.

Dialectics, Transaction, and Piaget's Theory

Klaus F. Riegel
and John A. Meacham

1. *Introduction*

Overton (1976) has criticized those perspectives that subordinate scientific metaphors to scientific inquiries themselves. From such perspectives, the use of metaphor in the context of discovery must be followed by acts of verification, and the use of metaphor is permitted only until it can be reduced to empirical concepts. In agreement with Overton, however, we claim that metaphor is an essential part of the activity of science, guiding the relationship between scientists and the object of their study. As Overton (1976) himself suggests, the metaphors one employs to capture the essential character or image of one's object of study may have "a continuing determining influence on the formulation of more concrete models and ultimately on the types of theories constructed; the questions asserted as significant or nonsignificant; and even the types of methods preferred" (p. 76). In this chapter, the use of two metaphors, dialectics and transaction, is explored.

Dialectics has had a consistent influence in philosophy since the sixth century B.C. At first, it was employed as a method to generate knowledge by means of overcoming and resolving contradictions (Socrates and Plato). We prefer dialectics in a wider sense, as it came into use especially through Hegel's formulation, as a metaphor to generate knowledge and for theory construction. The dialectical metaphor emphasizes continuing activity and conflict, rather than passivity and stability. In particular, it explores the relations between individual development and cultural history (Meacham and Riegel, in press; Riegel,

Klaus F. Riegel • Late of the Department of Psychology, University of Michigan, Ann Arbor, Michigan 48104. John A. Meacham • Department of Psychology, State University of New York at Buffalo, Buffalo, New York 14266.

1973, 1975a, 1975c). The transactional model is also to be regarded as a metaphor, and not as an empirically verifiable concept. The transactional model provides a more concrete and specific focus upon the nature of the synchronizations or temporal coordinations implied by the dialectical model. Transaction and dialectics are consistent metaphors; the latter, however, is a more general world view and philosophy, encompassing development, activity, and history. We will present and illustrate these two models because the perhaps more familiar model of interaction does not provide a sufficient framework for our conceptualization and criticism of Piaget's theory. First, a further distinction between the metaphors of interaction and transaction will be briefly discussed.

2. *Interaction and Transaction*

The distinction between the metaphors of interaction and transaction (Dewey and Bentley, 1949/1960; Meacham, 1977a; Sameroff, 1975; Sameroff and Chandler, 1975) rests upon a consideration of whether elements or relations are assumed to be primary and which are assumed to be derived (Overton, 1975). As a typical example, Riegel (1970, 1975b) has pointed to the need for describing the communication process in terms of psychosocial relations from which the common linguistic units, such as words or syllables, are derived or abstracted in the process of communication, rather than in terms of words that are given and learned prior to the establishment of the relations by which the communication process takes place.

In the case of *interaction*, as defined here, elements are primary; they can be described and located independently of one another. The task for the scientist, then, is to inquire into the derived relations between such elements, that is, into the manner in which the elements act upon one another. In the case of *transaction*, activity is assumed as primary, and elements as derived and secondary within the system. In transactional models "systems of description and naming are employed to deal with aspects and phases of action, without final attribution to 'elements' or other presumptively detachable or independent 'entities,' 'essences,' or 'realities,' and without isolation of presumptively detachable 'relations' from such detachable 'elements' " (Dewey and Bentley, 1949/1960, p. 108).

An increasing variety of examples of the use of a transactional metaphor is found in the developmental literature. For example, Sameroff and Chandler (1975; Sameroff, 1975), in an effort to predict the consequences of trauma in infancy, have proposed a model in which the infant and the caretaking environment are altered continually as a result of transactions between the two. This model is contrasted with less adequate ones, such as main effects models, in which either constitution or environment is a factor, and interactional models, in which the effects of constitution and environment are combined additively to yield specific developmental outcomes. Parent–child relations are a most fertile ground for transactional models. Martin (1975) has called for moving beyond parent-causation models in the study of child development. Speier (1976) also warns of an implicit adult ideological viewpoint in much of our theory and research. Researchers "have neglected what we are calling the interactional foundation of human group life . . . instead of seeking to discover the interactional processes at work when children and adults say and do things together" (1976b, p. 170). Finally, Gutmann (1975) has suggested that the basic activity of parenting permits the derivation not only of the personality of the child but also of the adults participating in the transactional process.

2.1. *Remembering and Communicating*

For more detailed demonstrations of the transactional model let us consider briefly two cases: the relationship between the remembering person and his or her memories (Meacham, 1977a), and the dialogical relationship between two communicating individuals (Riegel, 1976a).

A commonly held view of the process of remembering is that the individual rememberer is a source of memories who remains unchanged despite having constructed numerous memories over time. The memories themselves are changeable. This view assumes an abstract isolated rememberer but neglects the impact upon the individual of the memories that he or she has constructed. As an alternative, a transactional model assumes at the outset a general system of activity, communication, and exchange. Memories are constructed in order to represent knowledge of past experience. As a derivative of these basic activities also a social context is constructed through the attribution of meaning to the environment. Thus, the system does not merely consider the individual rememberer but also includes the memories and the social context. Neither the rememberer nor the memories are stable entities, for both depend on the continuing activity of the system; as the system functions, the rememberer and the memories are changed. The relationship between the individual, the memories, and the social context is one of reciprocal causality (Overton and Reese, 1973). Memories, as products of transactions, act upon the individual, and change the nature of the individual's motor actions, cognitions, and personality (see Meacham, 1977a).

As a second example, let us consider the process of communicating, specifically the dialogues involving a parent and a child. Dialogues consist not merely of the addition of the independent contributions of two participants; rather, the contributions of the participants themselves are always intimately tied to the flow of the communicative transaction itself. Thus, the dialogue between a mother and a child requires temporal coordination or synchronization (Riegel, 1976a, 1977) that, at first, depends heavily on shared extralingual knowledge, demands, and affects. But, increasingly with age, the synchronization relies on their common language experience and selective cognitive operations. Their actions become finely tuned to one another, as they are derived from a shared transaction. A few weeks after birth, the child begins to look at the mother's face. When the mother moves, the child follows her with his or her eyes. When she speaks, the child looks at her mouth. When she stops, the child vocalizes and/or switches attention from her mouth to her eyes. The load for the child should be neither too heavy nor too light. Information has to be given at the right moment, in the right amount, and of the right kind. The mother has to speak, direct, and prevent, but she also has to listen and change her own activities according to the demands of her child. The synchronization of these derived activities, that is, the changes and the development of the child and the changes and the development of the mother, is of central importance in the shared transaction. The topic of synchronization of two time sequences is also a central issue from the perspective of dialectical theory.

2.2. *Comparison of Models*

Superficially, there seems to be little difference between the metaphors of interaction and transaction. For example, in considering from an interactional viewpoint the relationship between the individual and the social context, each may be considered to act upon the other in a unidirectional manner. However, the adoption of the interaction metaphor is likely to exert at least two limitations in theory construction and in research efforts (Meacham, 1977a, pp. 264–265). As explicitly recognized in Soviet dialectical psychology, often an insufficient role in development is attributed to such media as tools, verbal concepts, signs, memories, etc.; and further, the adoption of the interactional model makes difficult an adequate decentering from either the individual or the social context as factors in development (Meacham, 1977b). In the transactional model, on the other hand, activity is primary and both the individual and the social context have a derived status. Thus, the derived status of tools, verbal concepts, signs, memories, etc., is equivalent to that of the developing individual. Rather than isolating primary causes, a transactional model describes systems of regulation or coordination of activity through which various factors in development are interrelated.

Although we have tried to separate the terms "interaction" and "transaction" (as introduced by Dewey and Bentley, 1949/1960, and by Sameroff and Chandler, 1975) as much as possible from one another, both terms are often used interchangeably. Overton and Reese (1973; see also Overton, 1973), for example, have employed the term "interaction" as equivalent to reciprocal causation. In the present chapter, interaction is seen as implying unidirectional causality, with transaction reserved for models in which reciprocal causality is considered. Lewis and Lee-Painter (1974, 1975) have described an interactional approach to understanding relations between the individual and the environment, specifically the interindividual relations between the mother and the infant. Their use of the term "interaction" appears appropriate, both for their simple interaction model and for the flow model of interaction, in which both the child and the caregiver are defined independently before the onset of activity. In a transactional model, however, the child and caregiver would derive their characteristics following the specification of the relational activity.

Lewis and Cherry (1977) in considering intraindividual relations between language, social, and cognitive knowledge, have proposed a "Unified Model," which they contrasted with the elementalistic or reductionist model and with the interaction model. In the interaction model, "language, social, and cognitive knowledge are still discrete domains even though each affects the other" (1977, p. 5). Thus, their use of the term interaction is consistent with our own. In the unified model, "language, social, and cognitive knowledge are interrelated and dependent since all are aspects of the same unified development of the individual" (1977, p. 6). Thus, the unified model is consistent with the transactional model if language, social, and cognitive knowledge are understood to be derived from the more basic unified development (functioning or activity) of the individual. The unified model can be extended easily to include not only intraindividual but also interindividual transactions.

Lewis and Cherry (1977) suggest two versions of the unified model. In the first, consistent with the transaction metaphor, the interrelationship of knowledge domains is seen as "a dynamic flow in a state of constant change." In the second, however, the relationship between these domains is expressed as their "interaction," and is illustrated as an overlap of the domains. Such an image suggests, inappropriately for a transactional model, that the domains or some portions of the domains might exist independently of their relationship with one another, and expresses less adequately than the first model the extent to which the knowledge domains are derived from the more basic, overlapping activity or transaction. To summarize, within the transaction model, an ongoing activity or process is assumed to be basic, and individuals, their characteristics, and the social context are derived from these basic transactions.

2.3. *Models of Transactional Processes*

The metaphor of transaction calls for an analysis of activity, process, or functioning. What kinds of questions can be raised in the course of such an analysis? First, one can inquire into the *dynamic* itself, specifying not only the rate at which the process takes place, but also the qualitative aspects of the flow, that is, whether there is turbulence or perhaps stretches of relatively steady movement. For example, the rate at which various cognitive structures are manifested is found to vary between children raised under differing conditions of formal schooling and within differing cultural contexts. Similarly, the course of a dialogue between parent and child, or between teacher and pupil, may proceed steadily, or may be characterized by relative lulls followed by crescendos of exchanges. Second, one can inquire into the *consequences* of variations in the transactions. For example, a transactional model may be used to describe the exchange of self-disclosures between two persons over the course of time (see Pearce and Sharp, 1973). In this process, the number and intimacy of disclosures is likely to increase over time; however, deviations from this pattern, such as proceeding too quickly or too slowly, can lead, as a consequence, to the termination of the exchange (Fitzgerald, 1963). Third, one can inquire into the *conditions* that permit or set limitations on the transactions. Among the many possibilities that are conceivable here are that a transaction may proceed only if a certain condition exists, or if two conditions are met, or if first one condition exists and then the other, etc. For example, Kuypers and Bengtson (1973) have described a process of social breakdown during aging in which negative labeling leads to the atrophy of skills and to self-labeling as incompetent. The condition that permits this process to be initiated and to continue is role loss during aging (for example, upon retirement or widowhood) accompanied by vague or inappropriate normative information.

A further indication of the possible questions to be asked and models to be proposed in the course of an analysis of behavioral transactions can best be elucidated by drawing an analogy between processes in chemistry and these transactions. Certain processes in chemistry have been understood best by focusing not upon the reactants themselves, but rather upon unique aspects of the processes in which the reactants are involved. Similarly, the understanding of certain behavioral transactions awaits the construction of more precise models of the processes involved.

2.3.1. Seeding. By cooling very carefully a solution that has been heated while in contact with excess solute, a supersaturated solution may be obtained. For example, a solution of sodium acetate may be produced that has a concentration of the solute higher than what is the usual maximum concentration at a given temperature. The supersaturation may be destroyed and crystallization of the excess solute will occur by seeding, that is, by dropping a tiny seed crystal of sodium acetate into the supersaturated solution. Alternatively, a sudden shock to the container or imperfections on the sides of the container may initiate the process of crystallization.

Seeding may not necessarily be brought about by means of an element of the solute itself, but rather may involve only the provision of a focal point for, or a slight impetus to, a process that is latent. Waddington (1957; see Scarr-Salapatek, 1975) has introduced in this context the concept of genetic canalization, according to which a developing phenotype has available several potential outcomes. The force required to direct the phenotype in an alternative course of development can be very slight, depending on the degree of genetic control, the timing of the deflection, etc. As a second example, there are an increasing number of studies relating illness to stressful events in the individual's life pattern (Rabkin and Struening, 1976). These studies do not imply that a particular event, such as the loss of a job, may be the efficient cause in the later onset of a chronic disease, but the loss of a job may provide the focus for distortions in the processes of adaptation that, subsequently, increase the risk that the individual will become ill.

2.3.2. Catalysis. Some chemical reactions may be speeded by the presence of catalysts that themselves remain unchanged during the course of a reaction. For example, potassium chlorate may be decomposed rapidly into potassium chloride and oxygen by adding a pinch of manganese dioxide. At the end of the accelerated reaction, the initial amount of manganese dioxide is still remaining. A more familiar example of catalysis is the enzymes in biochemical processes, such as ptyalin in the saliva, which accelerates the conversion of starch into sugar. A special case is autocatalysis or self-catalysis; a product of the reaction serves as the catalyst to further speed the reaction. For example, in the reaction of permanganate and oxalic acid, the production of manganese ions permits the reaction to take place at an increasing rate.

A number of processes familiar in psychology may be interpreted in terms of catalysis. For example, in psychoanalytic therapy the patients often are said to be reacting to the analyst as they had reacted to other important persons earlier in their lives; subsequently, the analyst and the patients are able to learn about these earlier relationships that might have created the problem and, ultimately, led to the involvement in therapy. The transference is a catalyst in psychoanalytic therapy. Similarly, in group therapy one person serving as a scapegoat may act as a catalyst for more important group processes from which other members of the group may be benefiting. Strictly speaking, the therapist and the scapegoat are changing during these processes, unlike the catalyst in chemistry. Nevertheless, these changes are less significant in view of the outcomes by which the process would typically be assessed. Thus, as catalysts they are essential to the process but are not incorporated into the product and remain relatively unchanged at the conclusion.

In somewhat different situations, which may still be described as examples of catalysis, processes take place at the usual rapid rate only when certain limiting conditions are absent. One might refer to these conditions as negative catalysts. For example, the absence of racial discrimination may be an important catalyst for the processes of formal education; the absence of sensory defects may be a catalyst in the transaction between parents and children. A further example is given by Sameroff and Chandler (1975). Research on reproductive risk and caretaking casualty suggests that the long-range effect of trauma consists in blocking equilibratory processes or in interfering with the caretaking process. Thus, they call for "a change in orientation from focusing upon single events or even combinations of events, to focusing upon an understanding of the integrative and organizing capacities of the whole organism" (1975, p. 204).

Autocatalysis or self-catalysis is illustrated also by the production of verbal concepts, tools, signs, etc. that, once produced, constitute changes in the environment and act as catalysts for more rapid and qualitatively different developments at a later time. For example, the words amount, equal, order, profit, etc. might lead to a sudden integration of previously acquired knowledge that, thus far, had been disconnected. Similarly, the introduction of a statement by one of the speakers in a dialogue might suddenly remove a great deal of uncertainty, disagreement, and conflict and will, in turn, lead to the development of new ideas and new exchanges. The notion of generalized expectancy (Lewis and Goldberg, 1969), the increasing belief by the infant that his or her actions can affect the environment, might also be interpreted within a model of self-catalysis.

In summary, a chemistry that emphasizes only the nature and the concentration of the reactants, that is, those elements that are incorporated and changed from one time to the next, will not yield a complete understanding. It is only by including apparently minor and nonparticipating elements or conditions in the analysis that the entire process can be comprehended. Similarly, in the case of behavioral processes, what appear at first to be the most important factors leading to a particular outcome may be the least informative, and the least may be the most. However, the impact of minor factors becomes important only in the context of ongoing transactions.

Our discussion has touched upon a recurring problem in the social sciences, namely, that our input–output, additive models that focus on the nature and the concentration of the reactants can account for embarrassingly little of the variance in the resulting behavioral products. We continue to expect naively that large differences in inputs (for example, in compensatory education) will lead to large differences in output and that the specification of those major inputs or factors is our most important goal. However, we need to be more open to the possibility that in behavioral development, as in seeding and catalysis in chemistry, minor inputs in the context of ongoing processes may lead to major changes in what we observe as the products of transaction.*

3. *Dialectical Model of Development*

Consistent with the model of transaction, the dialectical model of development (Riegel, 1975a, 1975c, 1976a, 1976b, 1977; Meacham and Riegel, in press) emphasizes processes and activities. In this model, event sequences are seen as occurring along arbitrary but interdependent progressions that provide the conditions for development: the inner-biological, the individual-psychological, the cultural-historical, and the outer-physical. Development is determined by asynchronies between movements along one progression or by asynchronies in sequences of events along two or more progressions. When such

*An alternate perspective on the relationship between small inputs and large outputs is provided by the topological models of "catastrophe theory," which predict, for example, how a very slight increase in a fear-inducing stimulus may lead a dog to attack rather than to flee, that is, may lead to a dramatic change in behavior (see Freedle, 1977; Zeeman, 1976).

asynchronies occur, they manifest themselves in crises, conflicts, or breakdowns. At the same time they also generate opportunities for development as new coordinations are constructed. For example, events in the biological progression provide the conditions by which the individual is prepared for marriage and parenthood, but development results only if a synchronization has been constructed between these events and events on the psychological as well as the cultural progression. Thus, in the dialectical model, development consists in the synchronization of the activities within several progressions; it does not depend upon any one of the progressions alone nor upon any additive combination of events in two or more of the progressions. Within the dialectical model, activity or transaction is primary and the importance of event sequences in any one of the progressions depends on their relationships with event sequences in all the other progressions.

For a demonstration of the dialectical model numerous examples could be introduced, for example, describing the synchronization or the developmental negotiations between mother and child, brother and sister, husband and wife, teacher and student, employer and employee, and, equally convincing, between various social groups, classes, and generations. Before exploring some of these examples in detail (for fuller discussion, see Riegel, 1976a, 1976b; Hefner, Rebecca, and Oleshansky, 1975), we call attention again to the temporal movements in dialogues. In comparison to developmental sequences and episodes, dialogues represent short-term temporal transactions that, like developmental progressions, are dependent on at least two event sequences, that is, those produced by the dialogue partners in the negotiation of their discourse.

3.1. *Dialogues*

A dialogue has temporal structure because the speakers alternate in their presentation. Each successive statement reflects at least the two immediately preceding it, and has to be consistent with the speaker's own previously expressed views. Each statement must also represent equally consistent or systematically modified reactions to statements made by the other participants in the dialogue. If such a reflective coordination did not take place, dialogues would degenerate into alternating monologues in which both speakers merely reflect upon their own earlier statements without reacting to the other speaker's elaborations. The other speaker's statements would, thus, appear as distracting interruptions. If these alternations cease, too, we approach conditions that Piaget (1926) has described as "collective monologues," in which two or more speakers continue, uncoordinatedly, their productions on parallel tracks, comparable to the tuning of instruments before the music begins.

In contrast to monologues, dialogues are composed of triangular subsections that are called *dialogical units*. Such units reflect the dialectical character of the communication process. The original statement represents a *thesis* that will be denied, challenged, or modified by the other speaker. The second statement, therefore, represents an *antithesis*. Even a simple confirmation by a nod of the head is a dialogical response, and thus a challenge to the first speaker who will take notice of it and integrate this message in the form of a *synthesis*. But as this synthesis is uttered, the second speaker may propose a different interpretation that integrates his or her own former statement (thesis) with that of the opponent (antithesis). The contradictory relationship between any two statements makes the empirical description of dialogues exceptionally difficult. Traditionally, we are accustomed to categorizing observations on the basis of their identity or at least their similarity, but not on the basis of their divergence. For the analysis of dialogues, we have to do both.

The relationship between thesis and antithesis may vary widely. But even mere repetitions of the thesis, as employed in nondirective therapy, imply an antithetical challenge. Such a challenge cannot be comprehended, however, within the overt exchanges between the two individuals but has to be located in the conflicting experience of the listener who is forced into a double reflection about his or her own statement, once when he or she has uttered it, and once when it is thrown back at him or her by the other speaker. The result is an inner dialogical process that leads the person to improved self-awareness. In this case, too, the condition forced upon him or her and the apparent solitude that results reflect the dialogical character not only of the overt exchange but of each listener's internal thought process as well.

The dialectical process that constitutes a dialogical unit makes us also aware of the reflective character of all dialogical transactions. An antithesis is not merely a reaction to but reflects upon the thesis. The thesis provokes and anticipates the antithesis; the antithesis modifies and reinterprets the thesis. Neither can be understood without the other. And what holds for the thesis and the antithesis also holds for their relationship to the synthesis. Thus, each utterance in the dialogical exchange represents a thesis, an antithesis, and a synthesis at one and the same time.

If a statement never becomes a part of some outer or inner dialogue, it is of no interest at all and bare of any meaning. It becomes significant only if it is incorporated into a dialogical temporal structure. A statement in complete isolation is like sounds in the forest in the absence of a listener; it represents material conditions without an observer in a developmental and historical context. One might question with Wittgenstein their existence but as one begins to think about these sounds, they enter into an inner dialogical interaction and, therefore, gain meaning regardless of whether they "really" exist in the material world or not. All reality lies in the dialogical or, rather, in the dialectical process.

The development of the dialogue between a mother and her child depends heavily on shared extralingual knowledge, actions, and emotions. Shortly after birth the necessary synchronization of their activities is determined by their joint physiology that, though disrupted, continues to function in unison (like Leibniz's perfectly synchronized clocks). But temporal coordination will increasingly depend on the mother's and the child's experience and selective actions. Early in life the dialogues between mother and child are out of balance. Like an experienced musician, the mother has at her disposal a large repertoire of signs, rules, topics, and roles. The child has virtually none of these acquired forms of communication available. Thus, the mother has to be highly restrictive in her interactions with the child, and she retreats to the mode of "primitive" dialogues (Lawler, 1975). Only on a few occasions does she engage in conscious efforts at naming objects or giving instructions to the child. Most of the time she talks and sings along, and the child follows her activities and participates in them.

Most important in the mother's task is the synchronization of her efforts with those of her child. This is achieved in dialogical transactions with the child. A mother may become too abstract and remote; she may progress too fast or lag behind. In a more concrete sense, she has to speak as she tries to influence her child, but she also has to listen and change her own activities in accordance with the development of her child. Thus, the synchronization of two time sequences is of central importance, that is, the development of the child and the development of the mother.

3.2. Negotiated Development

The study of dialogues represents a concrete case of the investigation of dialectical change. It is concrete because it lends itself to observations and descriptions. The study of dialectical development and change represents the more general case, which is not limited to communicative exchanges based on language. But, like the study of dialogues, these changes are interrelated with at least two temporal sequences that may represent inner-biological, individual-psychological, cultural-sociological, or outer-physical progressions. Development results from the synchronization of any two and indirectly of all of these progressions. Taken separately, these sequences are mere abstractions.

Development and change do not consist in stages or plateaus at which equilibrium is achieved, but in continuing modifications. Critical leaps occur whenever two sequences are in conflict, that is, when coordination fails and synchronization breaks down. These conflicting or contradictory conditions are the basis for development and change. Stable plateaus of balance, stability, and equilibrium occur when a developmental or historical task is completed. However, developmental and historical tasks are never completed. At the very moment when completion seems imminent, new questions and doubts arise in the individual and in society. The organism, the individual, society, and even outer nature are never at rest and in their restlessness they are rarely in perfect harmony. In the following paragraphs, a few of the many possible conflicting or contradictory conditions, and the resulting developments and changes, are described.

Critical problems arise for individuals when events occurring on the inner–biological progression, such as illness, incapacitation, or death, are not synchronized with individual-psychological events. Nevertheless, synchronization remains a goal in these situations. Development occurs when a synchronizing reinterpretation has taken place. Crises may be prevented when asynchronies, for example, widowhood, are foreseen and reinterpretations are achieved prospectively. Inner-biological and individual-psychological progressions are not always synchronized with the cultural-sociological or outer-physical conditions. For example, inner-biological progressions lead the individual away from home to work, marriage, and parenthood (Riegel, 1975a). Synchronization can be difficult to achieve, however, with certain traditions or laws about marriage or with reduced availability of marriage partners after wars. Under favorable conditions, coordination is achieved, that is, individuals marry when they are mature enough and when the social conditions are conducive and appropriate.

Numerous forms of coordination may exist between two or more progressions along the individual-psychological dimension. The progressions within a family are quite dependent upon one another, and may often be crisis producing. For example, if a child is not wanted, difficulties and further changes arise for the child, the parents as individuals, and the parents in their development with one another. Progressions outside the family retain greater independence and flexibility, yet nevertheless lack of coordination may exist among relatives, friends, teachers and students, employers and employees, creditors and debtors, etc.

As illustrated previously in the case of parent–child dialogues, the degree of mutuality or symmetry may vary among individual-psychological progressions. The synchronization of the career developments of marriage partners, for example, has been achieved traditionally by subordinating the wife's progression to that of her husband, and so coordination was achieved asymmetrically, that is, at the expense of the wife's individual-psychological development. Liberation movements provide a means to change this form of solution. Development consists neither in the individual alone nor in the social group, but in the dialectical transactions in which both are enmeshed. The development and status of social groups depends on individual efforts, yet simultaneously these groups strongly influence the individual's development as they provide means of existence, of communication, and of organization, including laws and traditions. Crises result when progressions between individuals and social groups are not in synchrony (Riegel, 1975a).

The range of organizational units and the forms of developmental transactions at the cultural-sociological dimension are more extensive than those at the individual-psychological level. The family is traditionally the fundamental group. Although different families within the kin or tribe may compete for leadership, they also cooperate in order to provide a common welfare and security for the larger society. These functions have been taken over in part by interest groups, political parties, manufacturing companies, and business organizations. Of course, a variety of other groups and stratifications in society participate in these functions: linguistic, political, religious, economic, occupational, and scientific groups, and, most important, cohorts or generations. Each of these makes its contribution, through competition and coordination with others, until it is replaced in the historical progression (Mannheim, 1952). The crises created by the breakdown of coordination between groups often lead to new artistic styles, provocative scientific interpretations, elaborated manufacturing technologies, restructuring of economic systems, and new and more equitable social orders.

Outer-physical events, such as earthquakes, climatic changes, droughts, floods, and changes in energy resources, also have their impact on entire cultures. The task of societies, therefore, consists through new coordinations in protecting themselves and their individual members from these catastrophes. In summary, development results from the renewed synchronization of any two or more of these progressions, which taken separately are mere abstractions. Thus, the lack of coordination should not be viewed in a negative manner, for this provides the basis for the further development of the individual and for the history of the society. Only the inner-biological and the outer-physical sequences include events that appear as catastrophes to the individual and as disasters to society. But even here, refined structural transformations at the individual-psychological or cultural-sociological level will succeed in assimilating these disruptive conditions by coordinating them in a manner that gives meaning to every event in the development of the individual and in the history of society.

4. Piaget's Developmental Theory

4.1. Causes and Conditions

Our discussion sets forth two contrasting models that may guide inquiry in the field of developmental psychology. In the first, the interaction model, various inputs are assumed to add together to yield behavioral outputs; the second, the transactional model, emphasizes the activities or processes that may work to accentuate or to depress the impact of a specified input. Which of these models is the more popular one in developmental psychology? On the assumption that what is taught in our classes represents what is commonly accepted knowledge in the field, eight current introductory developmental textbooks were surveyed. Each of these was found to include, either as a section of a chapter or by division of the material into two chapters, a discussion of the "causes," "determinants," "factors," "influences," etc. in human development. But only two major categories were mentioned, namely, heredity, biology, or internal influences on the one hand, and environmental or external influences on the other. In some textbooks these categories are identified explicitly as causes, in others the identification is only implicit. Thus, the development of the child is said to be "caused" by heredity and by the impact of the parents and the surrounding environment upon the child. Even from an interactional perspective, such a statement is overly simple.

A number of inappropriate inferences and severe limitations in understanding are likely when heredity and environment, or internal and external determinants, are identified as causes. First, the reader is likely to infer that heredity and environment may act as independent causes, and that they may contribute in an additive manner to the course of development, leading to the conclusion common among undergraduates that the composition of intelligence is 80% heredity and 20% environment. Recently, this viewpoint has been thoroughly discussed and rejected by Overton (1973). Bee's (1975) *The Developing Child* is unusual and commendable in identifying not only internal and external influences on development, but also, as a separate and equal category, interaction effects that, as she cautions the reader, include not merely additive effects of internal and external influences, but instead complex combinations.

Most authors provide isolated examples to show that both heredity and environment are important, but no conceptual framework is offered to the students, indeed, it cannot be offered, for guiding them in the choice as to whether a biological or an environmental explanation is more appropriate, or in combining the two categories of explanations in an interactional manner. Of course, most authors would agree that these factors must be interrelated, but more than lip service is required to explicate their mutual significance. Once heredity and environment have been identified as independent causal factors, it is conceptually impossible as long as one continues to regard them as additive to put them back together again. Only a few of our textbooks include even a very general discussion of this problem (Anastasi, 1958).

Second, the typical textbook leads too easily to the inference that these isolated factors are themselves fixed and unchanging. In contrast, individual development needs to be seen within the progressions of history that provide a continually changing cultural context. In particular, Boocock (1976) has argued that much of our developmental research has been carried out under unusual conditions, for example, during a period of high birth rate, strong familistic orientations, and economic affluence following World War II. Elder (1977) has also recently reviewed historical changes in family structure and function and the impact of such changes upon family members.

In order to avoid inappropriate inferences textbooks should include an emphasis at the outset on the processes of regulation or coordination by which the various factors in development are interrelated, reserving the terms "cause" or "determinant" of development for those processes or mechanisms. Such a framework would be consistent with the metaphor of transaction. Although our discussion has been derived from the contrast between the metaphors of interaction and of transaction, our preference is congruent with that of Przetacznikowa (1976), who has called attention to the distinction between conditional and causal analyses of individual psychological development. The conditional analysis is directed toward an exploration of the biological basis of individuals and the exploration of the environmental conditions in which they grow. The causal analysis inquires into the mechanisms by which developmental changes occur. Conditions are not the same as causes; causes or determinants are "found in the whole complex of conditions and in their mutual interaction." Self-activity is one of the determinants of development identified by Przetacznikowa. It involves the adaptive regulation by individuals of their relations with the external world.

Given the framework adopted by many textbook authors, that is, one that neglects to distinguish between conditions and causes of development, and one that identifies only biological and environmental factors as major "causes," it is not surprising that Piaget's theory is often miscategorized and misunderstood. As Kohlberg (1968) has noted, even those who are enthusiastic about Piaget's ideas often adapt these to a framework different from Piaget's own. Piaget (e.g., 1964, 1966, 1970a; see also Furth, 1973) identifies four main factors that are required for an explanation of structural development. Three of these factors are compatible with those of other theories of development: maturation; physical experience (including logicomathematical experience that derives from actions performed upon objects); and social experiences (transmitted by the particular culture in which the child develops). The principal factor in Piaget's theory, however, and one that plays a fundamental role in regulating the other three factors, is the factor of equilibration. Equilibration is the process by which a balance is maintained in the child's transactions (assimilation and accommodation) with the environment. Thus, heredity and environment, in particular, are not independent primary entities or separately existing processes (Furth, 1973) as would be expected for the interactional model. In addition, equilibration is the process that promotes the construction of more stable cognitive structures. Thus, equilibration may be compared to self-activity as described by Przetacznikowa, and to the synchronization of the dialectical model of development (where, however, its temporality rather than its simultaneity is emphasized). Within the framework of the present chapter, maturation, physical experience, and social experience may be considered as conditions for development, while equilibration may be considered as the cause of development in Piaget's theory.

The categorization of Piaget's theory, with the equilibrating process as a cause of development, has been a source of difficulty in those textbooks that provide as categories only biological as opposed to environmental or learning theories. Generally, Piaget's theory has been considered a maturational theory rather than, more appropriately, an interactional or, better yet, a transactional theory, which is conceptually distinct from either biological or environmental perspectives (Furth, 1973).

Kuhn (1974) has reviewed recently a number of studies in which attempts have been made, from an environmental perspective, to induce conservation in nonconserving children. Success through some short-term experiential training would not be consistent with Piaget's view that conservation reflects a reorganization of cognitive structures brought about by the process of equilibration. Among the training techniques that have been employed with little success are the elimination of misleading perceptual inputs, provision of specific information that may be necessary for judgments of conservation, and training of presumed underlying cognitive operations such as reversibility. The only method of training congruent with Piaget's theory is that of inducing cognitive conflict (see Kuhn, 1974). The resolution of this conflict will then lead to the reorganization of cognitive structures.

In the perspective of this chapter, development occurs when there is a transaction involving the organism and the environment. One of the products of that transaction may be a change in the structure of the organism. As an illustration of such a conflict or disequilibrium, consider the concept of inclusion, which may be assessed by asking the child whether he or she has more brown beads or more wooden beads, when all of many brown beads and of a few white beads are wooden. Conflict may be induced by asking the child to put all the wooden beads in one box and all the brown beads in another (see Langer, 1969).

Thus, it is inappropriate to seek an understanding of Piaget's theory within an interactional framework, specifying causal inputs to the developmental process. The theory is best understood within a transactional framework in which the equilibration process is primary and serves to relate the various biological and environmental conditions to one another. To refer to our analogy with chemistry, for Piaget's theory a specification of the nature and concentration of the reactants is not sufficient; a formal description of the developmental process is needed as well.

A variety of additional examples may be provided in which specification of the inputs is inadequate to predict developmental outcomes: the college or professional football season, for which the composition of the teams and the schedule of games are known at the outset; jazz sessions, in which the players and their instruments and the music they will play and the type of audience are known; politics, for example, the American presidential campaigns, in which the strengths and weaknesses of the candidates as well as the preferences of the voters are often assessed far in advance of the election. Each of these situations retains an unpredictability and an excitement because, despite our foreknowledge of the inputs, there occurs during the course of the activity and as a product of that activity a reorganization of the team's spirits, of the musicians' and the audience's mutual appreciation, of the candidates' match with the issues, etc. At the conclusion of each of these transactions, the sportscaster, the music reviewer, or the political columnist may attempt to identify the cause of the final outcome, but the true cause lies, as Przetacznikowa (1976) suggests, "in the whole complex of conditions and in their mutual interaction."

Despite the contrast between Piaget's theory and nontransactional approaches to understanding individual development, Piaget has been criticized for not conforming sufficiently to the transactional approach. Wilden (1975), for example, has suggested that Piaget differentiates too sharply between the child and the environment, between the knower and the known, for a primary assumption in the theory "is that the child's first relation is to objects, rather than to information" (1975, p. 104). Wilden suggests that the child, therefore, is forced to overcome this artificial boundary. The problem of the boundaries, according to Wilden, constitutes the critical problem of the metaphor of interaction, rather than the boundary being recognized as a "locus of information and exchange." Wilden's criticism neglects the important role of activity, especially of logicomathematical experience, in Piaget's theory; however, he is justified in criticizing Piaget's general disregard of the cultural-historical dimension that derives from the transactions between the child and the environment. For example, what impact do young children with their constant questioning and their changing understanding of the world have upon other members of the family? Almost exclusively, Piaget's theory emphasizes the role of the individual as agent in the transaction. In his own words, "the subject performs in, sometimes even composes these plays; as they unfold, he adjusts them by acting as an equilibrating agent compensating for external disturbances; he is constantly involved in self-regulating processes" (Piaget, 1970b, p. 59).

4.2. Dialectical Extensions

Piaget's theory can be extended and incorporated within the dialectical model of development by deemphasizing the equilibrium model that describes the child's development as a succession of plateaus at which the cognitive structures are in balance. Interpretations in terms of an equilibrium model fail to explore the fact that every change has to be explained by the process of imbalance or asynchrony that forms the basis for any movement or development. Once this is recognized, the stable plateaus can be seen as transitory conditions in a stream of ceaseless change.

Piaget's (1947/1950; 1970a) work has been concerned primarily with the question of how children solve problems, in tasks such as conservation, grouping, and seriation. Children are asked to resolve conflicting or contradictory evidence. Rarely, however, does Piaget report how children come to question their earlier judgments and how they create their own questions. This preference for studying how problems are solved rather than generated, how questions are answered rather than raised, is derived from the commitment to an equilibrium model and is revealed in the experimental methods used. The experimenter always poses the question and asks the child to solve it. Little concrete attention is given in Piaget's theory to the question of how transitions are initiated, that is, how the child proceeds from the tranquility of balance within each stage to the next higher stage of cognitive balance. From a dialectical perspective, greater efforts in research ought to be directed toward understanding how new questions and doubts arise in the child, so that the balance is disturbed and the conditions are created for further changes and developments.

Piaget's theory can be incorporated within the dialectical model of development also by giving greater consideration to the implications of event sequences on the individual-psychological dimension for changes in events on the inner-biological and the cultural-sociological dimensions, as well as the impact of changes in these latter dimensions upon individual development (Meacham and Riegel, in press). Piaget's theory does not consider that the social context of development changes in a regular or systematically patterned way. There is increasing evidence that this development may be as significant as the development that occurs at a psychological level within the individual. According to Buck-Morss (1975), elaborating upon arguments by Lukács (1968), the cultural-sociological conditions strongly influence the cognitive structures described in Piaget's work. She notes a correspondence between the logical structures and the abstract, formal transactions of production and exchange that are carried out in modern, industrialized societies.

This view that not only the contents of the mind but also cognitive processes are dependent upon the practical activities under differing social conditions is consistent also with Luria's (1971, 1974/1976) conclusions based on a series of investigations in Central Asia during the 1930s, a period of rapid change in social and economic structure. With increased complexity of social life, Luria argues, cognitive processes become less concrete and practical in nature; they may be characterized instead as abstract, verbal, and logical. The impact of cultural change is illustrated dramatically in an investigation by Nesselroade and Baltes (1974), in which adolescent personality was found to depend more strongly upon the time of measurement, that is, upon cultural conditions and historical changes, than upon the age of the individuals being tested. The impact of cultural change upon cognitive development is equally dramatically documented by Coleman (1971). In past generations the role of the schools was to supplement what children were learning in their direct personal experiences by providing vicarious experiences, that is, through reading and from the teacher's own knowledge. More recently, however, television has led to great increases in the child's vicarious experiences, and with productive activities no longer found in most families there are fewer possibilities for direct action by the child. According to Coleman, the child's world has become information rich and action poor, a change that alters some of the essential conditions for development in Piaget's theory.

Piaget has addressed recently the issue of cultural change and its relationship to individual development, acknowledging that cross-cultural research can be useful in differentiating the roles of the family and of formal education in development (Piaget, 1966), and that the construction of advanced structures of formal operations may depend upon opportunities provided in work or by the demands of one's career (Piaget, 1972). In confirming these expectations, Sinnott (1975) has shown that performance on various Piaget tasks can vary according to the materials used in assessment, with the advantage to using familiar materials rather than the standard, formal materials being greater for adults of retirement age than for younger adults. The adults in both groups were highly educated, and so the question of how experiences and opportunities for development by these two cohorts or generations have varied is left unanswered. In summary, Piaget's theory focuses on individual development; the dialectical model of development is concerned with the processes of synchronization from which developments of the individual and of the cultural-sociological context are derived.

5. *Conclusion*

The purpose of this chapter has been to provide a framework for discussing developmental interaction and, in particular, to examine Piaget's theory of development from such a perspective. A distinction was introduced between two metaphors or models, interaction and transaction; the latter is stronger in its recognition of reciprocal causality. The transactional model is consistent with the more encompassing dialectical model of development. Transactions may be said to describe the synchronization or temporal coordinations between various dimensions of development. A second distinction, between causes and conditions in development, was employed to interpret development in Piaget's theory. Finally, the importance of mutual relations between the developing individual and the changing cultural-historical context was acknowledged and reviewed.

In conclusion, we can make a brief effort to answer the question, what is to be gained by adopting the metaphors of dialectics and transaction as opposed to the metaphor of interaction. From the transactional perspective, there is no need to isolate causes in development as, for example, heredity and environment, or mother and child, and then secondarily to be concerned with how these isolated factors or entities interact with one another. Rather, a transactional interpretation focuses from the outset upon the processes by which these various conditions of development are interrelated. Thus, our perspective is consistent with the unified model of Lewis and Cherry (1977), with Piaget's process of equilibration as a fundamental cause in development, and with the notion of self-activity as described by Przetacznikowa (1976).

In addition, we must also recognize the need for a greater repertoire of models to describe such regulating or coordinating processes. Some possibilities for such models may be seeding and catalysis. These models provide a contrast with traditional, interactional models, in showing how the relationship between inputs and outputs in development need not be necessarily linear. Indeed, the smallest change in the conditions of an ongoing process or transaction may in time lead to the greatest observable change in the products of that process. The dialectical model, in particular, calls attention to the need to include an account of the mutual relations between the individual-psychological dimension and the cultural-sociological context. Although in this chapter the consequences of events on the cultural-sociological dimension for individual change have been emphasized, the impact of individuals upon changes in the cultural-sociological context must not be neglected.

References

Anastasi, A. Heredity, environment, and the question "How?". *Psychological Review*, 1958, *65*, 197–208.

Bee, H. *The developing child.* New York: Harper & Row, 1975.

Boocock, S.S. Children in contemporary society. In A. Skolnick (Ed.), *Rethinking childhood: Perspectives on development and society*. Boston: Little, Brown, 1976.

Buck-Morss, S. Socio-economic bias in Piaget's theory and its implications for cross-culture controversy. *Human Development*, 1975, *18*, 35–49.

Coleman, J. Children, schools, and the informational environment. In M. Greenberger (Ed.), *Computers, communications, and the public interest.* Baltimore: Johns Hopkins Press, 1971.

Dewey, John, and Bentley, A.F. *Knowing and the known*. Boston: The Beacon Press, 1960. (Originally published, 1949.)

Elder, G.H., Jr. Family history and the life course. *Journal of Family History*, 1977, *2*, 279–304.

Fitzgerald, M.P. Self-disclosure and expressed self-esteem, social distance, and areas of the self revealed. *Journal of Psychology*, 1963, *56*, 405–412.

Freedle, R. Psychology, Thomian topologies, deviant logics, and human development. In N. Datan and H.W. Reese (Eds.), *Life-span developmental psychology: Dialectical perspectives on experimental research*. New York: Academic Press, 1977.

Furth, H.G. Piaget, IQ, and the nature–nurture controversy. *Human Development*, 1973, *16*, 61–73.

Gutmann, D. Parenthood: A key to the comparative study of the life cycle. In N. Datan and L.H. Ginsberg (Eds.), *Life-span developmental psychology: Normative life crises.* New York: Academic Press, 1975.

Hefner, R., Rebecca, M., and Oleshansky, B. Development of sex role transcendence. *Human Development*, 1975, *18*, 143–158.

Kohlberg, L. Early education: A cognitive-developmental view. *Child Development*, 1968, *39*, 1013–62.

Kuhn, D. Inducing development experimentally: Comments on a research paradigm. *Developmental Psychology*, 1974, *10*, 590–600.

Kuypers, J.A., and Bengtson, V.L. Social breakdown and competence: A model of normal aging. *Human Development*, 1973, *16*, 181–201.

Langer, J. Disequilibrium as a source of development. In P. Mussen, J. Langer, and M. Covington (Eds.), *Trends and issues in developmental psychology*. New York: Holt, Rinehart, & Winston, 1969.

Lawler, J. Dialectic philosophy and developmental psychology: Hegel and Piaget on contradiction. *Human Development*, 1975, *18*, 1–17.

Lewis, M., and Cherry, L. Social behavior and language acquisition. In M. Lewis and L. Rosenblum (Eds.), *Communication and language: The origins of behavior* (Vol. 5). New York: Wiley, 1977.

Lewis, M., and Goldberg, S. Perceptual-cognitive development in infancy: A generalized expectancy model as a function of the mother–infant interaction. *Merrill-Palmer Quarterly*, 1969, *15*, 81–00.

Lewis, M., and Lee-Painter, S. An interactional approach to the mother–infant dyad. In M. Lewis and L. Rosenblum (Eds.), *The effect of the infant on its caretaker*. New York: Wiley, 1974.

Lewis, M., and Lee-Painter, S. The origin of interactions: Methodological issues. In K. F. Riegel and G.C. Rosenwald (Eds.), *Structure and transformation: Developmental and historical aspects*. New York: Wiley, 1975.

Lukács, G. *History and class consciousness*. Cambridge, Mass.: MIT Press, 1968.

Luria, A.R. Toward the problem of the historical nature of psychological processes. *International Journal of Psychology*, 1971, *6*, 259–272.

Luria, A.R. *Cognitive development: Its cultural and social foundations* (M. Lopez-Morillas and L. Solotaroff, trans.). Cambridge, Mass.: Harvard University Press, 1976. (Originally published, 1974.)

Mannheim, K. The problem of generations. In K. Mannheim (Ed.), *Essays on the sociology of knowledge*. London: Routledge & Kegan Paul, 1952.

Martin, B. Parent–child relations. In F.D. Horowitz (Ed.), *Review of child development research* (Vol. 4). Chicago: University of Chicago Press, 1975.

Meacham, J.A. A transactional model of remembering. In N. Datan and H.W. Reese (Eds.), *Life-span developmental psychology: Dialectical perspectives on experimental research*. New York: Academic Press, 1977a.

Meacham, J.A. The decentration of developmental psychology: A review of recent books. *Merrill-Palmer Quarterly*, 1977b, *23*(4), 287–295.

Meacham, J.A., and Riegel, K.F. Dialectical perspectives on Piaget's theory. In G. Steiner (Ed.), Piaget and beyond *The Psychology of the 20th Century* (Vol. 7). Zurich: Kindler, in press.

Nesselroade, J.R., and Baltes, P. B. Adolescent personality development and historical change: 1970–1972. *Monographs of the Society for Research in Child Development*, 1974, *39*(1, Serial No. 154).

Overton, W.F. On the assumptive base of the nature–nurture controversy: Additive versus interactive conceptions. *Human Development*, 1973, *16*, 74–89.

Overton, W.F. General systems, structure, and development. In K.F. Riegel and G.C. Rosenwald (Eds.), *Structure and transformation: Developmental aspects*. New York: Wiley, 1975.

Overton, W.F. The active organism in structuralism. *Human Development*, 1976, *19*, 71–86.

Overton, W.F., and Reese, H.W. Models of development: Methodological implications. In J.R. Nesselroade and H.W. Reese (Eds.), *Life-span developmental psychology: Methodological issues*. New York: Academic Press, 1973.

Pearce, W.B., and Sharp, S. M. Self-disclosing communication. *Journal of Communication*, 1973, *23*, 409–425.

Piaget, J. *The language and thought of the child*. New York: Harcourt Brace, 1926.

Piaget, J. *The psychology of intelligence* (M. Piercy and D.E. Berlyne, trans.). London: Routledge & Kegan Paul, 1950. (Originally published, 1947.)

Piaget, J. Development and learning. In R. Ripple and V. Rockcastle (Eds.), *Piaget rediscovered*. Ithaca: Cornell University, 1964.

Piaget, J. Need and significance of cross-cultural studies in genetic psychology. *International Journal of Psychology*, 1966, *1*, 3–13. (Also in B. Inhelder and H.H. Chipman (Eds.), *Piaget and his school*. New York: Springer-Verlag, 1976.)

Piaget, J. Piaget's theory. In P.H. Mussen (Ed.), *Carmichael's manual of child psychology* (Vol. 1). New York: Wiley, 1970a.

Piaget, J. *Structuralism* (C. Maschler, Ed. and Trans.). New York: Basic Books, 1970b.

Piaget, J. Intellectual evolution from adolescence to adulthood. *Human Development*, 1972, *15*, 1–12.

Przetacznikowa, M. Conditions and determinants of child development in contemporary Polish psychology. In K.F. Riegel and J.A. Meacham (Eds.), *The developing individual in a changing world* (Vol. 1). The Hague: Mouton, 1976.

Rabkin, J.R., and Struening, E.L. Life events, stress, and illness. *Science*, December 3, 1976, 1013–1020.

Riegel, K.F. The language acquisition process: A reinterpretation of selected research findings. In L.R. Goulet and P.B. Baltes (Eds.), *Life-span developmental psychology: Research and theory*. New York: Academic Press, 1970.

Riegel, K.F. Dialectic operations: The final period of cognitive development. *Human Development*, 1973, *16*, 346–370.

Riegel, K.F. Adult life crises: A dialectic interpretation of development. In N. Datan and L.H. Ginsberg (Eds.), *Life-span developmental psychology: Normative life crises*. New York: Academic Press, 1975a.

Riegel, K.F. Semantic basis of language: Language as labor. In K.F. Riegel and G.C. Rosenwald (Eds.), *Structure and transformation: Developmental and historical aspects*. New York: Wiley, 1975b.

Riegel, K.F. Toward a dialectical theory of development. *Human Development*, 1975, *18*, 50–64. Also in K.F. Riegel (Ed.), *The development of dialectical operations*. Basel: Karger, 1975c.

Riegel, K.F. From traits and equilibrium toward developmental dialectics. In W.J. Arnold (Ed.), *1974–75 Nebraska symposium on motivation*. Lincoln: University of Nebraska Press, 1976a.

Riegel, K.F. The dialectics of human development. *American Psychologist*, 1976b, *31*, 689–700.

Riegel, K.F. The dialectics of time. In N. Datan and H.W. Reese (Eds.), *Life-span developmental psychology: Dialectical perspectives on experimental research*. New York: Academic Press, 1977.

Sameroff, A. Transactional models in early social relations. *Human Development*, 1975, *18*, 65–79. Also in K.F. Riegel (Ed.), *The development of dialectical operations*. Basel: Karger, 1975.

Sameroff, A.J., and Chandler, M.J. Reproductive risk and the continuum of caretaking casualty. In F.D. Horowitz (Ed.), *Review of child development research* (Vol. 4). Chicago: University of Chicago Press, 1975.

Scarr-Salapatek, S. Genetics and the development of intelligence. In F.D. Horowitz (Ed.), *Review of child development research* (Vol. 4). Chicago: University of Chicago Press, 1975.

Sinnott, J.D. Everyday thinking and Piagetian operativity in adults. *Human Development*, 1975, *18*, 430–443.

Speier, M. The adult ideological viewpoint in studies of childhood. In A. Skolnick (Ed.), *Rethinking childhood: Perspectives on development and society*. Boston: Little, Brown, 1976.

Waddington, C.H. *The strategy of the genes*. London: Allen & Unwin, 1957.

Wilden, A. Piaget and the structure as law and order. In K.F. Riegel and G.C. Rosenwald (Eds.), *Structure and transformation: Developmental aspects*. New York: Wiley, 1975.

Zeeman, E.C. Catastrophe theory. *Scientific American*, 1976, *234*, 65–83.

Situational Analysis and the Study of Behavioral Development

MICHAEL LEWIS

In the study of human development a great deal of effort has gone into the study of the measuring of behavior and its change over time. Even those studies sensitive to the need to look at the complexity of behavior and its interaction with other behaviors have failed, in general, to study the context in which the behavior occurs. Thus, while some progress has been made in increasing the level of complexity of the analysis of the behavioral flow through the use of interactional analyses (see, for example, Lewis and Rosenblum, 1974) little attention and still less systematic effort has been directed toward the study of the context in which the behavioral flow is emitted.

This lack of interest and information has been acceptable as long as the situations in which behaviors have been observed remain few, were laboratory based, and the behavior observed assumed to be invariant to situational constraints. Thus, help, approval, or affection seeking, all supposed measures of dependency, could be measured in any situation, and individual differences in the amount of behavior shown were reported to reflect an individual trait or characteristic. Likewise, the same case could be made for attachment behaviors. Differences in the attachment relationship between the mother and infant could be measured in a variety of situations, since attachment reflected an underlying relationship between the dyad (something akin to a trait on an individual basis).

Developmental theory focusing on the ontogenetic flow of behavior, its causes and consequences, has also been somewhat unresponsive to the need to take into account a situational consideration, that is, studying the context of behavior. In part, this was due to the fact that the thrust of genetic epistemology theory focused on the emergence of similar structures under different contexts. In fact, the major, important determinant of behavior, although immersed in an

---

MICHAEL LEWIS • The Infant Laboratory, Institute for Research in Human Development, Educational Testing Service, Princeton, New Jersey 08540.

interactional approach between the organism and its environment, has been the genetic unfolding of invariant sequences and behavior. As Riegel and Meacham have noted in this volume, this lack of situational or contextual concern, as affecting both structures and such processes as equilibrium–disequilibrium, has been a major theoretical obstacle in approaching the study of context.

Recently, some interest in situational analysis has appeared in developmental inquiry (Lewis and Freedle, 1973; Lewis and Freedle, 1977; Parke and O'Leary, 1975). In addition to this interest, there has been some concern about the issue of field versus laboratory studies as the appropriate situation in which to study behavior.

While the exercise that some have set, namely, discussing the differences between laboratory or field work (in the case of humans the field becomes the home or school or playground), is an attempt to deal with situation or context, its scope is too narrow. The laboratory versus field research controversy centers around the belief in natural situations and natural behavior. The argument that having found the natural situations of the organism where one can observe the natural behaviors of the subject, negates the basic assumption that behavior is influenced by context and that there may be no one situation in which all behavior can be observed. The issue of laboratory versus field study is a limited case of the broader question of the role of situation. A situational analysis will be the focus of our concern, not because of its central role in behavior (see, for example, Mischel, 1973) but because of the belief that the understanding of development, in general, requires that we turn our attention to the interaction between internal and external determinants of behavior.

1. The Nature of the Stimulus

American psychology has, for the most part, been unreceptive to the study of the nature of the stimulus and has concerned itself as a discipline with the questions of categorizing, observing, and assigning meaning to organisms' responses. By ignoring or holding constant the stimulus it has been thought that through the careful study of responses it would be possible to understand and predict the organism's perception, motivation, cognition, and action within its environment. Much empirical effort can be characterized as the control of the stimulus and the observation of varying responses. In the traditional experimental design the *E* and *C* groups receive different stimuli (or stimulation) and responses are observed. In any such manipulative design the careful manipulation of both the stimulus (stimulation) and response was essential since a cause and effect relationship was being tested. While techniques for observation, measurement, and classification of responses were developed (a taxonomy of the responses), little attention was paid to the stimulus. In addition, there was a strong asymmetry in our procedures since the responses emanated from the subject while the stimuli were controlled by the experimenter. For example, it was the experimenter who varied the size or shape of the stimulus, while it was the subject who responded. This asymmetry is confusing since the causal relationship between stimulus and response demanded as much knowledge of the stimulus as it did of the response.

In 1960 J. J. Gibson reflected on this problem and our lack of concern about the stimulus: "It seems to me that there is a weak link in the chain of reasoning by which we explain experience and behavior, namely, *our concept of the stimulus*" (Gibson, 1960, p. 694). While Gibson had several interesting ideas about the stimulus and how we might set about studying it, his article caused little change in the traditional research approach. Not surprisingly, in light of the historical and philosophical context of the issue of the stimulus (Hamlyn, 1961), it was thought best to leave it alone.

More recently, Orne (1973) has challenged the traditional view that the stimulus dimension is and can be well controlled by the experimenter, independent of the subject. He pointed out that the mind of the subject and its past experience affects the stimulus meaning, and therefore the subject's response is dependent on the subject's perception of the stimulus and its meaning.

These problems have direct bearing on research with infants and young children as well. A decade ago Lewis (1967) was interested in individual differences in infants' responses to frustration. In this particular study individual differences in young infants' responses to the interference of an ongoing instrumental response was studied. Each infant was placed in front of a glass screen behind which a toy was presented. The infant reached forward, came in contact with the screen, and either (1) continued reaching forward and contacting the screen, (2) reached around the screen, or (3) stopped reaching and often cried. Individual differences became apparent in these six-month-olds, but what were the causes of the individual differences observed? It could have measured individual differences in response to a frustration or individual differences in motivation to get the particular toy placed behind a screen. The bright red truck might not have been of interest to some infants but of great interest to others. How could we be sure the response being measured reflected some attribute independent of the particular stimulus used? It would appear that there would be no solution as long as one saw the problem from the point of view of controlling the stimulus by using the same object (toy) for each child. While one could present many toys (the same) to each child, there might always be a toy that would alter the results. The solution could only be reached by concluding that the same toy was not the same for each infant. Having reached that conclusion, it was possible to vary the object but to control its sameness, in this case its interest and value. In this particular case each mother was asked to bring her child's favorite toy to the experiment. Thus, the objects were different but were the same along the dimension of value. Parenthetically, this procedure produced a set of problems itself since mothers brought toys they thought the research scientist would consider to be better, that is, more educational. However, the toys received were not the infants' favorites but rather the perceived favorites of psychologists.

This example makes clear that the control of the stimulus by using the same event may be no control at all. Consider the clinical psychology literature and, in particular, projective techniques. The very rationale of these techniques is based upon the premise that the stimulus event, a fixed and constant stimulus (as in a scene for the TAT or an ink blot as in the Rorschach), is not perceptually the same event for each subject. Subjects see different things although the event is the same; it is this difference that is reported to reflect some underlying psychological structure.

The interaction of stimulus and subject characteristics can be seen even more clearly in the infant perception and development field. Salapatek (1969) and Haith (1976) have indicated that the scanning ability of infants varies as a function of age, a finding reported for older children by Zaporozhets (1965). Salapatek (1969) has demonstrated an increase in whole-part perception with younger infants engaging in less whole perception. For example, given a triangle they are more likely to fixate on an angle than to scan the whole figure. Haith (1976) has shown a similar finding for faces; the contour of a face is scanned initially and only after five weeks of age do infants fixate on the internal features. These developmental changes in what the infant fixates upon when an entire stimulus is presented must have important implications for the understanding of the meaning of their responses.

Consider that the problem under study involves the change in infants' responses to a stimulus as a function of age; it is found that a two-day-old infant responds differently from a two-month-old infant. Since each has been presented with the same stimulus, the difference in response has something to do with some aspect of an age x response dimension; perhaps increased cognition or some explanation such as this would be offered. Careful analysis, however, would reveal that although the same stimulus event was presented to each aged child—thus, differences in response were age related—it in fact turns out that it is not the same stimulus. In particular, imagine that the perception of the eyes elicits a smile from the infant. In the preceding example, the two-day-old does not smile while the two-month-old does. Age differences in smiling would have been assumed since the stimulus was the same. We know, however, that this was not the case. If the neonate did look at the eyes, it might have smiled.

Few would disagree that in any stimulus–response paradigm, the nature and meaning of the stimulus must receive appropriate attention. To understand behavior we must understand the context of that behavior. The stimulus cannot be taken for granted.

2. *Toward a Taxonomy of Situations*

Once having perceived that the problem lies in the emphasis on responses rather than stimuli, it becomes necessary to address the issue of the stimulus. For the purpose of this chapter, let us center our attention on the situation, recognizing that stimulus, situations, and environments can be subsumed under the same general problem (see, for example, Frederiksen, 1972; Lowenthal 1972; and a review by Pervin, 1975).

What is necessary is the development of a taxonomy of situations. This study of the situation is not an easy task and is full of complications (see, for example, Murray, 1938; Pervin, 1968; Mischel, 1973). First, everything must be included. Pavlov, as noted in Gibson (1960), believed that a "stimulus (in our case, situation can be substituted) could be anything in the terrestrial world," a rather inclusive statement. Given the first problem of the inclusive nature of our problem, the second problem offers us little relief.

This is the problem of who shall define this taxonomy. Barker (1965), Rotter (1955), and Sells (1963), for example, hold to the view that the situation can be defined in objective and measurable characteristics. Barker, for example, would have the experimenter define the situation in terms of a room size as an example of a measurable characteristic. The alternative approach would be to define the situation in terms of the subject's perception of it (Endler and Magnusson, 1974). In this approach one would wish to study how the organism characterizes its world and that any situation must be specified in terms of the particular organism experiencing it (Bowers, 1973). A middle position would argue for some interaction between the situation as is and the organism's perception of it. While we will not pursue this issue, it is necessary to consider that these various views of the stimulus or situation carry with them concomitant ways of characterizing it.

If the conception of the environment is "real," existing independent of the organism's perception of it, then there is no reason to ask the subject to define the stimulus. In this case, it becomes the experimenter who defines these situations. If, on the other hand, the situation exists only as the subject experiences it, the definition or characterization requires the organism's participation.

Independent of these considerations is the issue of how the situation should be defined. For example, it is possible to define the situation in terms of its physical properties. These properties themselves could vary along several dimensions, for example, temperature, area, etc. Situations can be defined in terms of *location*, such as rooms or buildings. Daily activities, such as washing, going to bed, etc., or *adaptation* functions are still other methods of dividing situation. *Requirements* of situations, *skills* involved or *affect* elicited, are still other dimensions. Finally, *people involved* in the situation would be another. For this consideration, classification across specific dimensions or combinations would be possible, and in addition it would seem that certain dimensions might be more interrelated than others. Recently Pervin (1975) has undertaken some exploration of some of these dimensions and their interrelatedness; however, the enormity of the problem remains. The taxonomy of situations involves an enormous problem at both the levels of characterization and interrelationship.

One solution to this problem is to characterize the situation in relation to the particular problem to be studied. The taxonomy or methods derived will not fit all cases and thereby represent only a limited solution. Nevertheless, until more empirical attempts are made the problem will remain at its abstract and unusable level.

The issues of objective versus perceived classification of the situation and the manner of classification (dimensions) has been shown to be complex. The consideration of situation in perceived terms is extremely hazardous with adult subjects; with infants and young children, the subjects of our interest and study, it is impossible. For this reason, the choice of perceived situation must be left to the caregiver; unfortunately, this has not been undertaken. More often the experimenter defines the situation. As for the dimensions of classification, a combination of location, function, and activity has been chosen in the study of mother–infant interaction, the subject of the examples to be presented.

3. *Situation Analysis in Mother–Infant Interaction*

There were several alternatives in how to approach and define the concept of situation in the study of the mother–infant relationship. For the study of communication it was necessary to characterize the setting with respect to early vocalization of very young infants.

One method was to take note of those locations that our culture says are significant (for adults, at least) and to assume that this has consequences for the infant, even though its behavior might not reflect any real differences across all the situations so defined. Another approach was to try to define situation objectively apart from cultural presuppositions about what is and is not important and salient in the environment. Since the isolation of objective features of any environment apart from any cultural value system has not been undertaken, this second possibility was not feasible.

Another possibility was to conduct elaborate studies of how adults seem to partition their world of experience, to objectively isolate (perhaps through some method as factor analysis) those dimensions of the experience that account for all the situations these adults experience, and to use these features or dimensions as basic concepts in defining the infant's situational experience. It would be necessary to accept on faith that such features will have the same perceptual impact on the young as it seems to have for adults.

In the Lewis and Freedle studies of the mother–infant communication system (Lewis and Freedle, 1973, 1977; Freedle and Lewis, 1977) we initially assumed the situation might be defined by the space in which the infant and mother were located. For adults, physical space usually carries with it a high degree of contextual meaning. Thus, a kitchen has associated with it food, eating, drinking, certain somatic sensations; whereas the bedroom as a space is associated with sleeping, quiet play, etc. With this in mind, the observation of the infant–mother communication system as a function of physical space was attempted.

Much to our surprise, it was found that the physical space or location by function of the very young infant was not yet differentiated by his caregiver. The child typically was not fed in the kitchen, played with in the living room or family room, washed in the bathroom, and put to sleep in the bedroom. Each of the activities most usually associated with a room in the house was performed by and large in any room. Physical space, such as a room, could not be used as a clear indicator of context. Interestingly enough, further observation of infants' activities in their home does reveal that by 12 months the physical

TABLE I
Some Potentially Important Aspects by Which Main Situations Differ

	Suggested critical features for vocalization							
		Distance between dyad			Function			
Situation	New sensory stimulation?	Large	Medium	Small	Social?	Other?	Free movement for infant?	Eye contact and gesture freely viewable?
Tub-table	Yes (water, powder)			X	Not	Clean	Not much	Yes
Jump-swing	Yes (proprioceptive feedback)		X		No	Mother busy	Semi-	Not necessarily
Couch	Maybe (texture)			X	Semi-	Mother rest?	Semi-	Semi-
Floor	Yes (rug, no rug, smells) (wide muscular movement)	X			No	?	Yes	Not necessarily
Mother's lap	Maybe			X	Yes	—	Not much	Maybe
Crib-bed	Intended lack of new stimulation	X			No	Rest infant	Not intended	No
Infant seat	Maybe		X		No	Mother busy	Not much	Not necessarily
Playpen	Maybe (toy, textures, . . .)	X			No	Mother busy	Semi-	Not necessarily

space as well as functional differentiation have been associated. This change over the first year speaks to important changes in the contextual relationship of space for the infant.

In order to study context another approach was considered. For this analysis the enclosure or where in a room a child was situated was observed and eight specific categories seemed to account for almost all of the observed time and, as a matter of pragmatics, these location-physical properties were considered; they were infant seat, playpen, mother's lap, crib or bed, couch or sofa, floor, changing table or bathtub, and jumper or swing. An "other" category was included to contain the few remaining cases.

Lewis and Freedle (1973) were interested in studying prelinguistic forms of communication in order to relate them to subsequent formal linguistic activity (language). They hoped to be able to demonstrate the occurrence, at least by three months, of nonrandom vocalization patterns as a function of situational context. They were interested in situational context because of the hypothesized possibility that meaning may initially rely upon the perceptual location and recognition of features or relational differences in the external world. Meaning is generated because the organism probably perceives such differences by noting a significant shift in the behavioral patterns that occur in different situations. It seemed, therefore, that an exploration of the origins of semantics could be found in the communication network of the very young infant by studying situational differences.

Before turning to the data generated by a situational analysis, consider for a moment the difficulties of choosing even an objective classification system of situation. Even here, the taxonomy is multidimensional.

Table I, taken from a paper by Freedle and Lewis (1977), presents these eight situations. Observe that they can vary along at least five continua such as new sensory stimulation, distance between the dyad, function (only social and other have been listed although many more would be possible), movement, and eye contact and visibility. Clearly, more could be thought of or the present categories expanded. Thus, even the restriction to location–space does not produce a problem-free solution to situation taxonomy!

For the purposes of the study of mother–infant interaction and vocalization behavior, two questions were asked of the situational analysis: (1) do these situations produce differences in the behaviors that are of interest (in this case, vocalization), and (2) do these differences by situation make any sense to the phenomena under study (in this case, vocalization interaction)?

One hundred infants were seen in their homes for two hours of

TABLE II
Mean Number of 10-Second Intervals Spent in Each Situation

	Infant seat	Play pen	M-lap	Crib/ bed	Couch sofa	Floor	Table/ tub	Jumper	Other
Total	100.9	29.2	288.4	118.2	46.2	28.0	62.5	26.7	19.9
Male	80.2	33.0	329.5	91.6	42.0	35.1	52.9	29.7	24.0
Female	121.6	25.4	247.4	144.8	50.5	21.0	72.1	23.7	15.8
SES I	111.8	18.8	231.8	204.8	51.0	19.5	54.8	12.0	15.8
II	108.5	11.5	222.5	163.1	44.2	48.0	60.7	19.1	41.5
III	88.2	64.8	308.4	75.6	30.6	38.8	68.4	27.6	15.0
IV	112.8	00.0	286.8	68.4	51.6	32.4	52.8	99.6	14.4
V	90.6	36.0	387.0	67.2	57.6	00.0	69.6	9.6	00.0

awake observation. A trained observer recorded by 10-second periods the occurrence of a large number of infant and mother behaviors. Figure 1 presents the scan sheet. Note the infant and maternal behaviors on the left; the 6 10-second periods run from left to right; and the situational coding in the upper right-hand corner. The particular coding procedure has been elaborated elsewhere (see Lewis, 1972).

Table II presents the amount of time spent in these various locations. A situation analysis reveals a distribution of time across these situations such that the mother's lap was the most frequent situation in the two hours of observation followed by the crib/bed and infant seat. Relatively little time was spent on the floor or in the jumper at this age. When these data are segmented by sex and social class, interesting situation-by-subject characteristics emerge. For example, over 54% of the observational time for the poor (SES V) the infant was in its mother's arms, while for only 32% of the time was this true of middle-class subjects (SES I). Interestingly, no SES V mother ever put her infant on the floor, while SES I babies were on the floor 3% of the observational time. Thus, situational observation differed markedly between individuals and groups.

Not only were there different situations for different infants, but these different situations had consequences for the frequency with which vocalization behaviors are engaged in by both the infant and its caregiver.

Table III presents these data. For example, one can see that even though the mother's lap is the most frequent situation it has the lowest percentage of infant vocalization of all the situations (17.1% out of the 288.4, 10-second occasions in which a vocalization could have been realized). On the other hand, some of the least frequent situa-

SUBJECT NAME ______________________

SUBJECT NUMBER ____________________

LOCATION

ACTIVITY

MINUTE NO.

Infant	0–10	11–20	21–30	31–40	41–50	51–60
1. Eyes Closed	A B C	A B C	A B C	A B C	A B C	A B C
2. Vocalization	A B C	A B C	A B C	A B C	A B C	A B C
3. Extra Movement	A B C	A B C	A B C	A B C	A B C	A B C
4. Fret/Cry	A B C	A B C	A B C	A B C	A B C	A B C
5. Feed — Bottle	A B C	A B C	A B C	A B C	A B C	A B C
6. Spoon	A B C	A B C	A B C	A B C	A B C	A B C
7. Play — Object	A B C	A B C	A B C	A B C	A B C	A B C
8. Person	A B C	A B C	A B C	A B C	A B C	A B C
9. Self	A B C	A B C	A B C	A B C	A B C	A B C
10. Smile/Laugh	A B C	A B C	A B C	A B C	A B C	A B C
11. Burp, Sneeze, Cough	A B C	A B C	A B C	A B C	A B C	A B C
12. Looking at Mother	A B C	A B C	A B C	A B C	A B C	A B C
13. Sucking — Non-feed	A B C	A B C	A B C	A B C	A B C	A B C

Mother	0–10	11–20	21–30	31–40	41–50	51–60
1. Touch	A B C	A B C	A B C	A B C	A B C	A B C
2. Hold	A B C	A B C	A B C	A B C	A B C	A B C
3. Vocalization	A B C	A B C	A B C	A B C	A B C	A B C
4. Vocalization to Other	A B C	A B C	A B C	A B C	A B C	A B C
5. Look	A B C	A B C	A B C	A B C	A B C	A B C
6. Smile/Laugh	A B C	A B C	A B C	A B C	A B C	A B C
7. Play w/S	A B C	A B C	A B C	A B C	A B C	A B C
8. Change diaper/Bathe	A B C	A B C	A B C	A B C	A B C	A B C
9. Feed	A B C	A B C	A B C	A B C	A B C	A B C
10. Rocks S	A B C	A B C	A B C	A B C	A B C	A B C
11. Reading/TV	A B C	A B C	A B C	A B C	A B C	A B C
12. Kiss	A B C	A B C	A B C	A B C	A B C	A B C
13. Give Toy/Pacifier	A B C	A B C	A B C	A B C	A B C	A B C

694VV123P12M

FIGURE 1. The behavior check list for mother-infant interaction observation.

TABLE III
Relative Frequency of Occurrence of Infant and Maternal Vocalizations as a Function of Amount of Time Spent in Each Situation

	Infant seat	Play pen	Lap	Crib	Sofa	Floor	Table/ tub	Jumper	Other
					Infant vocalization				
Total	.233	.303	.171	.214	.200	.285	.216	.228	.211
Male	.308	.261	.183	.186	.170	.292	.225	.200	.228
Female	.179	.400	.150	.210	.227	.278	.207	.277	.137
SES I	.113	.345	.107	.204	.280	.350	.153	.130	.130
II	.222	.175	.097	.166	.133	.203	.153	.155	.240
III	.160	.460	.208	.280	.214	.345	.174	.420	.145
IV	.297	—	.168	.155	.320	.160	.200	.213	.180
V	.337	.050	.244	.262	.126	—	.464	.230	—
					Maternal vocalization				
Total	.338	.257	.404	.325	.474	.518	.475	.365	.337
Male	.332	.265	.313	.385	.481	.562	.447	.393	.298
Female	.350	.243	.441	.272	.468	.466	.503	.310	.387
SES I	.244	.100	.342	.270	.480	.430	.456	.495	.240
II	.395	.300	.400	.318	.553	.600	.425	.170	.285
III	.376	.297	.423	.408	.562	.455	.630	.400	.535
IV	.312	—	.460	.625	.320	.553	.496	.130	.350
V	.407	.180	.398	.216	.205	—	.340	.515	—

tions (such as playpen and floor) account for the highest percentage of infant vocalizations (30.3% and 28.5% respectively). In other words, the frequency of infant vocalization is a function of the situational setting. Parenthetically, this is also the case for the mother.

Particularly important in any situational analysis is whether the situation dimensions are useful in understanding behavior or individual differences. For example, in this study of mother–infant vocalization it was found that the probability of a conversation (both mother and infant vocalizing to each other) continuing from one 10-second period to the next is .49 if the infant is in its mother's lap, .63 if it is in the infant seat, and only .21 when the infant is in its crib or bed (Freedle and Lewis, 1977). Thus, vocal interaction is lowest when the infant is in its crib or bed and highest when the infant is in its mother's lap or infant seat. Since the assumed function of placing an infant in its crib or bed is to allow it to rest, the probability that the mother will allow for simultaneous vocalizations in this particular situation will be low. On the other hand, when the infant is supposed to be wide awake as it is when in the infant seat, the mother will take the opportunity of strongly engaging the infant in conversation. Thus, a situational analysis may provide for an analysis of function through observation of differentiated behavior as a function of those situations.

3.1. *Individual Differences*

A situational analysis is also invaluable in understanding individual or group differences. It may be the case that true group differences or similarities are hidden without taking situations into account. The situation may interact with group or individuals so that these individual or group differences may be exaggerated or reduced. Consider as an example differences between two mothers. If mother A was to hold her infant more than mother B and if holding is related to vocalization, then differences in vocalization may be due to differences in situations between mothers rather than in the quality of mothering *per se.* In order to deal with the possibility that individual differences may be differences in situation rather than behavior it is necessary to equate for time in each situation. For the study of individual or group differences, this procedure is necessary in order to be confident of differences *per se,* and for the study of the processes underlying these differences this procedure is critical.

An example of this type of analysis, taken from a study of Lewis and Freedle (1977), is presented below. In this particular study Lewis and Freedle were interested in the interaction patterns of vocalization rather than the amount of vocalization. Interactions were determined by observing the sequential vocalizations of both mother and infant. For both infant and mother an occurrence of vocalization was scored for each 10-second period over a total of 720 such periods; six vocalization states were possible for each 10-second period. *State 0,* no one was vocalizing; *state 1* infant was, mother was not; *state 2* mother was, infant was not; and *state 3* both were vocalizing. Other states were possible but not considered here (see Lewis and Freedle, 1977). A conditional probability analysis was undertaken to determine the likelihood of switching states (see Table IV for switching state definitions).

Figure 2 presents the conditional probabilities associated with these state changes in conversation compared across two of the eight situations. Since mother's lap and infant seat account for approximately 50% of location time, these two situations were chosen. For the example of group differences, 20 SES level 5, which have been labeled *p* for poor and 20 SES level 1, which have been labeled *w* for wealthy, mother–infant dyads were observed (Hollingshead, 1957).

Of particular interest for the present discussion is the state change from 1⇆2, which represents what has been called an interaction pattern. When observation in the infant seat is compared to the mother's lap, there is relatively little interaction in the infant seat (a mean of 4%) and considerable interaction in the mother's lap (over 25%). Note that this says nothing about the overall level of vocalization of the mother, which was as great or greater in the infant seat than the lap. This analysis refers to interaction, the change from 1⇆2. In the infant seat the probability of exchange between speakers is less than what would be expected by chance and represents a suppression of the possible level of exchange. There were no social class differences in the attempt by the mother to separate herself from interaction with her infant (not a reduction in amount of vocalization just its interaction). For mother's lap there are social class differences, with poor mothers showing 40% less interaction than middle-class mothers. The causes of such a difference will not be pursued (see Lewis and Freedle, 1977) except to point out that without a situational analysis individual and group differences might be masked by summing across situations.

TABLE IV
Various State Changes

State 1→State 1	Infant continues to vocalize alone
State 1→State 2	Infant vocalizes, mother listens switches to infant listens, mother vocalizes
State 1→State 3	Infant vocalizes, mother listens switches to infant and mother vocalizes
State 2→State 2	Mother continues to vocalize alone
State 2→State 1	Mother vocalizes, infant listens switches to infant vocalizes, mother listens
State 2→State 3	Mother vocalizes, infant listens switches to infant and mother vocalizes
State 3→State 3	Infant and mother continue to vocalize
State 3→State 2	Infant and mother vocalize switches to mother vocalizes, infant listens
State 3→State 1	Infant and mother vocalize switches to infant vocalizes, mother listens

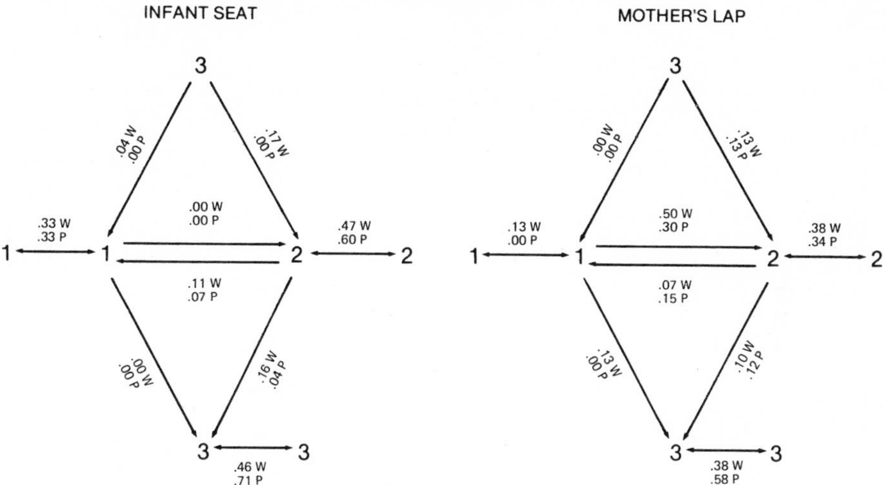

Figure 2. Conditional probabilities associated with conversational states under two different situations.

Equally alike is the case where individual or group differences would not be apparent if situational analysis is undertaken. For example, there is a strong indicator that father–infant and mother–infant interactions do not differ significantly when fathers and mothers are in interaction with their infant (Parke and O'Leary, 1975). What is different is the amount of time they are in interaction (Ban and Lewis, 1974).

The type of situational analysis that has been undertaken is limited. More work varying the dimensions of situation need to be considered. Functional analysis, looking at mother–infant interaction as it relates to what the parent wants to do and accomplish (feed, play, nurture), needs to be undertaken. This may take the form of observing her behavior or by asking the mother herself to define the function of her actions.

4. *Other Situational Analyses in Parent–Child Interaction*

The parent–child interactions have been studied using a variety of situations, under the general hope that a situational analysis would yield similarity across situations. That is, most studies of attachment hope to find a set of behaviors that would reflect an underlying structure within the dyadic relationship of parent and child. It was hoped that although the behaviors subsumed under the construct might undergo some transformation (Lewis and Ban, 1971), the quality of attachment might be measured across different situations.

Ainsworth and Wittig (1969) suggested three or four situations in which to observe the mother–infant relationship. These included a free-play situation in which mother and infant are free to play as they will; a *separation* and *departure situation* in which the mother separates herself from the child and leaves the child alone in a room; a *reunion situation* in which the mother returns to the child after being gone; in addition, the *stranger situation* in which an adult or child stranger enters the room with the child (with or without the mother). Each of these has been used to assess the mother (and father)–child relationship. These proceedings have been used by many (see Weinraub, Brooks, and Lewis, 1977 for a review). While designed initially for use in the laboratory setting, these procedures have also been used in the home (e.g., Clarke-Stewart, 1974). The results of these studies have been summarized by Zarin-Ackerman (1975) and Weinraub and Lewis (1978) and indicate only a very weak correspondence across situations.

Moreover, in terms of the more limited situational analysis, there appears to be more consistency from laboratory to home, holding situation constant. While these findings are in need of more exploration—there is relatively little home study of mother–infant relationships—what these findings point up is that a situational analysis is what is critical, not whether it is home or laboratory based. The question then is not which situation is natural or "real" but rather the nature of the situation. One should no longer believe that the mother leaving the child alone in a laboratory room is any more related to the mother's normal relationship than the relationship between the mother's free play and separation behavior within the laboratory setting. The stability within a situation is important, not its generalization to all situations, a less than likely occurrence.

Situations and situational analysis requires that situations be selected (if the perceived situation approach is not used) that characterize the phenomenon under study. The ethologist's selection of situations meets this by looking at situations in relationship to responses,* e.g. aggressive situations for fighting, eating situations for feeding, etc. In any event, having chosen a situation, two requirements seem important. First, these situations produce stable and consistent outcomes when reproduced. If a situation does not produce this, and it might not especially if not subject perceived, the situational analysis

*This point of the interembeddedness of situation and behavior may necessitate a study of interaction rather than separating out stimulus and response.

fails. Secondly, a situation produces an outcome that is meaningful, that is, captures an important percentage of the variance of the phenomena. It matters little whether such situations are laboratory or home based, real or fictitious. What matters is their relationship to the phenomena under study. Thus, it is possible to make up a totally unreal situation, for example, a marble-dropping situation, if one can demonstrate that performance on this "unreal" task can predict other more real-life situations such as test-taking in school.

Toward such a goal more effort needs to be directed. Situational analyses are difficult and they have just started to be considered. Even the most simple of situational taxonomies pose overwhelming questions. Taxonomies based on the perceiver are only beginning to be evolved. Nonetheless, situational analysis becomes important if we wish to capture the interface between the developing organisms and the context in which that development takes place.

References

Ainsworth, M.D.S., and Wittig, B.A. Attachment and exploratory behavior of one-year-olds in a strange situation. In B.M. Foss (Ed.), *Determinants of infant behavior IV*. London: Methuen, 1969, pp. 233–253.

Ban, P., and Lewis, M. Mothers and fathers, girls and boys: Attachment behavior in the one-year-old. *Merrill-Palmer Quarterly*, 1974, *20*(3), 195–204.

Barker, R.G. Explorations in ecological psychology. *American Psychologist*, 1965, *20*, 1–14.

Bowers, K.S. Situationism in psychology: An analysis and a critique. *Psychological Review*, 1973, *80*, 307–336.

Clarke-Stewart, K.A. Interactions between mothers and their young children: Characteristics and consequences. *Monographs of the Society for Research in Child Development*, 1974, *38* (5, Serial No. 153).

Endler, N.S., and Magnusson, D. Interactionism, trait psychology, and situationism. *Reports from the Psychological Laboratories*, University of Stockholm, #418, 1974.

Frederiksen, N. Toward a taxonomy of situations. *American Psychologist*, 1972, *27*, 114–123.

Freedle, R., and Lewis, M. Application of Markov processes to vocalization states. Paper presented at the meetings of the Psychometric Society, Princeton, March 1972.

Freedle, R., and Lewis, M. Prelinguistic conversations. In M. Lewis and L. Rosenblum (Eds.), *Interaction, conversation, and the development of language: The origins of behavior*. Vol. V. New York: Wiley, 1977.

Gibson, J.J. The concept of the stimulus in psychology. *American Psychologist*, 1960, *15*, 694–703.

Haith, M.M. Visual competence in early infancy. In R. Held, H. Leibowitz, and H. L. Teuber, (Eds.), *Handbook of sensory physiology (VIII)*. Berlin: Springer-Verlag, 1976.

Hamlyn, D. W. *Sensation and perception*. London: Routledge & Kegan Paul, Ltd., 1961.

Hollingshead, A.B. *Two factor index of social position*. New Haven: Author, 1957.

Lewis, M. The meaning of a response or why researchers in infant behavior should be oriental metaphysicians. *Merrill-Palmer Quarterly*, 1967, *13*(1), 7–18.

Lewis, M. State as an infant–environment interaction: An analysis of mother–infant interaction as a function of sex. *Merrill-Palmer Quarterly*, 1972, *18*, 95–121.

Lewis, M., and Ban, P. Stability of attachment behavior: A transformational analysis. Paper presented at the Society for Research in Child Development meetings, Symposium on Attachment: Studies in Stability and Change, Minneapolis, April 1971.

Lewis, M., and Freedle, R. Mother–infant dyad: The cradle of meaning. In P. Pliner, L. Krames, and T. Alloway (Eds.), *Communication and affect:Language and thought*. New York: Academic Press, 1973, pp. 127–155.

Lewis, M., and Freedle, R. The mother and infant communication system: The effects of poverty. In H. McGurk (Ed.), *Ecological factors in human development*. Amsterdam: North Holland Publishing Company, 1977, 205–215.

Lewis, M., and Rosenblum, L. (Eds.). *The origins of fear: The origins of behavior*. Vol. II. New York: Wiley, 1974.

Lowenthal, D. Research in environmental perception and behavior: Perspectives on current problems. *Environment and Behavior*, 1972, *4*, 333–342.

Mischel, W. Toward a cognitive social learning reconceptualization of personality. *Psychological Review*, 1973, *80*, 252–283.

Murray, H. A. *Explorations in personality*. New York: Oxford University Press, 1938.

Orne, M. T. Communication by the total experimental situation: Why it is important, how it is evaluated, and its significance for the ecological validity of findings. In P. Pliner, L. Krames, and T. Alloway (Eds.), *Communication and affect: Language and thought*. New York: Academic Press, 1973, pp. 157–189.

Parke, R. D., and O'Leary, S. Father–mother–infant interaction in the newborn period: Some findings, some observations, and some unresolved issues. In K. Riegel and J. Meacham (Eds.), *The developing individual in a changing world. Vol. II. Social and environmental issues*. The Hague: Mouton, 1975.

Pervin, L. A. Performance and satisfaction as a function of individual–environment fit. *Psychological Bulletin*, 1968, *69*, 56–68.

Pervin, L.A. Definitions, measurements, and classifications of stimuli, situations, and environments. *Research Bulletin 75-23*. Princeton, N.J.: Educational Testing Service, 1975a.

Pervin, L.A. A free-response description approach to the analysis of person–situation interaction. *Research Bulletin 75-22*. Princeton, N.J.: Educational Testing Service, 1975b.

Rotter, J.B. The role of the psychological situation in determining the direction of human behavior. In M.R. Jones (Ed.), *Nebraska symposium on motivation*. Lincoln: University of Nebraska Press, 1955, 245–268.

Salapatek, P. The visual investigation of geometric patterns by the one- and two-month-old infant. Paper presented at meetings of the American Association for the Advancement of Science, Boston, December 1969.

Sells, S.B. (Ed.) *Stimulus determinants of behavior*. New York: Ronald Press, 1963.

Weinraub, M., Brooks, J., and Lewis, M. The social network: A reconsideration of the concept of attachment. *Human Development*, 1977, *20*, 31–47.

Weinraub, M. and Lewis, M. The determinants of children's responses to separation. *Monographs of the Society for Research in Child Development*, 1978, *42* (4, Serial No. 172).

Zaporozhets, A.V. The development of perception in the preschool child. In P.H. Mussen (Ed.), European Research in Cognitive Development. *Monographs of the Society for Research in Child Development*, 1965, *30* (2, Whole No. 100).

Zarin-Ackerman, J. A study of the mother infant relationship in the first year of life. Unpublished doctoral dissertation, Graduate School for Political and Social Sciences, New School for Social Research, May, 1975.

Theoretical Approaches to the Analysis of Individual–Environment Interaction

LAWRENCE A. PERVIN

In the introductory chapter the dichotomy between internal and external determinants of behavior was discussed. Emphasis was placed on the interaction between internal and external determinants in terms of their interdependent character. Thus, the need for a focus on the internal and external units to be employed and on the processes involved—what in the organism interacts with what in the environment and how? In this chapter there will be a review of five models for analyzing the process of individual–environment interaction. The five models do not cover all such past efforts in the field. However, they are representative and cover drive (need), cognitive, and behavioral points of view. Indeed, one point of interest is the extent to which the models tend to focus on one or another set of variables to the exclusion of others, as if cognitive, behavioral, and affective activities occurred in isolation from one another. The five models vary in a number of ways: the extent to which they have been formalized or systematized, the extent to which they have evolved out of and have subsequently influenced interactional research, whether the conceptual roots are in psychology or in other fields, and the clarity with which they address the question of how. What ties them together, however, is the claim of each, in one form or another, to represent an interactionist model of behavior.

1. *Murray's Need–Press Model*

The personologist Henry Murray was keenly aware of the issues toward which this book is directed. In his *Explorations in Personality*,

LAWRENCE A. PERVIN • Department of Psychology, Rutgers University, Livingston College, New Brunswick, New Jersey 08903.

Murray (1938) drew a distinction between two types of psychologists, peripheralists and centralists. According to Murray, the peripheralist defines personality in terms of action qua action and focuses attention on the external stimulus or the perception of it as the origin of psychological phenomena. Attention is directed to that which is observable and can be reliably measured. The facts that are observed are based on relationships between manipulated environmental objects and the behaving, physically responding organism. Mechanical laws are emphasized so that, as observed by Watson, personality is the sum total of habitual responses. The interest is in similarities among people and that which holds for all people. Basically man is seen as inert, passive, and responsive to outer stimulation.

In contrast to the peripheralist, the centralist defines personality in terms of central processes that action or behavior manifests. Instead of limiting themselves to the study of overt behavior, centralists are prepared to try and study, and at times infer, such intangibles as wishes, needs, impulses, desires, and intentions. While not disregarding the study of overt behavior, they crave to know the internal life of their subject. Rather than being passively driven or pulled by outer stimuli, man is seen as active and influenced in virtually all spheres of activity by internal energies. Activity occurs in the absence of external stimulation. Finally, often the centralist is the clinician or social philosopher who has no stomach for experiments conducted in the artificial laboratory and prefers instead to concern himself with man enmeshed in his environment.

While clearly leaning in the direction of the centralists, Murray attempted to give attention to both centralist and peripheralist concerns, to both internal and external determinants of behavior. The concepts developed to give expression to these internal and external determinants of behavior were need and press. The concept of need gave expression to the organized, directed, unitary trend aspects of behavior. The concept of press gave expression to the responsiveness of the organism to external stimulation.

For Murray, a need was a hypothetical process or force within the organism that influenced fantasy and perception, and induced effectively organized activity. Needs both lead to behavior and affect responses to external stimuli. In terms of the former, if the organism is hungry it will explore for food. In terms of the latter, if hungry it will eat food whereas if angry it may throw food. Whether in terms of initiating activity or influencing responsiveness to stimuli, needs account for consistent individual differences in the intensity, duration, and direction of goal-directed behaviors. In this sense, the concept of need may seem similar to that of trait. Therefore, it may be of interest to note that while Murray saw many parallels between the two concepts, he also emphasized two major differences. First, whereas a trait refers to a recurrent reaction pattern, a need refers to a process that may operate infrequently and in only a limited number of situations. Second, the trait concept refers to an observed behavioral regularity whereas the need concept refers to an internal process that may or may not manifest itself directly or overtly. When needs are frequently expressed directly in overt behavior, they can easily be linked to trait concepts. However, it would be difficult to link a need that is infrequently and/or indirectly expressed to any trait. Murray was interested in both stability and change as the organism interacted with its environment and felt that trait psychology was overconcerned with recurrences-consistency and too little concerned with environmental factors (Murray, 1938, p. 715).

While needs could be provoked by internal processes, Murray felt that it was more often the case that they were provoked by forces or press in the environment. A number of different ways of conceptualizing press were considered, involving alternatives that continue to be debated today (Magnusson and Ekhemmar, 1975; Pervin, 1978). Thus, for example, Murray considered whether the environment should be defined in objective or perceived terms, whether the environment should be defined in terms of actual as opposed to potential effects, and finally, the question of how to classify situations or environments. In relation to these issues his concept of press included the actual environment (alpha press) and the perceived environment (beta press), both actual and potential-expected environmental effects, and a classification scheme based on effects on the organism (i.e., what is done to the organism or may be done to him before he makes a response.)

What is the relationship between needs and press, and how do they account for the flow of behavior? Murray suggested that needs and press be defined in parallel terms so as to facilitate interpretation and analysis. In terms of process, the organism activated by a need may seek a press or act to avoid one, or, more frequently, the organism encounters a press and a need is activated by the encounter. Thus, complex behavior expresses need–press combinations expressed in terms of episodes or single organism–environment interactions. The complete behavioral event is seen as the result of an interaction between internal and external forces.

Murray's scheme, a valiant effort to attend to the relationships between internal and external forces, contains many ambiguities and relatively little interactional research has been done with it. An effort to incorporate the views of Murray in an assessment program was made by Stern, Stein, and Bloom (1956). Furthermore, Stern (1970) made an effort to develop parallel need and press indexes, and then to analyze need–press relationships in terms of transactions between persons and environments. However, these and related efforts pointed to the difficulties of developing parallel person and environment measures and, following from such measures, the difficulty of analyzing processes of individual–environment interaction (Landis, 1964; Walsh, 1973). In sum, Murray's need–press model has a certain appeal to it and stands as a significant early effort to give attention to both individual and environment variables in explaining behavior. In a certain sense, it is basically a simple reward–punishment model. However, in fact, a great deal of complexity is added by suggesting that the values of rewards and punishments (i.e., press) are tied to the needs of the individual, that the organism functions in terms of both actual and anticipated press, that the need-activated organism may seek out press as well as be stimulated by them, and that the need-activated organism may serve as a press for another organism. While seemingly making a great deal of sense and having a certain intuitive appeal, at least to dynamically oriented psychologists, the model clearly has major pitfalls that account for its limited systematic use in research. First, there remain considerable problems in translating the need and press concepts into measurable phenomena. Second, the relationship between needs and press is not really clear, at least not in terms of questionnaire scales. For example, one would assume that need–press congruence would be represented by parallel scores on the parallel scales. However, theoretically a person with a low need will be satisfied with a press that is any level above that need; that is, if the environment is considered to be a source of rewards and gratifications, then all that is necessary is that it have an adequate amount of rewards and benefits to meet the person's needs; anything above that is gravy. On the other hand, if one considers the environment to be exerting a force or pressure upon the individual, then a high press–low need relationship could express dissonance and lead to dissatisfaction. In other words, different aspects or functions of the environment have different implications for the individual's need system. Such differing implications, however, were never fully spelled out. Undoubtedly, part of the reason for this is that while the need–press schema serves as a potential model for the analysis of individual–environment interactions, in fact it has never been systematically applied to a process analysis of behavior. The emphasis upon the process of adaptation to the environment, within the context of organismic needs and environmental press, has remained abstract and intuitive rather than concrete and applied.

2. *Cognitive, Informational Approaches to Organism–Environment Interaction*

For a long time in the history of psychology, cognition was neglected as an important area of research and conceptual effort. The situation has changed dramatically over the past two decades and even within the drive-oriented framework of psychoanalysis there has been increased attention to cognitive variables. Of particular significance in this regard has been the development of information processing models based on computer analogies and the work of Piaget.* Piaget's emphasis is clearly on the interaction between the organism and the environment in the development and functioning of cognitive structures. Both purely internal and purely external views are rejected. The organism is active both in terms of spontaneous activity and in terms of processing information from the environment into already existing structures. Knowledge, in other words, is not just a simple copy of reality. At the same time, the organism remains responsive to external events and modifies its structures in accordance with them. Interaction with the environment involves the constant interplay between these processes of assimilation and accommodation. Discrepancies between information from events and existing structures produces strain and efforts to achieve equilibrium.† Heavy emphasis is placed here on the concept of autoregulation, a concept we will return to in considering the biologically based general systems theory. According to Piaget, the organism functions as an organized system to preserve its structures while remaining responsive to changing conditions. Life is essentially autoregulation or the maintenance of stability in the face of outside perturbations. Indeed, cognitive processes represent the most highly differentiated organs for regulating the interactions of the organism with the environment. The essential function of logical operations is to set up systems of control and autocorrection. Cognitive processes develop out of the organism's exchanges with the environment and then

*It is interesting to note the extent to which Piaget has been influenced, and continues to be influenced, in his thinking by his background in biology (Piaget, 1971). Thus, for example, there is an emphasis on structure ("All knowledge presupposes a physical structure"), organization ("These action schemata . . . comprise an organization, and this fact immediately brings us into the realm of biology"), and adaptation ("It is impossible to dissociate organization from adaptation, because an organized system is open to the environment, and its functioning therefore entails exchanges with the external world, the stability of which defines the adapted character of the system" p. 171).

†The issue of the conditions under which the organism will move toward equilibrium and the theoretical explanation for the process have been considered by Langer (1975), Riegel (1975), and Sigel (Sigel and Cocking, 1977) among others.

functions in the service of regulating such exchanges. A parallel is thereby drawn between the openness of physiological systems to influences from the environment while a constancy in the interior environment is preserved through homeostasis, and the functioning of the cognitive system:

> Behavior is at the mercy of every possible disequilibrating factor, since it is always dependent on an environment which has no fixed limits and is constantly fluctuating. Thus, the autoregulatory function of the cognitive mechanisms produces the most highly stabilized equilibrium forms found in any living creature, namely, the structures of intelligence. (Piaget, 1971, p. 37)

In sum, in Piaget we find an emphasis on the constant interplay between exogenous factors that cause disequilibria and endogenous factors that act as equilibration agents. Life is made up of this interplay between the internal and the external, with special emphasis on the organism's efforts to preserve organization while responding to outside perturbations: "This means that anyone who sees . . . a belief in the systematic primacy of one or the other of these factors will have failed to understand me, my central idea being that of interaction" (Piaget, 1971, p. 348).*

Another relevant cognitive view is that of Hunt (1963, 1965). Hunt's emphasis is on motivation, particularly on motivation that inheres in the organism's informational interaction with its environment. Basing his view on the feedback loop and the TOTE unit of Miller, Galanter, and Pribram (1960), Hunt suggested that incongruity or discrepancy between the incoming information of the moment and the relevant information already stored in the brain provides the basis for instigating actions on the part of the organism. Congruity provides the basis for stopping these actions. In this sense, the basis for action inheres neither in the organism nor in the environment, but rather in the informational interaction between the two. An incongruity between present input and past constancies instigates the search for new information. Such a search is ended when the organism is informed.

Hunt tied this view to an arousal theory. Thus, it was assumed that incongruity leads to emotional arousal. In other words, information processing has arousal or emotional implications. It was furthermore assumed that there was a curvilinear relationship between incongruity and arousal; too little or too much incongruity produces high arousal whereas a medium level of incongruity leads to an optimum level of arousal. The former conditions of high arousal would

*Piaget has suggested that since psychologists emphasize the environment so much he tends to emphasize internal factors when speaking before them whereas he emphasizes external factors when speaking before biologists who tend to focus on the internal.

be experienced as unpleasant and lead to withdrawal behavior whereas the latter condition (i.e., optimum incongruity) would be experienced as pleasant and lead to approach behaviors. While connecting incongruity to arousal, the focus remained on information processing and incongruity. The important point for Hunt was that incongruity in information processing not only instigated action but had something to do with the direction of behavior. Thus, it was assumed that the organism abhors boredom (i.e., too little incongruity) and extreme novelty (i.e., too much incongruity), and seeks an optimum amount of novelty or the mildly incongruous.

Many questions remain with the Hunt view: How is the optimum amount of incongruity to be defined and established for each individual? What determines the way in which incongruity is reduced? Is there not a contradiction between the argument that congruity stops behavior and that too little incongruity results in withdrawal behavior? Would the individual seek unpleasant news where it would result in an optimum amount of incongruity? What is the relationship between motivation inherent in the informational interaction between organism and environment and other sources of motivation? While questions such as these and others can be raised, the theory does bring together diverse pieces of research and establishes an alternative view of significant phenomena. Most significantly, within the context of this chapter, it focuses attention on the need for considering the cognitive activity of the organism in relation to both internally stored information and new information from external sources. It is this emphasis upon the dialectic between cognitive operations within the organism and information to be processed from the environment that ties Piaget and Hunt together in a cognitive interactional model. Both address the process question in terms of the interaction between cognitive structures or bits of information that are present within the organism and input from the outside world. Both view the organism as inherently active and as placing its own stamp upon events in the world. Both view the relationship between information stored within the organism and new input as having emotion-producing significance. Finally, both emphasize the dialectic between preserving cognitive organizations that have been developed while remaining open to change, and that between the desire for predictability while appreciating novelty and surprise.

3. *Behavioral and Social Learning Models of Individual–Environment Interaction*

The third model of person–situation interaction follows from Skinner's behavioral emphasis and represents a direct contrast both with Murray's need–press model and with the cognitive models discussed in the previous section. Whereas these earlier models clearly recognized the importance of environmental characteristics, they also clearly assumed the existence of internal states. The existence of internal motivational states, which could not be measured directly and which were associated with the assumption of stable and enduring personality characteristics, was rejected by Skinner in favor of a model emphasizing directly observed behaviors governed by maintaining conditions in the environment. Skinner's behavioral emphasis had an appeal to personality and clinical psychologists who were frustrated, conceptually and practically, with the psychodynamic model. At the same time, however, it seemed to suggest that there was little about the person, as an organized entity, that was worth studying, other than its behavioral repertoire. What kinds of units then could be used for the analysis of person–environment interaction? In this section we shall begin by considering an organism–environment interaction model that attempted to stay as close as possible to the Skinnerian behavioral emphasis. We will then consider how the behavioral model was extended to consider additional aspects of the organism that play a role in its transactions with the environment.

An important extension of the behavioral approach to personality was Wallace's (1966, 1967) suggestion of an abilities conception of personality. In contrast to response disposition views of personality, such as Murray's need concept and Allport's trait concept, Wallace construed personality in terms of skills or abilities. Instead of talking about a need for aggressiveness, or a trait of sociability, one could talk about the ability of the person to behave in an aggressive or sociable way under defined stimulus conditions. A response capability picture of the person was substituted for an essence, motivational determinant picture. The response capability conception of the person asks two questions: (1) Response Capability: Is the behavior in the person's repertoire? (2) Response Performance: What are the conditions necessary for the performance of the response? Thus, one could consider concepts such as response repertoires, response deficits, response inhibitions, and conditions in the environment that affect the acquisition, maintenance, and modification of individual responses.

A further development of this conception is found in the work of Goldfried (D'Zurilla and Goldfried, 1971; Goldfried and D'Zurilla, 1969; Goldfried and Pomeranz, 1968). Goldfried suggested that the environment be analyzed in terms of problems or situations that the person encounters that require an appropriate response for effective functioning. According to this view, behavior–environment interaction involves the process of the organism being faced with a situation requiring a response, being able to make a decision concerning the best response, and then having that response or acquiring it as part of its repertoire. Problem-solving behavior involves the ability to generate response alternatives and to make appropriate decisions or choices among alternatives. Life, then, is viewed as a continuous process of meeting new problematic situations and finding ways of coping with them. According to this analysis, the competent individual is the person who possesses a versatile response repertoire and the ability to make decisions concerning the best response to make in a given problem situation. Such an analysis is contrasted with Murray's need–press analysis in two specific ways: (1) There is a more detailed analysis of the situation, specifically in terms of relevant adaptive behavior; (2) instead of emphasizing hypothetical internal forces and dynamics, the model emphasizes various possible specific behavior–environment (i.e., problem) interactions.

One further aspect of the Goldfried model is worthy of note since it represents a departure from a strict Skinnerian position and points the way toward later consideration of the cognitive social learning position. Goldfried assumes that while some relevant stimulus elements originate in the external environment, other stimulus elements arise from within the organism in the form of thoughts and emotional responses. Thus, internal as well as external stimuli are recognized, and cognitive as well as motoric behavior is emphasized.

The Wallace conception of abilities can be seen as an effort to examine the implications of Skinnerian views for personality, assessment, and psychopathology. As a model of individual–environment interaction, however, it offers no new units for looking at persons or situations and provides no new answers to the question of how. Looking at the person in terms of response repertoire and at conditions in the environment that affect response acquisition, maintenance, and modification hardly represents a new departure in behavioral thinking. We are still left with a passive organism that responds to specific external stimulus conditions. The Goldfried conception goes beyond the Wallace one in two ways. First, it opens up a new avenue of analysis of situations, one that is specifically linked to characteristics of the organism. In viewing the environment as presenting problems to the organism, one is reminded of the synthetic evolutionist's view that in the course of evolution the environment presents challenges to the species. Second, greater recognition is given to internal properties of the organism, both in terms of stimuli that originate in the organism and in terms of the role of cognitive processes in complex behavior. However, how internal stimuli and cognitive activities may themselves generate activity and engagement with the environment is left unanswered.

The development of social learning theory within a behavioral framework is interesting in this regard. An early effort to consider the role of internal forces, including cognitive activity, within the context of learning theory was made by Julian Rotter (1954, 1967). Rotter rejected both generalist and specifist views, both purely internal and purely situational views, in favor of an interaction model. Indeed, Rotter emphasized the interaction between the individual and his meaningful environment as the proper unit of investigation. The basic hypothesis in Rotter's theory is that the potential occurrence of a behavior is a function of the expectation that a particular reinforcement or goal will occur following that behavior in a specific situation and the value to the person of the reinforcement. What is inside the organism is important since for any given situation the individual may have a variety of potential behaviors, each of which is associated with an expectancy for a reinforcement, with the specific reinforcement having a value for the individual. What is in the situation is important because the direction of behavior is determined by reinforcements that are likely to occur for different behaviors.* Through their ability to arouse expectancies, situations elicit more human social behavior than is true of cyclical internal states. While often emphasizing the individual's perception of the situation, Rotter also suggested that situations could be categorized in terms of objective similarities in reinforcements for behaviors.

While Rotter emphasized the importance of situational variables, his thinking and research were mainly concerned with the development of expectancies inside the individual, including individual differences in generalized expectancies in the areas of trust and locus of control. In contrast to this, Bandura's early social learning view represented an effort to avoid all spurious inner causes and to explain the acquisition and maintenance of social behavior strictly in terms of antecedent social stimulus events (e.g., the social models the person was exposed to as a child) and the reinforcement contingencies of the past and present environments. Biological and individual difference variables were not rejected out of hand. However, it was suggested that more could be gained from the study of situational variables that influence the acquisition and maintenance of social behavior than from the study of internal variables and individual differences. This was the basis for Bandura's sociobehavioristic approach.

Bandura's recent book on aggression is of interest here both in

*From a behavioral standpoint, Franks has been critical of Rotter's concept of the environment: "While it is true that Rotter does take the external environment more seriously than do most personality theorists, he does so in terms of a theoretical model which stresses intervening variables. Thus, while Rotter 'talks the talk' of objective psychology, whether he actually 'walks the walk' is a debatable issue" (Franks, 1974, p. 303).

terms of its comparison of internal and situationist views of aggressive behavior and in terms of how far his social learning theory has come in emphasizing an interactionist position (Bandura, 1973). Bandura is critical of instinct and drive theories of aggression on both conceptual and methodological grounds; the inner determinants emphasized are inferred from behavior and result in pseudo-explanations that cannot account for the variation found in behavior according to the situational context. The shift in emphasis toward external variables is described as follows:

> Developments in learning theory shifted the focus of causal analysis from hypothesized inner determinants to detailed examination of external influences on responsiveness. Human behavior was extensively analyzed in terms of the stimulus events that evoke it and the reinforcing consequences that alter it. Researchers repeatedly demonstrated that response patterns generally attributed to underlying forces could be induced, eliminated, and reinstated simply by varying external sources of influence. These impressive findings led many psychologists to the view that the causes of behavior are found not in the organism, but in environmental forces. (Bandura, 1973, p. 41)

Bandura himself, however, rejects the view that man's actions are exclusively under external control and his reasons for this are of interest since they parallel the situationists' rejection of the trait point of view. First, just as a person's behavior is not consistent across situations, the effects of a situation are not consistent across persons. Second, just as a person's behavior is not always predictable from an analysis of his or her personality, behavior is not always predictable from an analysis of the external sources of influence. An exclusively situationist position is inadequate because it fails to take into consideration cognition (i.e., the fact that people can interpret and represent stimulus events) and self-regulation (i.e., people produce consequences for their own actions).

Bandura thus rejects the view that behavior is exclusively under internal control and the view that behavior is exclusively under external control, both the view that man is driven by inner forces and the view that man is buffeted helplessly by environmental influences. Behavior is continuously regulated by the interplay of internal and external sources of influence. Environmental stimuli activate physiological reactions and emotions, direct behavior because of their association with differential response consequences, and generally serve as an informational basis for behavioral decisions. At the same time, internal processes mediate between the actual external event and psychological representation of that event. In addition, internal processes influence the anticipated consequences of prospective actions and guide the development of behavioral plans or strategies. What a person thinks influences what he does and, thereby, what happens to him. At the same time, what a person thinks is influenced by current stimulus conditions and past reinforcement conditions. In the course of phylogenetic and ontogenetic development, man has become increasingly free of control by innate releasing and inhibiting mechanisms and of control by stimuli in the immediate environment. Developments in cortical control enable the organism to represent as well as to respond to its current situation and to influence as well as be influenced by its environment.* Organism and environment are engaged in a two-way causal process or a continuous reciprocal interaction.†

The shift in Bandura from an exclusive concern with social stimulus events and reinforcement contingencies to an interactionist position is paralleled by the change in Mischel from a view in which behavior is seen as dependent upon the details of evoking situations to a view in which equal attention is given to person variables and their interaction with "psychological situations" (Mischel, 1973). It is true that in Mischel's earlier critique of trait and dynamic theory the roles of intrapsychic activities and mediating cognitive processes were not denied. At the same time, however, his 1968 book did little to spell out the nature of these variables or their relation to influential environmental events. In contrast to this, his 1973 *Psychological Review* paper focused on the role of person variables in mediating between environmental inputs and behavior and their role in enabling the organism to affect, indeed overcome, the environment as well as being affected by it.

Mischel's cognitive social learning position is based on the view that the individual has a unique organization of stimulus equivalences and response equivalences so that it is what is in the organism's head that counts in terms of behavior. The relevant person variables represent a conglomeration of variables already discussed or to be discussed in the next section. They relate to what the individual can do in a situation, how events are categorized, expectancies about environmental reinforcement contingencies, subjective reinforcement preferences, self-regulation by self-imposed standards, and the organization of covert and overt activity in relation to long-term goals or plans.

*Bandura's emphasis on phylogenetic development of cortical control may be related to Piaget's emphasis upon knowledge as mediating between the organism and the environment. However, the difference in terms of research efforts is clear. Whereas Piaget is interested in cognitive processes and the epistemology of knowledge, Bandura continues to be primarily interested in conditions in the environment that regulate the acquisition and maintenance of behavior.

†For a more expanded version of his views concerning individual-environment interaction and reciprocal determinism, see Bandura, 1977.

However, global dispositional concepts are rejected and the emphasis is on how expectancies tend to become relatively specific rather than on their being broadly generalized.

From a cognitive social learning standpoint the relationship between situations and persons can be understood as follows. Situations evoke, maintain, and modify behavior through their informational value. They act as information inputs and influence behavior through their effect upon the person's mediating cognitive variables. Some situations are highly structured and provide clear information concerning incentives, rewards, and appropriate behavior. Such situations tend to place severe constraints upon the individual. On the other hand, some situations are ambiguous and leave considerable room for individual differences in interpretation and construction. Person variables are important in terms of the way in which the informational input gets encoded, transformed, and organized. Through cognitive activity the individual can overcome stimulus control. Through self-regulation and planning the individual may select and influence situations as well as be influenced by them. Thus, the effects of situations may be strong or weak depending on the characteristics of the situation, and the effects of persons may be strong or weak depending on the person's idiosyncratic organization of cognitive activity. The danger of oversimplifying human behavior is "equally great whether one is searching for generalized (global) person-free situational effects or for generalized (global) situation-free personality variables" (Mischel, 1976, p. 499). The relationship between situations and persons is interdependent and reciprocal; situations, through their informational value, modify and change the behavior of the person while the person both organizes environmental input in an idiosyncratic way and selects or generates his own conditions.*

4. *General Systems Theory*

General Systems Theory (GST) was first introduced by von Bertalanffy (1966) as an outgrowth of his thinking about biological organisms and extended from there to a model for all systems. Associated

*The concept of reciprocal interaction is not new to behavior theory or specific to social learning theory. Thus, for example, Skinner has made the following point: "In analyzing any social episode from this point of view a complete account must be given of the behaviors of both parties as they contribute to the origin and maintenance of the behavior of each other. . . . In noticing how the master controls the slave or the employer the worker, we commonly overlook reciprocal effects. . . . The slave controls the master as completely as the master the slave" (Skinner, 1961, p. 540).

with its roots in biology is the emphasis on the relationships between processes going on within the organism and between the organism and its surrounding external environment. Inherent in the theory is a view of man as an active organism engaged in processes of selection, organization, coding of stimuli, and self-regulation.

While it is impossible to present a complete discussion of GST, certain concepts are particularly worthy of note because of their relevance to questions of individual–environment interaction. Basic to GST is an analysis of the properties of open systems, particularly living systems. First, living systems exhibit a degree of distinctiveness, self-regulation, or purposefulness. The functioning of such a system may be planned and guided in its activity by a particular goal or end-point. This is not teleology in the sense of a final effect being interpreted as the cause of a previous movement but rather a statement concerning the goal-directed nature of organismic functioning. In orienting itself toward some end-point the organismic makes use of feedback, sometimes from its internal environment and often from the external environment.

A second concept, and one of particular significance in relation to the current discussion, is that of the distinction between open and closed systems. Whereas closed systems are self-contained and isolated from influence by the external environment, open systems are involved in a continuous exchange of inputs and outputs with the surrounding environment. Living systems are both responsive to and act upon the environment. GST is particularly concerned with ongoing processes within a living system and between such a system and its environment. Thus, for example, there is interest in how a system remains responsive to changes internal and external to it while still retaining its basic identity.

Concepts such as homeostasis, adaptation, and conflict are illustrative of the GST approach to an understanding of such processes. Cannon's concept of homeostasis, developed in the 1930s and prior to the development of GST, refers to the process through which the organism maintains a constancy of its internal environment in the face of changing external influences. This process of self-regulation is seen as characteristic of open systems in contrast with the immobile, stagnant quality of conditions associated with closed systems. The process of homeostasis, like many other aspects of organismic functioning, is adaptive in terms of the organism's favorable response to both internal and external demands. Finally, the concept of conflict is used to refer to a condition where the internal parts of a system are incompatible with one another or where the system as a whole may be incompatible with the surrounding environment. Conflict may also be represented in terms of input from the environment in terms of messages that are incompatible or in conflict with one another. Thus, conflict may exist exclusively within the system, in the relationship between the system and its environment, or in the input from the environment. In each case conflict expresses a basic antagonism between the interacting parts. In a sense, conflict expresses a failure in adaptation. In both cases there is a concern with the relationship between interacting parts. Concepts such as conflict and adaptation could not exist in the absence of units, such as organism and environment, interacting with one another.

The GST approach has important conceptual and research implications. For example, there is an emphasis on multivariable interaction. Simple cause–effect or if-then explanations are eschewed in favor of explanations that consider the interaction of many internal and external variabilities. In addition, there is a concern with the temporal aspect or behavioral processes. Important aspects of systems functioning generally take place over a period of time. To stop behavior at one point in time may be to distort one of the system's most fundamental properties, its ability to maintain the same state or move toward a final goal in the face of varying internal and external conditions.

GST concepts have been applied to perception (Allport, 1955), to groups and organizations (Berrien, 1968; Katz and Kahn, 1966), and to psychopathology and psychotherapy (Menninger, Mayman, and Pruyser, 1963). Part of the reason for the diversity of application lies in the generality of the concepts. GST is at an abstract level and says little about the specific units that are most suitable for analyses of individuals and environments. At the same time it provides a useful model for focusing attention on ongoing processes of exchange or influence between organisms and their environments.

5. *Overview and Summary*

A variety of approaches to individual–environment interaction have been reviewed. These approaches vary in their level of abstraction, in the extent to which they have been systematized and developed, in the extent to which they evolved out of and have led to systematic research, whether they developed from within psychology or were borrowed from other fields, and in the clarity with which they address the question of how. In some, such as General Systems Theory, the process of exchange between individual and environment is central, whereas in others, such as in social learning theory, the emphasis tends to be on the effects of internal or external variables in relative isolation from one another. In some approaches, such as Hunt's emphasis on incongruity, it is the match or relationship between internal and external that is of interest, whereas in others it is the reciprocal cause–effect relationships that are of interest. In some there remains an interest in a single event whereas in others the emphasis is on the pattern and flow exhibited by a sequence of events. While all are interested in both stability and change, there are differences in the extent to which one or the other is emphasized or even on the interconnectedness between the two.

All of the approaches emphasize person variables, situation variables, and process variables, but the kinds of variables emphasized and relative significance among them remain different. Person concepts utilized include the following: needs, expectancies, abilities, behavioral repertories, constructs-schema, reinforcement values, organizations of stimulus equivalences and response equivalences, and plans-goals. As noted earlier, the emphasis tends to be on drives, cognitions, or behaviors rather than on the person as a total integrated system. None of the approaches gives much attention to the role of affects, though with the exception of theorists such as Tomkins (1962) and Izard (1971) this tends to be true of personality theorists generally. While there are differences in views of man, all of the approaches would appear to view man as actively involved in initiating activity, transforming stimuli, and representing the world rather than copying it, anticipating events rather than merely responding to them, and engaged in self-regulatory and self-maintaining activities. In other words, while it is true that the organism responds to the environment, it is also true that the organism anticipates, transforms, and acts upon the environment.

In terms of environment variables, we can again see a diversity of concepts employed. Such environmental variables as the following are emphasized by one or more theorists: press related to needs, reinforcers, task requirements-problem situations, and informational input-cues. Not only is there a variety of conceptual units, but diverse roles are emphasized for the environment. Thus, the environment may *spur* (initiate, evoke, activate, stimulate, provoke), *guide,* or *restrain* (constrain, inhibit) behavior, it may satisfy–benefit or frustrate–harm, it may facilitate or obstruct, attract or repel, upset the organism's equilibrium or leave it undisturbed, and, in a general way, challenge the organism to adapt. While all emphasize the importance of the environment, there are differences in whether to interpret the environment in objective terms or in perceived terms, as composed of potential stimuli or limited to actual stimuli, and differences in whether it makes sense to try and classify situation variables as opposed to concluding, as does Mischel, that such classificatory efforts will be as fruitless as efforts to classify behaviors into traits.*

To a great extent, the nature of the organism and environment variables define the nature of the processes emphasized in the interaction between the two. From a drive theory standpoint, it is the need–press relationship that is important, from a behavioral standpoint the relationship between abilities and task requirements, and, from a cognitive standpoint, the relationship between existing cognitive structures and new informational input. The theoretical approaches differ not only in the content of the processes emphasized, but in the extent to which there is a true dialectic between organism and environment. In the cognitive models emphasized, for example, it is not just that the environment provides information and the organism possesses constructs or schema, but there is a point of contact between the two that has implications for current and future cognitive structures. It is not just that the organism and environment have characteristics of importance for one another, or that each is continually influencing one another, but the focal point of interest is on the point of engagement between the two. Such an emphasis is also clear in the general systems theory concepts of adaptation and conflict. Such emphases may be contrasted with other approaches (e.g., Murray, Bandura, Mischel) where organism and environmental variables are emphasized, and the relationship between the two is recognized, but relatively little attention is given to the point of contact between the two.

To a certain extent, this last point calls attention back to the fact that approaches within the field have tended to emphasize internal or external determinants, and some approaches that claim to be interactional are primarily based upon one or another set of determinants. As was noted in the introductory chapter, it is not enough to talk about both internal and external determinants, or to say that both are important, or to say that they interact with one another. What is needed is a conceptualization of the process of interaction with an emphasis on the point of engagement between organism and environment. In terms of understanding what is occurring at that point of engagement, it may be important to recognize two things. First, a variety of events are occurring simultaneously within and outside of the organism. In other words, there is multidetermination of events. Second, in a related way, it may be that an event can only be understood in relation

*See Pervin (1978) for a discussion of the various issues relevant to defining, measuring, and classifying stimuli, situations, and environments.

to the sequence, phase, or pattern of which it is a part. Such conclusions would again dictate the kind of long-term process observations that are all too infrequently found in personality research.

References

Allport, F.H. *Theories of perception and the concept of structure.* New York: Wiley, 1955.

Bandura, A. *Aggression: A social learning analysis.* Englewood Cliffs, N.J.: Prentice-Hall, 1973.

Bandura, A. *Social learning theory.* Englewood Cliffs, N.J.: Prentice-Hall, 1977.

Berrien, F.K. *General and social systems.* New Brunswick, N.J.: Rutgers University Press, 1968.

D'Zurilla, T.J., and Goldfried, M.R. Problem solving and behavior modification. *Journal of Abnormal Psychology,* 1971, *78,* 107–126.

Franks, C.M. Social learning theory after two decades. *Contemporary Psychology,* 1974, *19,* 302–303.

Goldfried, M.R., and D'Zurilla, T.J. A behavioral-analytical model for assessing competence. In C.D. Spielberger (Ed.), *Current topics in clinical and community psychology.* New York: Academic, 1969.

Goldfried, M.R., and Pomeranz, D.M. Role of assessment in behavior modification. *Psychological Reports,* 1968, *23,* 75–87.

Hunt, J.McV. Motivation inherent in information processing and action. In O.J. Harvey (Ed.), *Motivation and social interaction: Cognitive determinants.* New York: Ronald, 1963, pp. 35–94.

Hunt, J.McV. Traditional personality theory in the light of recent evidence. *American Scientist,* 1965, 53, 80–96.

Izard, C.E. *The face of emotion.* New York: Appleton-Century-Crofts, 1971.

Katz, D., and Kahn, R.L. *The social psychology of organizations.* New York: Wiley, 1966.

Landis, H.L. Dissonance between student and college variables related to success and satisfaction. *Dissertation Abstracts,* 1964, *25,* 1047.

Langer, J. Interactional aspects of cognitive organization. *Cognition,* 1975, *3,* 9–28.

Magnusson, D. and Ekehammar, B. Perceptions of and reactions to stressful situations. *Journal of Personality and Social Psychology,* 1975, *31,* 1147–1154.

Menninger, K., Mayman, M., and Pruyser, P. *The vital balance.* New York: Viking, 1963.

Miller, G.A., Galanter, E., and Pribram, K.H. *Plans and the structure of behavior.* New York: Holt, 1960.

Mischel, W. *Personality and assessment.* New York: Wiley, 1968.

Mischel, W. Toward a cognitive social learning reconceptualization of personality. *Psychological Review,* 1973, *80,* 252–283.

Mischel, W. *Introduction to personality.* New York: Holt, Rinehart, and Winston, 1976.

Murray, H.A. *Explorations in personality.* New York: Oxford University Press, 1938.

Pervin, L.A. Performance and satisfaction as a function of individual–environment fit. *Psychological Bulletin,* 1968, 69, 56–68.

Pervin, L.A. Definitions, measurements, and classifications of stimuli, situations, and environments. *Human Ecology,* 1978, *6,* 71–105.

Piaget, J. *Biology and knowledge.* Chicago: University of Chicago Press, 1971.

Riegel, K.F. From traits and equilibrium toward developmental dialectics. In W.J. Arnold and J.K. Cole (Eds.), *Nebraska symposium on motivation.* Lincoln: University of Nebraska Press, 1975.

Rotter, J.B. *Social learning and clinical psychology*. New York: Prentice-Hall, 1954.

Rotter, J.B. Personality theory. In H. Helson and W. Bevan (Eds.), *Contemporary approaches to psychology*. Princeton, N.J.: Van Nostrand, 1967, pp. 461–498.

Sigel, I.E., and Cocking, R.R. Cognition and communication: A dialectic paradigm for development. In M. Lewis and L. Rosenblum (Eds.), *Communication and language: The origins of behavior* (Vol. 5). New York: Wiley, 1977.

Skinner, B.F. The design of cultures. *Daedalus*, 1961, 534–546.

Stern, G.G. *People in context*. New York: Wiley, 1970.

Stern, G.G., Stein, M.I., and Bloom, B.S. *Methods in personality assessment*. Glencoe, Illinois: Free Press, 1956.

Tomkins, S.S. *Affect, imagery, consciousness*. New York: Springer, 1962.

Von Bertalanffy, L. General systems theory and psychiatry. In S. Arieti (Ed.), *American handbook of psychiatry*. Vol. 3. New York: Basic Books, 1966, pp. 705–721.

Wallace, J. An abilities conception of personality: Some implications for personality measurement. *American Psychologist*, 1966, *21*, 132–138.

Wallace, J. What units shall we employ? Allport's question revisited. *Journal of Consulting Psychology*, 1967, *31*, 56–64.

Walsh, W. B. Theories of person–environment interaction: Implications for the college student. *American College Testing Monograph Number 10*, Iowa City, Iowa, 1973.

Predicting Prosocial Behavior: A Model for Specifying the Nature of Personality–Situation Interaction

ERVIN STAUB

The issues of consistency in behavior has been extensively discussed by personality and social psychologists in the last few years. To what extent is behavior consistent across many situations, and to what extent is it predictable in a single situation on the basis of our knowledge of the situation and the persons in it? It has long been assumed that behavior is a function of the person, the situation, and the interaction between the two. Under certain circumstances most people may act similarly in a particular situation, because the situation activates very basic common goals or needs, such as the desire for survival or for respect by one's peers. Usually, however, people will behave differently in a particular situation as a function of their individual characteristics (Bowers, 1973; Ekehammar, 1974).

Although the concept of interaction has a long history (Ekehammar, 1974) most personality research employed a single measure of some personal characteristics and related it to behavior; situation–personality interactions were not tested. The writing of Mischel (1968, 1973) and of Jones and Nisbett (1971), who also questioned consistency, gave rise to controversy and renewed vigorous interest in an interactionist approach. The still limited research on interaction has been primarily demonstrative. In most research the influence of some personality characteristic and some situation on behavior have been jointly considered, without proper specification of the classes of personality characteristics and situations that are regarded as important in determining particular types of behavior. Moreover, most studies explored the influence of a single personality characteristic in conjunction with some situational variation. We will need to consider the joint influence of a variety of personality characteristics, in interaction

ERVIN STAUB • Department of Psychology, University of Massachusetts, Amherst, Massachusetts 01002.

with situations, if we are to improve our understanding of how behavior is determined, and the prediction of behavior.

The underlying assumption in the reasoning that follows is that consistency in behavior will be limited. Most behavior is determined in a complex manner. Varied personality characteristics, their combination, and their activation by characteristics of the situation will together determine whether a person will or will not behave prosocially in a specific instance. With the proper specification of the most important personality characteristics, relevant situational influences and their manner of interaction, reasonably accurate predictions about behavior in specific settings will be possible.

Although this discussion implies limitation in consistency and focuses on predictability, the existence of consistency in behavior ought to be also recognized. Block (1975) suggested that while consistency in behavior across laboratory situations has been limited, with other data sources both consistency and stability over time have been found. Block's longitudinal research showed a moderate to high degree of consistency in dependency and other personal characteristics. These characteristics were evaluated by extensive observations of interaction with peers in childhood, and by in-depth interviews and other means in young adults. An important aspect of such research is the collection of extensive samples of data, not just a few instances of behavior. In laboratory research investigators usually exposed participants to circumstances that in their view have certain properties and would instigate particular kinds of behavior. However, the manner in which these situations are perceived by the subjects is rarely determined, only deduced from the behavior itself. Consequently, apparent inconsistency in behavior across several situations may result from differences in the meaning of these situations to the experimenters and to subjects. Moreover, most situations have varied elements, place varied demands on people, even if some similarity in components can be identified, e.g., they are all relevant to prosocial behavior. When many samples of behavior are taken, the influence of certain personality characteristics, mainly motivational in nature, may become apparent. Across many situations additional determinants may, in a sense, average out, and the influence of important motives will gain expression. This further implies that people will be consistent primarily in domains of activity that are important for them, not in any domain (Bem and Allen, 1974).

A theoretical model will be schematically presented below that specifies personality characteristics that are important in affecting prosocial behavior and the nature of personality situation interaction. This model has been elaborated in other writing (Staub, 1974; 1976;

1978, Staub and Feinberg, 1978). Here it will be briefly described, and attempts to test some aspects of the model will be presented. Some aspects of this model are relevant to the determination of any kind of social behavior, others are specific to prosocial behavior. The determination of prosocial behavior, or "moral behavior" in general, can be understood, in part, by understanding the manner in which social behavior is determined. However, prosocial and moral behavior also have unique aspects and unique determinants.

By prosocial behavior I mean behavior that benefits other people and usually demands some form of self-sacrifice from the actor. An extended definition of prosocial behavior also includes behavior that benefits the self as well as others, such as cooperation, and positive acts that are part of a person's attempts to initiate a relationship with another person or are aspects of an ongoing relationship. The motivation for any prosocial behavior can vary, being partly selfish, for example, in the sense that a person wants to create or maintain a positive image in the eyes of other people. However, even in instances of cooperation and reciprocal positive interaction, when both parties make sacrifices and derive gains, the major reason for a person's positive behavior can be to benefit the other person. Psychologists writing about the motivators of prosocial behavior have focused, on the one hand, on external influences; the behavior guided by the desire for approval or to avoid disapproval, by the hope of material gains, or by other forms of self-interest. On the other hand, prosocial behavior may be guided by internalized values, norms, or beliefs, or motivated by empathic emotion, the vicarious experience of other people's emotions. The nature of internalized values that lead to prosocial behavior can vary, of course. I think that a distinction between behavior guided by concern for other people's welfare and the desire to benefit others, particularly others in need, and behavior guided by a feeling of obligation or duty to help others, may be useful. This distinction refers to differences in value orientation among people, which have different consequences on behavior, at least under certain circumstances. Moreover, the tendency to react empathically to others needs may be associated with a value orientation characterized by concern for other people's welfare (Staub, 1978).

1. *Personal Goals and the Activating Potential of Situations*

There has been a long history in psychology of concern with and emphasis on motivational constructs in attempting both to understand why people behave as they do and to predict how they will behave.

The names of constructs varied: drive, need, reinforcement, reward value, and other terms have been used. The purported properties of these constructs also varied. A primary characteristic of human behavior does seem to be its purposefulness. I assume that personal motives or goals, the construct I will use to denote motivation, direct our behavior, and many other personality characteristics that need to be considered are mainly important in determining whether personal goals are activated and/or their satisfaction is pursued or not. The word "goal" implies a preference for certain outcomes or end states, or an aversion for certain outcomes and the desire to avoid them. It also implies a striving toward or away from these outcomes. The word "personal" implies that a person's goals have a special individual character. Nonetheless, there is likely to be enough similarity among goals of different individuals that people can be grouped on the basis of communality in goals. Mischel (1973; Mischel and Mischel, 1976) argued that people are highly idiosyncratic in the outcomes they value. However, for each individual there is probably a range of similar valued outcomes: minimally, a person who values diminishing others' physical pain is likely to hold this value with varied sources of pain. Moreover, certain classes of outcomes are valued by many people or even by most people to some degree: positive evaluation and approval rather than negative evaluation and disapproval (the latter might be regarded as a negative goal, something to be avoided), physical safety, enhancing material gain, and others.

Internalized values, norms, beliefs, and the tendency to react empathically to others' needs can all increase the value or desirability of benefiting other people and thus contribute to a prosocial goal. Depending on the nature of the values, the extent to which empathy is involved, and so on, the specific character of the goal may differ. For some people, the desired outcome might be to improve others' welfare; for other people, acting in a helpful manner might itself be the desired outcome. Variation in the nature of personal goals is likely to be found in most domains, not only the prosocial one. Some individuals who are characterized by a strong achievement goal may want to do the best job they can when their goal is activated, others may want to experience success, and so on. These and other achievement goals may all gain expression in hard work and attempts to do well in varied activities.

Personal goals are likely to have a number of defining characteristics. One I already noted is the desirability of certain outcomes. Another is a network of cognitions that is usually associated with a goal. It does happen, of course, that the inclination to reach some goal—or the desire to avoid an outcome, a negative goal—is primarily emotional. Usually, however, we have varied thoughts, beliefs, values associated with outcomes that are desirable (or aversive) to us. These cognitions function, in part, to tune us perceptually to the kind of circumstances that make it possible to satisfy our goal. They are also applied to the interpretation of situations. The manner in which events or situations or outcomes are interpreted is likely, in turn, to determine our emotional reactions to them. This view is consistent with current cognitive theories of emotion (Arnold, 1960; Lazarus, 1966; Leventhal, 1974: Averill, 1979). Thus, the cognitive network presumably leads to interpretations that make the goal desirable and lead to the arousal of emotion that motivates attempts to reach the goal.

A third related characteristic of personal goals is the arousal of tension upon the activation of the goal, which continues to exist until either the goal has been reached or it has been deactivated in some manner. The notion that tension is aroused and maintained by the activation of a goal has been proposed by Lewin (1948; Deutch, 1968) and currently extended to the realm of prosocial behavior by Hornstein (1976). The limited evidence that is available about tension systems and their properties supports the concept. For example, consistent with Lewinian assumptions, interrupted tasks are remembered better than completed tasks, and tasks that are interrupted nearer their completion—nearer the achievement of the goal—are remembered better than tasks interrupted further from completion (Deutch, 1968).

It is important, I think, that even if certain people have similar personal goals, for example, the goal of benefiting other people, the range of applicability of their goals can vary. Some people might have learned to apply their concern about others' welfare at times when another person is in physical need, but not in psychological distress; others might have learned to apply such concern to people of certain kinds, perhaps people whom they think of as similar to themselves, or coming from the same ethnic or racial background, but not to other people. Thus, the personal goal that functions as a motive for prosocial action might have different specific ranges of applicability. In some cases the range might be narrow, in others the range might be broad, applicable to varied circumstances, varied needs. We have to develop measurement devices not only to measure the existence of various personal goals and their intensity, but also the specific ranges in which they are applicable, and their breadth or narrowness.

In any particular situation varied motives or personal goals may be aroused in a person. Sometimes when a person is faced with another's need for help, that is the only force acting on him or her: if he or she possesses some degree of motivation to be helpful, he or she will act. Other times a person might be faced with a situation that potentially activates a variety of motives: to be helpful, to achieve well on some task, to behave in proper social ways. Whether such goals are activated will depend on the nature of the situation, its activating potential, as well as on the characteristics of the person, the degree to which the person possesses the personal goals that might be activated by the situation.

I am suggesting, then, that the nature of the situation and the personal goals of an individual will jointly affect behavior. For example, someone might be working on a task or might be simply sitting in a room waiting. Somebody in another room seems to be in distress. If it is important for this person to both do well on tasks and to help other people, he will experience conflict when he is working on the task. His two goals conflict with each other. This will not happen when he is simply waiting, because then his goal of achievement will not be activated. Neither will this happen if doing well on tasks is unimportant to him.

What is the utility of a conception of personal goals when the nature of the goals, as well as their ranges of applicability, may vary across individuals? If it is to have utility, we will have to be able to measure personal goals, ranges of applicability, and the activating potential of situations, and assign people to groups with similar characteristics. The utility of the concept lies in the recognition that frequently when people face particular circumstances varied personal goals are activated. In understanding how prosocial behavior in particular and social behavior in general are determined, we have to consider the joint influence of varied motives. Different goals may sometimes conflict, sometimes join and support each other. For example, the goal to achieve may lead a person to work hard on a task and diminish the likelihood of helping another person, or it may be applied to helping someone in need, adding to the influence of a prosocial goal. Using motivational constructs that apply to varied motives and classes of outcomes may improve our ability to understand and predict social behavior.

2. *Goal Conflict and the Measurement of Goals and Activation Potentials*

What determines which personal goal in a particular situation will exert dominant influence on behavior? The strength or intensity of an activated personal goal must be a joint function of the strength or importance of the personal goal to the individual and the strength of the activation potential of the environment for that goal. As an initial assumption, I will suggest that the intensity of the activated goal will be a function of the multiplicative relationship between intensity of the personal goal and of the activating potential. The greatest sum that results from this multiplication will determine which activated goal will be dominant and influence behavior. When the intensity of two or more activated goals is nearly identical, action required to pursue any of them may be inhibited, and/or various processes may be involved in conflict resolution. (Although the full implication of this will not be discussed here, it is important to note that personal goals and activating potentials of situations are not independent. An aspect of this will be discussed below.)

How can personal goals be measured? One possibility is to ask people to rank order them, similar to Rokeach's (1973) method for rank ordering values. Values and goals are quite similar concepts, in fact, in that values also imply the desirability of certain outcomes. Rokeach's measure showed that rank ordering has reasonable stability over time intervals of a year and a half. However, in measuring personal goals in this manner we must recognize that the hierarchy of personal goals may not only change over time, but vary over the circumstances of a person's life. For example, such a hierarchy may be different for students during the academic year and during their summer vacation.

A second index of personal goals may be the cognitive network associated with them. With regard to prosocial goals, I believe that the important aspects of a cognitive network that lead to a prosocial goal of some generality and breadth are: (a) positive orientation toward other people, positive evaluation of human beings, (b) concern about, value placed on others' welfare, and (c) a feeling of personal responsibility for others' welfare. Clearly, these three dimensions of thinking are interrelated. There is a substantial amount of research evidence for the importance of the last one of these, and some evidence for the second one (Staub, 1978). The first one, positive orientation to people, is likely to provide a basic orientation that in some sense is a precondition for the other two (Staub, Erkut, and Jacquette, as described in Staub, 1974: Staub, 1976; Wrightsman, 1966; Midlarz, 1973). A third measure of individual differences in personal goals may be the extent to which the first two are affected by varying conditions of activation. That is, if a prosocial goal moves up in a person's hierarchy of goals and/or a person's thinking shows greater evidence of the prosocial goal under activating conditions, that would provide further evidence for the importance of the goal for that person.

To evaluate the activating potential of situations it seems necessary to consider personal goals and activating potentials of situations in relation to each other. Although people who do not possess a certain goal may perceive a particular situation as relevant to that personal goal, they may do so to a smaller degree than a person for whom that goal is important. There is some evidence of a meaningful relationship between personal needs, as measured by the Edwards Personal Preference Scale, and perceptual dimensions that people employ in describing other people (Cantor, 1976). Further, implicit personality theories that people hold affect the manner they perceive other people (Schneider, 1973).

Even with identical perception of the relevance of particular situations to particular goals, a person for whom a certain goal is important will evaluate the situation, and the importance of pursuing that goal in that situation, quite differently from one who is unconcerned about that particular goal. Thus, we may ask people who possess personal goals to varied degrees to evaluate the meaning of situations that we believe vary in their activating potential for those goals, and to describe what they would do in those situations, and why. Thus, personal goals and activating potential would be measured and validated, in part, in relation to each other. Measures of activation potentials would also have to be validated by differences in the behavior of people with the same and with different personal goals under varied conditions of activation, as well as by other criteria.

Although the necessity to conceptualize, categorize, classify situations for understanding the manner in which situations and personality interact in determining behavior has been increasingly recognized (Frederickson, 1972; Mischel, 1976; Moos, 1976), little progress has been achieved so far in doing so.

A number of writers have suggested that person measures and situation measures should be in the same units (Murray, 1938; Rotter, 1954). The concepts of personal goal and goal activating potential of a situation are consistent with this view. While a great deal of current interest has developed in an interactionist view, theories about the aspects of individuals and of situations that are particularly important to consider, although not absent (Mischel, 1973), have been minimal. Using concepts somewhat similar to those suggested by Murray (1938) and Rotter (1954), who emphasized respectively needs and the value of outcomes, and in some ways to those of Lewin (1948), the present conception proposes basic dimensions along which personality and situations interact. A future task is to progressively identify dimensions of situations that are relevant to the activation of various goals, and then locate particular situations along those dimensions. In the realm of prosocial behavior there are many and varied research findings on the basis of which such dimensions can be tentatively identified (Staub, 1978).

3. *Other Important Personality Characteristics*

Obviously, personal motivation is not the only determinant of behavior. For example, people may vary in habitual ways of accomplishing their goals. In the present conception habitual modes of behavior can sometimes be autonomous, be of intrinsic value to people, but usually are in the service of satisfying personal motives. Being polite and kind (in superficial ways) can serve the personal goal of gaining approval, or the desire of making others feel good, or satisfy an internalized value of a certain conception of proper social behavior, or all these goals. In general, there are a number of classes of personal characteristics that seem important in determining whether personal goals will be activated and their satisfaction pursued. The following brief discussion will focus on characteristics relevant to prosocial goals.

Perceptual tendencies represent one class. I am primarily referring to role taking, to the capacity and/or tendency to take other people's perspective, to view events from other people's point of view. Although role taking has frequently been viewed as a capacity, having the capacity to correctly perceive how others feel does not necessarily mean that people will actually consider events from others' point of view, will put themselves into another's place. The tendency to actually do so may also depend on prosocial values that can motivate role taking. In addition to role taking, individual differences in the speed of making judgment about the meaning of events (Denner, 1968) may affect the likelihood, particularly in emergencies, that people respond to another's need.

Competencies of varied kinds may be somewhat important in determining whether relevant goals will be activated or not, and essential in determining whether a goal, once activated is acted upon. There are several potentially important kinds of competencies. First, individuals vary in their beliefs of their ability to influence events, to bring about important and/or desirable outcomes: in what is usually referred to as locus of control. This is the most general kind of competence that may influence whether a person will initiate action and pursue attempts to help another person. Individuals also vary in the extent that they have plans of action for dealing with varied circumstances, and perhaps even more importantly in their capacity to generate appropriate plans to satisfy some personal goal in a particular situation. Finally, specific competencies to engage in particular acts that are necessary for helping someone are, obviously, an important determinant whether a person will help another and in what manner. The capacity to swim is essential if one is to jump into a river to save someone from drowning; interpersonal sensitivity and skills are necessary if a person is to be of genuine help to someone in psychological distress.

Individual differences in the capacity and tendency to generate justifications for not helping someone in need, and thereby "neutralizing" personal values and norms, can also be important in determining whether a person will help others or not (Schwartz, 1977; Walster, Berscheid, and Walster, 1973; Staub, 1978) Particularly when prosocial and other goals are in conflict, one way to reduce conflict is to minimize the need for help, the degree to which a person in need deserves to be helped, or in other ways to deactivate the prosocial goal. The tendency to use justifications seems to depend, in turn, on certain values and beliefs, such as a strong belief in a "just world" (Rubin and Peplau, 1973). This can lead people to justify others' suffering as deserved or just.

Individual differences in "hedonic balancing" is a further characteristic that seems important in determining the manner in which prosocial and certain other goals are applied to particular situations (Staub, 1978). This concept is derived from equity type notions, and it is supported by findings about the influence of positive and negative experiences on prosocial behavior. Hedonic balancing refers to people's tendency to consider their own current welfare and its deviation from their usual, accustomed level of well-being, in comparison to the current welfare of the person who provides the stimulus for prosocial behavior and its deviation, in the potential helper's view, from that person's usual or accustomed level of well-being. The judgment that is made on the basis of these elements, as a function of the potential helper's personality and the specific circumstances, affects the likelihood of help.

The importance of these and other personality characteristics has been discussed at greater length elsewhere (Staub, 1978).

4. *Supporting Research*

The findings of the first experiment that we conducted to extensively explore personality–situation interaction have in turn contributed to the formulation of our model (Staub, Erkut, and Jaquette, as described in Staub, 1974). In this study, we administered a large number of personality tests to male undergraduates in one session, and in the first hour of a second session. These measures were either related to prosocial values, evaluation of other human beings, and a feeling of concern for and obligation to others, or they were related to a sense of competence and speed of reacting to events. (Scores on these latter measures were expected to be associated with speed of reacting to an emergency, but were not, probably because the reaction time and other tests that we used are not very good measures of speed of judgment and action). Following the personality tests, the subjects were individually exposed to one of three experimental treatments. Either it was communicated to them that it is permissible to interrupt work on the task they were starting, and to enter the adjoining room (permission) by telling them that they could get some coffee from the adjoining room; or they were prohibited from interrupting their work, by being told that they are working on a timed task and asked not to interrupt their work (prohibition); or they were given no relevant information (control). After the lapse of a period of time they heard live sounds of distress from the adjoining room, produced by a confederate. If the subject entered the adjoining room, the confederate asked if he could go into the subjects' room and lie down on the couch; if the subjects did not enter, after 180 seconds the confederate opened the door and asked the same question. This was followed by several sequences of activities by the confederate that provided opportunities for helpful responses. Thus, we collected a number of measures of helpfulness. These included the original response to the distress sounds, as well as the amount of effort the subject was willing to extend to have a prescription for the confederate filled fast and thereby help reduce the confederate's stomach cramps.

Analyses of variance with treatments as one factor and the subjects divided on several personality measures into high and low groups, one at a time, each of which was regarded as relevant to prosocial values, produced significant interactions. In general, particularly in filling the prescription, subjects whose score fell on the prosocial side of a personality measure tended to help significantly more in the permission group, but not in the other group.

A number of personality characteristics significantly correlated with measures of help. Since many of these measures appeared to be relevant to prosocial values or action—the values helpfulness, equality, Schwartz's (1977) measure of ascription of responsibility to the self for others' welfare, Kohlberg's (1969) measure of moral judgment, Christie's test of a Machiavellian orientation and others—a factor analysis was performed. All of the mesures that I mentioned had high loading on a single factor. A summary "prosocial orientation" score was computed for each subject: their scores on measures that had high loading on the above factor were weighted by the factor loading and summed. These scores correlated significantly and often substantially with measures of helping ($r = .46$ with average help). Moreover, analyses of variance showed no interaction between treatments and this index of personality in affecting prosocial behavior. It is possible that the prosocial orientation scores represented a broad-based prosocial goal, perhaps one that combined the desire for benefiting others out of concern with others' welfare and a sense of obligation and personal responsibility. Moreover, due to the varied tests that were used, the measure may have tapped a broad range of applicability of the prosocial goal. Unfortunately, we included in the factor analysis a couple of value indices that were not prosocial in nature. Of particular importance is ambition, which had a negative loading on the factor. That is, high prosocial orientation score in this study represented subjects who were high on what in subsequent studies I will continue to refer to as prosocial orientation, and also low on a potentially conflicting goal with helping, that of ambition. When both a prosocial goal and one related to accomplishments on tasks are activated, subjects high on the first and low on the second would experience little conflict, according to the model, and would tend to act prosocially. The relevance of this is shown by the finding that in the prohibition condition, where the instruction to work without interruption on the "timed task" could be expected to activate achievement goals, there was a significant negative relationship between the importance to subjects of the value of ambition and their helpful behavior. The above considerations, combined with the findings, make a reanalysis of the data desirable, with prosocial orientation and ambition separated. We are in the process of doing this. Some other findings also showed the interacting influence of prosocial orientation, impulsivity, locus of control, and treatments in affecting prosocial behavior.

Our first primitive attempts to specifically test some aspects of the model that I presented have been made in two dissertations (Feinberg, 1977; Grodman, 1978). Several years ago I conducted a small study that explored female subjects' reactions to another female's psychological distress. I thought that studying reactions to psychological distress is in some ways even more meaningful than studying reactions to physical need, because the former is ever present, we encounter it all the time. The methodology we used seemed effective. The findings did not support the basic hypothesis we tested, that if a person is responsible for the events that created her distress people will respond less than if a person is not responsible. However, the interaction was transactional, as one would expect in real life, in the sense that there was a positive relationship between the amount the subject and the distressed confederated talked.

Using the basic approach of this study, that two people are working on a task as one of them, the confederate begins to communicate that she is distressed, upset, in psychological need, Feinberg carefully designed a situation in which the confederate was upset about suddenly having been left by her boyfriend, without understanding the reasons for it. The relationship had lasted for two years and included discussions of marriage. As is the Staub, Erkut, and Jaquette study, in the studies of psychological distress the confederates' communications were carefully organized into units, providing the other person with opportunities to respond following each unit. Moreover, additional units were prepared, which the confederate was to use in response to relevant questions and comments by the subjects. While the interactions were seemingly highly natural and freeflowing, the confederate's behavior was highly structured and standardized.

Previously a variety of personality tests were administered to the subjects, some of which we developed. The tests included many of those that we used in the study described above and had high loadings on the prosocial orientation factor, but not all, and some new ones. This group of tests was intended to measure a prosocial goal. Another group of tests was intended to measure an achievement goal, an orientation to wanting to do well in specific realms of activities or in all activities. Separate factor analysis of these two groups of tests produced a meaningful prosocial factor and a meaningful achievement factor. The design of the study was a $2 \times 2 \times 2$ design, with subjects divided into high and low groups on the basis of each of the two factor scores, and experimental variation in degree of need. In the high need condition the confederate lost her boyfriend the day before, in low need a year ago; in each case the confederate was reminded of it and the discussion of it was elicited by a story in the task that the subject and confederate were working on.

The manner in which nonverbally the subjects oriented themselves to the confederate and the task was coded by observers who were observing through one-way mirrors. The extent to which they looked at, were attentive to, and smiled at the confederate, or alternatively looked at or worked on the task, was noted. On several nonverbal measures there was a need by prosocial orientation interaction. In high need, high prosocial subjects looked at or worked on the task much less than low prosocial subjects; in low need, high prosocial subjects looked at or worked on the task more than low prosocial subjects. In high need high prosocial subjects oriented themselves toward the person in need, rather than the task. High prosocial, low achievement subjects in high need looked at and worked on the task least (Table I). Thus, with regard to nonverbal interaction, Feinberg tended to find what the model would predict.

TABLE I
Nonverbal Responses:
Looking at Work and Writing

Achievement	Low need		High need	
	Prosocial		Prosocial	
	Low	High	Low	High
Low	77	93	99	58
High	71	76	125	68

[a]Adapted from Feinberg, 1977.

The participants' responses to some of the items on a postexperimental questionnaire gives some meaning to the nonverbal data, as well as to some of the findings reported below. The high prosocial subjects expressed more of a feeling of obligation to the experimenter—e.g., to do the task—than did low prosocial subjects. Moreover, high prosocial subjects expressed less desire to help the experimenter in the high than in the low need condition, and more desire to help the confederate. These subjects apparently felt an obligation to help the experimenter, to do what they agreed to, but in the high need condition their desire to help the confederate became dominant, this expressed in their behavior.

The verbal communications by the subjects to the confederate were coded on a number of dimensions, and scores on each dimension were used as a dependent variable in the analyses of variance. High achievement subjects tended to speak more than low achievement subjects. On several dimensions there was a prosocial by achievement interaction: subjects in the low prosocial and high achievement group were more verbal than subjects in other groups. The total of verbalizations in this group was substantially higher than in other groups (Table II). Also, in several specific categories of seemingly helpful verbalizations the amount subjects talked in this group was higher in other groups (e.g., "problem-directed questions"). It is unclear, however, whether being more verbal is necessarily more helpful. A purported helper may monopolize the interaction and thereby limit a distressed person's opportunity to express feelings.

How does one determine what behavior of a person who responds to another's psychological need is really helpful? External criteria can be wrong. We have little or no empirical guidance in this; even psychotherapists of different schools disagree what behavior directed at their patients is helpful. The subjective experience of the

TABLE II
Cell Means of Analyses of Variance by Need (N), Prosocial Goal (P) and Achievement Goal (A): Total Verbal Responses[a]

Achievement	Low need		High need	
	Prosocial		Prosocial	
	Low	High	Low	High
Low	11.23	12.30	11.82	14.24
High	25.8	11.00	26.75	14.38

Note. Significant effect: $P_x A$; P; A.
[a] Adapted from Feinberg, 1977.

person at whom help is directed is one important criterion. The impressions of a "bystander" are also relevant. Feinberg had both the experimenter (observing from behind a one-way mirror) and the confederate rate the behavior of the subject on a variety of dimensions. Their combined ratings on the dimensions where ratings were similar and thus "reliable" were used as dependent measures in analyses of variance. The raters knew, of course, what degree of need the subjects responded to, but not their personality. In subjects relating their own experience, presumably to help the confederate, there was a need by prosocial interaction. High prosocial subjects did it more under high need, less under low need, than low prosocial ones (Table III). Both high need, and high achievement, resulted in greater expression of "sincere sympathy." A major dependent variable was the subjects' expression of willingness to later continue the interaction with the

TABLE III
Relates Own Experience: Confederate's and Experimenter's Ratings[a]

Achievement	Low need		High need	
	Prosocial		Prosocial	
	Low	High	Low	High
Low	5.18	3.83	2.92	4.22
High	5.38	4.50	4.40	5.57

Significant effect: $N_x P$.
[a] Adapted from Feinberg, 1977.

confederate. The confederate at some point indicated that she did not want to keep the subject any more from working on the task, expressed satisfaction from having had the opportunity to talk, and indicated her interest in later continuing the conversation. Analyses of the ratings of the subjects' expressed willingness for future interaction again resulted in a need by prosocial interaction. Low prosocial subjects were more willing under low need, high prosocial ones were more willing under high need. Finally, subjects high on achievement were rated significantly more friendly than subjects low on achievement.

Some further ratings of the postexperimental questionnaire may add to the understanding of the data. Although the analyses of variance of these ratings only showed trends, given the pattern of findings it is important that low prosocial high achievement subjects in the high need group tended to dislike the confederate; they judged her cold, depressed and unemotional. In contrast, high prosocial low achievement subjects in the high need condition judged her warm, liked her most.

Clearly, in this study high achievement orientation tended to manifest itself by people making efforts to verbally, and in other ways, respond to the confederate. Feinberg refers to Stein's (1970) review of the literature on achievement orientation in women: those with high achievement will strive for success in sex-typed activities. Interpersonal relations and help for another woman in distress seem such activities. The greater responsiveness by the high achievement women tended to occur both in high and low need, was not only elicited by the confederate's distress. A high prosocial orientation resulted in differentiated responding, in greater attention to and work on the task in low need, and more help for and interest in the confederate in high need. However, the amount of verbal help that subjects provided was moderate. Mean verbalization by high prosocial subjects in high need was substantially less than in the low need high achievement group but greater than in the other groups. The low prosocial high achievement subjects provide an "interesting" picture. They talked a great deal, both in low and in high need. However, they looked at and worked on their task more than subjects in any other group in high need (Table I), and in the high need condition they also disliked the confederate. Finally, they reported more of a feeling of obligation to help the experimenter by doing their task in *high* need than in low need. Feinberg suggests that they tried to respond in ways that they perceived appropriate to the situation, rather than being lead by a desire to help. However, it seems that they not only tried to do what they considered appropriate and desirable, in the high need condition, but that they felt uncomfortable in facing the person in need. While making extensive effort to "help" verbally they concentrated on their task more than in low need, and reported dislike of the confederate.

The findings clearly show the complexity of lifelike human interactions. At the same time, they are promising in that they show that despite the complexity, behavior is predictable on the basis of the situation and personality, and provides some support for the model. Low need was, in essence, not a need but a control condition: the confederate reminisced about a distressful event but was not distressed. Consequently, a prosocial goal was not activated in low need. When it was activated, in high need, high prosocial subjects were responsive to the distressed person in varied ways. Probably even their moderate, rather than extremely high rate of verbal responses can be taken as an indication of their responsiveness. Finally, the findings do suggest that it is important to carefully establish what conditions are likely to function as activators of what goals. In this study another's request for attention—through expressing distress or describing past distress—seemed a more potent activator of women's achievement goal than performance on a task.

In another dissertation Grodman (1978) used the basic procedure that Feinberg developed, with some improvements, primarily in processing the data. The categories used to classify the subjects' verbal behavior were somewhat different and more elaborate. Since we came to realize the difficulty in determining what kinds of reactions are helpful to a person in psychological distress, Grodman had both observers and the confederate make more elaborate ratings of the subjects' behavior immediately after the interaction was concluded. Moreover, independently of other data analyses, naive judges listened to tapes of the complete interaction between the confederate and the subject, and rated the subject's global helpfulness. These ratings allowed consideration of the whole interaction, and both what the subjects said and the affects expressed by their voices.

Grodman first administered to female subjects a large number of personality measures, similarly to the two previous studies, to measure prosocial orientation. These included the measures that had high loadings on the prosocial factor in Feinberg's study, and a few others. Factor analysis again provided a prosocial factor, with most of the same tests as in the previous study loading high on this factor. (The following tests had high loading: Schwartz's ascription of responsibility, Berkowitz and Lutterman's social responsibility, the Machiavellian scale (negative), and some of Rokeach's values). Subjects were divided into high and low groups on the basis of their factor scores. They were exposed, several weeks after the administration of the personality tests, to a distressed confederate. Feinberg's high need condition was used. Grodman included two types of experimental variations in her study. The subjects were either told that at a later time they will meet the person who was working in the same room with them on the experimental task, that at that time they will discuss and have to draw some conclusions about several "case histories," or no expectations were created about meeting this person again. A second variation was in the cost of helping. In a high cost condition the subjects were told that feedback about their personality will be available to them, based on the personality measures they filled out. It was indicated to the subjects as they started to work on the task that "activated" the expression of distress by the confederate—the evaluation of people's personality described in passages taken from short stories (see Staub, 1974, VII)—that information on this task was relatively unimportant for the experimenter, but quite valuable in providing feedback to the subject. No feedback was mentioned in the low cost group. In high cost, by responding to and interacting with the confederate, the subjects would give up the opportunity to work on the task, and thereby diminished the value of the feedback to them.

In this study, the subjects were exposed to another person's relatively intense psychological distress. This was expected to activate their prosocial goal, as measured by prosocial orientation. One of the consistent findings, across varied measures, was that in comparison to low prosocial subjects high prosocial subjects acted in ways that appeared more helpful. Frequently, the difference was substantial. On a few measures, variation in the cost of helping had a significant influence, high cost resulting in less help than low cost. More frequently there was a cost by prosocial orientation interaction, in addition to a main effect of personality. In these cases usually the difference between high and low prosocial subjects was small in high cost, although numerically high prosocial subjects still helped more. In the low cost condition low prosocial subjects helped about as much as subjects in the high cost condition, while high prosocial subjects helped substantially more. Expecting or not expecting to meet the distressed person had relatively little effect on the subjects' behavior.

I will exemplify these generalizations by noting some of the many findings in greater detail. The consistency of these findings is quite impressive. High prosocial subjects looked at the task less than low prosocial subjects ($p < .01$) while high cost subjects looked more than low cost subjects ($p < .01$). High prosocial subjects smiled more at the confederate ($p < .01$). An analysis of variance of the sum of all the positive (helpful) verbalization by subjects again showed a significant

TABLE IV
Global Ratings of Help Provided by Subjects[a]

Prosocial orientation	Cost	Expect to meet: Yes	Expect to meet: No
Low	Low	2.1	2.0
	High	2.0	2.5
High	Low	3.1	3.1
	High	2.7	2.3

[a] Adapted from Grodman, 1977.

prosocial effect ($p < .05$) as well as a cost by prosocial interaction ($p < .01$). Similar findings were obtained when verbalizations were factors analyzed and the analyses of variance were based on scores on two emerging factors of positive verbalizations. Analyses of what the subjects said in response to the confederate's expression of the desire to talk after the experimental session showed a generally more positive attitude by high than low prosocial subjects ($p < .001$). Moreover, high prosocial subjects agreed sooner to meet the confederate ($p < .005$) and also to a definite meeting place ($p < .03$). The ratings of global help by independent raters who listened to the taped interactions again showed substantially more help by high prosocial subjects ($p < .002$) and a personality by cost interaction ($p < .05$) (Table IV).

Ratings by the confederates following their interactions with subjects showed that they perceived high prosocial subjects as substantially more helpful than low prosocial subjects, in varied ways. (Naturally, the confederate had no information about the subjects' personality scores). High prosocial subjects were perceived as more responsive, more sympathetic, less nervous, and less shy. On all except the last rating there was a personality by cost interaction. In response to the question, "If it was a life situation, do you think she would have done a good job making you feel better?" there were significant prosocial ($p < .002$), cost ($p < .01$), and prosocial by cost interaction effects ($p < .05$) (see Table V). Ratings by the observers also supported these findings. The confederates' (and observers') ratings are valuable because even though they were trained participants, they responded to the total behavior of the subjects.

Postexperimental responses by subjects to a questionnaire were consistent with other findings. High prosocial subjects liked the con-

TABLE V
Confederate's Ratings of How Helpful Subject Would Be in Real Life

Prosocial orientation	Cost	Expect to meet: Yes	No
Low	Low	1.44	1.75
	High	1.57	1.44
High	Low	2.75	2.12
	High	1.80	1.60

[a]Adapted from Grodman, 1977.

federates substantially more than low prosocial subjects, with a significant personality by cost interaction. The former believed more than the latter that they could be helpful. It was more important for subjects in the high cost than in the low cost condition to do well on the test. Surprisingly, however, subjects in the high cost condition reported stronger belief than those in the low cost group that it mattered to the experimenter whether they finished the test or not.

The expectation of meeting the confederate had relatively little influence. Subjects who expected to meet the confederate looked more at her, but after the confederate said she would like to talk more later they made more attempts to disengage—mainly the subjects low in the prosocial orientation—and said more negative things than subjects who did not expect to meet the confederate. It seemed that under the conditions that existed in the experiment the expectation of further involvement with the distressed person led to some attempts by subjects, mainly those less prosocially oriented, to distance themselves.

5. *Concluding Comments*

Our initial attempts to test the model provided some support. Conditions that would be expected to activate a personal goal to benefit others have resulted in more attempts to help by high than by low prosocial subjects. These findings were unequivocal in Grodman's dissertation, more complicated in Feinberg's study. One of the immediate tasks for further testing the model is to develop measures of a prosocial goal, and perhaps of other personal goals, based on our experience with the kind of measurement that we have relied on so far, that of using varied tests of the domain of prosocial values and beliefs. Another immediate task is to develop measures of activation potential of situations. Then additional relevant personality characteristics have to be measured and used as the basis of more refined prediction. We would expect, for example, that competence and a prosocial orientation would jointly affect prosocial behavior. In one study Liebhart (1972) did find, in fact, that subjects scoring high on both a measure of sympathy and of instrumental activity were more likely to respond to sounds of distress than other subjects.

Our findings clearly show that a general personality characteristic, which I referred to as prosocial orientation and considered as the index of a prosocial goal, tends to lead people to behave prosocially. We found this in all three studies that I described. It is also true that this personality orientation tended to exert influence jointly with other characteristics of the person or with characteristics of the situation. Although prosocial orientation had a substantial influence on subjects' behavior in the Grodman study, a high cost reduced this influence. In light of the postexperimental questionnaire it is not certain whether this was only due to subjects' desire to gain information about themselves—and my guess is that this may be important to high prosocial people—or also to their belief in the high cost condition that it was important to the experimenter that they finish the task.

Of particular importance is that some "general" personality characteristic, such as prosocial orientation, may affect prosocial behavior across varied situations, in predictable fashion. Gergen, Gergen, and Meter (1972), whose views about personality situation interaction are somewhat similar to my own, came to conclusions quite different from those suggested by this research. They found, in a class of students whose personality was evaluated, and who were then asked to volunteer their help with various projects in the psychology department, that different personality characteristics were associated with volunteering to help in different projects. For example, need for nurturance in males was significantly related to their willingness to help with counseling other males, but not to volunteering with other forms of help. Sensation seeking as a personality characteristic was positively related to helping with research on unusual states of consciousness, but negatively related to research on deductive thinking. The pattern of correlations also differed for males and females. Gergen *et al.* stress that helping behavior is determined by situational payoffs, and discourage the notion that "trait dispositions" or individual difference variables will be found that predict helping behavior across situations or across types of help. The subjects in this study did not actually help, they only volunteered; moreover, they were not confronted with anyone's direct need. The findings are clearly consistent with the theoretical model I presented, in that people seemed to volunteer for tasks that appeared satisfying and meaningful from the standpoint of their various needs, characteristics, perhaps goals. However, no attempt has been made by Gergen *et al.* to measure a personality characteristic relevant to helping itself, some form of orientation to others' welfare or to helping. Only a characteristic that makes helping a desirable activity could be expected to relate to different kinds of helping acts. Only a high degree of motivation for prosocial behavior can one reasonably expect to lead to any generality in helping behavior, or generality in the expressed intention to be helpful, and even that only under certain conditions. An "irrelevant" characteristic, such as sensation seeking, would be expected to sometimes add to, other times detract from, the influence of a prosocial goal. When considered by itself it can be expected to lead to helping only when it so happens that the helping behavior satisfies sensation seeking, that is, for accidental reasons. However, given the existence of a strong prosocial motivation, a positive relationship between such motivation and several helping acts can be expected under certain, specifiable conditions. The theoretical model that I presented in this paper is an initial attempt to specify such conditions.

One purpose of this theoretical model is to go beyond attempting to demonstrate that situations and persons jointly determine behavior, by specifying the characteristics of persons in conjunction with characteristics of situations that are important to consider. The model points to a variety of characteristics of people that enter into the determination of behavior. Considering at the same time all the relevant characteristics that the model points to, the varied motives and their different hierarchies, their ranges of applicability, and differences in activating potentials they imply, perceptual tendencies and competencies, each person would end up as unique. By considering a limited number of relevant personal characteristics at one time, however, we can make meaningful predictions for groups of individuals who possess varied combinations of these characteristics. The larger the number of characteristics we consider, the better will our predictions be, but the smaller the number of individuals to whom such predictions apply.

References

Arnold, M. *Emotion and personality*. New York: Columbia University Press, 1960.

Averill, J. Emotion, mood, and personality. In Staub, E. (Ed.), *Personality: Basic issues and current research*. Englewood Cliffs, N.J.: Prentice-Hall, 1979.

Bem, D.J., and Allen, A. On predicting some of the people some of the time: The search for cross-situational consistencies in behavior. *Psychological Review,* 1974, *81,* 506–520.

Block, J. Recognizing the coherence of personality. Paper presented at the Symposium on Interactional Psychology, Stockholm, June, 1975.

Bowers, K.S. Situationism in psychology: An analysis and a critique. *Psychological Review,* 1973, *80,* 307–336.

Cantor, J.H. Individual needs and salient constructs in interpersonal perception. *Journal of Personality and Social Psychology,* 1976, *34,* 519–525.

Denner, B. Did a crime occur? Should I inform anyone? A study of deception. *Journal of Personality,* 1968, *36,* 454–466.

Deutch, M. Field theory in social psychology. In Lindsey, G. and Aronson, E. (Eds.), *Handbook of social psychology.* Reading, Mass.: Addison-Wesley Publishing Co., 1968.

Ekehammar, B. Interactionism in personality from a historical perspective. *Psychological Bulletin,* 1974, *81,* 1026–1048.

Feinberg, H.K. Anatomy of a helping situation: Some determinants of helping in a conflict situation involving another's psychological distress. Unpublished dissertation, University of Massachusetts, 1977.

Frederiksen, N. Toward a taxonomy of situations. *American Psychologist,* 1972, *27,* 114–124.

Gergen, K.L., Gergen, M., and Meter, K. Individual orientations to prosocial behavior. *Journal of Social Issues,* 1972, *8,* 105–130.

Grodman, S.M. The role of personality and situation variables in responding to and helping an individual in psychological distress, Unpublished dissertation, University of Massachusetts, 1978.

Hornstein, H.A. *We and they: Socio-psychological origins of kindness and cruelty.* Englewood Cliffs, N.J.: Prentice-Hall, 1976.

Jones, E.E., and Nisbett, R.E. *The actor and the observer: Divergent perceptions of the causes of behavior.* New York: General Learning Press, 1971.

Kohlberg, L. Stage and sequence: The cognitive-developmental approach to socialization. In Goslin, D. (Ed.), *Handbook of socialization theory and research.* Chicago: Rand McNally, 1969.

Lazarus, R.S. *Psychological stress and the coping process.* New York: McGraw-Hill, 1966.

Leventhal, H. Emotions: A basic problem for social psychology. In Nemeth, C. (Ed.), *Social Psychology: Classic and contemporary integrations.* Chicago: Rand McNally College Publishing Co., 1974.

Lewin, K. *Resolving social conflicts.* New York: Harper, 1948.

Liebhart, E. Empathy and emergency helping: The effects of personality, self-concern, and acquaintance. *Journal of Experimental Social Psychology,* 1972, *8,* 404–411.

Midlarz, S. The role of trust in helping behavior. Unpublished masters thesis, University of Massachusetts, Amherst, 1973.

Mischel, W. *Personality and assessment.* New York: Wiley, 1968.

Mischel, W. Towards a cognitive social learning reconceptualization of personality. *Psychological Review,* 1973, *80,* 252–283.

Mischel, W. *Introduction to Personality.* 2nd ed. New York: Holt, Rinehart, and Winston, 1976.

Mischel, W., and Mischel, H.N. A cognitive social-learning approach to morality and self-regulation. In Lickona, T., *Moral development and behavior.* New York: Holt, Rinehart, and Winston, 1976.

Moos, R. *The human context: Environmental determinants of behavior.* New York: Wiley, 1976.

Murray, H.A. *Explorations in personality*. New York: Oxford University Press, 1938.

Rokeach, M. *The nature of human values*. New York: Macmillan Publishing Co., 1973.

Rotter, J.B. *Social learning and clinical psychology*. Englewood Cliffs, N.J.: Prentice-Hall, 1954.

Rubin, Z., and Peplau, L.A. Belief in a just world and reactions to another's lot: A study of participants in the national draft lottery. *Journal of Social Issues*, 1973, *29*, 73–93.

Schneider, D.J. Implicit personality theory: A review. *Psychological Bulletin*, 1973, *79*, 294–309.

Schwartz, S. Normative influences on altruism. In Berkowitz, L. (Ed.), *Advances in experimental social psychology*, (Vol. 10). New York: Academic Press, 1977.

Staub, E. Helping a distressed person: Social, personality, and stimulus determinants. In Berkowitz, L. (Ed.), *Advances in experimental social psychology* (Vol. 7). New York: Academic Press, 1974.

Staub, E. The development of prosocial behavior: Directions for future research and applications to education. Paper presented at Moral Citizenship/Education Conference, June 1976, Philadelphia.

Staub, E. *Positive social behavior and morality* (Vol. 1). New York: Academic Press, 1978.

Staub, E., and Feinberg, H.K. Personality, socialization, and the development of prosocial behavior in children. In Smith, D.H., and Macauley, J. (Eds.), *Voluntary social action research*. San Francisco: Jossey-Bass, 1978.

Stein, A. The socialization of achievement orientation in females. *Psychological Bulletin*, 1973, *80*, 345–366.

Walster, E., Berscheid, E., and Walster, G.W. New directions in equity research. *Journal of Personality and Social Psychology*, 1973, *25*, 151–176.

Wrightsman, L.S. Personality and attitudinal correlates of trusting and trusting behaviors in a two-person game. *Journal of Personality and Social Psychology*, 1966, *4*, 328–332.

Altruism and Human Kindness: Internal and External Determinants of Helping Behavior

C. Daniel Batson, John M. Darley, and Jay S. Coke

1. *Introduction*

In several incidents, of which the Kitty Genovese tragedy is the best known and best publicized, bystanders have watched without offering assistance while other humans have suffered and even died. In the Genovese case, thirty-eight persons witnessed a woman being repeatedly stabbed; not one intervened, not one called the police.

A very different sort of incident occurred recently on a Los Angeles freeway. George Valdez, forty-nine, rescued two girls involved in a serious car accident. At considerable risk to his own life, he ran across four lanes of fast-moving freeway traffic to give first-aid to one of the victims lying helpless in the fast lane (Blank, 1970).

Another incident that seems to show compassion rather than callousness comes from developmental psychologist Martin Hoffman (1975). In this case a twenty-month-old male child responded to the plight of a young playmate. When about to go home, the visiting friend burst into tears, complaining that her parents would not be there (they were away for two weeks). His immediate reaction was to look sad; he then offered her his beloved teddy bear to take with her. Reminded by his parents that he would miss the teddy if he gave it away, he still insisted on her taking it.

Why do some people fail to help others in desperate need? Why do other people help, even when helping involves considerable cost?

C. Daniel Batson • Department of Psychology, University of Kansas, Lawrence, Kansas 66044. John M. Darley • Department of Psychology, Princeton University, Princeton, New Jersey 08540. Jay S. Coke • Department of Psychology, University of Kansas, Lawrence, Kansas 66044.

After a period of relative neglect in psychology, these questions have recently generated considerable interest and controversy (Hebb, 1971; Krebs, 1970, 1971; Macaulay and Berkowitz, 1970; Severy, 1974; Wispé, 1972). Answers have obvious social relevance; they also have theoretical relevance. Incidents such as the Genovese case, in which bystanders failed to assist someone in desperate need, provide an embarrassment to society. They generate cries of outrage; in the words of one *New York Times* editorial, "Creatures in the jungle could not be more unfeeling." Incidents like the last two cited above, in which someone helps with apparent disregard for self, seem more reassuring about human nature. But they provide an embarrassment to psychologists. Since Thorndike formulated his famous Law of Effect (1898) and before, the prevailing psychological models of human motivation have been egoistic. People are assumed to act for their own gains, benefits, or rewards. Our faith in this egoistic principle is so strong that it has almost become a tautology. If a person acts in an apparently unselfish fashion, we immediately look for hidden sources of personal gain that we assume must be present: George Valdez was motivated by a desire to see his name in the headlines; the young boy was amply compensated for the temporary loss of his teddy by his parents' proud smiles.

It is worth noting that modern psychology's devotion to egoistic models of motivation is breathtakingly extreme. Historically, even relatively cynical observers of human behavior have not been willing to limit motivation exclusively to selfish desires. For example, Adam Smith, a noted champion of egoism and *laissez-faire*, asserted:

> How selfish soever man may be supposed, there are evidently some principles in his nature which interest him in the fortune of others, and render their happiness necessary to him. (1759, p. 1)

Thus, incidents of helping behavior not only provide psychologists with a timely, socially relevant arena for research, they also provide potential anomalies that may eventually force a change in our basic paradigm (Kuhn, 1962) of human motivation. They force us to reconsider whether all human behavior is motivated by egoistic concerns for personal benefit or whether at least some motivation for at least some behavior might be altruistically directed toward benefiting someone else.

2. *Internal versus External Determinants of Helping*

In contemporary discussions the altruism versus egoism question has usually been cast in terms of internal versus external determinants of helping behavior. Researchers have asked: Is there some internal disposition within at least some people that leads them to care about the fortune of others, or is the only difference between persons who help and persons who do not that the two groups are confronted with different external social situations having different egoistic reward structures? When considered in the light of recent research on internal and external determinants of helping, one is likely to answer the question of what motivates helping in purely egoistic terms. Clear empirical demonstrations that internal, dispositional factors affect helping have not been forthcoming. There has been, however, considerable evidence that external, situational factors affect helping.

2.1. *Internal Determinants*

2.1.1. Individual Difference Variables. A natural point to begin the search for internal determinants of helping is to assume that certain individuals possess dispositions, learned or innate, that are conducive to helping. Helpers possess these dispositions in sufficient measure; nonhelpers do not. One might assume that George Valdez was an unusually sensitive person or had a well-developed sense of social responsibility, while the 38 witnesses of the Genovese murder lacked these characteristics. Certainly the most frequent explanations of the Genovese incident by psychiatrists and social commentators at the time were individual difference explanations: apathy, indifference, depersonalization, alienation (Rosenthal, 1964). Such explanations for helping have considerable intuitive appeal. They are straightforward; they can explain helping or failure to help in a wide range of situations; and they can even be reconciled with the prevailing view that human behavior is egoistic ("he helped because he's the type that gains pleasure from helping"). But there is a problem: Individual difference explanations have received at best limited empirical support.

Researchers have examined the relationship between helping and a wide range of personality and demographic variables: social responsibility, Machiavellianism, authoritarianism, social desirability, alienation, autonomy, deference, submissiveness, trustworthiness, independence, agreement with New Left beliefs, awareness of consequences, ascription of responsibility, and size of home town (Berkowitz and Daniels, 1964; Darley and Latané, 1968; Korte, 1971; Midlarsky and Midlarsky, 1973; Rutherford and Mussen, 1968; Schwartz, 1968; Schwartz and Clausen, 1970; Schwartz and Gottlieb, 1976; Staub, 1971; Weiner, 1976; Yakimovich and Saltz, 1971). None of these variables, by itself, has proven to be a consistent predictor of helping behavior. More encouraging results were reported by Staub (1974), who successfully predicted helping in one study with an index of prosocial orientation based upon subjects' responses to several personality measures (ascription of responsibility, social responsibility, Machiavellianism, moral reasoning, and prosocial values). But a number of individual personality measures have predicted helping in one study only to fail to predict in subsequent studies; therefore, we cannot yet assume that Staub's index will prove to be a consistent predictor of helping. This is especially true since Staub's findings were not expected, but instead resulted from post hoc exploration of his data.

To generalize from the studies conducted thus far, the notion that individual difference variables affect whether a person will help has not received consistent support. Support has been more consistent for the effect of individual differences on how a person helps. Schwartz and Clausen (1970) found a relationship between ascription of responsibility and whether a person helped directly or indirectly. Those higher in ascribing responsibility to self were more likely to help by going directly to the victim instead of seeking someone else to aid the victim. Darley and Batson (1973) found a correlation between another personality variable, religious orientation, and how individuals helped. A doctrinally orthodox orientation to religion correlated positively with a relatively persistent form of helping. This form of helping appeared insensitive to the expressed needs of the person in trouble. In contrast, an open, questioning orientation to religion correlated positively with relatively tentative, need-responsive helping. Batson (1976) provided a generalized replication of the relationship of these two religious orientations to these two ways of responding to needs.

Although more research is needed on the relationships between individual difference variables and type of help, the Schwartz and Clausen (1970), Darley and Batson (1973), and Batson (1976) results suggest that individual differences may play a greater role in determining the type of help offered than in determining whether help will be offered. Whether a person helps is often a quick decision and may be little influenced by dispositional characteristics. How one helps involves a more complex series of decisions occurring over a longer time span; there may be greater leeway for dispositions to shape responses.

It seems unlikely, however, that researchers will or should abandon the search for a relationship between individual difference variables and whether a person will help. Still, some changes in research strategy may be in order. Reviewing previous research and their own results, Gergen, Gergen, and Meter (1972) have suggested that it may have been unreasonable to expect any one personality variable to predict with consistency whether a person will help. Instead, a given personality variable may predict who will help in one type of situation;

other personality variables may predict who will help in other types of helping situations. This suggests that before we can expect to observe a relationship between individual differences and helping it may be necessary to develop an explicit taxonomy of need situations, indicating the important dimensions on which these situations may differ and the implication of differences along these dimensions for the individual differences under consideration.

Alternatively, Huston and Korte (1976) have suggested that the research methods used to investigate the relationship between personality variables and helping may be to blame for the failure to find a relationship. Samples have typically been rather small and homogeneous; this could reduce correlations by restricting variance on the personality variable. Further, Huston and Korte suggest that research to date may not have looked at the right personality variables, or the right combination of variables. They feel that Staub's (1974) composite prosocial index may overcome this weakness. While such suggestions for methodological improvement are always in order, considering the research to date it is difficult not to be impressed by the array of failures to find any consistent relationship between what would seem to be relevant individual differences and whether one will help.

2.1.2. Norms. Another frequently invoked internal determinant of helping is the norm of social responsibility (Berkowitz, 1957; also see Leeds, 1963). This norm specifies individuals should help another who is in need and is dependent upon them. Once socialized to accept this rule for appropriate behavior, it has been argued, one should feel internal pressure to act accordingly. This should be especially true when one is reminded of the norm. But, once again, while a normative explanation has been popular the empirical evidence that adherence to the norm of social responsibility produces helping has not been convincing.

Beginning with Berkowitz and Daniels in 1963 the results of a number of studies have been consistent with the assumption that the norm of social responsibility motivates helping (Berkowitz, 1968; Berkowitz and Daniels, 1963, 1964; Horowitz, 1968; Schaps, 1972; Schopler and Bateson, 1965; Schopler and Matthews, 1965). None of these studies, however, has provided unequivocal evidence that this norm elicits helping, and few were even designed to test this assumption.

In 1970, Darley and Latané challenged the usefulness of norms to explain helping. They contended that although norms may provide a general disposition to help others, they are not particularly useful in predicting when helping will occur. First, norms are often contradictory. One norm says help dependent others; another says mind your own business. Second, norms are both too general and too vague to direct behavior. Norms can be used after the fact to explain helping or lack of helping in virtually any situation, but they are far less useful in generating precise predictions of when helping will or should occur.

The Darley and Latané (1970) challenge reopened the question of whether the norm of social responsibility actually motivates helping. Berkowitz and Macaulay (reported in Berkowitz, 1972) and Darley and Batson (1973) attempted to answer this question by manipulating the salience of this norm without also manipulating the ability to help or receipt of prior help, serious confounds in several previous studies of the norm-helping relationship. Berkowitz and Macaulay interviewed women in shopping centers, asking them questions either about whether they and others were helpful or about whether they were smart consumers. It was assumed that the interview about being helpful would make the norm of social responsibility salient. Yet, the women interviewed about helpfulness were subsequently no more likely to help a man needing 40¢ for a bus ticket than were the women interviewed about shopping. Berkowitz (1972) concluded, "The findings do not provide any clear-cut support for the normative analysis of help-giving" (p. 77). . . . The potency of the conjectured 'social responsibility norm' was greatly exaggerated in (the) early formation" (p. 68).

Darley and Batson (1973) used what, by any standard, should have been a very powerful manipulation of salience of the norm of social responsibility. In a high salience condition students at Princeton Theological Seminary read the parable of the Good Samaritan. In the low salience condition, seminarians read a message concerning nontraditional job opportunities for ministers. The seminarians were then directed to another building where they anticipated giving a talk on the message they had read. As they went, they passed through an alley where a young man was slumped in a doorway, coughing and groaning. Seminarians going to talk about the Good Samaritan were not significantly more likely to help the victim than were seminarians going to talk about jobs.

Greenwald (1975) has pointed out that a Bayesian analysis of Darley and Batson's (1973) data indicates that the norm salience manipulation did have a detectable effect. Yet, while detectable, the effect seems surprisingly small; the norm salience manipulation accounted for only 6.25% of the variance in whether seminarians helped the victim.

One might tentatively conclude, as Berkowitz (1972) and Darley and Batson (1973) did, that the norm of social responsibility is not a very potent motivator of helping. Of course, one might also conclude that manipulating salience of the norm is not the most appropriate technique for assessing its causal efficacy. If the norm is well internalized by all members of society, making it salient for some may have little effect. It may already be salient for everyone. While this could explain the weak effect of norm salience manipulations, it creates new problems for a normative analysis of helping. If a norm is universal within society, the norm cannot account for why some people help and others do not.

Shalom Schwartz (1973, 1975, 1977) has attempted to rescue the concept of norm as a predictor of helping by proposing that we must look not to general social norms but to "specific personal norms." Personal norms are internalized rules of conduct learned from social interaction. They vary from individual to individual, even within the same society. Their stability, strength, and scope also vary. The sanctions attached to a personal norm are tied to the self-concept: guilt, self-depreciation, or loss of self-esteem (Schwartz, 1973). Unlike general social norms, these specific norms are linked to particular behavioral responses. Specific norms are "crystallized" out of one's structure of values and general norms to provide directives for action in a particular situation. Need situations initiate a decision process concerning appropriate response; situation-specific personal norms provide direction in deciding which response is best.

The notion of specific personal norms overcomes several problems with general social norms. First, the emphasis on personal internalization of norms allows, even predicts, wide-ranging individual differences and situational variation in helping responses. Second, the concepts of specific norms and norm crystallization meet a criticism leveled against social norms, that they are too general and too vague to direct behavior.

But the notion of specific personal norms also poses several unanswered questions. First, what is the relation of specific personal norms to other cognitive-evaluative concepts? The answer to this question carries implications for how one operationalizes specific personal norms. At times such norms seem to be personality variables, at times attitudes, and at times moral judgments. Second, can one provide empirical evidence that specific personal norms, however operationalized, affect responses to need situations? Schwartz has attempted to answer this central question by appealing to correlations between helping and presumed individual differences in the strength of specific personal norms (see Heberlein and Black, 1974; Rothstein, 1974; Schwartz, 1968, 1973). But while Schwartz (1975, 1977) addressed the problem of trying to infer causation from correlations in this context, the problem is not easily overcome. One cannot be sure that a correlation is not the result of some other factor that affects helping and, as a result, affects self-reported feelings of obligation to help (the index of strength of specific personal norms). Some method of directly manipulating the strength of specific personal norms may be needed before their causal power can be assessed. As Schwartz has admitted, "Much of the argument remains speculative" (1975, p. 133).

Finally, unlike most normative explanations of helping, Schwartz suggests that a sense of responsibility to help activates the search for relevant norms, not vice versa. What leads to this sense of responsibility? Schwartz (1975) notes that a number of external, situational factors—having caused the other's need, having distinctive suitability to act, or being given explicit responsibility to act—could produce a sense of responsibility. But he also notes that people seem to feel a sense of responsibility even when none of these external conditions pertain. The source of this sense of responsibility remains unclear.

To summarize thus far, attempts to find internal determinants of helping have not been very successful. The empirical support for individual difference variables has been inconsistent; the empirical support for norms has been weak. But there are developments that deserve further exploration with regard to each, most notably Staub's (1974) proposal of a composite prosocial orientation as a helping-relevant personality variable and Schwartz's (1973, 1975, 1977) proposal of specific personal norms.

2.2. *External Determinants*

Given the general lack of success in uncovering internal determinants of helping, it is not surprising that a large proportion of recent social psychological research on helping behavior has addressed the question of external determinants. Perhaps because present research methods are better attuned to assessing situational effects, attempts to uncover external determinants of helping have been far more successful than attempts to uncover internal determinants. We cannot begin to review all the relevant studies; instead we shall simply mention some of the more reliable findings.

As a heuristic aid in studying external determinants, Latané and Darley (1970; see also Schwartz, 1970) developed a model of the cognitive decision process involved in helping in an emergency. Emergencies are rare, unusual, and often ambiguous events. Are screams in the night a woman being attacked or, as some witnesses of the Genovese murder apparently thought, two lovers having a quarrel? If the situation is an emergency, something should be done. But what? The appropriate response is frequently not clear, and to respond at all may be dangerous. Further, the action of one bystander is often sufficient. One call to the police is as helpful, if not more helpful, than 38 calls.

Latané and Darley suggested that in responding to such a situation, a bystander must first notice that something is happening; he must next interpret the event as an emergency; he must then decide that it is his personal responsibility to act; he must consider what form of assistance he can give; and, finally, he must decide how to implement his action. They further propose that the social context of an emergency will influence this cognitive decision process, especially at the second and third stages, interpretation and responsibility.

Overall, this cognitive decision model has received consistant support. Studies have shown that social cues from other bystanders suggesting that they have or have not interpreted an event as an emergency (e.g., facial displays of alarm versus displays of calmness) affect the likelihood that a bystander will act (Bickman, 1972; Darley, Teger, and Lewis, 1973; Latané and Darley, 1968; Latané and Rodin, 1969; Ross and Braband, 1973). Further, several studies have shown that focusing responsibility for helping upon a bystander (e.g., no other bystanders who could help are present) makes it more likely that he or she will help (Bickman, 1971, 1972; Darley and Latané, 1968; Korte, 1971; Schwartz and Clausen, 1970).

The power of situational variables in determining when helping will occur has led a number of researchers (e.g., Rosenhan, Moore, and Underwood, 1976) to conclude that the answer to the question of why people help is to be found, not in any internal characteristics of the individuals in question but in characteristics of the social situation. Although it must be remembered that there is more than sufficient error variance in any study to leave room for the discovery of internal determinants that are strong predictors of helping, research to date seems to justify this conclusion.

3. *Factors Leading to Renewed Interest in Internal Determinants*

But, despite the rather dismal empirical track record, several factors have led to renewed interest in internal determinants of helping. First and most fundamental, external determinant models such as the one developed by Latané and Darley (1970) are simply not sufficient to explain why a person helps. While these models have proven quite successful in explaining when a person will help and when he will not, they cannot explain why a person helps at all. The notion of diffusion of responsibility, for example, assumes that there is a sense of responsibility to diffuse. Individuals apparently are concerned that others' distress be reduced. Where does this sense of responsibility come from and how does it operate? Is it a function of some individual difference variable? Of some norm? Or, could it stem from some aspect of the psyche not considered previously?

Such questions raise again the issue of internal determinants, but in a new way. They highlight a fundamental error in stating the research problem as one of seeking internal versus external determinants of helping. This statement juxtaposes analytic dimensions that are logically uncorrelated. Behavior can be under perfect "external control" in the sense that some change in the external stimulus conditions can cause the behavior to be totally absent or present and yet still be totally dependent on internal processes to occur at all.

Second, an aspect of the psyche not considered in previous social psychological research as a possible internal determinant of helping has recently come to the fore. Evidence is mounting that internal emotional states are related to helping (Rosenhan, 1972). The evidence comes from two sources. There is considerable anecdotal evidence that bystanders in emergencies are physiologically aroused (Greenberg, 1968; Latané and Darley, 1970; Piliavin and Piliavin, 1972; Weiss, Boyer, Lombardo, and Stich, 1973). Symptoms of arousal such as sweaty hands, shortness of breath, and general tenseness are exhibited. As Piliavin, Piliavin, and Rodin (1975) have noted, a number of factors can contribute to the overall level of arousal during an emergency: vicarious arousal (arousal produced by observing another's affective state), startle, shock, disgust, curiosity, and fear. Of course, the mere presence of emotional arousal does not mean that it motivates helping; it may be an unimportant by-product of experiencing an emergency.

There is also experimental evidence that one's emotional mood affects helping in less extreme situations. People in a good mood are more likely to do favors than people in a neutral or bad mood. Succeeding at a task (Berkowitz and Connor, 1966; Isen, 1970; Isen, Horn, and Rosenhan, 1973), unexpectedly receiving cookies or a dime (Batson, Coke, Chard, Smith, and Taliaferro, 1977; Isen and Levin, 1972) or a packet of stationary (Isen, Clark, and Schwartz, 1976), or simply thinking happy thoughts (Moore, Underwood, and Rosenhan, 1973; Rosenhan, Underwood, and Moore, 1974) all increased the likelihood of helping. These effects have been found with males and females, children and adults. Precisely why mood affects helping, however, remains unknown (but see Isen, Shalker, Clark, and Karp, 1978).

The emergence of interest in the role of emotion in helping seems to be part of a more general shift in emphasis in psychology that is reflected in social psychology. In the recent past, a strong cognitive orientation has developed in social psychology. This cognitive orientation has fitted hand-in-glove with an emphasis on external, situational determinants of behavior. The cognitive emphasis, reflected to some degree in cognitive dissonance (Aronson, 1969, Festinger, 1957) and person perception (Tagiuri, 1969) research, came to reign supreme in the rational information-processing models proposed by some attribution theorists (Bem, 1972; Kelley, 1967, 1972; Valins, 1966). Man was characterized as a fallible but dispassionate sense-making machine. Motivational and emotional constructs—the hopes, fears, and needs that used to be so prominent in social psychological discussions—were dealt with simply as biases in or inferred products of cognitive processes.

But the pendulum swings, and there are people who currently contend that some of the older motivational and emotional concerns require reconsideration, albeit in a new form. It is felt that a model of human functioning that is limited to cognitive processing of external stimuli is not adequate to account for human behavior, for cognitive processes are affected by internal states of the organism.

4. *Emotional Arousal as an Internal Determinant of Helping*

Two quite different approaches have been taken in conceptualizing the role of emotional arousal as a determinant of helping behavior. The two approaches are not logically exhaustive nor are they mutually exclusive, but they do provide clearly distinct logical alternatives. Both assume that emotional arousal provides an important component of the motivation to help others; both also assume that this motivation may or may not lead to actual helping, depending upon external situational pressures. The two approaches differ, however, in the type of motivation they assume emotional arousal produces. For one, the motivation is considered to be purely egoistic, for the other, it is considered to be at least partly altruistic. The first view contends that the arousal caused by witnessing another's distress creates an aversive state of personal distress in the witness that he or she is egoistically motivated to reduce. The second view contends that witnessing at least some others' distress can create empathic emotional arousal that leads to altruistic motivation to reduce not one's own arousal but the others' distress.

4.1. *Aversive Arousal as an Egoistic Motivator*

The Piliavins first suggested the importance of emotional arousal in motivating helping (Piliavin and Piliavin, 1972; Piliavin, Rodin, and Piliavin, 1969). They have systemized their thinking in an unpublished, but widely circulated paper (Piliavin and Piliavin, 1973). The Piliavin's model has two major components, an arousal component and a decision component. The decision component employs a cost-benefit calculus. Relative costs to self and to the victim determine whether the bystander will leave the scene, will help directly or indirectly, or will cognitively reinterpret the situation either by derogating the victim or by deciding the situation is not an emergency. Other theorists have employed similar cost-benefit models (Latané and Darley, 1970; Schwartz, 1975), and there is consistent evidence for the intuitively obvious prediction that increasing the cost of a given helping response decreases the likelihood of it occurring (Piliavin and Piliavin, 1972; Piliavin, Piliavin, and Rodin, 1975; Piliavin, Rodin, and Piliavin, 1969; Schaps, 1972; Wagner and Wheeler, 1969). The decision component of the Piliavin model is not especially novel or controversial.

The arousal component is both more novel and more controversial. Piliavin and Piliavin (1973) suggested a number of sources for arousal in emergencies: vicarious arousal or empathy, surprise, shock, uncertainty, and fear. These different types of arousal are assumed to summate, creating an overall level of personal distress. While Piliavin and Piliavin (1973) note that sudden, nearby emergencies can lead to a rapid onset of extremely high arousal and a reflexive response to reduce the arousal, arousal typically develops more slowly and is interpreted cognitively (Schachter, 1964). If interpreted as a positive emotion (excitement, interest, or amusement), the bystander will not be motivated to reduce it. If interpreted as a negative emotion (disgust, shame, fear, anger, empathic pain), he will. Piliavin and Piliavin make no distinction among these negative emotions; each is assumed to contribute to an overall level of personal distress that the individual is egoistically motivated to reduce. The bystander is "an aroused individual whose primary concern is with the reduction of his own distress" (Piliavin and Piliavin, 1973, p. 33).

There has been some research that is consistent with the Piliavin model. A number of studies have indicated that emergencies can be arousing (Bandura and Rosenthal, 1966; Berger, 1962; Nomikos, Opton, Averill, and Lazarus, 1968; Stotland, 1969). Further, several recent studies have been interpreted as suggesting that personal distress leads to helping (Ashton and Severy, 1976; Gaertner and Dovidio, 1977; Piliavin, Piliavin, and Broll, 1976; Piliavin, Piliavin, and Rodin, 1975). None of these studies has, however, provided direct evidence that the various forms of arousal evoked by an emergency summate, or that reduction of one's own personal distress is the primary motivation for helping.

The Piliavins' model is clearly egoistic. In their view, response to the other's need is an instrumental response made only because it will reduce one's own arousal. If other more immediate means of arousal reduction are available, the other's need should be ignored. While this rather chilling prescription may be correct, there is another possibility, that under at least some circumstances individuals are motivated to reduce not their own but the other's distress. Several researchers have proposed that this altruistic motivation is mediated by an emotional state, but a very different one from the aversive personal distress discussed by the Piliavins. Empathic concern is the emotion assumed to evoke altruistic motivation to help.

4.2. Empathic Emotion as an Altruistic Motivator

4.2.1. Definitions. Before discussing the possibility of empathic concern producing altruistic motivation for helping, we must make explicit how we are using two key terms: altruism and empathy.

4.2.1a. Altruism. A little thought makes one conclusion warranted: There are many motivations that lead one person to help another. Sometimes the motives involve the possibility of personal gain: the hope of reward or of gaining regard of others either because that regard is intrinsically valued or will lead to some material gains. In other situations, one helps to avoid some sort of punishment for not doing so: either direct losses (e.g., incurring a fine or other punishment when one fails to help in those few situations in which one is legally obligated to do so) or the loss of other's regard or one's self-regard suffered when one fails to help when it is expected. Finally, there is the possibility that some helping is altruistically motivated.

An individual's behavior is altruistically motivated to the degree that it is directed toward the end-state goal of reducing another's pain or increasing another's pleasure. This is contrasted with the various kinds of helping that are motivated by concern for one's own rewards and punishments, that is, egoistically motivated helping. This distinction leads to three observations: (a) Helping can be either egoistically or altruistically motivated; it is the goal not the behavior that distinguishes an act as altruistic. (b) Motivation for helping may be a mixture of altruistic and egoistic desires; it need not be solely or even primarily altruistic to have an altruistic component. (c) Reduction of the other's need is both necessary and sufficient to reduce altruistic motivation; to the degree that an act is altruistically motivated, reducing the other's need is not an intermediate, instrumental response directed toward reducing one's own need. Most simply, then, behavior of organism A is altruistically motivated to the extent that the responses of organism A are directed toward producing pleasure or reducing pain for organism B. (This conception of altruism seems entirely consistent with Webster's definition, "unselfish concern for the welfare of others.")

We believe that we have given a definition of altruism that is well within the standard range of definitions for it. Having done so, we can suggest one conclusion immediately: No experimental evidence is going to convince anybody who doesn't want to be convinced that altruistic helping actually exists. Putting this another way, the existence of actual altruistic motivation is a metaexperimental, rather than an experimental question, at least given our present levels of experimental sophistication. One is likely to be able to find some not totally implausible post hoc egoistic explanation for any helping behavior displayed within an experimental context. For example, one can argue that the subject was aware that his helping behavior, no matter how unexpectedly the need for it arose, might become known to the experimenter, and that he responded in order to look good in the experimenter's eyes. This is equivalent to saying that, for any naturally occurring helping act, we cannot totally rule out the possibility that it was dictated by phenomenological considerations of personal gain or loss in the decision processes of the helper. The evidence will not require the postulation of altruistic motivation. Yet it may be that postulation of such motivation is not inconsistent with the data, and may in the long run provide a more parsimonious account of results that egoistic theories deal with in an awkward and nonpredictive fashion. In the next several sections of this chapter, we will attempt to develop an account of altruistic motivation that is consistent with psychological research and theory.

4.2.1b. Empathy. For a relatively new term (apparently coined by Titchener in 1909 to translate the German "Einfühlung"), "empathy" has seen a wide range of definitions (Wispé, 1968). Not only has its meaning varied, its relation to associated concepts such as sympathy has also varied. Since empathy has been used by different people in contradictory ways, it would be impossible to propose a definition that would capture the essence of the term. Instead, we can only try to make clear what we shall mean by empathy. Empathy, as we shall use it, is an emotional state elicited by and congruent with the assumed emotional state of someone else. We do not require, as some have, that an empathic response involves feeling the same emotion that the other person is feeling. We do, however, require that it be affectively congruent. By this we mean that it involves a negative emotion when the other is experiencing a negative emotion and a positive emotion when the other is experiencing a positive emotion. Someone else's fear may, however, produce an empathic response of sorrow or unhappiness rather than fear; their elation may produce happiness or pride rather than elation. This emotional congruence implies caring.

Three comments need to be made about this conception of empathy. First, as an emotion it involves both a state of physiological arousal and a cognitive label for that arousal (Schachter, 1964; Stotland, 1969). In order to experience empathy one must feel (or believe one feels), and one must perceive this feeling to involve concern that another's pain be reduced or pleasure be increased. Such a perception seems to imply a special type of relationship between the person empathizing and the person being empathized with. An "empathic bond" is perceived to exist; the two individuals are tied together in some way so that one feels that he has some awareness of the other's internal state and that he has some investment in the quality of that state. Possible sources of such a bond is an issue we will consider shortly. For now, we shall simply observe that such relationships suggest a different view of the self than is popularly held (although not different from the view held by classic self-theorists like William James and Gordon Allport): One's self is probably not limited to the confines of his or her body. Certain individuals, most notably relations and friends, may be seen as part of "us." As part of us, it is only natural that when they hurt we hurt. This view of the self as extended beyond the body suggests a modified view of egoism. To say that one is self-centered may no longer be opposed to saying that he is responding in an attempt to reduce another's distress. Considered in this light, the neat juxtaposition of egoism and altruism begins to break down. This is because altruism is defined at the organismic level, as it should be, while egoism is defined in terms of the self, which may extend beyond the organism.

Second, our conception of empathy does not permit a clean distinction between empathy and sympathy. Some have suggested that sympathy be applied to congruent emotions, at least emotions elicited by another's suffering. "Empathy" is then reserved for feeling the identical emotion as the other, a feeling that may lead to sympathy but is not sympathy. Were one to follow such an analysis one would soon begin to speak of something like an "empathy–sympathy complex," and this more general complex would be essentially what we have called simply "empathy."

Third, our consideration of empathy as an emotion must be distinguished from a currently popular alternative conception of empathy, as a cognitive process (Borke, 1971; Dymond, 1949; Regan and Totten, 1975). For these cognitive theorists empathy means taking another person's perspective and seeing the world as he or she sees it. So long as one takes the perspective of the other, any emotions that might accompany this cognitive process are assumed to be epiphenomenal. While we consider perspective-taking important in that taking another's perspective is likely to intensify any empathic emotion one might feel, we consider the emotional state to be the defining characteristic of empathy.

4.2.2. Empathic Emotion as a Source of Altruistic Motivation. Given these definitions of altruism and empathy, the role of empathic emotion in motivating helping can be stated quite succinctly: Perception of at least certain others in distress arouses empathic emotion. Analogous to innate egoistic desires to have one's own distress relieved, this empathic emotion leads to an altruistic desire to see the other's distress relieved. Situational factors will determine whether and how this altruistic motivation is acted upon.

There is growing empirical evidence not only that humans do experience empathy as we have defined it but also that this emotion plays an important role in motivating helping. Berger (1962) found that observers became aroused (as evidenced by GSR responses) upon seeing a target person jerk his arm in response to a supposed electric shock. Less arousal occurred when either the arm movement or the supposed electric shock was absent. Subjects apparently reacted to the inference that the target person was experiencing pain and not to the direct stimuli of arm movement or electric shock. Berger concluded that empathic arousal does occur. Subsequent research (Bandura and Rosenthal, 1966; Craig and Lowery, 1969; Craig and Wood, 1969) has provided further support for this conclusion. Further, Stotland (1969) reported research supporting the more specific hypothesis that taking the perspective of a person in need increases physiological arousal. Stotland's research also indicated that the arousal experienced under these conditions tends to be labeled as empathic.

Aronfreed and Paskal (cited in Aronfreed, 1968) and Aderman and Berkowitz, (1970) set up experimental conditions designed to encourage or inhibit empathic response to the distress of a target person. Subjects were then given opportunities to help. In the Aronfreed and Paskal study they could help the target person; in the Aderman and Berkowitz study, the experimenter. More helping occurred in the experimental conditions designed to encourage empathic arousal, and both pairs of authors concluded that empathy had mediated helping. Subjects' physiological responses were, however, not measured in either study. Krebs (1975) attempted to measure both physiological responses and helping. He found that a high empathy condition (a similar other in great need) created the greatest physiological arousal and the most self-sacrificing help. Subjects in this condition reported identifying most with the victim and feeling the most concern about his plight.

While Krebs demonstrated that empathic arousal and helping were highly correlated, he did not demonstrate that empathic arousal caused helping. A study by Harris and Huang (1973) provided clearer evidence that some form of arousal can play a causal role in mediating helping. As subjects performed a mathematics task, a confederate with a bandaged knee limped into the experimental room and tripped over a chair, falling to the floor and crying out in pain. Some subjects were induced to misattribute arousal caused by this incident to an aversive noise being broadcast during the math task; others were not. Harris and Huang reasoned from Schachter's (1964) theory of emotion that if arousal motivates helping, it should do so only when attributed to a victim's plight. As predicted, subjects induced to misattribute their arousal to the aversive noise offered less help to the confederate than did subjects not so induced.

Unfortunately, because of the need situation Harris and Huang used it was not clear that the arousal experienced by subjects was empathic or that responses were directed toward reducing the other's need. Consistent with the Piliavins' egoistic model, the confederate's fall may have led subjects to experience an unpleasantly high level of personal distress, which they then sought to reduce. Given the strong constraints against leaving the experimental setting, helping may have been the least costly means of reducing personal distress.

Coke and Batson (1977), using a misattribution of arousal procedure similar to that used by Harris and Huang, provided results that suggested that specifically empathic emotion could mediate helping. They had subjects listen to a taped radio newscast describing the plight of a victim. Following Stotland's (1969) standard empathy manipulation, subjects were instructed either to observe the broadcast techniques (low empathy) or to imagine how the victim felt (high empathy). Just prior to hearing the newcast, subjects were given a placebo in the context of another study. Some were told that the placebo would be relaxing; others were told it would be arousing. It was assumed that empathic emotion would be experienced and acted upon only in the high empathy-relax condition. In the two low empathy conditions little empathic arousal should occur, and in the high empathy-arousal condition empathic arousal should occur but be misattributed to the pill. Results indicated the importance of perceived empathic arousal as the mediator of helping. Seventy-seven percent of the people in the imagine-relax condition offered help. In contrast, only 30% of the subjects across the other three conditions offered help. It should be noted that Coke and Batson (1977) employed a situation where, according to the Piliavins' model, the costs of not helping should have been low, so egoistic motivation should not have led to helping: (a) At the time they were exposed to the need, subjects did not anticipate having an opportunity to help; (b) they only learned of the victim's need by listening to an audio tape; and (c) their helping responses were anonymous.

Finally, Coke, Batson, and McDavis (1977) not only provided a generalized replication of the effect of empathic arousal on helping, they demonstrated that this effect was due to subjects labeling their arousal as empathic concern and not personal distress. In this study, a false-feedback of arousal paradigm (Valins, 1966) was used to lead some subjects to believe that they were aroused by a tape-recorded appeal for help. Other subjects were given false feedback indicating that they were not aroused. Subjects were then asked to indicate the degree to which they were experiencing various emotional states. Factor analysis of subjects' ratings indicated that empathic concern and personal distress were unrelated. Emotions such as "empathic," "concerned," and "compassionate" loaded most highly on one factor (loadings $>.70$); adjectives such as "upset," "alarmed," and "troubled" loaded most highly on a different, orthogonal factor (loadings $>.60$).

After indicating their emotional state, subjects were unexpectedly confronted with an opportunity to respond to the tape-recorded appeal. Results indicated that, as predicted, subjects given false feedback indicating that they were aroused perceived themselves to be significantly more aroused by the broadcast ($p<.001$), rated themselves as feeling significantly more empathic concern ($p<.005$), and offered significantly more help ($p<.002$). It should also be noted that the false-feedback manipulation did not have a significant effect on ratings of personal distress.

These studies provide consistent evidence that increased empathic emotion leads to increased helping. But does empathy motivate helping, as we have proposed, or does it simply function as a cognitive cue, affecting helping because it provides a potential helper with additional information that he uses to interpret the need situation as one in which he should help? If empathic emotion serves as a cognitive cue for interpreting the need situation, the effect of increased empathic emotion on helping should be a result of increased perceived need (see Schwartz, 1977). In neither the Coke and Batson (1977) study nor the Coke, Batson, and McDavis (1977) study was there an indication of such a relationship. In the Coke and Batson study subjects in the high empathy–relax condition, who helped more and presumably experienced more empathic emotion than subjects in the other three conditions, actually perceived the victim's need to be slightly less than did subjects in the other three conditions. In the Coke, Batson, and McDavis study, subjects led to believe that they were aroused did tend to rate the victim's need somewhat higher than other subjects, but the difference was not statistically reliable ($p = .09$). Further, perceived need did not predict a significant proportion of the variance in helping. Thus, in neither study did perceived need appear to mediate the effect of empathic emotion on helping.

To propose that empathic emotion in response to another's distress leads to altruistic motivation to help raises two further questions. First, how does the empathic-altruistic motivation develop? Second, how do we relate this motivational model to the clear evidence that external, situational determinants have a powerful influence on helping? These two questions will concern us for the remainder of this chapter.

4.2.3. Development of Empathic-Altruistic Motivation

4.2.3a. Possible Genetic Bases for an Empathic Bond. Martin Hoffman (1975, 1976) has argued persuasively that we must not dismiss too quickly the possibility that some form of altruistic motivation may have developed through the process of natural selection. There seem to be two ways one could argue for a genetic basis for empathic-altruistic motivation. First, one could argue that the protective concern that is shown most dramatically in maternal behavior may find more general expression in a genetically based proclivity to care for the small and defenseless. Leonard Berkowitz long ago pointed to the importance of dependency relationships in motivating helping (Berkowitz, 1957), but his attempts to find a basis for this effect in a norm of social responsibility proved less than successful (Berkowitz, 1972). Perhaps we should consider a genetic rather than a normative basis for the tendency to respond to the needs of dependent others.

Second, inclusive fitness (Hamilton, 1964, 1971) may provide a basis for altruistic concern for one's kin, those with whom one shares at least some genes. Functionally, a kinship-based altruistic impulse may extend to those who are like oneself or with whom one shares some identifying characteristic. Consistent with this possibility Stotland (1969) and Krebs (1975) both report stronger empathic responses to similar others. Of course, their findings could easily be accounted for entirely in terms of social learning.

How one reacts to the idea of a genetically based motive for altruism depends on both one's reading of the arguments and the evidence, and on one's predilections toward this sort of evolutionary theorizing. It is possible to suggest that people possess an impulse toward altruism without holding that it is genetic in origin. For example, Donald Campbell (1972, 1975) has called psychologists' attention to the possibility of what he calls "sociocultural evolution," and proposes that cultural factors create rather than extend altruistic impulses. Emphasizing the great social interdependence of human societies when compared to those of other vertebrates, Campbell contends that the human need for prosocial behavior is far greater than it was for our genetic ancestors. In order to meet this need, he suggests, societies use cultural preachments to ingrain and support altruistic impulses. Sociocultural evolution, it appears, is Lamarkian; altruistic principles that emerge in one generation are taught to other people, and to later generations, and thus preserved.

4.2.3b. Cognitive and Social Intensification and Extension. Regardless of the ultimate source of empathic-altruistic motivation, the empirical evidence makes it clear that expression of the motivation to help is greatly affected by one's cognitive and social development. Martin Hoffman has recently (1975, 1976) devoted considerable effort to tracing the interaction of basic, perhaps genetic, altruistic impulses and cognitive and social development. He suggests that initially an infant does not differentiate between self and others, so a distinction between egoistic and altruistic orientations is not appropriate. Based on the work of Simner (1971), Hoffman suggests that infants may, however, have an innate empathic reaction to others' distress. As the child's sense of separateness of self and other develops, cognitive factors become more important in empathic emotion (Schachter, 1964) and empathy tends to be followed by helping. Empathic-altruistic motivation emerges.

Hoffman suggests that the transformation of innate empathic reactions into empathic-altruistic motivation occurs in three stages: (a) Initially, the child reacts to another's distress as though self and other were simultaneously or alternately in distress. The child feels concern for the other as distinct from self, but any attempts to help may be misguided due to limited understanding of the other's need and of appropriate responses. (b) At about two years, the child begins to recognize that others' inner states are distinct from his, but that their feelings often resemble his own. He also begins to develop the ability to imagine how he would feel in their situation. At this "Golden Rule" level, his responses are more adaptive and effective. (c) Around six to nine years, the child develops conceptions of himself and others as distinct continuous persons with personal histories and identities. Another's general plight (as opposed to immediate needs) can be recognized, felt, and responded to. Issues of injustice and victimization loom large (Kohlberg, 1976).

Reflection upon Hoffman's developmental sequence suggests that five cognitive potentialities may play an important role in transforming an undifferentiated empathic reaction into empathic-altruistic motivation as it is found in adults. These five potentialities are: emotional labeling, perspective taking, awareness of future consequences, conceptual generalization, and unit formation. We will discuss each in turn.

Emotional labeling: As the child develops a clear sense of self and other, the ability to label his arousal as empathic (concern, compassion, care, etc.) seems crucial in maintaining a link between another person's distress and his response (Schachter, 1964; Stotland, 1969). The child knows that he is aroused by the other's plight, but what does his arousal mean? Interpretation as shock, disgust, surprise, or fear does not imply that reduction of the other's need is necessary to reduce the arousal. An empathic label, on the other hand, does.

Perspective taking: The growing ability to experience a situation from another's perspective also helps to bridge the gap between self and other. Some (Flavell, 1968; Selman, 1976) have suggested that this cognitive ability is a crucial element of moral thinking and may itself mediate prosocial behavior. In light of the Coke and Batson (1977) results, it seems more likely that perspective taking affects helping by intensifying one's empathic emotional response to the person in need and therefore increasing the motivation to help. Perspective-taking ability allows the child to detect and respond empathically to increasingly subtle distress cues. Finally, it seems that the empirical evidence (e.g., donations to charity when the plight of the eventual recipients of the charity is not directly observable) requires the recognition that eventually the child does not have to be confronted directly with the other's distress; mere knowledge that another has experienced some catastrophe is sufficient to evoke images of how the other feels and an empathic response.

Awareness of future consequences: A sense of personal history and the future has two major effects on empathic-altruistic motivation. As Hoffman (1975) has pointed out, it enables one to perceive enduring need or injustice. It also enables one to understand and employ reciprocity (Gouldner, 1960). To say, "I owe you one," implies a sense of personal history and future interaction.

Conceptual generalization: Development of language and conceptual categories introduces the possibility for a major transformation in empathic-altruistic motivation. Whatever the initial targets of the helping impulse, the development of skills at symbolic representations and conceptual processing means that the impulse can be generalized considerably beyond its initial benefactors. For example, one may be initially inclined to help only his closest kin, his brother, but through conceptual generalization he may come to call a total stranger "brother" and respond accordingly.

Unit formation: Heider (1958) pointed out that certain characteristics of another person or of a social situation may lead an individual to perceive himself and another person as a unit. Similarity, proximity, and sharing a common fate can all lead to unit formation. A unit bond would presumably increase the chances that the other would come within the purview of cognitively generalized empathic-altruistic motivation. Consistent with this view, it has been found that if potential helpers have met or even previously observed a person, they are more likely to help him (Latané and Darley, 1970; Macaulay, 1975). Further, Sole, Marton, and Hornstein (1975) found that people were more likely to help a person with similar attitudes, and Dovidio and Morris (1975) found that people were more likely to help another who was to share their fate of receiving electric shock.

5. *Situational Constraints on Altruistic Motivation: Integrating Internal and External Determinants of Helping*

We have suggested that the distress of at least some others causes the witness to feel empathic concern for the person in distress and that this emotional state leads to altruistic motivation, the desire to have the other's distress reduced. Various factors contributing to the presence of this motivation have been considered, both possible genetic sources and cognitive and social influences. The current state of the evidence does not permit a decision as to which of these factors, together or singly, are most important in the emergence of altruistic motivation. But, fortunately, the question of the origins of altruistic motivation need not be precisely resolved before its effect on helping behavior can be considered. Even one who believes that an altruistic impulse is innate must concede that it goes through a developmental transformation approximately like the one suggested by Hoffman. Therefore, although there are different accounts of the origins of altruism, there seems to be a convergence of opinion on its final form.

Empathic-altruistic motivation may provide an internal desire to have the need of another relieved in many helping situations, but obviously this desire is not always acted upon. External, situational constraints must also be taken into consideration. In an attempt to do this we shall try to integrate this emotional-motivational process with the cognitive-decision process outlined by Latané and Darley (1970). Our hope is to provide a model that can account for both why one person helps and another does not, and to account for why anyone helps at all.

Recall that Latané and Darley (1970) suggested a five-stage decision sequence in a bystander's response to an emergency: (1) Notice something unusual may be happening, (2) interpret the situation as an emergency, (3) accept personal responsibility for helping, (4) consider the best form of assistance, (5) help. Recall also that this sequence has been criticized for lacking a motivational component. We would suggest that empathically induced altruism may provide the motivational component.

If an individual decides that he is witnessing an emergency, that there is someone in need (stage 2), he may experience empathic emotion and a desire to see the other's need reduced. Existence and intensity of the empathic emotion will depend upon the strength of the empathic bond linking bystander to victim. Perceived unit relations as well as dependency and vulnerability of the victim may affect the strength of the empathic bond. It may also be affected by the degree to which the bystander is self-focused at the particular time. Self-concern can inhibit ability to take the other's perspective and therefore one's ability to experience empathic concern (Hoffman, 1976; Duval and Wicklund, 1972).

Empathic emotion creates a desire to have the other's need reduced, but it does not require that the bystander himself reduce it. If the situation does not demand an immediate, impulsive response (Piliavin and Piliavin, 1973), the bystander must decide whether he should help or let someone else help (stage 3). If he knows or can convince himself (realistically or not) that someone else has helped, empathic emotion declines and with it the motivation to help. Responsibility has been diffused. If he thinks no one else has helped, empathic emotion remains. It can be effectively reduced only if he helps, learns that someone else has helped, or redefines the situation as one not involving need. If the bystander decides others have not helped, he will be motivated to seek ways of helping (stage 4). And if a viable means is found, he will help (stage 5). If no one helps and the situation cannot be redefined, empathic emotion will gradually decay over time. But this is a less than optimal solution. Tentatively, it could be suggested that if not reduced, the empathic emotion will be reinterpreted as (a) moral indignation directed toward others who should have helped but have not, (b) guilt directed toward the self, or (c) contempt and derogation directed toward the victim, severing the empathic bond.

While this empathic-altruistic motivation model incorporates several aspects of the Piliavins' egoistic model, it differs from their model in two major respects. First, the Piliavins suggest that all forms of emotional arousal contribute to an aversive arousal state. We suggest instead that there is a qualitative difference between empathic emotion and the other forms of emotional arousal that an emergency evokes (surprise, shock, fear). This qualitative difference has motivational consequences. While other emotions may be reduced by escape as well as helping, empathic emotion cannot. For this reason, it seems likely that leaving the scene will occur, if it occurs, before one defines the situation as an emergency (stage 2). Once the situation is defined and empathy is aroused, leaving seems less viable, for leaving cannot reduce empathic emotions, except to the degree that turning to some other activity increases distraction. Studies showing that unambiguously defining an event as an emergency increases helping (Bickman, 1972; Clark and Word, 1972, 1974) are entirely consistent with this reasoning; but they are, of course, also subject to other interpretations.

Second, the Piliavins' egoistic model suggests that a bystander's action, whether helping, leaving, or reinterpreting, is egoistically directed toward reduction of his own needs. We cannot entirely agree. While nonempathic emotions no doubt occur and are almost certainly subject to egoistic arousal reduction, we believe that empathic emotion is not. It is linked to the other's need state and, if it is effectively to be reduced, the other's needs must be reduced. Thus, it produces altruistic motivation.

As for empirical support for this integrated model, evidence for the role of empathic emotion in engendering altruistic motivation has been reviewed, as has the evidence for the cognitive decision process outlined by Latané and Darley (1970). But a number of questions remain. Are other forms of emotional arousal as effective in motivating helping as is empathy? Is empathic emotional arousal reduced by helping? What happens to empathic emotion not reduced by helping; is it transformed into indignation, guilt, or derogation? Are there individual differences in empathic responsivity, and if so, do they affect helping (see Mehrabian and Epstein, 1972)? What is the effect on helping of inhibiting empathic arousal with, for example, tranquillizers? Does empathic responsivity diminish among helping professionals who are continually exposed to others' need, and if so, what are the consequences? These questions and more await further study.

6. *Summary and Conclusion*

Research during the past decade provides convincing evidence for the importance of external, situational factors in determining why one person helps and another does not. It does not provide much evidence relevant to the critical question of why anyone helps at all. While possible answers in terms of individual difference variables and norms are being and should be pursued, we have followed the lead of the Piliavins and focused on emotional arousal as a possible internal instigator of the desire to help. We differ from the Piliavins, however, in what we consider to be the nature and motivational consequences of emotional arousal in response to another's need. They suggest all such arousal is aversive, leading to egoistic motivation to reduce it. Based on some recent research, we suggest instead that one form of emotional arousal, empathic concern, directs attention outward and, further, that it produces an altruistic desire to have the distress of the person in need relieved. Finally, we suggest that this emotional-motivational analysis may be combined with the cognitive decision analysis developed by Latané and Darley (1970) to provide an integrated model in which both internal and external determinants interact in shaping response to another's need. This integrated internal–external model can provide answers to both the question of why one person helps and another does not, as well as the question of why anyone helps at all. At the same time, it questions the general assumption that all human behavior is egoistically motivated. It suggests instead that an empathic bond may lead us to respond to the needs of at least some others as if they were our own, altruistically acting with a goal of reducing the other's distress. Truly a social animal, man's behavior may at times be directed not toward maximizing his own pleasures and minimizing his own pains, but toward maximizing the pleasure and minimizing the pain of others.

References

Aderman, D., and Berkowitz, L. Observational set, empathy, and helping. *Journal of Personality and Social Psychology*, 1970, *14*, 141–148.

Aronfreed, J.M. *Conduct and conscience: The socialization of internalized control over behavior*. New York: Academic Press, 1968.

Aronson, E. The theory of cognitive dissonance: A current perspective. In L. Berkowitz (Ed.), *Advances in experimental social psychology* (Vol. 4). New York: Academic Press, 1969.

Ashton, N.L., and Severy, L.J. Arousal and costs in bystander intervention. *Personality and Social Psychology Bulletin*, 1976, *2*, 268–272.

Bandura, A., and Rosenthal, L. Vicarious classical conditioning as a function of arousal level. *Journal of Personality and Social Psychology*, 1963, *3*, 54–62.

Batson, C.D. Religion as prosocial: Agent or double agent? *Journal for the Scientific Study of Religion*, 1976, *15*, 29–44.

Batson, C.D., Coke, J.S., Chard, F., Smith, D., and Taliaferro, A. *Activation as a mediator of the effect of mood on helping: A second look.* Unpublished manuscript, University of Kansas, 1977.

Bem, D.J. Self-perception theory. In L. Berkowitz (Ed.), *Advances in experimental social psychology* (Vol. 6). New York: Academic Press, 1972.

Berger, S.M. Conditioning through vicarious instigation. *Psychological Review*, 1962, *69*, 450–466.

Berkowitz, L. Liking for the group and the perceived merit of the group's behavior. *Journal of Abnormal and Social Psychology*, 1957, *54*, 353–357.

Berkowitz, L. Social motivation. In G. Lindzey and E. Aronson (Eds.), *The handbook of social psychology* (Vol. 3). Reading, Mass.: Addison-Wesley, 1968.

Berkowitz, L. Social norms, feelings, and other factors affecting helping and altruism. In L. Berkowitz (Ed.), *Advances in experimental social psychology* (Vol. 6). New York: Academic Press, 1972.

Berkowitz, L., and Connor W.H. Success, failure, and social responsibility. *Journal of Personality and Social Psychology*, 1966, *4*, 664–669.

Berkowitz, L., and Daniels, L.R. Responsibility and dependency. *Journal of Abnormal and Social Psychology*, 1963, *66*, 429–236.

Berkowitz, L., and Daniels, L.R. Affecting the salience of the social responsibility norm: Effects of past help on the response to dependency relationships. *Journal of Abnormal and Social Psychology*, 1964, *68*, 275–281.

Bickman, L. The effect of another bystander's ability to help on bystander intervention in an emergency. *Journal of Experimental Social Psychology*, 1971, *7*, 367–379.

Bickman, L. Social influence and diffusion of responsibility in an emergency. *Journal of Experimental Social Psychology*, 1972, *8*, 438–445.

Blank, J. Rescue on the freeway. *Reader's Digest*, 1970, *96* (577), 73–77.

Borke, H. Interpersonal perception of young children: Ego-centrism or empathy? *Developmental Psychology*, 1971, *5*, 263–269.

Campbell, D.T. On the genetics of altruism and the counter-hedonic components in human culture. *Journal of Social Issues*, 1972, *28*, 21–37.

Campbell, D.T. On the conflicts between biological and social evolution and between psychology and moral tradition. *American Psychologist*, 1975, *30*, 1103–1126.

Clark, R.D., III, and Word, L.E. Why don't bystanders help? Because of ambiguity. *Journal of Personality and Social Psychology*, 1972, *24*, 392–400.

Clark, R.D., III, and Word, L.E. Where is the apathetic bystander? Situational characteristics of the emergency. *Journal of Personality and Social Psychology*, 1974, *29*, 279–288.

Coke, J.S., and Batson, C.D. Empathy as a mediator of helping behavior: A dose of kindness. Paper presented at the annual convention of the American Psychological Association, San Francisco, California, August, 1977.

Coke, J.S., Batson, C.D., and McDavis, K. *Empathic mediation of helping: A two-stage model.* Unpublished manuscript, University of Kansas, 1977.

Craig, K.D., and Lowery, J.H. Heart rate components of conditioned vicarious autonomic responses. *Journal of Personality and Social Psychology*, 1969, *11*, 381–387.

Craig, K.D., and Wood, K. Psychophysiological differentiation of direct and vicarious affective arousal. *Canadian Journal of Behavior Science*, 1969, *1*, 98–105.

Darley, J.M., and Batson, C.D. "From Jerusalem to Jericho": A study of situational and dispositional variables in helping behavior. *Journal of Personality and Social Psychology*, 1973, *27*, 100–108.

Darley, J.M., and Latané, B. Bystander intervention in emergencies: Diffusion of responsibility. *Journal of Personality and Social Psychology*, 1968, *8*, 377–383.

Darley, J.M., and Latané, B. Norms and normative behavior: Field studies of social-interdependence. In J. Macaulay and L. Berkowitz (Eds.), *Altruism and helping behavior.* New York: Academic Press, 1970.

Darley, J.M., Teger, A.L., and Lewis, L.D. Do groups always inhibit individuals' responses to potential emergencies? *Journal of Personality and Social Psychology*, 1973, *26*, 395–399.

Dovidio, J.F., and Morris, W.N. Effects of stress and commonality of fate on helping behavior. *Journal of Personality and Social Psychology*, 1975, *31*, 145–149.

Duval, S., and Wicklund. R.A. *A theory of objective self-awareness.* New York: Academic Press, 1972.

Dymond, R. A scale for the measurement of empathic ability. *Journal of Consulting Psychology*, 1949, *13*, 127–133.

Festinger, L. *A theory of cognitive dissonance.* Stanford: Stanford University Press, 1957.

Flavell, J.H. *The development of role-taking and communication skill in chilren.* New York: Wiley, 1968.

Gaertner, S.L., and Dovidio, J.F. The subtlety of white racism, arousal, and helping behavior. *Journal of Personality and Social Psychology*, 1977, *35*, 691–707.

Geer, J.H., and Jarmecky, L. The effect of being responsible for reducing another's pain on subject's response and arousal. *Journal of Personality and Social Psychology*, 1973, *26*, 232–237.

Gergen, K.J., Gergen, M.M., and Meter, K. Individual orientations to prosocial behavior. *Journal of Social Issues*, 1972, *28*, (3), 105–130.

Gouldner, A.W. The norm of reciprocity: A preliminary statement. *American Sociological Review*, 1960, *25*, 161–178.

Greenberg, J. *The effect of relative and absolute distance on helping behavior in an emergency situation.* Unpublished manuscript, University of Pennsylvania, 1968.

Greenwald, A. Does the Good Samaritan parable increase helping? A comment on Darley and Batson's no effect conclusion. *Journal of Personality and Social Psychology*, 1975, *32*, 578–583.

Hamilton, W.D. The genetic evolution of social behavior. *Journal of Theoretical Biology*, 1964, *7*, 1–51.

Hamilton, W.D. Selection of selfish and altruistic behavior in some extreme models. In J.F. Eisenberg and W.S. Dillon (Eds.), *Man and beast: Comparative social behavior.* Washington, D.C.: Smithsonian Institution Press, 1971.

Harris, M.B., and Huang, L.C. Helping and the attribution process. *Journal of Social Psychology*, 1973, *90*, 291–297.

Hebb, D.O. Comment on altruism: The comparative evidence. *Psychological Bulletin*, 1971, *76*, 409–410.

Heberlein, T.A. and Black, J.S. The land ethic in action: Personal norms, beliefs, and the purchase of lead-free gasoline. Paper presented at the meeting of the Rural Sociology Association, Montreal, August, 1974.

Heider, F. *The psychology of interpersonal relations.* New York: Wiley, 1958.

Hoffman, M.L. Developmental synthesis of affect and cognition and its implications for altruistic motivation. *Developmental Psychology*, 1975, *11*, 607–622.

Hoffman, M.L. Empathy, role-taking, guilt, and development of altruistic motives. In T. Lickona (Ed.), *Moral development and behavior: Theory, research, and social issues.* New York: Holt, Rinehart and Winston, 1976.

Horowitz, I.A. Effect of choice and locus of dependence on helping behavior. *Journal of Personality and Social Psychology*, 1968, *8*, 373–376.

Huston, T.L., and Korte, C. The responsive bystander: Why he helps. In T. Lickona

(Ed.), *Moral development and behavior: Theory, research, and social issues.* New York: Holt, Rinehart and Winston, 1976.

Isen, A.M. Success, failure, attention, and reactions to others: The warm glow of success. *Journal of Personality and Social Psychology*, 1970, *15*, 294–301.

Isen, A.M., Clark, M., and Schwartz, M.F. Duration of the effect of good mood on helping: "Footprints on the sands of time." *Journal of Personality and Social Psychology*, 1976, *34*, 385–393.

Isen, A.M., Horn, N., and Rosenhan, D.L. Effects of success and failure on children's generosity. *Journal of Personality and Social Psychology*, 1973, *27*, 239–247.

Isen, A.M., and Levin, P.F. The effect of feeling good on helping: Cookies and kindness. *Journal of Personality and Social Psychology*, 1972, *21*, 384–388.

Isen, A.M., Shalker, T.E., Clark, M., and Karp, L. Affect, accessibility of material in memory and behavior: A cognitive loop. *Journal of Personality and Social Psychology*, 1978, *36*, 1–2.

Kelley, H.H. Attribution theory in social psychology. In D. Levine (Ed.), *Nebraska symposium on motivation* (Vol. 15). Lincoln: University of Nebraska Press, 1967.

Kelley, H.H. Attribution in social interaction. In E.E. Jones, D.E. Kanouse, H.H. Kelley, R.E. Nisbett, S. Valins, and B. Weiner (Eds.), *Attribution: Perceiving the causes of behavior.* Morristown, N.J.: General Learning Press, 1972.

Kohlberg, L. Moral stages and moralization: The cognitive-developmental approach. In T. Lickona (Ed.), *Moral development and behavior: Theory, research, and social issues.* New York: Holt, Rinehart, and Winston, 1976.

Korte, C. Effects of individual responsibility and group communication on help-giving in an emergency. *Human Relations*, 1971, *24*, 149–159.

Krebs, D.L. Altruism—an examination of the concept and a review of the literature. *Psychological Bulletin*, 1970, *73*, 258–302.

Krebs, D.L. Infrahuman altruism. *Psychological Bulletin*, 1971, *76*, 411–414.

Krebs, D. Empathy and altruism. *Journal of Personality and Social Psychology*, 1975, *32*, 1134–1146.

Kuhn, T. *The structure of scientific revolutions.* University of Chicago, 1962.

Latané, B., and Darley, J.M. Group inhibition of bystander intervention in emergencies. *Journal of Personality and Social Psychology*, 1968, *10*, 215–221.

Latané, B., and Darley, J.M. *The unresponsive bystander: Why doesn't he help?* New York: Appleton-Century-Crofts, 1970.

Latané, B., and Rodin, J. A lady in distress: Inhibiting effects of friends and strangers on bystander intervention. *Journal of Experimental Social Psychology*, 1969, *5*, 189–202.

Leeds, A. Altruism and the norms of giving. *Merrill-Palmer Quarterly*, 1963, *9*, 229–240.

Macaulay, J. Familiarity, attraction, and charity. *Journal of Social Psychology*, 1975, *95*, 27–37.

Macaulay, J., and Berkowitz, L. *Altruism and helping behavior: Social psychological studies of some antecedents and consequences.* New York: Academic Press, 1970.

Mehrabian, A., and Epstein, N. A measure of emotional empathy. *Journal of Personality*, 1972, *40*, 525–543.

Midlarsky, E., and Midlarsky, E. Some determinants of aiding under experimentally induced stress. *Journal of Personality*, 1973, *41*, 305–327.

Moore, B.S., Underwood, B., and Rosenhan, D.L. Affect and altruism. *Developmental Psychology*, 1973, *8*, 99–104.

Nomikos, M., Opton, E., Jr., Averill, J., and Lazarus, R. Surprise versus suspense in the production of stress reaction. *Journal of Personality and Social Psychology*, 1968, *8*, 204–208.

Piliavin, J.A., and Piliavin, I. The effect of blood on reactions to a victim. *Journal of Personality and Social Psychology*, 1972, *23*, 253–261.

Piliavin, J.A., and Piliavin, I.M. The Good Samaritan: Why *does* he help? Unpublished manuscript, 1973.

Piliavin, J.A., Piliavin, I.M., and Broll, L. Time of arrival at an emergency and likelihood of helping. *Personality and Social Psychology Bulletin*, 1976, *2*, 268–272.

Piliavin, I.M., Piliavin, J.A., and Rodin, J. Costs, diffusion, and the stigmatized victim. *Journal of Personality and Social Psychology*, 1975, *32*, 429–438.

Piliavin, I.M., Rodin, J., and Piliavin, J.A. Good Samaritanism: An underground phenomenon? *Journal of Personality and Social Psychology*, 1969, *13*, 289–299.

Regan, D.T., and Totten, J. Empathy and attribution: Turning observers into actors. *Journal of Personality and Social Psychology*, 1975, *32*, 850–856.

Rosenhan, D.L. Learning theory and prosocial behavior. *Journal of Social Issues*, 1972, *28* (3), 151–163.

Rosenhan, D.L., Moore, B.S., and Underwood, B. The social psychology of moral behavior. In T. Lickona (Ed.), *Moral development and behavior: Theory, research, and social issues.* New York: Holt, Rinehart, and Winston, 1976.

Rosenhan, D.L., Underwood, B., and Moore, B. Affect moderates self-gratification and altruism. *Journal of Personality and Social Psychology*, 1974, *30*, 546–552.

Rosenthal, A.M. *Thirty-eight witnesses.* New York: McGraw-Hill, 1964.

Ross, A.S., and Braband, J. Effect of increased responsibility on bystander intervention, II: The cue value of a blind person. *Journal of Personality and Social Psychology*, 1973, *25*, 254–258.

Rothstein, H.R. Attitudes and behavior: The effects of perceived payoffs and facilitating intrapersonal conditions. Unpublished master's thesis, The Hebrew University, 1974.

Rutherford, E., and Mussen, P. Generosity in nursery school boys. *Child Development*, 1968, *39*, 755–765.

Schachter, S. The interaction of cognitive and physiological determinants of emotional state. In L. Berkowitz (Ed.), *Advances in experimental social psychology*. Vol. 1. New York: Academic Press, 1964.

Schaps, E. Cost, dependency, and helping. *Journal of Personality and Social Psychology*, 1972, *21*, 74–78.

Schopler, J., and Bateson, N. The power of dependence. *Journal of Personality and Social Psychology*, 1965, *2*, 247–254.

Schopler, J., and Matthews, M. The influence of perceived causal locus of partner's dependence on the use of interpersonal power. *Journal of Personality and Social Psychology*, 1965, *2*, 609–612.

Schwartz, S.H. Words, deeds, and the perception of consequences and responsibility in action situations. *Journal of Personality and Social Psychology*, 1968, *10*, 232–242.

Schwartz, S.H. Elicitation of moral obligation and self-sacrificing behavior. *Journal of Personality and Social Psychology*, 1970, *15*, 283–293.

Schwartz, S.H. Normative explanations of helping behavior: A critique, proposal, and empirical test. *Journal of Experimental Social Psychology*, 1973, *9*, 349–364.

Schwartz, S.H. The justice of need and the activation of humanitarian norms. *Journal of Social Issues*, 1975, *31* (3), 111–136.

Schwartz, S.H. Normative influences on altruism. In L. Berkowitz (Ed.), *Advances in experimental social psychology* (Vol. 10). New York: Academic Press, 1977.

Schwartz, S.H., and Clausen, G.T. Responsibility, norms, and helping in an emergency. *Journal of Personality and Social Psychology*, 1970, *16*, 229–310.

Schwartz, S.H., and Gottlieb, A. Bystander reactions to a violent theft; Crime in Jerusalem. *Journal of Personality and Social Psychology*, 1976, *34*, 1188–1199.

Selman, R.L. Social-cognitive understanding: A guide to educational and clinical practice. In T. Lickona (Ed.), *Moral development and behavior: Theory, research, and social issues*. New York: Holt, Rinehart, and Winston, 1976.

Severy, L.J. Comment on: "Positive forms of social behavior: An overview." *Journal of Social Issues*, 1974, *30* (2).

Simner, M.L. Newborn's response to the cry of another infant. *Developmental Psychology*, 1971, *5*, 136–150.

Smith, A. *The theory of moral sentiments*. London: A. Miller, 1759.

Sole, K., Marton, J., and Hornstein, H.A. Opinion similarity and helping: Three field experiments investigating the bases of promotive tension. *Journal of Experimental Social Psychology*, 1975, *11*, 1–13.

Staub, E. Helping a person in distress: The influence of implicit and explicit "rules" of conduct on children and adults. *Journal of Personality and Social Psychology*, 1971, *17*, 137–144.

Staub, E. Helping a distressed person: Social, personality, and stimulus determinants. In L. Berkowitz (Ed.), *Advances in experimental social psychology* (Vol. 7). New York: Academic Press, 1974.

Stotland, E. Exploratory investigations of empathy. In L. Berkowitz (Ed.), *Advances in experimental social psychology* (Vol. 4). New York: Academic Press, 1969.

Tagiuri, R. Person perception. In G. Lindzey and E. Aronson (Eds.), *Handbook of social psychology* (Vol. 3). Reading, Mass.: Addison-Wesley, 1969.

Thorndike, E.L. Animal intelligence: An experimental study of the associative process in animals. *Psychological Review*, 1898, Monograph Supplement No. 8.

Valins, S. Cognitive effects of false heart-rate feedback. *Journal of Personality and Social Psychology*, 1966, *4*, 400–408.

Wagner, C., and Wheeler, L. Model, need, and cost effects in helping behavior. *Journal of Personality and Social Psychology*, 1969, *12*, 111–116.

Weiner, F.H. Altruism, ambiance, and action: The effects of rural and urban rearing on helping behavior. *Journal of Personality and Social Psychology*, 1976, *34*, 112–124.

Weiss, R.F., Boyer, J.L., Lombardo, J.P., and Stich, M.H. Altruistic drive and altruistic reinforcement. *Journal of Personality and Social Psychology*, 1973, *25*, 390–400.

Wispé, L.G. Sympathy and empathy. In D.L. Sills (Ed.), *International encyclopedia of the social sciences*, (Vol. 15), New York: Free Press, 1968, 441–447.

Wispé, L.G. Positive forms of social behavior. *Journal of Social Issues*, 1972, *28* (3).

Yakimovich, D., and Saltz, E. Helping behavior: The cry for help. *Psychonomic Science*, 1971, *23*, 427–428.

Person by Treatment Interactions in Personality Research

NORMAN S. ENDLER
AND JEAN EDWARDS

1. *The Issue of Internal versus External Determinants of Behavior*

Historically, one of the recurring issues in personality theorizing and research concerns the determinants of actual behavior. Is behavior determined primarily by situations (external factors) or by dynamic sources within individuals (internal factors)? The type, trait, and psychodynamic models have assumed that actual behavior is determined by latent, stable dispositions, whereas situationists and many social learning theorists have assumed that behavior is determined by situational factors (see Endler and Magnusson, 1976a, 1976b).

1.1. *Persons as Sources*

Hippocrates (ca. 400 B.C.E.) was probably the first *type* theorist. He proposed four basic types of temperament (choleric, melancholic, sanguine, and phlegmatic) and assumed that these temperaments were due to different bodily humors (yellow bile, black bile, blood, and phlegm, respectively). William Shakespeare, in *Julius Caesar*, Act I, Scene ii, makes a similar assumption about the relationship between personality and body build, when Caesar says:

> Let me have men about me that are fat;
> Sleek-headed men, and such as sleep o'nights.
> Yon Cassius has a lean and hungry look;
> He thinks too much; such men are dangerous.

NORMAN S. ENDLER and JEAN EDWARDS • Department of Psychology, York University, Toronto, Ontario, Canada. The research reviewed in this chapter was partially supported by Grant No. S75–1208 from the Canada Council.

Many of the typologies espoused by psychologists and psychiatrists also emphasize constitutional and biological factors, and often assume that the expression of temperament or personality is a function of constitutional factors.

Type theory, which is a precursor of the trait model, proposes discrete categories of personality, whereas the trait model postulates that there are various continuous dimensions along which individuals differ. It is assumed that these latent traits (mediating variables) are the prime determinants of behavior, and serve as a predispositional basis for consistency of behavior across a variety of situations. The trait model also assumes that person variance contributes more to behavior than situation variance. The trait model does *not* propose that people behave exactly the same in different situations, but it does assume that the rank order of people with respect to a specific personality trait (e.g., affiliation) is the same across different situations (consistency).

Clinicians and many personologists support the trait approach. Alker (1972), for example, proclaims, "that personality variables can explain people's behavior even though that behavior varies from situation to situation" (p. 1). Allport (1937) believed that traits were not linked to specific stimuli or responses, but were instead general and enduring predispositions to respond. Cattell (1950, 1957, 1965) also postulated that traits are the basic units of personality. Cattell does, however, recognize the influence of situations, and conceptualizes two basic types of traits, namely, *surface traits* and *source traits*. *Surface traits* are clusters of overt trait elements or responses that covary and *source traits* (both environmental and constitutional) are the causal entities that determine the surface responses. Source traits may be specific, operating in one situation only, or general, affecting behavior in many situations. Theoretically, Cattell has been cognizant of situations, as exemplified by his "specification equations," but in his empirical research he has paid little attention to situations.

The various trait theorists disagree as to the types, numbers, and specific structure of traits. They do, however, agree that traits, which are usually derived by factor analytic procedures, are dispositions and that they account for cross-situational consistency. Consistency of behavior across situations is congruent with a stimulus response generalization model of learning theory. According to trait theorists, the major determinants of behavior reside within the individual, but there is an increasing awareness that traits (person factors) interact with situation factors in eliciting behavior.

Psychodynamic theories are more complex than trait theories, but they too emphasize inner determinants of behavior. Psychodynamic theories assume a basic personality core, which serves as a predispositional basis for behavior in a variety of different situations. Psychoanalytic theory is concerned with personality structure, personality dynamics, and personality development. Freud's (1959) psychodynamic theory is basically instinctual (biological), with experiences serving primarily to modify and influence the expression of the instinctual (sexual, aggressive, etc.) impulses. Neo-Freudians have focused on the ego, social and cultural factors, and psychosocial stages of development, and have de-emphasized psychosexual stages and the role of instincts.

Although both the trait and psychodynamic theories emphasize persons as sources of behavior, they differ in their interpretations as to the relationships between mediating variables representing psychological processes and overt behavioral reactions that are indicators of these processes (Magnusson, 1976; Magnusson and Endler, 1977). That is, they differ in their measurement models which assume a relationship between indicators of reaction variables and hypothetical constructs. The trait measurement model assumes a monotonic positive relationship between test scores, representing the underlying trait, and the person's position on the latent trait dimension. The psychodynamic measurement model suggests that for some variables the relationship between overt reactions and hypothetical processes may be linear, whereas for others, due to defense mechanisms, etc., it may be curvilinear (Magnusson, 1976). For the psychodynamic model, therefore, consistency at the mediating level does not necessarily lead to consistency at the reaction level. For example, an increase in aggressiveness (a mediating variable) may, at a certain level of intensity, lead to a decrease in aggressive behavior (a reaction variable) because of fear of retaliation, defensiveness, etc.

1.2. *Situations as Sources*

Ichheiser (1943) has pointed out that one of the mechanisms that has led to misinterpretations of personality is "the tendency to overestimate personal factors and underestimate situational factors in interpreting personality" (p. 151). He suggests that behavior is always determined by two groups of factors, namely personal and situational, and notes that the situation helps to determine behavior in two main ways: as a set of stimuli that provoke responses, and as *opportunities* for action or *obstacles* to action. Ichheiser (1943) believes that the emphasis on personal factors and the neglect of situational factors has its roots in the social system and ideology of 19th-century liberalism, which postulated that "our fate in social space depended exclusively, or at least predominantly, on our individual qualities—that we, as individuals, and not the prevailing social conditions, shape our lives" (Ichheiser, 1943, p. 152). However, the sociopsychological and sociopolitical forces of the last five decades (e.g., the Depression, unemployment, World War II, the Cold War, Vietnam, the revolution of rising expectations) have tended to shift the emphasis toward explaining behavior in terms of social conditions.

Within the psychology of personality, situationism has postulated that situational factors are the basic determinants of individual behavior. Social psychologists and sociologists have emphasized the role of social learning in the development of personality, but have not negated individual differences. As indicated elsewhere (Endler and Magnusson, 1976b), the various social learning theorists do not represent a homogeneous set of theoretical propositions, although they all emphasize situational factors as determinants of behavior. For example, Skinner (1953, 1960) focuses on an empirical analysis of the stimulus conditions, and the reinforcement contingencies that shape behavior, but refuses to impute traits, motives, or drives to individuals. Classical behavior theorists, e.g., Dollard and Miller (1950), emphasize situation factors and learning but are also concerned with organismic variables such as motives, drives, response-produced cues, and conflict. Modern social behavior theories (e.g., Bandura, 1971; Mischel, 1968, 1976; Rotter, 1954, 1975) have been concerned with the organism's behavior rather than with underlying dispositions such as attributed traits and motives. These social behavior or social learning theorists attempt to understand the situational factors or stimulus conditions that influence behavior. However, they are cognizant of person factors as indicated by Rotter's (1954, 1975) concept of expectancy and by Mischel's (1973) recent focus on cognitive factors. Mischel (1976) states that "while behavior theories emphasize learning they recognize that the structure and capacities of the organism limit what it can learn and do" (p. 94). Theoretically, but not necessarily empirically, the modern social behavior learning theorists have focused on the *reciprocal* interaction between person and situation.

The impact of situation factors on personality is well documented. For example, Milgram (1965) in his classic study on obedience has demonstrated the impact of situational factors in causing normal people to administer adversive shock. Zimbardo, Haney, Banks, and Jaffe (1973) in their simulated prison study, have shown that situational factors play an important role in eliciting abnormal social and personal reactions in normal subjects.

In addition to sociologists and social psychologists, ecological psychologists (e.g., Barker, 1965) have also focused on situational factors as determinants of behavior. However, as Endler (1975b) has indicated, there have been few attempts at studying situations psychologically. There are at least two approaches to studying situations psychologically, namely, situation *perception* studies and situation *reaction* studies (see Magnusson and Ekehammar, 1975a, 1975b; Endler and Magnusson, 1976b). Situation *perception* studies analyze the meanings that situations have for subjects, and situation *reaction* studies analyze situations on the basis of individuals' reactions to situations. The meaning (perception) that an individual ascribes to a situation seems to be the most influential situation factor affecting the person's behavior (Endler and Magnusson, 1976b). Situations, using a situation perception approach, cannot be investigated independently of the person.

1.3. Person by Situation Interactions

Interactional psychology emphasizes the importance of person by situation interactions in personality. "Behavior involves an indispensable, continuous interaction between individuals and the situations they encounter. Not only is the individual's behavior influenced by significant features of the situations he or she encounters but the person also selects the situations in which he or she performs, and subsequently affects the character of these situations" (Endler and Magnusson, 1976b, p. 958).

Staats (1971) and Endler and Magnusson (1976b) point out that the major influences in personality research have come from theories (e.g., psychodynamic, trait, etc.) that assume that the primary determinants of behavior reside within the individual. Behavioristic theories, on the other hand, "look for the determinants of behavior in the directly observable principles of learning and in presently acting environmental conditions" (Staats, 1971, p. 6). Both person factors and situation factors are important, but as pointed out elsewhere (Endler, 1973), the question of persons versus situations or internal versus external determinants of behavior is a pseudo-issue. The more sensible question is, How do person and situations interact in evoking or restricting behavior?

Endler and Magnusson (1976b) and Endler (1977) have discussed the four essential features of modern interactionism, which can be summarized as follows: (a) overt behavior is a function of a continuous process or feedback (multidirectional interaction) between the person and the situation she or he encounters or selects; (b) the person is an intentional and active agent in this interaction process; (c) cognitive factors are the essential determinant of behavior on the person side of the interaction, but emotional factors play an important role as they interact with strategies for information processing and cognitions; and (d) the psychological meaning of the situation for the person is an important determining factor of behavior. Since these basic four features operate simultaneously, it is often difficult, in practice to treat them separately, especially if we accept the assumption that interaction is an ongoing and continuous process. Basically, interactionism proposes that behavior is a function of person by situation interactions, and that functional equations of behavior must include a person factor, a situation factor, and the interaction between the two.

Endler (1976) and Endler and Magnusson (1976a, 1976b) have discussed the strategies that have been used to study person by situation interactions and the consistency versus specificity issue and have reviewed the relevant literature. The three basic strategies have been the multidimensional variance components research strategy, the correlational research strategy, and the personality by treatment experimental design.

The review of the literature using the variance components strategy, for various personality variables, indicates that persons and situations per se each account for less variance than person by situation interactions. These results demonstrate interactions, they do not explain them. In those instances in which the variance due to interactions is low, the variance components results indicating that both situations and persons each contribute very little to variance may not have direct implications for situationism nor for trait psychology. For example, it is possible for the stability of rank orders to be high (high consistency) even in those cases in which the variance due to persons is small (see Endler, 1977). "However, the existence of strong Person X Situation interaction variance is an indirect indication of the lack of stable rank orders (i.e., the lack of consistency) and provides direct evidence for interactionism" (Endler and Magnusson, 1976b, p. 964).

The review of the literature using the correlational research strategy, for various personality variable, fails to provide evidence for cross-situational consistency with respect to personality and social variables. There is, however, some evidence for moderate consistency (a) with respect to cognitive and intellectual variables (see Rushton and Endler, 1977; Mischel, 1968, 1969), (b) across situations that are similar (Magnusson, Gerzén, and Nyman, 1968; Magnusson and Heffler, 1969; and Magnusson, Heffler, and Nyman, 1968), and (c) with respect to longitudinal studies (stability over time) across similar situations (Block, 1971, 1977). The degree of situational specificity or cross-situational consistency, however, differs as a function of the variable under investigation.

Both the variance components strategy and the correlational strategy indicate what the state of affairs is, i.e., interactions are important. They do not tell us why (see Sarason, Smith, and Diener, 1975) or how persons and situations interact in evoking behavior (see Endler, 1973). Investigations that incorporate both situation and personality variables in their experimental designs would enable us to predict the nature of the interactions. Later in this chapter we will provide an extensive review of the person by situation (treatment) interaction experimental designs with respect to anxiety, locus of control, and conformity. The various studies, using the different strategies, seriously question some of the major assumptions of the trait theory of personality, and its traditional measurement model, and suggest that an interactional model of personality may be more congruent with the empirical data.

2. *Mechanistic versus Dynamic Models of Interaction*

With respect to an interactional psychology of personality, the concept of interaction has been discussed in at least two ways: (a) statistically, in terms of interactions of main factors such as persons, situations, and modes of response, within a data matrix, and (b) in process models of behavior concerned with reciprocal causation or reciprocal action between situational events and behavior. The first sense of the term would be concerned with interactions in terms of structure, and the second sense would be concerned with the process of interaction. This distinction is analogous to the one made by Overton and Reese (1973) between the reactive organism (mechanistic) and the active organism (organismic) models of man and to Pervin's (1968) distinction between interaction and transaction. Elsewhere (Endler, 1975a, and Magnusson and Endler, 1977) we have used the terms "mechanistic" and "dynamic interaction."

2.1. *The Interaction of Independent Variables—Structure*

The mechanistic model of interaction, which uses analysis of variance procedures in its measurement model, makes a clear distinction between independent and dependent variables, and assumes an additive and linear relation between situational and person factors (both independent variables) in determining behavior. Here interaction is concerned with the interdependency of determinants (independent variables) of behavior. It says nothing about the interaction between independent variables and dependent variables. The "interaction is not between cause and effect, but between causes" (Overton and Reese, 1973, p. 78). It is concerned with the structure of the interaction and not with the process.

Magnusson and Endler (1977) suggest that four different subcategories of mechanistic interaction, which influence behavior, can be investigated, namely: interactions between persons and modes of response (kinds of reactions), person by situation interactions, interactions of situations and modes of response, and finally interactions of persons, reactions (modes of response) and situations, in a three-way data matrix.

These types of interactions have been investigated via variance components techniques and via person by treatment (experimental) analysis of variance designs. The merit of the variance components approach is that it has demonstrated, but not explained, the existence of strong interactions. This provides us with insights as to the direction for formulating a more effective measurement model and a more effective behavioral model than the traditional trait personality and measurement models (see Magnusson and Endler, 1977). A person by treatment experimental design permits us to explain interactions. However, both the variance components strategy and the person by treatment design reflect a mechanistic model of man and are inadequate for studying the dynamic interaction process, within the interactional model of personality.

2.2. *The Interaction of Independent and Dependent Variables—Process*

The dynamic or organismic model of interaction is concerned with the reciprocal interaction between behavior and environmental or situational events. "*Reciprocal Causation* means that not only do events affect the behavior of organisms but the organism is also an active agent influencing environmental events" (Endler and Magnusson, 1976b, p. 969). Dynamic or organismic interaction is bidirectional (or multidirectional) and refers "to the mutual interdependence of persons–situations and behaviour so that persons–situations influence behaviour and vice versa" (Endler, 1975a, p. 18). Dynamic interaction is concerned with process and is concerned with attempting to integrate mediating variables, person reaction variables, and situations. Not only do individuals react to situations, but to a certain extent they select the situations in which they interact. Raush (1977) has suggested that within the dynamic model of interaction the traditional distinction between dependent and independent variables may not be a very fruitful one.

Most of the research until now has focused on mechanistic interaction and this is probably due to the fact that we have not yet perfected the techniques and measurement models for investigating dynamic interaction.

Let us first provide some brief illustrations of interactions within the context of both the mechanistic and dynamic models, and then examine in detail some of the interactional research on three variables, namely, anxiety, locus of control, and conformity. The research reviewed will focus primarily on person by treatment (situation) interactions within the mechanistic model. We will subsequently suggest some directions for future research, which might enable us to obtain some insights into the dynamic interaction process.

3. *Illustrations of Interactions*

3.1. *Mechanistic Models*

Sarason, Smith, and Diener (1975) have pointed out that the usual variance components studies are descriptive but not predictive. They do not tell us why interactions are important, nor do they tell us how persons and situations interact in evoking behavior. If recent and future person by treatment (situation) studies are designed in the context of an interactionist theory, it will enable us to predict the nature of mechanistic interactions.

Fiedler (1971, 1977) using both laboratory and field studies, has investigated how persons and situations interact with respect to leadership effectiveness. He found that leadership style (a person variable) interacts with situational variables in determining group effectiveness. Berkowitz (1973, 1977), although not using an interactional theoretical model for his investigations, found that person and situation variables interact in eliciting aggressive behavior. Moyer (1973) notes the interaction of biological and learning factors in evoking violent behavior. Schachter's (1968) studies on obesity have demonstrated the interaction of person and situational variables in affecting food consumption. Moore (1971), who has investigated language performance, has provided empirical evidence for "the interaction of characteristics of the speaker and characteristics of the situation in actual language performance" (pp. 18–19). Cronbach and Snow (1975) have provided an extensive review of studies on school achievement and found many aptitude (person) by treatment (situation) interactions with respect to school instruction. Domino (1971) has investigated college course outcome and found significant interactions between personality variables and instructor's style of teaching (situation) with respect to course grades, exam results, etc. Altman and Haythorn (1967) have demonstrated an interaction between group composition and social isolation with respect to territorial behavior and social activities.

3.2. *Dynamic Models*

While there have been a number of studies of interaction within the mechanistic models, there has been a paucity of research with respect to the dynamic models. Raush (1972, 1977) suggests the need to study dyadic transactions rather than unidirectional causality. He proposes that Markov models provide a useful methodological technique for investigating the process of interaction and change in interpersonal relationships, and demonstrates how this can be done with respect to marital relationships. Peterson (1977) has investigated interpersonal relationships by studying the recurrent interaction sequences of married couples. In his research strategy, Peterson examines the interaction sequences by focusing on the situational contexts, contractual rules, tactics, strategies, and reward–cost outcomes that are relevant to the interactions between dyadic pairs. Argyle (1977) has suggested that in order to understand the interaction process it may be necessary to examine rules and strategies rather than the content of interaction. He proposes that we develop a grammar of interaction that would be analogous to the grammar of language and suggests that we use a "generative rules approach" to social interaction rather than a predictive model.

Pervin (1977) and Wachtel (1977) have pointed out that not only do situations influence persons, but that persons influence situations as well. Pervin (1977) has been concerned with the stability of behavior as a function of both situation characteristics and person characteristics. He attempts to investigate the relationships between variations in person characteristics and variations in situation characteristics within the context of a process model of interaction. In his research Pervin (1976) asks subjects to generate a list of traits that can be applied to each environment or situation that they encounter in their daily lives. This approach enables Pervin to study the process of person by situation interactions. Pervin (1976) suggests that his approach can be used to develop a taxonomy of situations and behavior in situations. By factor analyzing the situations that persons generate and their type of reactions one can gain some insights into the ongoing interaction process.

Bales (1958) has investigated the interaction process that occurs in problem-solving groups. He finds that there is a predictable sequence, in that acts of orientation precede acts of evaluation, which in turn precede acts of control. He also finds that more questions are directed to the leader than to other members of the group. By examining who talks to whom and when and under what conditions, his approach provides us with a useful technique for investigating the person by situation interaction process.

Couch (1970) suggests that research in personality must consider the multiple determinants of interpersonal behavior, both in terms of personality factors and in terms of social environmental factors. For example, he examined the "accumulative effect on the predictability of individual behavior as these different determinants of Need, Defense and Press were successfully brought into the statistical formulation" (p. 84), and found that he improved the predictability of interpersonal behavior by investigating multiple (personality and environmental) factors. Path analysis (Land, 1969) seems to be another approach that may be useful in gaining some insights into the interaction process.

Much of the research on the dynamic process of interaction has been in the form of promise rather than fulfillment. Furthermore, most of the research in this area has focused on social interaction between persons, and although cognizant of situation factors, has not been primarily concerned with person by situation interactions. Although person by person interactions are an essential and almost pervasive component of person by situation interactions, in that other persons serve as situational or environmental events, it is hoped that future research will more actively investigate the broader context of environmental and situational impact.

Let us now turn to a more detailed examination of person by situation mechanistic interaction, with respect to anxiety, locus of control, and conformity. We will then suggest some directions for future research regarding the dynamic process oriented models of interaction.

The three content areas to be reviewed, anxiety, internal–external locus of control, and conformity were chosen because (1) each is an important area of empirical research and theory in social-personality psychology, and (2) the three constructs represent quite diverse types of research variables and activities. Anxiety, although defined in the literature in a variety of ways, has been associated primarily with the person. Conformity, however, is dependent upon a social situation for its meaning. Internal–external locus of control, although treated primarily as a person variable, is theoretically applicable to both persons and situations.

4. *Person by Situation Interactions in Anxiety*

Lewis (1970) states that anxiety "is an emotional state, with the subjectively experienced quality of fear or a closely related emotion (terror, horror, alarm, fright, panic, trepidation, dread, scare)" (p. 77). Although it is generally recognized that anxiety involves unpleasant subjective experiences and manifest bodily disturbances, anxiety has been defined in many different ways (Endler and Magnusson, 1976c; Spielberger, 1966, 1972). At various times it has been conceptualized as a response, as a stimulus, as a trait, as a motive and as a drive (Shedletsky and Endler, 1974). Spielberger (1966) attributes some of the conceptual and empirical confusion to a failure to distinguish between *trait* anxiety (A-Trait) and *state* anxiety (A-State). Spielberger (1972) defines A-State as an emotional reaction "consisting of unpleasant, consciously-perceived feelings of tension and apprehension, with associated activation or arousal of the autonomic nervous system" (p. 29). Trait anxiety is a measure of "anxiety-proneness—differences between individuals in the probability that anxiety states will be manifested under circumstances involving varying degrees of stress" (Spielberger, 1966, p. 15). The state–trait model of anxiety requires the effects of both person and situational variables to produce state anxiety. Under neutral or nonstress conditions there would be no differences predicted in the A-State of high and low A-Trait individuals. Under ego-threatening conditions, high A-Trait persons would be expected to manifest higher levels of A-State than would low A-Trait individuals. The State–Trait Anxiety Inventory (STAI) has been developed by Spielberger (Spielberger, Gorsuch, and Lushene, 1970) to measure state and trait anxiety, the A-Trait measure focusing on interpersonal or ego-threatening anxiety.

A number of studies by Spielberger and his colleagues have demonstrated the usefulness of the trait–state distinction. O'Neill, Spielberger, and Hansen (1969), Rappaport and Katkin (1972), Hodges (1968), and Auerbach (1973a) found that under ego-threatening conditions, for example, fear of failure or negative feedback, high A-Trait individuals showed larger changes in A-State than low A-Trait individuals. However for physical danger situations, e.g., threat of electric shock, there is no difference in the level of increase in A-State for high and low A-Trait individuals (Auerbach, 1973b; Hodges, 1968; Hodges and Spielberger, 1966; Katkin, 1965; Spielberger, Gorsuch, and Lushene, 1970). Thus the predicted person–situation interaction for state anxiety occurs when A-Trait is measured by a general trait measure such as the STAI A-Trait scale and the stressful situation involves ego or interpersonal threat but not other dimensions of stress, such as physical danger.

4.1. *A Multidimensional Model for Person by Situation Interaction for Anxiety*

Endler (1975a) has proposed a multidimensional interaction model of anxiety. Originally, individual differences in A-Trait were assumed to occur in three situational domains: interpersonal, physical danger, and ambiguous types of situations (Endler, Hunt, and Rosenstein, 1962). Recently, social evaluation threat was differentiated from the more global interpersonal situation and included as a separate scale of the S-R Inventory of General Trait Anxiousness (S-R GTA), which has been developed to assess the different facets of A-Trait (Endler and Okada, 1975). Empirical support for the multidimensionality of A-Trait has been found for Canadian and Swedish samples (Endler and Magnusson, 1976c; Endler, Magnusson, Ekehammar, and Okada, 1976).

Endler's multidimensional model of anxiety makes explicit predictions for person by situation interactions. In order for an interaction to occur, resulting in changes in A-State, the stress in the situation must be congruent with the A-Trait measure. That is, it would be predicted that interpersonal ego-threat A-Trait interacts with an ego-threat situation but not with physical danger nor an ambiguous threat situation. Similarly, physical danger A-Trait would be expected to interact with a physical danger threat situation but not with interpersonal threat. Support for the multidimensional interaction model of anxiety has been found in laboratory studies in which physical danger was manipulated (Endler and Okada, 1975; Hodges and Spielberger, 1966; Kendall, 1975), and in both field and laboratory studies that examined the effects of interpersonal evaluation or threat (Endler and Magnusson, 1977; Flood and Endler, 1976; Kendall, 1975; Lamb, 1973).

In addition to the interaction studies that have focused on self-report measures of A-State, several studies have also found behavioral consequences of person by situation interactions, including effects of interactions on test scores (Wrightsman, 1962), affiliation (Teichman, 1974), helping behavior (Wine, 1975), and conformity (Rule and Sandilands, 1969).

Interaction between A-Trait and reduction of stress or therapeutic intervention should also predict decreases in state anxiety and accompanying behavioral consequences. Consistent with the interaction hypothesis, Sarason (1973, 1975a) found that subjects high in test anxiety benefited more from a model who displayed effective coping behavior than did low anxious subjects. Modeling of task irrelevant or ineffective behavior did not improve the performance of subjects.

4.2. *The Multidimensionality of A-State*

In predicting interactions of facets of A-Trait and congruent situational stress, in evoking A-State, the predictions are complicated by the fact that A-State itself is multidimensional. The empirical results of Endler and Magnusson, (1976c) plus the theorizing of Liebert and Morris (1967) and Sarason (1975a) suggest that there are at least two components of A-State: a cognitive worry component and an emotional-arousal component. Differentiating these two components of A-State may have important implications for the person by situation interaction model of anxiety. For example, the predicted interaction may occur for only one of the A-State components and not be detected by a measure that confounds the two. In addition the two components may have different behavioral consequences. Sarason (1975b, 1975c) suggests that the high anxious person focuses on self-evaluation and self-worry rather than on the task, and that cognitive events, e.g., worry, have a more negative influence on performance than does autonomic arousal. However, these cognitive factors may also be more amenable to change or amenable to different therapeutic techniques, such as modeling of appropriate cognitive strategies, compared to the emotionality component that may be best treated by counterconditioning or relaxation therapy (see Meichenbaum, 1972, 1975; see also Morris and Liebert, 1973). Therefore, to predict person by situation interactions for reduction in A-State, it may be necessary to specify the component of A-State to which the therapeutic intervention was directed.

4.3. *Summary*

The interaction research in anxiety has focused on the trait-state model of Spielberger (1972) and the multidimensional interaction model proposed by Endler (1975a). The empirical evidence has supported the prediction that A-Trait interacts with situational stress in inducing A-State, when the stress is congruent with the dimension of A-Trait. In addition to self-report measures of state anxiety, the interaction of A-Trait and situation stress has been found to predict affiliation, altruism, and performance on complex tests. Interactions have also been found with coping behavior as the dependent variable.

5. *Person by Situation Interactions in Locus of Control*

The internal-external locus of control of reinforcement construct (I–E) is a cognitive expectancy or belief regarding the contingency between one's actions and reinforcements (Rotter, 1966). An internal locus of control denotes the belief that one's reinforcements are contingent upon one's own behaviors or characteristics. An external locus of control indicates the expectancy that reinforcements are not contingent on one's own actions but are "the result of luck, chance, fate, . . . under the control of powerful others, or . . . unpredictable because of the great complexity of forces. . . ." (Rotter, 1966, p. 1). Although Rotter presents I–E as a continuum, in much of the research, subjects are dichotomized into internals (I's) and externals (E's). In addition the I–E construct has most often been used as a global, person variable without regard for situational constraints. However, its basis in social learning theory emphasizes interaction between the individual and his meaningful environment in determining behavioral outcomes (Rotter, 1954; Rotter, Chance, and Phares, 1972).

5.1. *I–E and Situation Interaction Studies*

Although the definition of I–E indicates that I's attribute their outcomes to person variables and E's attribute their outcomes to situational variables, the research qualifies these conclusions. For example, it has been found that the I–E person variable interacts with the situational success–failure outcome variable to determine whether attributions are made to internal or external causes (Davis and Davis, 1972; Gilmor and Minton, 1974; see also Hochreich, 1974, 1975). Thus, characteristics of the situation as well as the I–E person variable must be considered in predicting causal attributions.

Locus of control is a situational dimension as well as a person variable (Rotter, 1966, 1975). Several person–situation interaction studies have examined the consequences of congruence and incongruence between an individual's generalized locus of control expectancy and the locus of control in the situation. When the situational locus of control is operationalized as a chance versus skill task description or perception, person–situation interactions have been found to effect reward value (Lefcourt, Lewis, and Silverman, 1968; Rotter and Mulry, 1965; Srull and Karabenick, 1975), information seeking (Davis and Phares, 1967), and performance (Houston, 1972; Petzel and Gynther, 1970; Watson and Baumal, 1967). Using a different operationalization of situational locus of control, Hrycenko and Minton (1974) found that for males I–E and the subject's degree of power in a communication network interact to effect satisfaction. Phares and Wilson (1971) report that subjects' I–E and the locus of control of a stranger interact to effect the rating given to the stranger on dimensions of interpersonal attraction. Sherman (1973) found an interaction between I–E and various attitude change procedures (e.g., writing a counterattitudinal essay versus reading a persuasive communication) and this interaction determined the degree of change. The effectiveness of therapy may also be the result of an interaction of the patient's locus of control and the degree of control allowed the patient by the structure of the treatment situation (Auerbach, Kendall, Cuttler, and Levitt, 1976; Kilmann, Albert, and Sotile, 1975).

Pines and Julian (1972) hypothesized that I's should respond more to task demands and E's more to social demands, particularly the threat of social evaluation. Their experimental results as well as those of others (Julian and Katz, 1968; Pines, 1973) support this hypothesis. The type of reinforcement, intrinsic or extrinsic, also interacts with I–E in affecting performance (Baron and Ganz, 1972; Baron, Cowan, Ganz, and McDonald, 1974; Kumchy and Rankin, 1975). Rotter (1954, 1966, 1975) hypothesized that the *value* of the reinforcement available, in a situation, is an important variable to be considered in predicting behavior. There appear to be few studies that include both reinforcement value and I–E although Seeman's (1963) work is suggestive.

5.2. *Interactions and Multidimensional Models of I–E*

One of the most active issues within the locus of control literature is whether it is most useful to formulate I–E as a unidimensional or multidimensional construct. The dimensionality of locus of control is important from an interactionist viewpoint since interactions would be expected to occur only when the person control dimension is congruent with the salient control dimension in the situation.

In Rotter's (1966) monograph, I–E was presented as unidimensional and his scale was constructed to measure a generalized expectancy of locus of control by sampling beliefs regarding a wide variety of situations. However, a number of more recent factor analytic studies of both the Rotter Scale and several modified scales have found two or more factors (see Lefcourt, 1976, and Phares, 1976, for reviews). The most consistently identified dimensions are Fatalism and Social System Control (Reid and Ware, 1973). Fatalism concerns the belief that one's outcomes are determined by luck, chance, or fate, versus hard work, ability, or person factors. The Social System Control factor reflects the extent to which people believe they can or cannot effect sociopolitical change in their society.

5.3. *Summary*

Although I–E has been treated primarily as a person variable with little attention given to situation constraints, a number of studies demonstrate the usefulness of the interactionist position. I–E has been shown to interact with locus of control as defined by the situation and with the success–failure outcome of the situation, although there are some conflicts in the observed patterns of the interaction which indicate the need for further work. The current concern over the multidimensional nature of I–E should now be directed toward further developing a multidimensional model and towards predictive person by situation interaction studies based on that model.

6. *Person by Situation Interaction in Conformity*

Conformity may be defined as a "change in behavior caused by social influence such that a conflict exists between a person's judgments and publicly presented social pressure by others" (Wiesenthal, Edwards, Endler, Koza, Walton, and Emmott, 1978, p. 43). This definition focuses on movement conformity rather than the more inclusive area of all types of social influence. It has been recognized for almost two decades that conformity behavior is the result of interactions between person and situation variables (Blake and Mouton, 1961; Endler, 1966; Rhine, 1968). Rhine (1968) states that conformity is "a complex behavior resulting from the interaction of an individual's motives and his perception of the relative instrumental value of conformity or nonconformity in the influence situation" (p. 989). However, little empirical research on person by situation interactions has been generated. The bulk of the conformity literature has examined the effects of either personality variables, for example, authoritarianism, need achievement, need affiliation, and need for approval, or situational variables such as stimulus characteristics, reinforcement, and the source and type of influence pressure. In a recent review of the conformity literature (Wiesenthal *et al.*, 1978) only 15% of the 326 articles reviewed included both personality and situational variables, and the majority of these articles did not examine the interaction of these variables.

Many of the predictive person by situation studies that have been done on conformity are based on the normative-informational influence distinction proposed by Deutsch and Gerard (1955). They contrast normative influence, based on the motivation to conform to the positive expectations of the source of influence, that is, to gain the reinforcements controlled by the influencer, with informational influence based on the need for information about reality. Although many of the interaction studies are based on this distinction, the specific person and situational variables included are quite diverse. The research to be presented will be organized according to the person variable included in the study. (It is also just as logical to organize the research reviewed on the basis of situational variables.)

6.1. Person by Situation Interaction Studies

McDavid (1959) and Sistrunk (1973), in investigating conforming behavior, both developed personality tests that measure differential responsiveness to normative versus informational influence. McDavid found that item difficulty and degree of discrepancy between the subjects' position and that of the group differentially affected conformity of subjects classified on this person variable. Sistrunk obtained an interaction between manipulations of task description, private versus public response conditions, and the normative informational person variable.

As discussed by Sistrunk and McDavid (1965), relationships between conformity and achievement and affiliation motivation have been studied, but little attention has been given to determining situational factors that might influence these relationships. Their experimental results demonstrated an interaction between achievement motivation and task difficulty.

Several investigators (Becker, Lerner, and Carroll, 1966) have proposed that first-borns are more sensitive to normative cues in an influence situation, whereas later-borns are more responsive to informational cues. Congruent with this proposition, Becker *et al.* (1966) found differential birth order effects for group reward and memory conditions. Similarly, Rhine (1968) found that birth order and task description interact to affect conformity.

Johnson and Steiner (1967) suggested that level of authoritarianism may interact with social and informational cues in the influence situation, in affecting conformity. Two studies lend support to this hypothesis. Saiyadain and Summers (1973) found a trend such that when there was a large discrepancy between the subject's and group's judgments on the experimental task, low authoritarians conformed under both individual and group reward conditions but high authoritarians conformed only in the group reward condition. Moore and Krupat (1971) found that low authoritarians conformed more to a highly positive status source compared to a mildly positive status source, whereas high authoritarians did not conform differentially to the two sources.

The review by Witkin and Goodenough (1976) of the literature on field dependence suggests that the relationship between this person variable and conformity is influenced by situational variables. Consistent with the above conclusions, Mausner and Graham (1970) found that field-independent subjects were relatively unaffected by prior reinforcement. However, field-dependent subjects, when led to believe that they were less competent than their partner, conformed more than when led to believe that they were more competent.

Several studies have examined interactions between person variables associated with anxiety, and the public–private response condition. For example, Rule and Sandilands (1969) found a significant interaction between the personality variable of test anxiety and public versus private response conditions. In addition, Snyder and Monson (1975) hypothesized that some individuals are more influenced by situational and interpersonal cues regarding the appropriateness of their behavior (self-monitoring persons) and are therefore more variable across situations. They found that the conformity of self-monitoring persons was affected by the situational manipulation of the subject's audience but not that of low self-monitoring persons.

6.2. *Summary*

Although most of the research on conformity has been concerned with either person or situational variables, a few studies based primarily on the normative-informational influence distinction have demonstrated person by situation interactions. The person variables examined included special measures developed to discriminate those differentially susceptible to normative or information influence, authoritarianism, and need achievement and need affiliation. The situational variables included manipulation of the explanation of the purpose of the conformity task, offering a group versus an individual reward, variations in task difficulty, and degree of disagreement between the group and the individual.

7. *Looking toward the Future*

7.1. *Goals of Science*

We would suggest that the goals of psychology as a science are threefold: (a) in the first instance we have to isolate the effective and predictive variables; (b) the second task is to examine the functional relationships between antecedent conditions (independent variables) and the behavior they influence or control (the dependent variables); (c) the third task is to examine behavioral processes so that we can explain and predict behavior. Although we have made some progress in isolating some important variables, we are only beginning to understand the functional relationships. Therefore, it may be premature to extensively investigate behavioral processes. The ideal approach would be to proceed simultaneously on all three fronts (isolating variables, examining functional relationships, and studying behavioral processes). Although "it is important to study dynamic interaction and to develop appropriate techniques for doing this, we have still not fully explored the nature of mechanistic interaction" (Endler, 1975b, p. 18).

7.2. *A Research Program for Studying Interactions*

As a research strategy for investigating interactions, we would suggest that in the first instance we should focus on mechanistic interaction or the structure of interactions in order to further our understanding of the effective and predictive variables and the functional relationships between antecedent conditions and the behavior they influence. The research on anxiety, locus of control, and conformity, reviewed in this chapter, provides a promising start for an understanding of person by situation interactions. Although the ultimate goal is an understanding of dynamic interactions, much research is still needed on how person and situations interact (mechanistic interaction) in effecting, modifying, and influencing behavior. This type of research has been done with a number of variables such as anxiety, hostility (see Endler and Hunt 1968, 1969), and social behavior of children (see Raush, 1965). However, many of these studies have used the variance components approach and have focused primarily on description. We need to experimentally examine the joint effects of persons and situations on behavior and subsequently to investigate the effects of behavior on persons and situations. Such an approach or strategy has to be done within the context of a theory (see Endler, 1977) so that we can predict interactions rather than merely providing post hoc explanations.

Most of the research on interactionism has been conducted in the context of the mechanistic model (e.g., see the research on anxiety, locus of control, and conformity), and has demonstrated the existence of strong person by situation interactions. As the research reviewed has demonstrated, promising starts have been made toward predicting how persons and situations interact. The person by treatment (situation) experimental designs do not investigate the dynamic multidirectional and process views of interaction. However, this research may serve as a starting point for developing an interactional psychology of personality, the ultimate goal of which is an understanding of the process of interaction (dynamic interaction).

With respect to situations, it is important to distinguish between perceptions of and reactions to situations (Magnusson and Ekehammar, 1975a) and between objective versus psychological situations (Endler and Magnusson, 1976b). However, equally important is the distinction between specific elements within the situation and differences between more global situations. For example, the mechanistic interaction studies reviewed have in general examined the macro aspects of situations and have been concerned with differences between situations, rather than studying the process of the various elements (e.g., contributions of participants) within a situation (cf. Magnusson and Endler, 1977). Future research should be directed toward examining the multicausal and multidirectional elements within the situation. Within situations the elements would include person by person interactions and person by situation interactions. Each person serves as a situational cue for other persons with whom he or she is interacting, and is in turn influenced by these other persons.

In most studies we arbitrarily take a subsample of behavior, in a static fashion, and rarely investigate the chain of events. Not only are persons influenced by situations but they actively seek the situations and persons with whom they interact. In order to understand this process it is important to conceptualize the person as an active intentional organism seeking stimulation, rather than as a passive victim of situational events.

Perhaps research and theorizing in personality have not made sufficient progress because we have been looking in the wrong place for the wrong thing. We should focus on rules and strategies of interaction perhaps rather than focusing on the content. Mischel (1973) has aruged the case for examining encoding and decoding strategies. Argyle (1977) has argued that we should analyze and investigate the generative rules of social interaction rather than attempting to make predictions about content. With respect to language behavior, although we cannot always predict the exact content of what someone will say, we can usually predict the rules of grammar that the person will use (e.g., each sentence will have a subject and a predicate). An analogous approach to investigating interaction may be useful.

Earlier, in discussing dynamic interaction, we have presented a number of approaches and methods that investigators have recently started using (e.g., Block, 1977, on longitudinal studies; Raush, 1977, on Markov chains; Pervin, 1977, on methods for having subjects generate their own situations; Argyle, 1977, on investigating rules for social interaction and Mischel, 1973, 1977, on encoding and decoding strategies). There is an intimate relationship between subject matter and methodology or technology, and they feed on one another. We are limited by the lack of appropriate methodologies for investigating dynamic processes. But science proceeds one small step at a time, rather than by leaps and bounds.

As Pervin suggests in this volume, perhaps we need to use general systems theory to investigate personality, in which we recognize that persons are open systems rather than closed systems. We have to develop new research strategies and new methods for investigating interaction processes and perhaps new ways of conceptualizing the problems involved. "Until and unless this occurs we will continue working within our own mythological framework—a convenient and satisfying illusion to some, but frustrating to many" (Endler, 1976, p. 179). *Caveat emptor!*

8. Summary

Theoretical positions that emphasize, as the major source of variance in behavior, either the person, i.e., type, trait, and psychodynamic theories, or the situation, i.e., situationism and some learning theories, were reviewed. Although these models have made important contributions, research findings indicate that the interaction of person and situational variables may be a more important source of variance than either persons or situations *per se*.

The modern interactionist position with its emphasis on how person and situation variables influence the ongoing interaction process was discussed. The distinction between mechanistic and dynamic models of interaction and the relevance of this distinction for research was pointed out, and illustrations of dynamic and mechanistic interaction presented. A more extensive examination of person by situation experimental studies in the areas of anxiety, conformity, and locus of control demonstrated the current utility of considering interactions within the mechanistic model. In conclusion, suggestions for future research were offered. These included the need to focus on process variables and the dynamic model of interaction, the need to intensively investigate the important elements within a situation, and to distinguish between perception of and reaction to situations, and the need to develop new research strategies, models, and theories.

ACKNOWLEDGMENTS

The authors wish to thank Michael Argyle for his helpful comments and suggestions.

References

Alker, H.A. Is personality situationally specific or intra-psychically consistent? *Journal of Personality*, 1972, *40*, 1–16.

Allport, G.W. *Personality*. New York: Holt, 1937.

Altman, I., and Haythorn, W.W. The ecology of isolated groups. *Journal of Behavioral Science*, 1967, *12*, 169–182.

Argyle, M. Predictive and generative rules models of P × S interaction. In D. Magnusson and N.S. Endler (Eds.), *Personality at the crossroads: Current issues in interactional psychology*. Hillsdale, N.J.: Lawrence Erlbaum Associates, 1977, pp. 353–370.

Auerbach, S.M. Effects of orienting instructions, feedback information and trait anxiety on state anxiety. *Psychological Reports*, 1973a, *33*, 779–786.

Auerbach, S.M. Trait-state anxiety and adjustment to surgery. *Journal of Consulting and Clinical Psychology*, 1973b, *40*, 264–271.

Auerbach, S.M., Kendall, P.C., Cuttler, H.F., and Levitt, N.R. Anxiety, locus of control, type of preparation information, and adjustment to dental surgery. *Journal of Consulting and Clinical Psychology*, 1976, *44*, 809–818.

Bales, R.F. Task roles and social roles in problem-solving groups. In E.E. Maccoby, T.M. Newcomb, and E.L. Hartley (Eds.), *Readings in social psychology*. 3rd Ed. New York: Holt, Rinehart and Winston, 1958, pp. 396–413.

Bandura, A. (Ed.), *Psychological modeling: Conflicting theories*. New York: Aldine-Atherton, 1971.

Barker, R.G. Explorations in ecological psychology. *American Psychologist*, 1965, *20*, 1–14.

Baron, R.M., Cowan, G., Ganz, R.L., and McDonald, M. Interaction of locus of control and type of performance feedback: Considerations of external validity. *Journal of Personality and Social Psychology*, 1974, *30*, 285–292.

Baron, R.M., and Ganz, R.L. Effects of locus of control and type of feedback on the task performance of lower-class black children. *Journal of Personality and Social Psychology*, 1972, *21*, 124–130.

Becker, S.W., Lerner, M.J., and Carroll, J. Conformity as a function of birth order and type of group pressure. *Journal of Personality and Social Psychology*, 1966, *3*, 242–244.

Berkowitz, L. The case for bottling up rage. *Psychology Today*, 1973, *7*, 24–31.

Berkowitz, L. Situational and personal conditions governing reactions to aggressive cues. In D. Magnusson and N.S. Endler (Eds.), *Personality at the crossroads: Current issues in interactional psychology*. Hillsdale, N.J.: Lawrence Erlbaum Associates, 1977, pp. 165–171.

Blake, R.R., and Mouton, J.S. Conformity, resistance, and conversion. In I.A. Berg and B.M. Bass (Eds.), *Conformity and deviation*. New York: Harper, 1961, pp. 1–37.

Block, J. *Lives through time*. Berkeley, Calif.: Bancroft, 1971.

Block, J. Advancing the psychology of personality: Paradigmatic shift or improving the quality of research. In D. Magnusson and N.S. Endler (Eds.), *Personality at the crossroads: Current issues in interactional psychology*. Hillsdale, N.J.: Lawrence Erlbaum Associates, 1977, pp. 37–64.

Cattell, R.B. *Personality: A systematic theoretical and factual study*. New York: McGraw-Hill, 1950.

Cattell, R.B. *Personality and motivation structure and measurement*. Yonkers-on-Hudson, N.Y.: World Book, 1957.

Cattell, R.B. *The scientific analysis of personality*. Chicago: Aldine, 1965.

Couch, A.S. The psychological determinants of interpersonal behavior. In K.J. Gergen and D. Marlowe (Eds.), *Personality and social behavior*. Reading, Mass.: Addison-Wesley Publishing Company, 1970, pp. 77–89.

Cronbach, L.J. and Snow, R.E. *Aptitudes and instructional methods*. New York: Irvington, 1975.

Davis, W.L., and Davis, D.E. Internal-external control and attribution of responsibility for success and failure. *Journal of Personality*, 1972, *40*, 123–136.

Davis, W.L., and Phares, E.J. Internal-external control as a determinant of information seeking in a social influence situation. *Journal of Personality*, 1967, *35*, 547–561.

Deutsch, M., and Gerard, H. A study of normative and informational social influence upon individual judgments. *Journal of Abnormal and Social Psychology*, 1955, *51*, 629–636.

Dollard, J., and Miller, N.E. *Personality and psychotherapy: An analysis in terms of learning, thinking and culture*. New York: McGraw-Hill, 1950.

Domino, G. Interactive effects of achievement of orientation and teaching style on academic achievement. *Journal of Educational Psychology*, 1971, *62*, 427–431.

Endler, N.S. Conformity as a function of different reinforcement schedules. *Journal of Personality and Social Psychology*, 1966, *4*, 175–180.

Endler, N.S. The person versus the situation—A pseudo issue? A response to Alker. *Journal of Personality*, 1973, *41*, 287–303.

Endler, N.S. A person–situation interaction model for anxiety. In C.D. Spielberger and I.G. Sarason (Eds.), *Stress and anxiety* (Vol. 1). Washington, D.C.: Hemisphere Publishing Corporation, 1975a, 145–164.

Endler, N.S. The case for person–situation interactions. *Canadian Psychological Review*, 1975b, *16*, 12–21.

Endler, N.S. Grand illusions: Traits or interactions? *Canadian Psychological Review*, No. 3, 1976, *17*, 174–181.

Endler, N.S. The role of personality situation interactions in personality theory. In I.C. Uzgiris and F. Weizmann (Eds.), *The structuring of experience*. New York: Plenum Press, 1977, pp. 343–369.

Endler, N.S., and Hunt, J. McV. S–R inventories of hostility and comparisons of the proportions of variance from persons, responses, and situations for hostility and anxiousness. *Journal of Personality and Social Psychology*, 1968, *9*, 309–315.

Endler, N.S., and Hunt, J. McV. Generalizability of contributions from sources of variance in the S–R Inventories of Anxiousness. *Journal of Personality*, 1969, *37*, 1–24.

Endler, N.S., Hunt, J. McV., and Rosenstein, A.J. An S–R Inventory of Anxiousness. *Psychological Monographs*, 1962, *76*, No. 17 (Whole No. 536), 1–33.

Endler, N.S., and Magnusson, D. Personality and person by situation interactions. In N.S. Endler and D. Magnusson (Eds.), *Interactional psychology and personality*. Washington, D.C.: Hemisphere Publishing Corporation (Wiley), 1976a, pp. 1–25.

Endler, N.S., and Magnusson, D. Toward an interactional psychology of personality. *Psychological Bulletin*, 1976b, *83*, 956–974.

Endler, N.S., and Magnusson, D. Multidimensional aspects of state and trait anxiety: A cross-cultural study of Canadian and Swedish students. In C.D. Spielberger and R.

Diaz-Guerrero (Eds.), *Cross-cultural research on anxiety*. Washington, D.C.: Hemisphere Publishing Corporation (Wiley), 1976c, pp. 143–172.

Endler, N.S., and Magnusson, D. The interaction model of anxiety: An empirical test in an examination situation. *Canadian Journal of Behavioural Science*, 1977, *9*, 101–107.

Endler, N.S., Magnusson, D., Ekehammar, B., and Okada, M. The multidimensionality of state and trait anxiety. *Scandinavian Journal of Psychology*, 1976, *17*, 81–93.

Endler, N.S., and Okada, M. A multidimensional measure of trait anxiety: The S-R inventory of general trait anxiousness. *Journal of Consulting and Clinical Psychology*, 1975, *43*, 319–329.

Fiedler, F.E. Validation and extension of the contingency model of leadership effectiveness: A review of empirical findings. *Psychological Bulletin*, 1971, *76*, 128–148.

Fiedler, F.E. What triggers the person situation interaction in leadership? In D. Magnusson and N.S. Endler (Eds.), *Personality at the crossroads: Current issues in interactional psychology*. Hillsdale, N.J.: Lawrence Erlbaum Associates, 1977, pp.151–164.

Flood, M. and Endler, N.S. The interaction model of anxiety: An empirical test in an athletic competition situation. *Department of Psychology Reports*, York University, 1976, No. 28.

Freud, S. *Collected papers*. Vol. I–V. New York: Basic Books, 1959.

Gilmor, T.M., and Minton, H.L. Internal versus external attribution of task performance as a function of locus of control, initial confidence and success-failure outcome. *Journal of Personality*, 1974, *42*, 159–174.

Hochreich, D.J. Defensive externality and attribution of responsibility. *Journal of Personality*, 1974, *42*, 543–557.

Hochreich, D.J. Defensive externality and blame projection following failure. *Journal of Personality and Social Psychology*, 1975, *32*, 540–546.

Hodges, W.F. Effects of ego threat and threat of pain on state anxiety. *Journal of Personality and Social Psychology*, 1968, *8*, 364–372.

Hodges, W.F., and Spielberger, C.D. The effects of threat of shock on heart rate for subjects who differ in manifest anxiety and fear of shock. *Psychophysiology*, 1966, *2*, 287–294.

Houston, B.K. Control over stress, locus of control, and response to stress. *Journal of Personality and Social Psychology*, 1972, *21*, 249–255.

Hrycenko, I., and Minton, H.L. Internal–external control, power position, and satisfaction in task oriented groups. *Journal of Personality and Social Psychology*, 1974, *30*, 871–878.

Ichheiser, G. Misinterpretations of personality in everyday life and the psychologist's frame of reference. *Character and Personality*, 1943, *12*, 145–160.

Johnson, H.H., and Steiner, I.D. Some effects of discrepancy level on relationships between authoritarianism and conformity. *Journal of Social Psychology*, 1967, *73*, 199–204.

Julian, J.W., and Katz, S.B. Internal versus external locus of control and the value of reinforcement. *Journal of Personality and Social Psychology*, 1968, *8*, 89–94.

Katkin, E.S. Relationship between manifest anxiety and two indices of autonomic response to stress. *Journal of Personality and Social Psychology*, 1965, *2*, 324–333.

Kendall, P.C. *Differential state anxiety reactions for subjects differing in measures of trait anxiety*. Unpublished doctoral dissertation, Virginia Commonwealth University, 1975.

Kilmann, P.R., Albert, B.M., and Sotile, W.M. Relationship between locus of control, structure of therapy, and outcome. *Journal of Consulting and Clinical Psychology*, 1975, *43*, 588.

Kumchy, C.G., and Rankin, R.E. Locus of control and mode of reinforcement. *Perceptual and Motor Skills*, 1975, *40*, 375–378.

Lamb, D.H. The effects of two stressor on state anxiety for students who differ in trait anxiety. *Journal of Research in Personality*, 1973, *7*, 116–126.

Land, K.C. Principles of path analysis. In E.F. Borgatta (Ed.), *Sociological methodology*. San Francisco: Jossey-Bass Inc., Publishers, 1969, pp. 3–37.

Lefcourt, H.M. *Locus of control: Current trends in theory and research*. Hillsdale, N.J.: Lawrence Erlbaum Associates, 1976.

Lefcourt, H.M., Lewis, L., and Silverman, I.W. Internal vs. external control of reinforcement and attention in a decision making task. *Journal of Personality*, 1968, *36*, 663–682.

Lewis, A. The ambiguous word "Anxiety." *International Journal of Psychiatry*. 1970, *9*, 62–79.

Liebert, R.M., and Morris, L.W. Cognitive and emotional components of test anxiety: A distinction and some initial data. *Psychological Reports*, 1967, *20*, 975–978.

Magnusson, D. The person and the situation in an interactional model of behavior. *Scandinavian Journal of Psychology*, 1976, *17*, 253–271.

Magnusson, D., and Ekehammar, B. Perceptions of and reactions to stressful situations. *Journal of Personality and Social Psychology*, 1975a, *31*, 1147–1154.

Magnusson, D., and Ekehammar, B. Anxiety profiles based on both situational and response factors. *Multivariate Behavioral Research*, 1975b, *10*, 27–43.

Magnusson, D., and Endler, N.S. Interactional psychology: Present status and future prospects. In D. Magnusson and N.S. Endler (Eds.), *Personality at the crossroads: Current issues in interactional psychology*. Hillsdale, N.J.: Lawrence Erlbaum Associates, 1977, pp. 3–36.

Magnusson, D., Gerzén, M., and Nyman, B. The generality of behavioral data: I. Generalization from observations on one occasion. *Multivariate Behavioral Research*, 1968, *3*, 295–320.

Magnusson, D., and Heffler, B. The generality of behavioral data: III. Generalization potential as a function of the number of observation instances. *Multivariate Behavioral Research*, 1969, *4*, 29–42.

Magnusson, D., Heffler, B., and Nyman, B. The generality of behavioral data: II. Replication of an experiment on generalization from observation on one occasion. *Multivariate Behavioral Research*, 1968, *3*, 415–422.

Mausner, B., and Graham, J. Field dependence and prior reinforcement as determinants of social interaction in judgment. *Journal of Personality and Social Psychology*, 1970, *16*, 486–493.

McDavid, John, Jr. Personality and situational determinants of conformity. *Journal of Abnormal and Social Psychology*, 1959, *58*, 241–246.

Meichenbaum, D. Cognitive modification of test anxious college students. *Journal of Consulting and Clinical Psychology*, 1972, *39*, 370–380.

Meichenbaum, D. A self-instructional approach to stress management. A proposal for stress innoculation training. In C.D. Spielberger and I.G. Sarason (Eds.), *Stress and anxiety* (Vol. 1). Washington, D.C.: Hemisphere Publishing Corporation, 1975, pp. 237–263.

Milgram, S. Some conditions of obedience and disobedience to authority. *Human Relations*, 1965, *18*, 57–76.

Mischel, W. *Personality and assessment*. New York: Wiley, 1968.

Mischel, W. Continuity and change in personality. *American Psychologist*, 1969, *24*, 1012–1018.

Mischel, W. Toward a cognitive social learning reconceptualization of personality. *Psychological Review*, 1973, *80*, 252–283.

Mischel, W. *Introduction to personality* (2nd Ed.). New York: Holt, Rinehart and Winston, 1976.

Mischel, W. The interaction of person and situation. In D. Magnusson and N.S. Endler (Eds.), *Personality at the crossroads: Current issues in interactional psychology*. Hillsdale, N.J.: Lawrence Erlbaum Associates, 1977, pp. 333–352.

Moore, D.R. Language research and preschool language training. In C. Stendler Lavatelli (Ed.), *Language training in early childhood education*. Champaign-Urbana, Ill.: University of Illinois Press, 1971, 3–48.

Moore, J.C., and Krupat, E. Relationships between source status, authoritarianism, and conformity in a social influence setting. *Sociometry*, 1971, *34*, 122–134.

Morris, L.W., and Liebert, R.M. Effects of negative feedback, threat of shock, and level of trait anxiety on the arousal of two components of anxiety. *Journal of Counseling Psychology*, 1973, *20*, 321–326.

Moyer, K.E. The physiology of violence. *Psychology Today*, 1973, *7*, 35–38.

O'Neill, J.F., Spielberger, C.D., and Hansen, D.N. The effects of state anxiety and task difficulty on computer-assisted learning. *Journal of Educational Psychology*, 1969, *60*, 343–350.

Overton, W.F., and Reese, H.W. Models of development: Methodological implications. In J.R. Nesselroade and H.W. Reese (Eds.), *Life span developmental psychology: Methodological issues*. New York: Academic Press, 1973, pp. 65–86.

Pervin, L.A. Performance and satisfaction as a function of individual–environment fit. *Psychological Bulletin*, 1968, *69*, 56–68.

Pervin, L.A. A free-response description approach to the analysis of person–situation interaction. *Journal of Personality and Social Psychology*, 1976, *34*, 465–474.

Pervin, L.A. The representative design of person–situation research. In D. Magnusson and N.S. Endler (Eds.), *Personality at the crossroads: Current issues in interactional psychology*. Hillsdale, N.J.: Lawrence Erlbaum Associates, 1977, pp. 371–384.

Peterson, D.R. A functional approach to the study of person–person interactions. In D. Magnusson and N.S. Endler (Eds.), *Personality at the crossroads: Current issues in interactional psychology*. Hillsdale, N.J.: Lawrence Erlbaum Associates, 1977, pp. 305–316.

Petzel, T.P., and Gynther, M.D. Effects of internal–external locus of control and skill or chance instructional sets on task performance. *The Journal of General Psychology*, 1970, *82*, 87–93.

Phares, E.J. *Locus of control in personality*. Morristown, N.J.: General Learning Press, 1976.

Phares, E.J., and Wilson, K.G. Internal–external control, interpersonal attraction, and empathy. *Psychological Reports*, 1971, *28*, 543–549.

Pines, H.A. An attributional analysis of locus of control orientation and source of informational dependence. *Journal of Personality and Social Psychology*, 1973, *26*, 262–272.

Pines, H.A., and Julian, J.W. Effects of task and social demands on locus of control differences in information processing. *Journal of Personality*, 1972, *40*, 407–416.

Rappaport, H., and Katkin, E.S. Relationships among manifest anxiety, response to stress, and the perception of autonomic activity. *Journal of Consulting and Clinical Psychology*, 1972, *38*, 219–224.

Raush, H.L. Interaction sequences. *Journal of Personality and Social Psychology*, 1965, *2*, 487–499.

Raush, H.L. Process and change. *Family Process*, 1972, *11*, 275–298.

Raush, H.L. Paradox, levels and junctures in person–situation systems. In D. Magnusson and N.S. Endler (Eds.), *Personality at the crossroads: Current issues in interactional psychology*. Hillsdale, N.J.: Lawrence Erlbaum Associates, 1977, pp. 287–304.

Reid, D.W., and Ware, E.E. Multidimensionality of internal–external control: Implications for past and future research. *Canadian Journal of Behavioural Science*, 1973, *5*, 264–270.

Rhine, W.R. Birth order differences in conformity and level of achievement arousal. *Child Development*, 1968, *39*, 987–996.

Rotter, J.B. *Social learning and clinical psychology*. Englewood Cliffs, N.J.: Prentice-Hall, 1954.

Rotter, J.B. Generalized expectancies for internal vs. external control of reinforcement. *Psychological Monographs*, 1966, *80*, 1–28.

Rotter, J.B. Some problems and misconceptions related to the construct of internal versus external control of reinforcement. *Journal of Consulting and Clinical Psychology*, 1975, *43*, 56–67.

Rotter, J.B., Chance, J., and Phares, E.J. (Eds.), *Applications of a social learning theory of personality*. New York: Holt, Rinehart and Winston, 1972.

Rotter, J.B., and Mulry, R.C. Internal versus external control of reinforcement and decision time. *Journal of Personality and Social Psychology*, 1965, *2*, 598–604.

Rule, B.G., and Sandilands, M.L. Test anxiety, confidence, commitment, and conformity. *Journal of Personality*, 1969, *37*, 460–467.

Rushton, J.P., and Endler, N.S. Person by situation interactions in academic achievement. *Journal of Personality*, 1977, *45*, 297–309.

Saiyadain, M.S., and Summers, D.A. The effects of influence conditions and discrepancy upon authoritarian conformity. *Bulletin of Psychonomic Society*, 1973, *1*, 357–358.

Sarason, I.G. Test anxiety and cognitive modeling. *Journal of Personality and Social Psychology*, 1973, *28*, 58–61.

Sarason, I.G. Test anxiety and the self-disclosing coping model. *Journal of Consulting and Clinical Psychology*, 1975a, *43*, 148–153.

Sarason, I.G. Test anxiety, attention and the general problem of anxiety. In C.D. Spielberger and I.G. Sarason (Eds.), *Stress and anxiety* (Vol. 1). Washington, D.C.: Hemisphere Publishing Corporation, 1975b, pp. 165–187.

Sarason, I.G. Anxiety and self-preoccupation. In I.G. Sarason and C.D. Spielberger (Eds.), *Stress and anxiety* (Vol. 2). Washington, D.C.: Hemisphere Publishing Corporation, 1975c, pp. 27–44.

Sarason, I.G., Smith, R.E., and Diener, E. Personality research: Components of variance attributable to the person and the situation. *Journal of Personality and Social Psychology*, 1975, *32*, 199–204.

Schachter, S. Obesity and eating. *Science*, 1968, *161*, 751–756.

Seeman, M. Alienation and social learning in a reformatory. *American Journal of Sociology*, 1963, *69*, 270–284.

Shedletsky, R., and Endler, N.S. Anxiety: The state-trait model and the interaction model. *Journal of Personality*, 1974, *42*, 511–527.

Sherman, S.J. Internal–external locus of control and its relationship to attitude change under different influence techniques. *Journal of Personality and Social Psychology*, 1973, *26*, 23–29.

Sistrunk, F. Two processes of conformity demonstrated by interactions of commitment, set and personality. *Journal of Social Psychology*, 1973, *89*, 63–72.

Sistrunk, F., and McDavid, J.W. Achievement motivation, affiliation motivation, and task difficulty as determinants of social conformity. *The Journal of Social Psychology*, 1965, *66*, 41–50.

Skinner, B.F. *Science and human behavior*. New York: Macmillan, 1953.

Skinner, B.F. Pigeons in a pelican. *American Psychologist*, 1960, *15*, 28–37.

Snyder, M., and Monson, T.C. Persons, situations, and the control of social behavior. *Journal of Personality and Social Psychology*, 1975, *32*, 637–644.

Spielberger, C.D. The effects of anxiety on complex learning and academic achievement. In C.D. Spielberger (Ed.), *Anxiety and behavior*. New York: Academic Press, 1966.

Spielberger, C.D. Conceptual and methodological issues in research on anxiety. In C.D. Spielberger (Ed.), *Anxiety: Current trends in theory and research* (Vol. 1). New York: Academic Press, 1972, pp. 481–493.

Spielberger, C.D., Gorsuch, R.L., and Lushene, R.E. *Manual for the state—trait anxiety inventory*. Palo Alto, Calif.: Consulting Psychologist Press, 1970.

Srull, T.K., and Karabenick, S.A. Effects of personality—situation locus of control congruence. *Journal of Personality and Social Psychology*, 1975, *32*, 617–628.

Staats, A.W. *Child learning, intelligence and personality*. New York: Harper and Row, 1971.

Teichman, Y. Predisposition for anxiety and affiliation. *Journal of Personality and Social Psychology*, 1974, *29*, 405–410.

Wachtel, P. Interaction cycles, unconscious processes, and the person–situation issue. In D. Magnusson and N.S. Endler (Eds.), *Personality at the crossroads: Current issues in interactional psychology*. Hillsdale, N.J.: Lawrence Erlbaum Associates, 1977, pp. 317–332.

Watson, D., and Baumal, E. Effects of locus of control and expectation of future control upon present performance. *Journal of Personality and Social Psychology*, 1967, *6*, 212–216.

Wiesenthal, D.L., Edwards, J., Endler, N.S., Koza, P., Walton, A., and Emmott, S. Trends in conformity research. *Canadian Psychological Review*, 1978, *19*, 41–58.

Wine, J.D. Test anxiety and helping behavior. *Canadian Journal of Behavioural Science*, 1975, *7*, 216–222.

Witkin, H.A., and Goodenough, D.R. Field dependence and interpersonal behavior. *Research Bulletin of the Educational Testing Service*, Princeton, New Jersey, 1976.

Wrightsman, L.S. Jr. The effects of anxiety, achievement motivation, and task importance upon performance on an intelligence test. *Journal of Educational Psychology*, 1962, *53*, 150–156.

Zimbardo, P.G., Haney, G., Banks, W.C., and Jaffe, D. The psychology of imprisonment: Privation, power and pathology. Unpublished manuscript, Stanford University, 1973.

Behavior Genetics from an Interactional Point of View

Louise Carter-Saltzman

The gradual emergence of behavior genetics as a field of legitimate inquiry is having a profound effect on the field of developmental psychology. The impact has not been to change the questions asked by developmental psychologists. Nor can behavior geneticists claim to have provided definitive answers to these questions. What has happened, rather, is that problems concerning the relative effects of genetic and environmental factors on behavioral development, problems that previously had seemed impervious to empirical inquiry, are being approached with a high level of focused attention and educated expertise. The increasing legitimacy of behavior genetics as a methodologically viable discipline has enabled psychologists to address questions that often were simply not allowed in the context of a behaviorist psychology. Because of some very real problems inherent in any attempt to specify the effects of genetic and environmental factors on behavioral development, the entire issue was frequently avoided by an affirmation of the impossibility of the endeavor.

One of the thorniest and most frequently misunderstood problems has been the one concerning the nonadditive, interactive effects of genetic and environmental factors on emerging behavioral patterns. Such nonadditive effects can be the results of either genotype–environment interactions or genotype–environment correlations. The presence of either can seriously complicate any estimation of independent genotypic and environmental effects.

1. *Some Definitions*

That both genes and environment contribute in important ways to the development of behavior is not seriously controversial at present.

Louise Carter-Saltzman • Department of Psychology, University of Washington, Seattle, Washington 98104.

In fact, it is only through the interaction of genotypic and environmental factors that observable behaviors are manifested at all. A genotype without an environment is, by virtue of its nonviability, impossible. Similarly, an environment that does not interact with genetic blueprints will never produce any behavioral phenotypes. The existence, then, of genotype–environment interaction at this very basic, individual level is not at issue. However, the nature of genotype–environment interactions, and the extent to which they contribute to differences among individuals in the population are not at all well understood.

In the field of behavior genetics, the term "genotype–environment interaction" has been used in a number of ways, and this multiplicity of usages has led to some confusion. In this chapter, various definitions of and approaches to genotype–environment interaction will be discussed, and a general unifying model will be considered. Finally, the problems of doing research on genotype–environment interaction in human populations will be discussed.

Genotype–environment interaction is most commonly defined as the differential responsiveness of different genotypes to the same environments. This is in contrast to environmental effects that are totally additive and constant across genotypes. A strictly additive model would propose that genetic and environmental factors each make some specific, quantifiable contribution to the differences that are observed among individuals.

For example, several factors affecting prenatal development that might be classified as environmental in origin include the following: mother's smoking, eating, and drinking habits; maternal stress and emotional condition; presence or absence of more than one fetus in utero; maternal levels of steroid hormones; and maternal ingestion of drugs. Under the assumptions of an additive model the effect of a mother smoking three packs of cigarettes a day throughout her pregnancy would be assumed to be equal across all genotypes if other relevant factors were controlled. For fetuses of different genotypes to interact differently with the same maternal intrauterine phenotype would not be admissible within a strictly additive model. In an interactive model, the effects of smoking during pregnancy would not be assumed to be equal for the fetal development of all genotypes. While smoking during pregnancy may be related to low birth weight for some genotypes, exactly the same amount of smoking may have no effect on fetuses differing genetically on some relevant dimension. Similarly, the fetuses predisposed to suffer adverse effects of smoking during pregnancy could be above average in birth weight under conditions of high levels of maternal milk-drinking, while those whose birth weights were unaffected by smoking could average lower-than-normal birth weights. Although the above example is purely hypothetical, it illustrates the limitations of purely additive models of genetic and environmental effects.

An example of additive effects of postnatal environmental factors would be a finding that extra handling and stimulation of infants in the first few weeks of life resulted in equal increments in motor activity across all genotypes (however they might be defined). These results would be interpreted as evidence for the additive effect of an environmental manipulation, but not for interaction between genotypes and environment. Table I presents hypothetical data that would support an additivity conclusion. For each of the three genotypes, the environmental intervention (extra handling and stimulation) led to an increment of two points on a motor activity scale. In this example, there is no indication of differential genotypic responses to the treatment.

Some of the best examples of genotype–environment interactions come from animal experiments, where it is possible to control both breeding and rearing conditions. Although many GE interactions have been demonstrated in species of *Drosophila* (Parsons and Kaul, 1966; Wright and Dobzhansky, 1946; Van Valen, Levine, and Beardmore, 1962), the present discussion will be limited to mammalian species.

Thompson and Olian (1961) compared the effects of maternal injections of adrenalin on the activity levels of offspring in three inbred species of mice. They found that adrenalin decreased activity of the high activity strain (C57BL/6), increased activity of the low activity strain (A/J), and had no effect on an intermediate activity-level strain (BALB/Ci).

Another investigation of GE interaction in mice was carried out by DeFries (1964). In an earlier study (Weir and DeFries, 1964), it had been found that two strains of mice differed in their responses to ma-

TABLE I
Motor Activity Scores of Three Genotypes with and without Early Stimulation (Scale from 0 to 10)[a]

	No intervention	Extra handling and stimulation
Genotype A	8	10
Genotype B	3	5
Genotype C	5	7

[a] Hypothetical results.

ternal stress during pregnancy. For one strain, activity level was higher in the offspring of stressed mothers, while in the other the offspring of the control mothers were more active. Further investigation (DeFries, 1964) revealed an additional interaction between maternal genotype and fetal genotype. Hybrids with mothers of one strain (BALB/cCrgl) showed increased activity in response to maternal stress, while those with mothers of the other strain (C57BL/Crgl) had decreased activity. When the offspring were not hybrids, but were the same inbred strain as their mothers, the direction of the effects of stress was reversed.

DeFries's (1964) results suggest that maternal genotype should not be ignored as a possible source of interactive effects. Probably the most common example of similar effects in humans is that of Rh incompatibility. Maternal genotype (Rh positive or negative) is a major determinant of whether an Rh positive fetus will suffer from erythroblastosis. In both the mouse and human examples, maternal genotype influenced the fetal environment, which was then subject to possible interactions with fetal genotype.

Although only two animal studies have been discussed here, there are other frequently cited examples of GE interactions from the animal literature (Cooper and Zubek, 1958; Freedman, 1958; Fuller and Collins, 1970; Henderson, 1970; Lynch and Hegmann, 1973; McGaugh and Cole, 1965; Satinder, 1971). In some of these cases the statistical interaction can be removed by a scale transformation (see Lubin, 1961), but care must be taken not to bury important effects in an effort to get rid of variance that complicates prevailing assumptions. An attempt is made in this chapter to consider the least ambiguous examples of interactions, but less drastic interactions should not be discounted without serious consideration.

A particularly good illustration of GE interaction in humans is that of phenylketonuria (PKU), which is a genetically caused metabolic disorder that, if undetected and untreated, results in severe mental retardation. The genetic defect leads to an inability to metabolize phenylalanine, which is a basic amino acid involved in protein synthesis. Unmetabolized phenylalanine accumulates in body cells until its high concentration becomes toxic. Without treatment, the syndrome is clinically manifested in severe mental retardation and a variety of other side effects. However, if PKU is detected early in development, the deleterious effects of the disorder can be avoided by radically altering the diet during the first few years of life. If a PKU child is put on a diet that is low in phenylalanine, the child will have a normal or near-normal level of intellectual functioning (McClearn and DeFries, 1973). In contrast, if a normal child were exposed to the same

TABLE II
Predicted IQ Levels of Two Genotypes Exposed to Two Different Nutritional Environments[a]

	Diet low in phenylalanine	Normal diet
PKU genotype	≈ 100	< 40
Normal genotype	$\lesssim 100$[a]	100

[a] Probable below-average IQ level due to severe protein deficiency, but data generally unavailable.

restricted dietary regime, he might exhibit signs of protein deficiency and general malnutrition. There is a growing body of data that indicate that malnutrition early in life may be related to later mental deficits (Cheek, 1975; Cravioto and DeLicardie, 1973; Dobbing, 1970). As indicated in Table II, across two quite different nutritional environments—one low in phenylalanine and one with normal concentrations of phenylalanine—the predicted mental development of PKU and normal genotypes would be quite different. While the PKU genotype will be optimally adapted to a low phenylalanine diet, a normal genotype will show optimal intellectual development with normal diet.

This sort of interaction during development could account for some of the variations in human behavior that are at present poorly understood. The classic example is of an environmental manipulation—either an enrichment or a deprivation—that has a profound effect on many individuals, but that seems either not to affect some people or to affect them in qualitatively different ways. Ideally, any claim of genotype–environment interaction should be supported by data on at least two genotypes reared under at least two sets of environmental conditions. This design prerequisite, however, is rarely met in studies of human phenotypes, and as a result, there are behavioral variations that are thought to be the products of GE interactions, but for which definitive data are not available.

For example, although about 50% of the offspring of mothers who contract rubella during the first month of pregnancy are afflicted with some kind of abnormality (deafness, cataracts, microcephaly, congenital heart disease, and mental retardation), the other 50% of the babies escape the damaging effects of their mothers' illnesses (Sever, 1970). The manifestation of defects seems unrelated to the severity of the mother's illness, since even mothers whose infections were subclinical have given birth to severely malformed babies (Wilson, 1973). Infants subjected to the same general kind of prenatal environmental experience (maternal rubella) at the same period of embryonic life show differential responses to that experience. Of course, it should be remembered that environmental conditions are not perfectly controlled, since the rubella experience is mediated through individual maternal phenotypes. In addition, it is not possible to observe infants of identical genotypes who were subjected to rubella and nonrubella pregnancies. If it were possible to obtain such data, what results would provide evidence for genotype–environment interaction?

Hypothetically, let us consider auditory sensitivity in childhood as the dependent measure of interest. An infant's auditory sensitivity can be affected by a variety of prenatal events. Rubella in the first trimester of pregnancy can lead to deafness in the infant, as can maternal ingestion of quinine during the last trimester (Wilson, 1973). Neither event results in deafness of all affected fetuses. In Figure 1, two genotypes with differential responses to the two prenatal conditions are represented. Individuals of genotype A were afflicted with deafness if their mothers contracted rubella early in pregnancy, but were unaffected by quinine in the latter part of gestation. Individuals of genotype B, however, were resistant to the effects of rubella, but became deaf if exposed to quinine. This pattern of results would provide empirical support for GE interaction.

The kind of interaction depicted in Figure 1 has been called a disordinal interaction by Erlenmeyer-Kimling (1972) and Lindquist (1953). Disordinal interactions are particularly striking because the rank orderings of phenotypes are altered depending upon the rearing conditions of the different genotypes. An equally plausible kind of in-

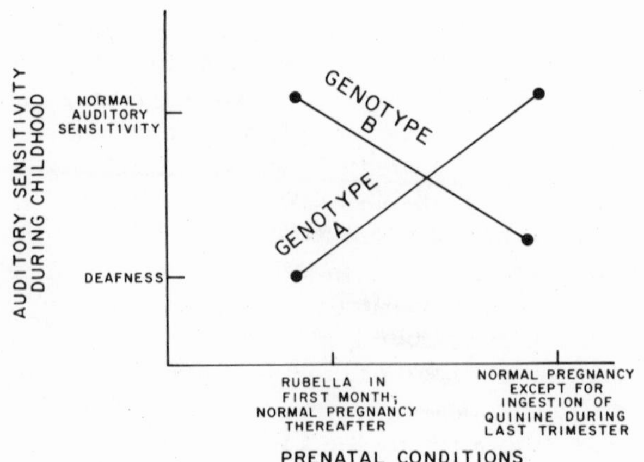

FIGURE 1. Hypothetical GE interaction during prenatal development.

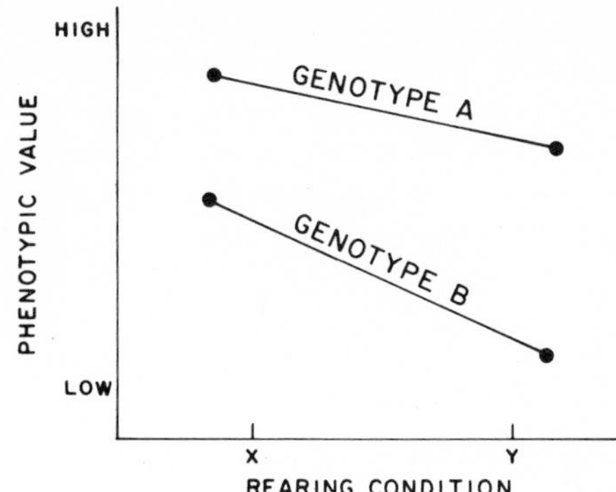

FIGURE 2. Ordinal interaction.

teraction, termed "ordinal" (Erlenmeyer-Kimling, 1972; Lindquist, 1953), is one in which the rank orderings of phenotypes are not altered by rearing conditions, but the effects of different environments are quantitatively different for different genotypes. Figure 2 illustrates such an interaction. Although the lines in Figure 2 do not intersect, their slopes differ, revealing the nonadditive effects of differential rearing environments. If differences between genotypes were constant across environments (see Fig. 3), no evidence of interaction would be present, and only an additive relationship could be inferred.

2. *Current Approaches to GE Interaction*

How do behavior geneticists approach questions about genotype–environmental interaction? Two approaches have dominated the field, and the extent to which they are congruent is not always clear. Medical geneticists and biochemists have usually worked from a known

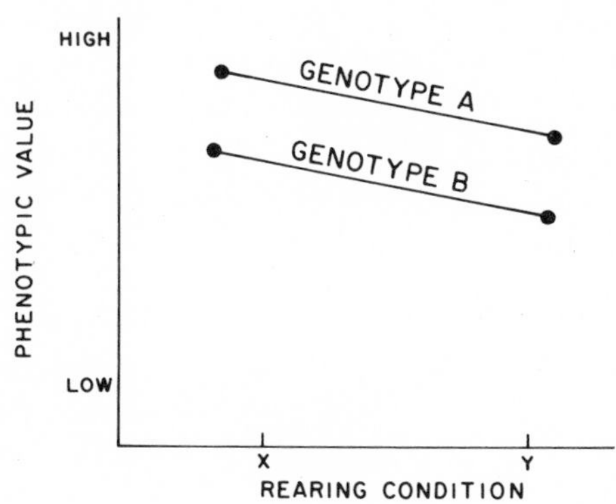

FIGURE 3. Addictive effect of rearing environment on phenotypic values.

genotype (such as PKU) and studied individuals with that genotype, contrasting them with individuals with a different genotype. Population biologists and psychologists have traditionally studied large populations of individuals who differ in the extent to which they share common genes and rearing environments. Variance analyses are carried out in order to obtain quantitative estimates of proportions of variance attributable to genetic and environmental factors.

2.1. *Medical Models*

From the medical perspective, the eventual goal of behavior genetic research is to be able to map the pathways linking genes and behavior. Although in research with animals it has been possible to control breeding and rearing environments quite closely, in human research, control over such factors has been minimal at best. Sometimes clinical manipulations are possible and desirable, but in most instances individuals are studied after having grown up in an uncontrolled setting.

For example, prior to 1950, no treatment was available to females who were masculinized due to a recessive genetic disorder that resulted in excessive androgen production. Without treatment these girls were subject to early maturation and development of male secondary sexual characteristics such as beard growth and deepening of the voice (Money and Ehrhardt, 1972). In 1950 it was discovered that with cortisone therapy from infancy through adulthood, females with the androgenital syndrome need not suffer the virilizing effects of excessive postnatal androgen. Obviously, the administration of cortisone to females who do not have the androgenization syndrome genotype may have quite different consequences: maturation into womanhood ordinarily occurs without the exogenous administration of any drugs or chemicals. By taking advantage of naturally occurring situations and by introducing appropriate biochemical interventions when they became available (post-1950), it was possible to fill three of the four cells necessary for an ideal research design: androgenital syndrome genotype in two biochemical environments (no treatment and cortisone treatment); and normal genotype in a biochemical environment that has not been tampered with.

For examples such as the one above, genetic factors other than those causing the defect are usually assumed to vary independently, and are not taken into consideration. Genotype is therefore broadly defined as a classification that discriminates individuals who exhibit clinical symptoms of the syndrome from those who do not. There may be undetected interaction among genes (epistasis) or multiple effects of a single gene (pleiotropy). For purposes of diagnosing individuals, however, these are all subsumed in the general category, genotype.

There are other instances, however, in which it may be inappropriate to define genotype so loosely. Precise specification of genotype may be necessary when one is interested in the observed variability among individuals known to have a particular genetic disorder. For example, homocystinuria is an autosomal recessive disorder that leads to an enzyme deficiency that in turn causes skeletal, visual, dermatological, and circulatory abnormalities. About 50% of those afflicted with this disease are mentally retarded, and there has been some speculation about increased incidence of schizophrenia among patients and members of their families (Omenn, 1976; Omenn and Motulsky, 1972). An intriguing question is, why are only half of the afflicted persons retarded? Although most psychologists ordinarily think of environmental factors as those that are not endogenous to the individual, it is possible that an individual's genotype can interact with cytological properties that are themselves the products of past genotype–environment transactions. Such interactions could contribute to variability in penetrance and expressivity of genetically caused disorders. One's genotype may set the cytological stage for development; a slightly different setting may interact in different ways with a common genetic event. Mayr (1954; 1970) has discussed the effects of introducing new genes into "genetic backgrounds" that have been firmly entrenched in response to past selection pressures. To this author's knowledge, no extensive studies of the sibships, parents, or rearing environments of retarded versus nonretarded homocystanuria patients have been done. It is unlikely that we will understand the variability in expression of the disease before such investigations have been carried out.

Clearly, the presence of a single known genetic difference may not adequately explain individual differences that are of interest. In such cases it is necessary to consider seriously the kinds of GE interactions that could lead to differential effects in what may have previously been thought of as a unitary genotypic disorder.

There are many examples of phenotypic expression that can be traced to specific environmental events, but not all individuals exposed to the same environments exhibit the same phenotype. Some of the best examples have come from studying the effects of teratogens on embryogenesis. Although morphological and behavioral disorders can often be traced to radiography, disease, or drug ingestion (thalidomide, tobacco, alcohol, birth control pills) during pregnancy, not all children who have been subjected to the same teratogens will demonstrate the same developmental sequelae.

Some clues about causes of individual differences in expression have been obtained from research with animals. Clearly, the effects of a given teratogen differ across species, and this imposes a serious limitation on the inferences that can be drawn from comparative research. It is appropriate, however, to use animal data to address questions about intraspecies variations. Although variability within a single litter of an outbred line is often attributed to genotypic factors, research on the effects of teratogens on rodents have revealed interactions related to the site of implantation in the uterus (Trasler, 1960) and maternal phenotype (Kalter, 1954).

Inquiries about GE interactions affecting development need not be confined to offspring alone. Parental germ cells may be affected by such interactions in ways that profoundly alter an offspring's genotype and phenotype. The incidence of Down's syndrome goes up dramatically for the offspring of women who are over the age of forty (Stern, 1973). In most cases this syndrome results from three chromosomes, number 21, rather than the normal chromosome complement of two. Apparently the chances of nondisjunction during meiosis are much greater for older mothers, although it is not know whether some older mothers are more susceptible to nondisjunction than others. For example, there may be individual differences in the extent to which mothers' germ cells are protected from ionizing radiation and other environmental insults.

About 10% of the cases of Down's syndrome are caused, not by nondisjunction, but by a translocation of part of the long arm of chromosome 21 with the short arm of another chromosome (McClearn and DeFries, 1973). Although no precipitating causes have been identified for translocation Down's syndrome, an increase in incidence has been reported for children born to Danish mothers under the age of thirty (Mikkelsen, 1970). In Manitoba (Uchida, 1970) a decrease in the mean age of mothers of Down's syndrome infants from 34.6 years in 1960 to 29.3 years in 1968 was accompanied by an increase in the incidence of Down's syndrome from 0.9 per 1000 live births to 1.35 per 1000 live births. The possibility that some general environmental factor may interact with maternal phenotypes and contribute to an increase in the incidence of translocation Down's syndrome in the offspring of younger mothers cannot be overlooked.

Although the number of good leads for biochemical geneticists has been small in terms of genetic specificity, there is a broad range of interesting phenotypes currently under investigation. The research usually begins with questions about the genetic sources of phenotypic variation. The best guesses of biochemists and clinicians are pursued in attempts to trace the origins of behavior in the genome. Once the genetic parameters have been specified, the task of describing and understanding the interactions among genotypic and environmental factors is greatly simplified. The problems of adequately specifying both genetic and environmental parameters is one that will be returned to later in this chapter.

2.2. *Biometrical Models*

For traits (such as IQ) that are continuously distributed in a population, it is probable that many genes affect phenotypic expression. To date it has not been possible to specify the effects of individual genes on overall performance. However, it has been observed that for some characteristics individuals who are genetically related are more similar than unrelated individuals. Quantitative analyses have been applied to estimate the extent to which these similarities are due to the effects of shared environments and shared genes, respectively. The end product of the quantitative analysis is frequently a heritability estimate; that is, a representation of the proportion of total phenotypic variation that can be attributed to genetic factors. It is clearly advantageous to have a method of quantification and objectification of one's observations, but it is important to be aware of the limitations of such a method.

Heritability estimates have been very useful in selective breeding of animals and plants. In selective breeding situations it is relatively easy to control both genotypic factors and environmental conditions. It is possible to do controlled experiments to test for possible genotype–environment interactions. If such interactions are detected within the ranges of the relevant genotypes and rearing environments of the population under consideration, then additive models leading to heritability estimates cannot appropriately be applied.

There has been considerable controversy over whether genotype–environment interaction in continuously distributed human characteristics presents serious problems for quantitative analyses of those traits (Block and Dworkin, 1974; Hirsch and Vetta, 1977; Jinks and Fulker, 1970; Layzer, 1974; Plomin, DeFries, and Loehlin, 1977). The issue is far from being resolved. Since the assumptions underlying various biometrical models are not always equivalent, variance due to genotype–environment interactions is sometimes attributed to genetic causes, and at other times is assumed to be mostly environmental in origin. Obviously, neither of these assumptions is justifiable without a clear understanding of the nature of the interactions.

Jinks and Fulker (1970) and Plomin *et al.* (1977) have proposed various methods of testing for the presence of significant GE interactions. Jinks and Fulker (1970) proposed a test for a specific kind of GE interaction that might affect behavior genetic studies of IQ. They suggested that individuals with "high IQ genotypes" might be more sensitive to environmental stimulation than low IQ genotypes, and that if this were so, one would expect to find larger intrapair IQ differences among monozygotic twin pairs with high IQs than among those with low IQs. When they tested for the presence of this kind of interaction, they did not find evidence for a substantial effect. It should be noted, however, that interactions other than the kind proposed could have been present, and would not necessarily have been detected by the analyses performed.

Plomin *et al.* (1977) discussed the nonadditive effects of genotypes and environments in terms both of GE interaction and GE correlation. They outlined a useful distinction among three types of GE correlation (broadly defined as the co-occurrence of certain genotypes with certain environments). The three types of GE correlation are: (1) passive, (2) reactive, and (3) active. Passive GE correlation refers to a co-occurrence of genotypic and environmental circumstances that are totally independent of a child's phenotype. For example, a child may be genetically predisposed to be overweight and may also have parents who serve hearty, rich meals. With reactive GE correlation, it is proposed that individuals of different genotypes may elicit different kinds of reactions from people. A child's genotypic tendency to be muscular, for example, might lead people to assume that the child liked sports, and therefore to provide him or her with more than average amount of opportunity to develop the skills necessary for excellent athletic performance. Active GE correlation refers to an individual, for genotypically determined reasons, actively seeking out certain kinds of environmental experiences. A person who has a genotypically influenced tendency to be introverted may often choose to be by himself rather than go to social gatherings. Plomin *et al.* (1977). also discussed the possibility of negative GE correlations within each of the three types.

Erlenmeyer-Kimling (1972) has pointed out that many GE correlations are the result of GE interactions that took place at some previous time. The relatively high incidence of sickle-cell anemia and glucose-6-phosphate dehydrogenase deficiency in areas where malaria was once prevalent is an example of a currently observed GE correlation (passive, in Plomin *et al.* (1976) terminology). Surely this correlation is the result of the increased resistance to malaria that was conferred on heterozygotes for either sickle-cell anemia or G-6-PD deficiency (Allison, 1954; Motulsky, 1964).

After carefully differentiating types of nonadditive effects of genotype and environment (GE interaction as well as the kinds of GE correlation outlined above), Plomin *et al.* (1977) proposed that data from adoption studies be used to assess the impact of such effects on quantitative behavior genetic analyses. In the absence of selective placement, the similarities among adoptive relatives are unaffected by many of the biases that contaminate such analyses in families in which both genetic and environmental factors are shared. The authors emphasized, however, that in order for their suggestions to be implemented meaningfully, more thoughtful conceptualizations of both genotype and rearing environment must be worked out. In most adoption studies parental genotype (of the natural parents of adopted children) has been estimated by natural parents' educational levels (Scarr and Weinberg, 1976; Skodak and Skeels, 1949) or IQ scores (Horn, Willerman, and Loehlin, 1977). The adoptive home environment has been similarly stratified. Although it has been known for some time that there is a positive correlation between parental demographics and child's IQ, as well as between parental IQ and child's IQ, such global classifications of genotype and environment are probably not precise enough to detect the kinds of interactions that may contribute meaningfully to individual differences. Not surprisingly, Plomin *et al.* (1977) did not find evidence of GE interaction in their reanalyses of data from adoption studies in which "genotype" and "environment" were classified in this very general way.

No one really believes that parental IQ or educational level are good indicators of parental genotype. They are clearly expressions of parental phenotype. The problem is that we don't have information that would enable us to classify natural parents or anyone else by genotypic factors. Even if we had unlimited access to data on natural parents, it is not clear which criteria would be most appropriate for the classification of genotypes.

The other aspect of the problem is that few serious attempts have been made to refine our very global conceptions of rearing environment. The notion that upper-middle class, white parents provide "good" environments and that parents with lower income, educational, and occupational levels provide "less good" environments has been tacitly accepted, if not openly embraced, by large segments of our society. Upward mobility carries an implicit acceptance of the belief that one is improving the opportunities for one's children by moving up the ladders of status, educational attainment, and income. Such global classifications of environments must give way to more precise identification of the effects of specific environmental manipulations on the development of particular behavioral phenotypes.

The first step in this identification process is to choose carefully those experiences that might contribute significantly to a particular aspect of psychological development. For example, one may want to learn what experiences most profoundly affect the development of musical ability. One may decide to study exposure in infancy to music and rhythm, opportunities to take music lessons at an early age, and availability of adult and child musicians as models. It would be more difficult, however, to justify the inclusion of other experiences, such as, the availability of tinker toys, interior decoration of the home, and opportunities to take horseback-riding lessons.

Since the covariance among relevant variables may be high, and since they may also have a strong relationship to broader demographic factors, it would be necessary to assess the contributions of each independent variable while holding the other variables constant. In this way the contributions of each environmental factor could be assessed independently from the natural ecology of the child's overall rearing circumstances. Multiple regression analysis is well suited to address problems of this sort (Cohen and Cohen, 1975; Kerlinger and Pedhazur, 1973), although it does not eliminate them.

No aspect of a child's experience with the world acts in isolation from the broad set of circumstances that we have come to call "environment" and no two children can be said to grow up in environments that are identical along all dimensions. Even within families, although some of the broader aspects of the environment may be consistent for all children, some very important ones may not be. For instance, with the possible exception of monozygotic twins, no child ever experiences having himself as a sibling. That is an experience, however, that each of his siblings has, and that experience must be considered as part of the family environment that may contribute to differences among individuals.

Siblings may also, by virtue of their differing genotypes, respond quite differently to the same set of environmental circumstances. While one child may welcome opportunities to take private lessons in art and music, attend museum openings and subscribe to the local symphony orchestra, another child may feel stifled in such an environment. Moreover, parents may (and probably do) respond to and interact with their children in quite different ways. These differences in parental behavior may be elicited by subtle differences among the children (subtle, because it would be difficult for a parent to specify exactly why his behavior differed with each child). Parents often say things like, "The kids were different from the day they were born. One of them cried all the time; the other was very good, never got upset about anything." That there are stable individual differences between infants in temperament and reactivity is well documented

(Thomas, Chess, and Birch, 1968, 1970). These differences may well be under some form of genetic control, but until we can identify developmentally consistent correlates of infant sociability and temperament, the appropriate family studies will be difficult to carry out.

With data from family studies, we might be better able to identify individuals who differed more or less from one another genotypically. We could then study two or more groups that were classified into genotypically differing groups, and observe their behavior and development in carefully defined environmental conditions.

3. A Conceptualization of Genotype–Environment Interactions

Although it is easy to say that genotype–environment interactions and correlations represent that proportion of variance that cannot be explained solely by either genetic or environmental causes, it is sometimes less simple to conceptualize how these nonadditive effects might come about developmentally, and how the notion might be incorporated into a developmental model.

3.1. Developmental Canalization

One of the most appealing models of development has its origin in embryology, but seems quite applicable to questions about behavioral development. This is Waddington's (1942; 1961; 1962; 1966) notion of developmental canalization. In Waddington's general scheme, an individual's genotype is conceived of as providing a landscape or setting for differentiation and development. Waddington has called this the epigenetic landscape. The terrain consists of a hierarchy of ridges and valleys that can branch at various critical points during ontogeny. The developing phenotype can be represented as the path taken by a ball rolling through the landscape over time, constrained by the contours of the valleys, and altered only to the extent that genotypic factors allow such diversions. For any given end state there may be alternative "stabilized or buffered pathways of change" (Waddington, 1962). These stabilized time trajectories have been labeled creodes by Waddington.

If one's path of development is highly canalized, or relatively unsusceptible to deflection from its genotypically determined developmental pathway, the ridges will be high and the valleys low in the landscape; it would take a powerful force to seriously change the course of development. If the creode is not so highly canalized (represented by a relatively flat terrain, with wide valleys and low ridges), then the effects of environmental manipulations may be quite strong. The individual's course of development would be malleable, and subject to deflections caused by external factors. In Waddington's formulation, a behavior for which the developmental course is highly canalized is probably that way because of a strong genetic predisposition to buffer that pattern of development against the effects of the external environment. For continuously variable traits, this buffering is probably affected by the combined action of many different genes that all affect the same course of development. For traits that do not vary continuously, and are affected by activity at only one or two gene loci (with little variability of expression), the notion of canalization may not be particularly useful in the present context, since serious environmental intrusion could either have no effect or severe results.

As Scarr-Salapatek (1976) has pointed out, one can consider behavioral canalization at two levels: at the species level and at the individual level. When one considers behaviors that appear to be highly canalized at the species level (language acquisition, for example), it is clear that both genetic and environmental factors operate to prevent deflection from a general developmental pathway. For behavioral development, then, one may be able to ask to what extent the degree of canalization is affected by genetic factors, and to what extent it is affected by environmental factors. The buffering of a developmental course against deviations may be accomplished in part through powerful cultural forces that have evolved along with biologically predisposing factors. Although each component may set limits on the expression of the other, it is difficult to know whether genotypic or environmental–cultural contributions are more powerful. Outside a certain range of environments, viable phenotypes will not develop; and although new and radically different genotypes are created continuously by mutation, most are never expressed as phenotypes. Presumably, some phenotypes might be viable if placed in suitable environments, but coadaptation of multigene complexes and "normal environment" make such an event unlikely (Dobzhansky, 1951).

The issue addressed in this chapter is the nature of the interaction between genetic and environmental factors during development. One could conceive of each exerting independent forces on the space–time trajectory of the phenotype. This would be in line with Waddington's model as discussed above, and would account for additive effects of genotype and environment. Such a conceptualization would probably not, however, be able to capture the possible interactive nature of genotypes and environments. That is, it is possible that the epigenetic landscape is not determined by genetic factors alone: an individual's genotype and the previous transactions of that genotype with the environment may jointly affect the unfolding of new contours in the landscape. An example should serve to illustrate the point.

A child may have a genotype that predisposes him to develop a left hemisphere superiority for processing linguistic, analytic, sequential information and a right hemisphere superiority for processing information in a holistic, synthesizing, gestalt manner. Injury to the left hemisphere has different implications for the functional relocation and overall quality of linguistic abilities, depending upon the age at which injury occurred. If the child were injured at age one, the chances that he would proceed through the normal sequence of language acquisition and that his right hemisphere would assume responsibility for linguistic processing would be quite high. However, if the same child were to suffer precisely the same injury at age ten, the prognosis for recover of linguistic function and the probability of right hemisphere assumption of functions previously subserved by the left hemisphere would be considerably lower (Basser, 1962; Lenneberg, 1967; Milner, 1974). Thus, for a younger child, the development of cerebral lateralization of function could be deflected to an alternative creode; for an older child, however, that optional creode may simply be unavailable.

Developmental progress, then, implies a loss of a previous range of potential for growth and differentiation. In one sense the epigenetic landscape is a delineation of all the potentialities of a genotype, but the extent to which those potentialities are under genetic control may vary as development proceeds. Once an organism has committed itself to a particular path of development, it may close off other genetically coded options that required external input for elaboration. In the hemispheric specialization example, the right hemisphere would not be expected to wait indefinitely in an equipotential state, prepared to take over the left hemisphere's function in the case of emergency or injury. It would proceed with its own pattern of development, and its versatility would decrease as it continued along that path. At age ten the right hemisphere may still have some potential for assisting with analytical thinking, but that potential will have been altered by the preceding ten years of functioning as an element in an integrated system.

Two points are central to this discussion: (1) The contour of the landscape at a given point in time is dependent on genotype–environment transactions that have taken place previously during growth; and (2) the possible range of phenotypic outcomes at an arbitrary point during development (for example, thirty years of age) may reflect a decrease in scope and a positional shift in epigenetic space as a result of previous developmental commitments. One may be able to specify a range of reaction (Gottesman, 1963) or range of potential phenotypes, for a given genotype over the life span, but where a person actually falls within that range will probably be the result of a hierarchy of contingent events. The total range of reaction may never be known. There may be a critical period when potential variability, or the range of possible outcomes, is greatest. After the critical period has passed and the system has committed itself in a particular direction, the potential reaction range may be considerably circumscribed by its developmental history.

Figure 4 depicts a two-dimensional schematization of this model. The predispositions of genotypes alone (at the time of conception) are shown at points A, B, C, D, E, and F. Since we began with an example of cerebral lateralization of function, let us extend that example here. The phenotype of interest will be strength of right ear superiority on a dichotic listening task. In a number of studies of nonimpaired, right-handed adults it has been found that when presented with two competing simultaneous verbal stimuli through a pair of earphones, most subjects are most accurate in reporting the sound presented to the right ear (Broadbent, 1974; Carter, 1976; Curry, 1967; Kimura, 1964, 1967). This is thought to reflect a general superiority of the left hemisphere in the processing of verbal information. Genotype A in Figure 4 has a genetic predisposition to develop in a direction that would result in a right ear superiority on this kind of task in adulthood. However, there is considerable plasticity in the nervous system early in development, so this individual could potentially develop in such a way that a left ear superiority in adulthood could be observed. Without any major events that would tend to deflect the developmental pathway leading to right ear superiority, however, he is likely to express the standard pattern.

There are some stresses that could lead to alteration of that pathway. One possibility would be perinatal cranial stress causing minimal cortical damage (probably undetectable in terms of its consequences on gross behavioral performance) that might result in a slight shift in the extent to which the left hemisphere served linguistic functions. Another might be selective injury to the right ear, which could result in a pattern of preferential presentation of verbal information to the right hemisphere and hence a deviation from the lateralization pathway with the strongest genetic predisposition. Still another stress causing such a change might be precipitated by the effort on the part of parents or teachers to alter a child's preferred handedness. Although the relationship between hand preference and cerebral lateralization is an imperfect one (Milner, Branch, and Rasmussen, 1964), some investigators believe that forced alteration of handedness may be

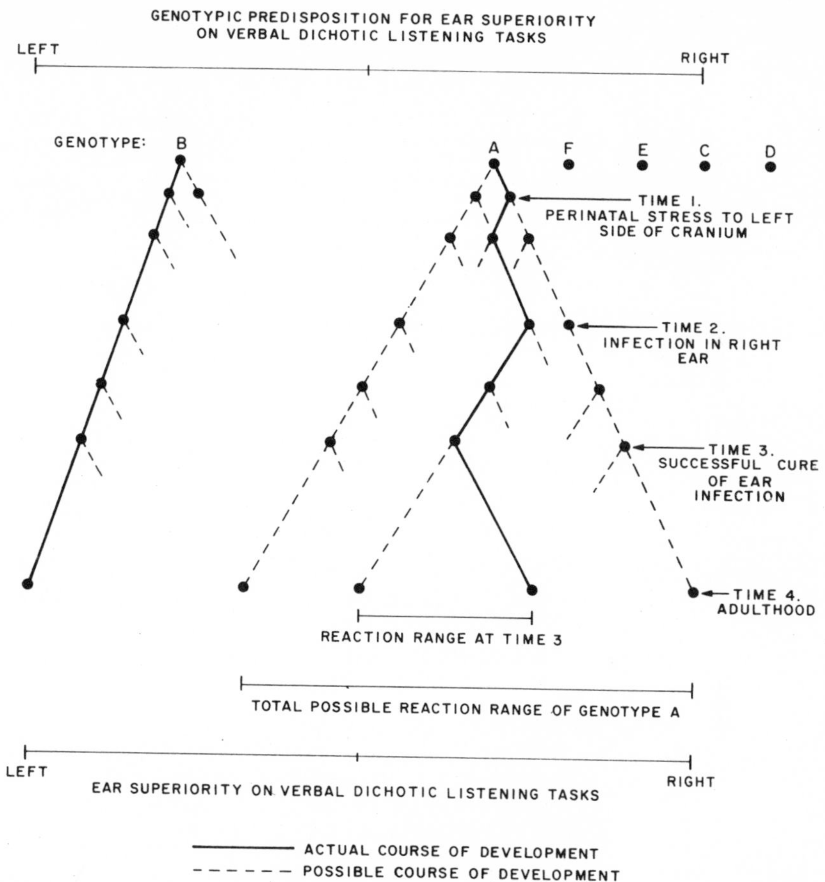

FIGURE 4. Two-dimensional schematization of possible genotype–environment model.

related to an increase in verbal dysfunction (Bloodstein, 1969; Kidd, personal communication).

In Figure 4, the extent to which Genotype A develops a right ear superiority on dichotic listening tests is shown to be affected by perinatal stress and by an ear infection. When the ear infection subsides, development returns to its original direction, but never finds the same pathway again. The range of reaction for Genotype A at the time of recovery from the ear infection has been considerably restricted by past events. Although Genotype B is not as fully elaborated, it is clear that exactly the same events (perinatal stress to the left side of the head and the onset of and recovery from an infection of the right ear) have *no* effects on cerebral lateralization for linguistic functioning.

A behavior, then, can be canalized to a greater or lesser extent, but as the individual develops, the contour of the epigenetic landscape will reflect the nature of past transactions with the environment. The genotype at conception may specify a reaction range for a particular behavior, and that reaction range is probably broader at conception than at any later period. The more highly canalized a developmental pathway, the less likely it is that previous developmental events can be reversed by subsequent events.

3.2. *Genotype–Environment Interaction*

If we accept the above as a general model of development, it is relatively easy to understand on a more concrete level how genotype–environment interactions might occur. The major prerequisite, of course, is the existence of genotypic variability with respect to the behavior of interest. Given such variability, differential responsiveness to environmental events could be empirically tested. Continuing with the hemispheric lateralization example, we can posit physiological individual differences that are genetically determined. Such differences may have quite different behavioral phenotypes for cerebral asymmetry when exposed to the same experiences in the environment.

Witelson (1977) has reported that a group of right-handed dyslexic boys performed as though both their left and right hemispheres were functioning in ways normally characteristic of only the right hemisphere. This deviation from the more common pattern of hemispheric specialization was substantiated both by a manual dichhaptic stimulation task and by selective presentation of nonverbal information to the right and left visual hemifields. These children had been diagnosed as dyslexic on the basis of multiple pediatric, psychological, and psychiatric assessments.

Additional support for the notion that laterality differences may be related to reading difficulty was supplied by Carter (1976). She found that adolescents who were in the lowest quartile of reading performance had significantly smaller inter-ear differences on a verbal dichotic listening task than subjects in the top quartile of reading achievement. That is, poor readers tended not to have the normal right ear superiority on the dichotic task and often showed no ear advantage. Although independent confirmation of these findings will be necessary, it is possible that strong differential hemispheric specialization is optimal for development of the skills necessary for processing verbal material.

This is at least potentially an example of a meaningful kind of GE interaction. Genotypically determined differences in cerebral lateralization patterns might be related to qualitative differences in individuals' responses to particular educational curricula. It should be emphasized that we do not yet have conclusive evidence that individual differences in lateralization processes are under genetic control. To date, there have been few family studies using measures of cerebral lateralization, and these have been hampered by poor reliabilities of the measures. Although Bryden (1975) found little evidence for genetic control, the results of a study of dyslexics and their families by Carter (1977) supported the notion that genetic factors are relevant. In another study of adoptive and biological families, Carter (1976) found that biologically related individuals were consistently more similar on a verbal dichotic listening task than adoptive relatives, although the differences between correlations were not statistically significant. The issue has not been resolved, and more reliable data on families must be collected before final conclusions can be drawn.

Can this kind of interaction be placed in a canalization framework? Consider the possibility that there are two (or more) relevant genotypes that affect hemispheric lateralization. Genotype A may show strong canalization in favor of developing a left hemisphere capacity for sequential, analytic thinking. Although Genotype B may also have that capability, it may show strong canalization for the development of a more gestaltlike, spatial type of processing in its left hemisphere.

If individuals of Genotype A and Genotype B are sent to the same school and are presented with the same set of curricular materials designed to teach them to read, their phenotypic outcomes may be quite different. Under standard instructional conditions, an individual with Genotype A might learn to read more quickly and more effectively than someone with Genotype B. However, if other individuals of Genotypes A and B, respectively, were sent to a school where the instructional emphasis was on visual pattern recognition and representation of spatial arrays rather than on sequential, verbal processing, Genotype B students might have an advantage, and might perform at higher levels than students with Genotype A. If this were found to be true, we would have evidence of a GE interaction that is relevant to cognitive functioning.

It is possible that Witelson's (1977) data on dyslexic boys, with corraborative support from Carter (1976) on individual differences in reading achievement, allow us to fill the first two cells in the GE interaction design. We know that some children whose left hemispheres share both verbal and spatial functioning perform at lower levels on verbal tasks (in standard educational settings) than children with the more prototypical pattern of laterality. We do not yet have data on the two kinds of genotypes (prototypical and nonprototypical) in nonstandard educational settings designed to teach children who are more dependent on right hemisphere types of processing.

Note that two conditions must be met before the presence of significant GE interaction can be concluded. First, the difference in hemispheric lateralization should be shown to be genetic in origin, and should not be due solely to random environmental events such as perinatal trauma. Second, the nonadditivity of the effects of at least two kinds of environmental conditions must be demonstrated in a comparison of the two genotypic groups. It is certainly possible that a new and innovative educational strategy would result in equal increments (or decrements) across genotypes, and hence provide no evidence for genotype–environment interaction.

It should also be noted that not all behaviors are equally likely to show evidence of GE interaction. First, behaviors that are highly canalized at the species level are not probable candidates since a wide range of different genotypes must have the capacity for differential responsiveness to environmental conditions in order to express functionally identical phenotypes. Many different genotypes would therefore result in the same phenotype regardless of transactions during development with widely differing environments. Second, and at the other extreme, behaviors that are weakly canalized (at the species or individual level) are not likely to express differences that are genetic in origin. A weakly canalized behavior would have a broad reaction range (over a wide range of environments) and identical genotypes could lead to many different kinds of phenotypic expression. In addition, different genotypes might easily be made to express the same phenotype, given a uniform environment across individuals. Finally, the behaviors that have the highest probability for detectable GE interaction are those that have a fairly high level of canalization at the individual level. If differences among individuals in a population can in part be attributed to their genetic differences, then questions about the presence of nonadditive effects of genotype and environment can reasonably be posed.

4. *Specification of Genotype*

Although the goal of genotypic specification is an admirable one, its practical implementation in research has been difficult. Often the existence of phenotypic differences between groups on traits that have been found to have high within-group heritabilities has been used inappropriately to infer genotypic between-group differences. In such instances, genotypic classification criteria are essentially based on phenotypic expression, with no real knowledge of the extent to which genetic factors may affect that expression.

Before individuals can be assigned to groups that are claimed to differ genotypically, there must be some indication that their differences are related to genetic differences. This prerequisite is easily met when the differences in behavioral phenotypes are known to have a specific genetic cause. Examples such as PKU, homocystinuria, Down's syndrome, and Tay Sachs disease are cases of behavioral disorders for which genetic causes are well established, and for which classification into affected and nonaffected groups can be unambiguous.

An example of a known genetic difference with possible behavioral correlates is sex. Genotypically normal females carry two X chromosomes, and genotypically normal males carry one X and one Y chromosome. It is possible, however, that this universally accepted genetic difference may not have many important behavioral correlates outside the realm of reproductive behavior. On many behavioral traits for which sex differences have been sought, no reliable evidence of such differences has been uncovered (Maccoby and Jacklin, 1974). However, for spatial visualization, a cognitive skill that involves the visualization and rotation of a two-dimensional representation of a three-dimensional figure, reliable and replicable differences in favor of males have been found (Carter, 1976; Maccoby and Jacklin, 1974; Spuhler, 1976; Vandenberg and Kuse, 1977; Wilson, DeFries, McClearn, Vandenberg, Johnson, and Rashad, 1975). While the origins of these differences have not yet been established, it seems likely that both genetic and environmental factors are important contributors. It is certainly possible, though, that the relative contributions of those factors differs as a function of sex. When provided with identically high or low levels of opportunity to develop spatial skills, males and females may respond differently to those opportunities for reasons that are genotypically mediated. If this is true, then it would be inappropriate to combine the sexes for analyses of variance and calculations of heritability estimates.

One can check for this possibility by calculating heritabilities for both sexes combined and for each sex separately. Preliminary analyses of WAIS Block Design scores from a large adoption study in Minnesota revealed such a possibility (Carter-Saltzman, unpublished data). The estimated heritability for the scores, as calculated on 209 biological midparent–child pairs and 107 adoptive midparent–child pairs, was .35. However, when heritabilities were calculated separately for sons and daughters, the values were .55 and .23, respectively. Although this does not constitute definitive evidence of GE interaction, it does indicate that a genotypic classification by sex might be appropriate for this (WAIS Block Design) phenotype.

Another candidate for classification by genotype might be schizophrenia. Data from a large number of family studies have led to the conclusion that there is a substantial genetic contribution to variation in the incidence of schizophrenia (Gottesman and Shields, 1972; Heston, 1966; Rosenthal and Kety, 1968). The number of genes involved, the locations of relevant genes, and the biochemical correlates of their action are all unknown. Nevertheless, it is possible to classify individuals into schizophrenic groups and nonschizophrenic groups, and then to test for GE interactions across a variety of environmental conditions.

The cerebral lateralization example that was used earlier is tenuous in terms of known genetic differences among individuals. Nevertheless, it provides clear-cut criteria for classification, and awaits further data for verification of the extent to which genetic factors affect differences on those criteria.

The main point is that any system of classification by genotype must be explicitly delineated and must be empirically verifiable. Just any genetic difference will not do. There must be reason to hypothesize that known genetic differences are meaningfully related to behavioral variation. This is crucial because of our paucity of knowledge about the extent to which behavioral phenotypes are correlated with genotypes. We know that the same phenotype can result from different genotypes, and that identical genotypes can produce differing phenotypes. The assumption of high genotype–phenotype correlations has often been made without adequate justification, and has perhaps been linked to premature acceptance of the assumptions underlying additive models of genetic and environmental effects.

5. *Specification of Environments*

The term "rearing environment" encompasses all dimensions of the developmental experience. It is not surprising that we have had difficulty in specifying the aspects of rearing environments that are most salient for the development of particular behaviors. Nevertheless, if the unfolding of behavioral patterns is to be properly understood, it is important that such specification be achieved. Large bodies of behavioral data exist for which the only indices of "home environment" are general SES classifications based on father's income, education, or occupational status. Few psychologists would seriously contend that demographics of the father are the best predictors of a child's behavioral development.

Despite such imprecision in much of the work in behavior genetics and developmental psychology, there are increasing numbers of studies that focus on the effects of specific environmental factors. For example, the nature of a particular social relationship (mother–infant attachment) during a specified period of infancy is thought to affect subsequent social development and adjustment (Bowlby, 1969; 1973). There is a growing body of research on the effects of early experience on behavioral development. Scarr-Salapatek and Williams (1973) have reported on the positive behavioral effects of a program of early tactile, visual, and social stimulation on a group of socially disadvantaged, low birthweight infants. Similarly, a program of visual stimulation and extra handling significantly accelerated the onset of visually guided reaching in institutionalized infants (White, 1967; White, Castle, and Held, 1964; White and Held, 1966).

Urie Bronfenbrenner (1977) has sketched a broad hierarchy of levels of childhood environments, and has proposed a program of research that should greatly enhance our understanding of the effects of growing up under differing circumstances. He has stressed the necessity for detailed descriptions of relevant aspects of rearing environments, but has in addition provided a conceptual umbrella for understanding the complex eco-systems in which development occurs. Within the context of Bronfenbrenner's suggestions, James Garabino (1977) has outlined a program for assessing the impact of various life experiences on the increasingly troublesome pheonomenon of child abuse.

Within a behavior genetic framework, Carter-Saltzman and Scarr (1977) have used multiple regression analyses to ascertain the extent to which demographic, attitudinal, and social environmental factors made independent contributions to differences in the IQ scores of adopted children in interracial families. Of 30 possible predictors, eight were found to contribute significantly when all other variables were held constant. Those eight were: (1) neighbors' reactions to transracial adoption; (2) percentage of blacks in the neighborhood; (3) number of siblings (negative effect); (4) mother's level of martyrdom as reflected on the Parental Attitude Research Instrument (PARI); (5) strictness of mother's attitudes as reflected on the PARI (negative effect); (6) difference between mother's educational level and median level of education in the census tract; (7) mother's education; and (8) median education level within the census tract. Some of the environmental factors that were not shown to have independent effects were parental age, father's education, orderliness of the home, and presence of other transracial adoptive families in the neighborhood. This study effectively isolated some aspects of home environments related to levels of intellectual performance of children growing up in those interracial homes. Although the level of environmental specification was rather remote from daily household activities, a relationship between a behavioral phenotype (IQ) and specific environmental parameters relevant to that phenotype was established.

6. *GE Interaction: An Empirical Question*

If it is possible to classify individuals according to genotypic differences, and to identify environmental parameters that are relevant to behavioral development in at least one population, then it is clearly possible to test for the existence of GE interactions that might contribute in a nonadditive way to the expressed differences among individuals. The investigation of such interactions can never be as elegant in human as in animal studies, because of the lack of control over breeding and rearing conditions. Still, by defining as closely as possible the relevant genotypes and environmental factors, we may be able to achieve a clearer understanding of the relative importance of additive and nonadditive contributions of these components to behavioral development.

To what extent should developmental psychologists concern themselves with the interactions discussed in this chapter? Only a minority of psychologists are currently doing behavior genetics research. It is extremely important for these people to know about possible GE interactions and correlations before attempting to fit their data to statistical models. Only in cases where there is no evidence of interactive effects should additive models be used. For other developmental psychologists, the perspective provided by knowledge of such interactions is important. Many research programs are designed to explain development of the "typical child." Unexplained variance is treated as a nuisance, and often more effort is devoted to getting rid of such variability than to explaining it. It should not be assumed that a given experimental treatment will affect all individuals in a similar manner. Such an assumption could bias the analyses and interpretations of data, and could result in the unintentional camouflaging of important effects.

Although the presence of GE interactions poses a problem for statistical models used by behavior geneticists, the study of such interactions should be motivated by additional considerations. Certainly, it would be reassuring to know when particular biometrical analyses are appropriate and when they are not. But the primary motivation must be to understand more fully the nature of the development of individual differences. Only with such understanding will we be able to optimize the opportunity for full development of children of all genotypes.

References

Allison, A.C. The distribution of the sickle trait in East Africa and elsewhere and its apparent relationship to the incidence of subtertian malaria. *Transactions of the Royal Society for Tropical Medical Hygiene*, 1954, *48*, 312–318.

Basser, L.S. Hemiplegia of early onset and the faculty of speech with special reference to the effects of hemispherectomy, *Brain*, 1962, *85*, 427–460.

Block, N.S., and Dworkin, G. IQ, heritability and inequality, Part 1. *Philosophy and Public Affairs*, 1974, *3*, 331–409.

Bloodstein, O. *A handbook on stuttering*. Chicago: National Easter Seal Society for Crippled Children and Adults, 1969.

Bowlby, J. *Attachment and loss. Vol. 1: Attachment*. London: Hogarth, 1969.

Bowlby, J. *Attachment and loss. Vol. 2: Separation, anxiety and anger*. New York: Basic Books, 1973.

Broadbent, D.E. Division of function and integration of behavior. In F.O. Schmitt and F.G. Worden (Eds.), *The neurosciences: Third study program*. Cambridge, Mass.: The MIT Press, 1974.

Bronfenbrenner, U. A theoretical model for the experimental ecology of human development. Paper presented at the biennial meetings of the Society for Research in Child Development, New Orleans, 1977.

Bryden, M.P. Speech lateralization in families: A preliminary study using dichotic listening. *Brain and Language*, 1975, *2*, 201–211.

Carter, B.F. Genealogical analyses of cerebral laterality and dyslexia. Paper presented at the 7th Annual Meeting of the Behavior Genetics Association, Louisville, 1977.

Carter, S.L. The structure and transmission of individual differences in patterns of cognitive ability. Unpublished doctoral dissertation, University of Minnesota, 1976.

Carter-Saltzman, L., and Scarr, S. The effects of integration in home, neighborhood and school settings on children in transracial adoptive families. Paper presented at the biennial meetings of the Society for the Research in Child Development, New Orleans, 1977.

Cheek, D.B. The fetus. In D.B. Cheek (Ed.), *Fetal and postnatal cellular growth: Hormones and nutrition*. New York: Wiley, 1975.

Cohen, J., and Cohen, P. *Applied multiple regression/correlation analysis for the behavioral sciences*. New York: Halstead Press, 1975.

Cooper, R.M., and Zubek, J.P. Effects of enriched and restricted early environment on the learning ability of bright and dull rats. *Canadian Journal of Psychology*, 1958, *12*, 159–164.

Cravioto, J., and DeLicardie, E.R. Nutrition and behavior and learning. *World Review of Nutrition and Dietetics*, 1973, *16*, 80–96.

Curry, F.K.W. A comparison of left-handed and right-handed subjects on verbal and nonverbal dichotic listening tasks. *Cortex*, 1967, *3*, 343–352.

DeFries, J.C. Prenatal maternal stress in mice: Differential effects on behavior. *Journal of Heredity*, 1964, *55*, 289–295.

Dobbing, J. Undernutrition and the developing brain: The relevance of animal models to the human problem. *American Journal of Diseases of Children*, 1970, *120*, 411–415.

Dobzhansky, T. *Genetics and the origin of species*. 3rd ed. New York: Columbia University Press, 1951.

Erlenmeyer-Kimling, L. Gene–environment interactions and the variability of behavior. In L. Ehrman, G. Omenn, and E. Caspari (Eds.), *Genetics, environment and behavior: Implications for educational policy*. New York: Academic Press, 1972, 181–218.

Freedman, D.G. Constitutional and environmental interactions in rearing of four breeds of dogs. *Science*, 1958, *127*, 585–586.

Fuller, J.L., and Collins, R.L. Genetics of audiogenic seizures in mice: A parable for psychiatrists. *Seminars in Psychiatry*, 1970, *2*, 75–88.

Garabino, J. The human ecology of child abuse and neglect. Paper presented at the biennial meeting of the Society for Research in Child Development, New Orleans, 1977.

Gottesman, I.I. Genetic aspects of intelligent behavior. In N. Ellis (Ed.), *Handbook of mental deficiency*. New York: McGraw Hill, 1963, 253–296.

Gottesman, I.I., and Shields, J. *Schizophrenia and genetics: A twin study vantage point*. New York: Academic Press, 1972.

Henderson, N.D. Brain weight increases resulting from environmental enrichment: A directional dominance in mice. *Science*, 1970, *169*, 776–778.

Heston, L.L. Psychiatric disorders in foster home reared children of schizophrenic mothers. *British Journal of Psychiatry*, 1966, *112*, 819–825.

Hirsch, J., and Vetta, A. *Misconceptions of behavioral genetics*. Unpublished manuscript, 1977.

Horn, J.M., Willerman, L., and Loehlin, J.C. Heritability of intelligence: Evidence from the Texas Adoption Project. Paper presented at the 7th Annual Meeting of the Behavior Genetics Association, Louisville, 1977.

Jinks, J.L., and Fulker, D.W. Comparison of the biometrical genetical, MAVA and classical approaches to the analysis of human behavior. *Psychological Bulletin*, 1970, *73*, 311–349.

Kalter, H. The inheritance of susceptibility to the teratogenic action of cortisone in mice. *Genetics*, 1954, *39*, 185.

Kerlinger, F.N., and Pedhazur, E.J. *Multiple regression in behavioral research*. New York: Holt, Rinehart & Winston, 1973.

Kimura, D. Functional asymmetry of the brain in dichotic listening. *Cortex*, 1967, *3*, 163–178.

Kimura, D. Left-right differences in the perception of melodies. *Quarterly Journal of Experimental Psychology*, 1964, *14*, 355–358.

Layzer, D. Heritability analyses of IQ scores: Science or numerology? *Science*, 1974, *183*, 1259–1266.

Lenneberg, E.H. *Biological foundations of language*. New York: John Wiley & Sons, Inc., 1967.

Lindquist, E.F. *Design and analysis of experiments in psychology and education*. Boston: Houghton, 1953.

Lubin, A. The interpretation of significant interaction. *Educational Psychological Measures*, 1961, *21*, 807–817.

Lynch, C.B., and Hegmann, J.P. Genetic differences influencing behavioral temperature regulation in small mammals. 2. Genotype–environment interactions. *Behavior Genetics*, 1973, *3*, 145–154.

Maccoby, E.E., and Jacklin, C.N. *The psychology of sex differences*. Stanford, Calif.: Stanford University Press, 1974.

Mayr, E. Change of genetic environment and evolution. In J. Huxley (Ed.), *Evolution as a process*. London: Allen and Unwin, 1954.

Mayr, E. *Populations, species, and evolution.* Cambridge, Mass.: Harvard University Press, 1970.

McClearn, G.E., and DeFries, J.C. *Introduction to behavioral genetics.* San Francisco: Freeman, 1973.

McGaugh, J.L., and Cole, J.M. Age and strain differences in the effect of distribution of practice on maze learning. *Psychonomic Science*, 1965, *2*, 253–254.

Mikkelsen, M.A. Danish survey of patients with Down's syndrome born to young mothers. *Annals of the New York Academy of Science*, 1970, *171*, 370–378.

Milner, B. Hemispheric specialization: Scope and limits. In F.O. Schmitt and F.G. Worden (Eds.), *The neurosciences: Third study program.* Cambridge, Mass.: The MIT Press, 1974.

Milner, B., Branch, C., and Rasmussen, T. Observations on cerebral dominance. In A.V.S. de Rench and M. O'Connor (Eds.), *Disorders of language.* Boston: Little, Brown & Co., 1964.

Money, J., and Ehrhardt, A.A. *Man and woman, boy and girl.* Baltimore: Johns Hopkins University Press, 1972.

Motulsky, A.G. Hereditary red cell traits and malaria. *American Journal of Tropical Medical Hygiene*, 1964, *13*, Part 2, 147–158.

Omenn, G.S. Inborn errors of metabolism: Clues to understanding human behavioral disorders. *Behavior Genetics*, 1976, *6*, 263–284.

Omenn, G.S., and Motulsky, A.G. Biochemical genetics and the evolution of human behavior. In L. Ehrman, G.A. Omenn, and E. Caspari (Eds.), *Genetics, environment, and behavior: Implications for educational policy.* New York: Academic Press, 1972.

Parsons, P.A., and Kaul, D. Mating speed and duration of copulation in *Drosophila pseudoobscura. Heredity*, 1966, *21*, 219–225.

Plomin, R., DeFries, J.C., and Loehlin, J.C. Genotype–environment interaction and correlation in the analysis of human behavior. *Psychological Bulletin*, 1977, *84*, 309–322.

Rosenthal, D., and Kety, S.S. (Eds.). *The transmission of schizophrenia.* Oxford: Pergamon, 1968.

Satinder, K.P. Genotype-dependent effects of D-amphetamine sulphate and caffeine on escape–avoidance behavior of rats. *Journal of Comparative and Physiological Psychology*, 1971, *76*, 359–364.

Scarr, S., & Weinberg, R.A. IQ test performance of black children adopted by white families. *American Psychologist*, 1976, *31*, 726–739.

Scarr-Salapatek, S. An evolutionary perspective on infant intelligence: Species patterns and individual variations. In M. Lewis (Ed.), *The origins of intelligence: Infancy and early childhood.* New York: Plenum, 1976.

Scarr-Salapatek, S., and Williams, M.L. The effects of early stimulation on low-birth-weight infants. *Child Development*, 1973, *44*, 94–101.

Sever, J. Viruses and embryos. In F.C. Fraser and V.A. McKusick (Eds.), *Congenital malformations.* Amsterdam: Excerpta Medica, 1970.

Skodak, M., and Skeels, H.M. A final follow-up on one hundred adopted children. *Journal of Genetic Psychology*, 1949, *75*, 85–125.

Spuhler, K.P. Family resemblance for cognitive performance: An assessment of genetic and environmental contributions to variation. Unpublished doctoral dissertation, University of Colorado, 1976.

Stern, C. *Principles of human genetics.* San Francisco: Freeman, 1973.

Thomas, A., Chess, S., and Birch, H.G. The origin of personality. *Scientific American*, 1970, *223*, 102–109.

Thomas, A., Chess, S., and Birch, H.G. *Temperament and behavior disorders in children.* New York: New York University Press, 1968.

Thompson, W.R., and Olian, S. Some effects on offspring behavior of maternal adrenalin injection during pregnancy in three inbred mouse strains. *Psychological Reports*, 1961, *8*, 87–90.

Trasler, D.G. The influence of uterine site on the occurrence of spontaneous cleft lip in mice. Paper presented at the Teratol Conference, New York, April 9–10, 1960.

Uchida, J.A. Epidemiology of mongolism: the Manitoba study. *Annals of the New York Academy of Science*, 1970, *171*, 361–369.

Vandenberg, S.G., and Kuse, A.R. Spatial ability: A critical review of the sex-linked major-gene hypothesis. In M.A. Wittig and A.C. Petersen (Eds.), *Determinants of sex-related differences in cognitive functioning*. New York: Academic Press, 1979.

Van Valen, L., Levine, L., and Beardmore, J.A. Temperature sensitivity of chromosomal polymorphism in *Drosophila pseudoobscura*. *Genetica*, 1962, *33*, 113–127.

Waddington, C.H. Canalization of development and the inheritance of acquired characters. *Nature*, 1942, *150*, 563–564.

Waddington, C.H. Genetic assimilation. *Advances in Genetics*, 1961, *10*, 257–293.

Waddington, C.H. *New patterns in genetics and development*. New York: Columbia University Press, 1962.

Waddington, C.H. *Principles of development and differeniation*. London: Macmillan, 1966.

Weir, M.W., and DeFries, J.C. Prenatal maternal influence on behavior in mice: Evidence of a genetic basis. *Journal of Comparative and Physiological Psychology*, 1964, *58*, 412–417.

White, B.L. An experimental approach to the effects of environment on early human behavior. In J.P. Hill (Ed.), *Minnesota symposium on child psychology*. Vol. 1. Minneapolis: University of Minnesota Press, 1967.

White, B.L., and Held, R. Plasticity of sensorimotor development in human infant. In J. Rosenblith and W. Allinsmith (Eds.), *The causes of behavior: readings in child development and educational psychology*. Boston: Allyn and Bacon, 1966.

White, B.L., Castle, P., and Held, R.M. Observations on the development of visually directed reaching. *Child Development*, 1964, *35*, 249–364.

Wilson, J.G. *Environment and birth defects*. New York: Academic Press, 1973.

Wilson, J.R., DeFries, J.C., McClearn, G.E., Vandenberg, S.G., Johnson, R.C., and Rashad, M.N. Cognitive abilities: Use of family data as a control to assess sex and age differences in two ethnic groups. *International Journal on Aging and Human Development*, 1975, *6*, 261–276.

Witelson, S.F. Developmental dyslexia: Two right hemispheres and none left. *Science*, 1977, *195*, 309–311.

Wright, S., and Dobzhansky, T. Genetics of natural populations. 12. Experimental reproduction of some of the changes caused by natural selection in certain populations of *Drosophila pseudoobscura*. *Genetics*, 1946, *31*, 125–156.

External Stimuli and the Development and Organization of Behavior

Jay S. Rosenblatt

1. *Introduction*

Animals interact with their environment in many ways during development and in the process of adapting their behavior to it. Sensory interaction with the environment is particularly crucial because effects of sensory stimuli on animal behavior are well known and there are few aspects of the physiological functioning of animals that are not affected by sensory stimuli. The close relationship between animals and their environments and between physiological and behavioral functioning in animals are always mediated through multiple effects of key sensory stimuli. Comparative psychology has traced the evolution of increasingly higher levels of psychological capacities through processes of sensory integration (Schneirla, 1949, 1962) in general treatments, and in the treatment of special areas of behavioral functioning (Beach, 1948; Nissen, 1951; Wheeler, 1928).

Ecological factors have played a crucial role in animal evolution as described by Alcock (1975), Crook (1970), Crook and Gartlan (1966), and Lack (1968). They have helped to shape individual and group behavior and behavioral interrelationships within groups, an area emphasized by current kin selection theory (Trivers, 1971, 1974; see Wilson, 1975).

One influence of studying animals under natural conditions is already seen in the growing tendency of those who are studying individual behavior in the areas of learning, sensory physiology, motivation, and the functioning of the nervous system to employ natural sources of stimulation instead of artificial ones, and to investigate a

---

Jay S. Rosenblatt • Institute of Animal Behavior, Rutgers-The State University of New Jersey, Newark, New Jersey 07102. The research from the author's laboratory reported in this chapter was supported by USPHS Grant MH–08604, Biomedical Support Grant, and a grant from the Alfred P. Sloan Foundation. Publication number 271 of the Institute of Animal Behavior.

wider range of natural motivational systems and naturally occurring behavior patterns. These studies have thus far yielded important new insights into behavioral and physiological processes, particularly in the area of sensory processes (Lettvin, Maturana, McCullough, and Pitts, 1959; Hubel and Wiesel, 1959, 1962; Konishi, 1973; Hailman, 1970) that would not have been discovered using traditional methods of study.

The fields of early behavioral development and reproductive behavior among birds and mammals have long been concerned with interrelationships among ecological stimuli, natural patterns of behavior, and internal physiological processes. Prenatal studies of behavioral development among birds arose from the effort to trace the development of the hatchling's early response to parental calls. Studies of neonatal behavior among mammals arose from the effort to understand early suckling and its role in the newborn's attachment to the mother. Investigation of mating among mammals has focused on the interaction between the male and female during sexual behavior in order to understand the organization of mating patterns (Adler, 1974; Diakow, 1974; Larsson, 1973), and the study of maternal behavior has shown that the influence of stimulation from the young is an essential part of the organization of this pattern (Noirot, 1972; Rosenblatt, 1975).

Perhaps the greatest advances in our understanding of how external stimuli, in the form of ecological and social influences, are intertwined with behavior and underlying physiological processes have been made in the study of the reproductive behavior of birds, as represented by the work of Lehrman and his colleagues (1959) on the ring dove and Hinde and his associates on the canary (1965). At the conclusion of his review of "Hormonal Responses to External Stimuli in Birds" Lehrman (1959) expressed most clearly this aspect of the subject in a paragraph that is worth quoting:

> The problems which we have been discussing are particularly interesting since they represent a borderline between, and the convergence of, the interests of workers in several different areas. Although the basic mechanisms have been worked out by endocrinologists and physiologists, many of the problems which are illuminated by knowledge of neuro-endocrine relationships arise from ecological work, since they have to do with the adjustment of breeding activity to the conditions in the environment. Many phenomenna which have long been known to ornithologists, such as the sexual flights of passerine birds, the prolonged mutual courtship ceremonies of colonial birds, indeterminate laying and the onset of incubation behaviour, changes in behaviour upon hatching of the eggs, re-nesting after destruction of nest and clutch, etc., acquire a new dimension as scientific problems in the light of recent advances in physiology. Similarly,

> students of bird behaviour may be enabled to give added physiological meaning to traditional knowledge of changes in behaviour during the reproductive cycle and of the effects of this behaviour upon the behaviour of fellow-members of the species. As in other areas of biology, the coalescence of ecology, ethology, and physiology can give added stimulation to all three.

The present article will review the progress that has been made in several areas of developmental study and the study of reproductive behavior and physiology in unraveling the relationship between external stimuli and internal processes in the development and organization of behaviour. These areas are: sensory influences in prenatal behavioral development among birds, suckling development and the role of sensory stimuli, the organization of reproductive cycles and behavior among birds, reproductive behavior in the rat, self-licking and mammary gland development during pregnancy, and the role of external stimuli in maternal behavior and reproductive physiology.

2. *Behavioral Development*

2.1. *Sensory Influences in Prenatal Behavioral Development among Birds*

Vince (1964, 1966, 1968, 1969, 1973) and Freeman and Vince (1974) have shown that bobwhite and Japanese quail eggs that are incubated in contact with one another, as they are in the nest under natural conditions, hatch within an hour or two of one another; eggs that are separated from one another by only a few inches, although they are kept in the same incubator, require a 10- to 24-hour period for all of them to hatch. By comparing the hatching times of grouped eggs and isolated eggs it was found that the grouped eggs tended to hatch at around the middle of the hatching period while isolated eggs hatched over the entire hatching period of 24 hours. Some of the grouped eggs had therefore been speeded up in hatching and others had been slowed down.

The acceleration of hatching could be demonstrated experimentally by removing one egg from a group for 24 hours, then replacing it: This egg hatched at the same time as the others of the group despite the 24-hour delay in development. When an older egg is placed in contact with a younger one, it hatches later than its isolated "clutch" mates, suggesting that its development has been slowed.

What are the sensory stimuli that are responsible for the retardation and for the acceleration of hatching during contact between incubating bobwhite quail eggs? Playing back to isolated quail eggs the recorded sounds that accompany the movement of embryos several days before hatching retards hatching whereas playing click sounds that are produced by somewhat older embryos during respiration, shortly before hatching, accelerates hatching (Freeman and Vince, 1974; Vince, 1973).

Shortly after hatching many precocial and semi-precocial birds approach the parent for feeding and often follow her, emitting soft sounds named pleasure calls in response to the parental "lure" call (Gottlieb, 1971; Freeman and Vince, 1974; Impekoven, 1976). Tschantz (1959, 1968) and Tschantz and Hirsbrunner-Scharf (1975) found that in the guillemot, a gull species that lives on cliff ledges in dense colonies, the newly hatched young respond immediately to "lure" calls of their parents and, moreover, they can distinguish the calls of their own parents from similar calls of neighboring parents. The young of the laughing gull, black-headed gull, and herring gull also respond to the luring call of their parents soon after hatching but individual recognition of the calls of their own parents appears at a somewhat later age (Beer, 1970a,b, 1972; Impekoven, 1976). Ducklings and chicks exhibit following responses to the calling parent shortly after hatching and these function in leaving the nest and subsequent trailing after her. These responses to parental calls have been used to establish imprinting in these species (Gottlieb, 1971).

Tschantz (1959) showed that early postnatal recognition of parental "lure" calls was based upon prenatal exposure to these calls. By playing the calls of a given parent to embryos at frequent intervals over 2½ days during the early phase of pipping (i.e., shortly before and after the embryo had penetrated the membrane and its head was in the air space) and testing them with familiar and unfamiliar "lure" calls before hatching, he showed that they were much more responsive to the calls they had been exposed to, as indicated in the frequency of their own vocalizations, than to unfamiliar calls. Posthatching they responded to the familiar calls by approaching the microphone, snuggling up against it, and vocalizing.

In the laughing gull, Beer (1970a,b) has shown that certain phrases of the long call serve in individual recognition of parents by the young, beginning during the first 24 hours after hatching, becoming better established after 1 to 3 weeks. Before that time, however, crooning, another call of the laughing gull which is used posthatching to attract the young to feeding, appears to be attractive to hatchlings from the start. However, Beer (see Impekoven, 1973) found that embryos incubated communally in incubators until 24 hours after hatching do not approach the parents when they utter the crooning call but crouch instead.

As Impekoven (1971) has shown, this call acquires its attractiveness for chicks during the embryonic period. Moreover, during this period chicks also develop their negative response to the "kow" call, a warning call that elicits immobilization or fleeing. Incubating embryos of the laughing gull taken from nests in the field were tested at 2-day intervals from the 15th to 21st day (hatching occurs at 23–24 days) for their responses to the crooning and kow calls. From the 15th day onward crooning stimulated an increase in motility compared to periods of silence; initially the kow call had an inhibiting effect on motility but then it had no effect (Impekoven, 1971). When groups of embryos were exposed to either crooning calls, kow calls, or no sound during late incubation, and all were tested posthatching for their pecking behavior to a rod with or without the sounds that were present during incubation, it was found that: (1) prenatal experience with crooning increased the frequency of pecking during crooning; (2) prenatal experience with the kow call reduced the frequency of pecking during kow calls; and (3) embryos that had no experience with either call were less responsive when either call was played and were more responsive when no sound was played.

A number of other investigators have also reported enhanced postnatal responsiveness in hatchings to calls that they have been exposed to prenatally. Gottlieb (1971) has shown that ducklings exposed to maternal or sibling calls are more responsive to maternal calls postnatally, and Grier, Counter, and Shearer (1967) reported that chick embryos exposed to intermittent 200 Hz tones from day 13 to day 18 of incubation were more responsive to this tone than a 2000 Hz tone. Recently Lien (1976) has found that Japanese quail exposed to 300 or 400 Hz tones from day 12 to day 15 of incubation are more responsive to these tones than to tones one harmonic above and below them, between 4 and 8 hours after hatching.

Even when duck embryos are incubated individually and in sound isolation they exhibit a strong preference for the maternal call of their species compared to the maternal calls of other avian species (Gottlieb, 1971). There remain, however, even in isolation, their own vocalizations as a source of auditory experience. However, when duck embryos were devocalized (Gottlieb and Vandenbergh, 1968) before they had begun to produce vocalizations, the postnatal preference for the maternal call was considerably reduced during the first 24 hours and later.

In an elegant series of studies Gottlieb (1975a,b,c) has analyzed how embryonic vocal self-stimulation contributes to postnatal discrimination of the maternal calls. Devocalized embryos, lacking auditory self-stimulation, are deficient in responsiveness to high frequency components of the maternal call (above 825 Hz), those that distinguish it from chicken and wood duck parental calls, the two calls that Gottlieb has used in choice tests in opposition to the Mallard parental call. Embryonic calls are in this high frequency range (about 3000 Hz) and prehatching experience with them appears to contribute, along with maturation of high frequency cochlear sensitivity, to the postnatal discrimination of the parental call of the Mallard from that of the chicken and the wood duck (Konishi, 1973).

Tschantz (1968) and others (see review by Impekoven, 1976) have noted that in many gull species parental vocalization during incubation is often accompanied by egg-rotation or shifting, which elicit embryonic vocalization and increased movement. Impekoven (1976) studying domestic chicks tested whether parental calls accompanied by egg rotation would be more effective in establishing postnatal responsiveness to the call than parental calls without egg rotation. Chicks were exposed to the prenatal treatments during the last 3½ to 6 days of incubation and tested 5–6 hours after hatching. She found that chicks that had experienced the parental calls with egg rotation emitted nearly 10 times more pleasure notes over a 5-minute test period during which the parental calls were played. Clements and Lien (1976) have recently reported a similar finding in the Common Murre, a cliff edge-nesting gull species.

2.2. *Suckling Development and the Role of Sensory Stimuli*

Suckling is one of the earliest responses to appear in the neonate of every mammalian species. Usually the first suckling takes place shortly after parturition but at times it has been observed during delivery of a sibling, by an earlier born young (Ewer, 1959; Schneirla, Rosenblatt, and Tobach, 1963). In several species where prenatal observations of the fetus have been made, such as the rabbit, guinea pig, and sheep, and by circumstantial evidence gleaned from an examination of the stomach contents of other species, including infants, swallowing of amniotic fluid occurs prenatally (Becker, Windle, Barth, and Schulz, 1940). The swallowing response is not simply passive mouth opening but is an active response in which the fetus is responding to the sensory qualities of the ingested fluid. This is suggested by recordings from the chorda tympani in sheep fetuses that show responses to some substances (e.g., ammonia chloride, amniotic fluid) and absence of response to others (e.g., glucose, fructose) Bradley and Mistretta, 1973).

Many of the earliest anterior end movements (i.e., of the head, shoulders, and forelimbs) in newborn mammals can best be understood as mechanisms for systematically sampling the environment in front of the neonate. Moreover, in the neonate these "scanning" movements often serve as the first step in the neonate's response to an appropriate stimulus when this is encountered. For example, the head side-to-side movements of the newly born rat and kitten (Prechtl, 1952) enable it to scan surfaces immediately in front of its face but they are also part of the eventual response that it makes to these stimuli. If there is an aversive stimulus (i.e., strong tactile, hot or cold thermal, strong olfactory stimulus) the head swing to one side, away from the stimulus, is extended into a turn away from the stimulus by recruitment of hind and forelimb actions. On the other hand, a low intensity stimulus (i.e., a soft, furry surface, warmth, or weak olfactory stimulus) encountered during side-to-side head movement elicits narrowing of the head swing and forward movement along a relatively straight path, bringing the neonate into closer contact with the stimulus (Langworthy, 1929; Schneirla, 1965; Tilney and Casamajor, 1924; Windle, 1930).

Welker (1964) has traced the gradual "assembling" of the sniffing response in the newly born rat pup during the first three weeks. This response can be considered an olfactory–tactile exploratory mechanism (i.e., it provides "pulses" of combined olfactory and tactile stimulation for processing by the nervous system). It incorporates synchronized respiratory, nasal, and vibrissae movements with advancing locomotion that enables the young rat to orient to the most significant objects in its environment even before its eyes have opened.

Among mammalian species in which the young are altricial (i.e., rat, cat, dog), that is, without vision and hearing at birth and limited to crawling, these initial movements enable them to receive combined tactile, thermal, and olfactory stimulation. In mammalian species with precocial young (i.e., sheep, cow, goat), in which hearing and vision are present at birth and the young are capable of walking, the young possess responses that enable them to combine visual, auditory, olfactory, and thermal stimulation at birth. In these species, there are movements that coordinate the reception of auditory and visual stimulation so that hearing a sound elicits head turning in the direction of the sound and therefore visual focusing on the object producing the sound. The familiar head-up alert posture of the newly born young among many species of ungulates (i.e., cows, goats, sheep, horses, deer, etc.) exposes the young simultaneously to olfactory, visual, and auditory stimulation. Any one of these stimuli is likely to elicit head turning toward the stimulus, bringing into play the other two sensory systems. Often the newborn approaches the stimulus shortly afterward and receives further olfactory, tactile, and thermal stimulation. Visual- and auditory-elicited head turning and arm reaching have been described in human neonates and some have even described "body" pointing to a visual or auditory stimulus that includes facing the trunk toward the stimulus and pointing the fingers and toes in the direction of the object (e.g., mother's face) (Brazelton, Koslowski, and Main, 1974).

Suckling arises from these neonatal sensorimotor coordinations as a specialized response that has certain special stimulus requirements and involves certain special motor responses. The newborn rat's and kitten's initial approach to the mother that eventuates in suckling is probably an unspecialized approach having no special relation at first to suckling. The newborn responds to the warmth, soft tactile and low intensity olfactory stimulation of the mother's body, and her licking when she approaches and lies down around or on top of the young to nurse them. These stimuli can be provided by artificial mothers (except the licking) and they are generally successful with rats, rabbits, kittens, and puppies (see review Rosenblatt, 1976) in eliciting and maintaining approach and contact but there are different requirements to elicit nipple grasping and sucking: thus far no one has been successful in constructing an artificial mother on which altricial newborn spontaneously suckle. This is not because the young are incapable of nipple grasping and sucking without help: rat pups do not need the help of the mother to grasp the nipple and suckle even on the first day of life provided they are placed on the mother's belly, while she is anesthetized and laid on her back, belly upward (Hall, 1975; Lincoln, Hill, and Wakerly, 1973). When the pup contacts her nipple with its nose and mouth, it grasps the nipple and begins to suckle quite well. Obviously, we have not been able to incorporate into our artificial mothers' nipples and surrounding areas the proper stimuli to elicit these responses from the newborn.

The immediate environment of the mother's body and of the home surroundings consist of stimulus patterns that guide the newborn to her from nearby and lead it to the nipple regions. These patterns consist of tactile, thermal, and olfactory stimuli that are structured in such a manner as to make it very likely that the newborn will reach the nipples. For example, in the cat, Freeman and Rosenblatt (1978a) measured surface temperatures around the nursing mother, starting at a distance of more than 2 ft, and on her body from her legs

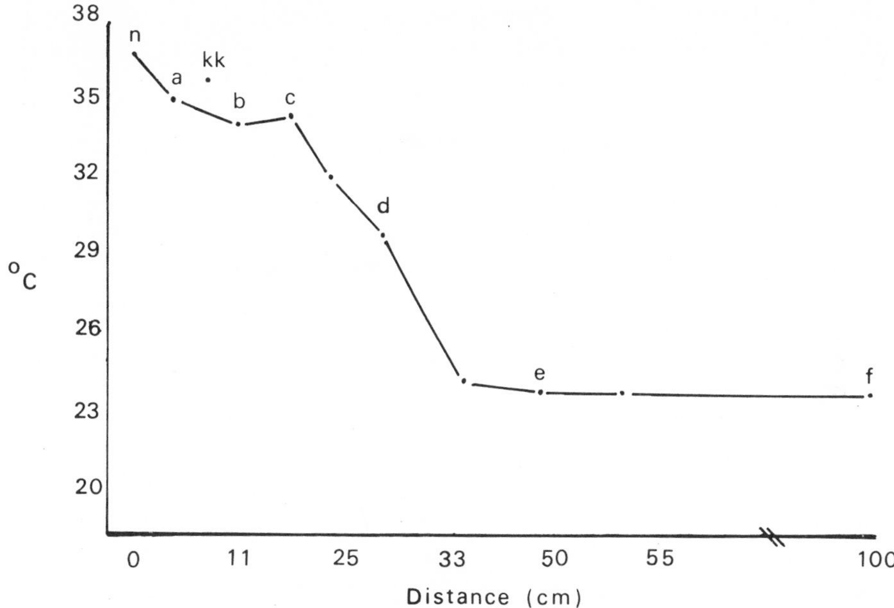

FIGURE 1. Schematic representation of thermal gradients that typically exist in the kittens' home cage environment: n = the temperature of a mother cat's aureole; a = ventrum; b = center of the home quadrant; c = mother's leg temperature; d = temperature of the floor at the border between the home and adjacent quadrants; e = center of the adjacent quadrant; f = center of the diagonal quadrant; kk = kitten huddles. (From N. Freeman and J.S. Rosenblatt, The interrelationship between thermal and olfactory stimulation in the development of home orientation in newborn kittens, *Developmental Psychobiology*, copyright by John Wiley and Sons, Inc., reprinted by permission.)

to her nipples, and found an increase in temperature: the temperature rises gradually until the mother's body is reached, then it increases sharply, increasing gradually again on her body until her nipples (see Fig. 1; Freeman and Rosenblatt, 1978a).

Moreover, an olfactory (i.e., odor) gradient that emanates from the mother closely parallels the above thermal gradient. Kittens respond to this odor gradient in orienting to the home site (Freeman and Rosenblatt, 1978a,b; Rosenblatt, Turkewitz, and Schneirla, 1969). The fur on the mother's body provides another source of guiding stimulation: it is heavily distributed over most of her body but around the nipples it begins to thin, becoming a short stubble and then simply a fuzzy texture or is almost entirely absent at the base of the nipple. Kittens find the nipple by nuzzling on the furry texture until they reach the nipple region (Rosenblatt, 1971; Shuleikina, 1977). Moreover, the nipples are located on mounds (i.e., areola) and are themselves oriented perpendicular to the body surface. This ensures that when the kitten encounters a nipple it will receive a prominent tactile stimulus against its nose and no other stimulus around the face area is present to elicit competing responses.

A rather different situation faces the newborn goat, sheep, calf, and deer: The mother stands during the initial nursing and the newborn must locate the udder and grasp the hanging teat. Interestingly, the characteristic exploratory head movement of these precocial young is an up-and-down movement, rather than the side-to-side head movement characteristic of altricial newborn. This is appropriate to the situation in which they must locate an udder "hanging" in space without guidance by a surface leading up to it. When the young's forehead makes contact with an object, it lifts its head upward and reaches toward the object with its mouth, a movement likely to enable it to respond to udder contact with nipple grasping.

In the rhesus monkey and chimpanzee and among primates generally, the mother forms a cradle with her whole body within which the newborn explores her body for the nipples. The nipples themselves are surrounded by bare skin and are prominent tactile, thermal, and olfactory stimuli (Rosenblum, 1967, 1971). The human infant is rarely required to approach the mother to suckle but is held to the nipple. It cannot be forced to suckle, however, but must be allowed to nuzzle the breast; the warmth and tactile stimulation, plus breast odors, at the cheek and lips elicit turning toward the nipple and eventual nipple grasping (Lewis and Rosenblum, 1974).

Nipple grasping among newborn rats requires special odor or taste stimuli to occur normally. Hofer and his associates (Hofer, Shair, and Singh, 1976) and Blass and his group (Teicher and Blass, 1976) have discovered substances that adhere to the nipple without which the young pup (i.e., five days and older) will not grasp the nipple. Hofer believes this to be a glandular secretion stimulated by oxytocin from the nipple surface while Blass believes it is saliva from the pup itself. Both have provided evidence in support of their proposals. In a recent study Teicher and Blass (1977) have shown that the initial suckling may be based on the presence of amniotic fluid spread on the nipple during parturition to which the newborn respond by nipple grasping. Amniotic fluid may be a precondition for nipple attachment in the newborn rat as Ewer (1959) suggested for kittens.

This does not preclude the role of other stimuli, however, and Hall (unpublished) has shown that anesthetizing the upper lip prevents rat pups from grasping the nipple although they are perfectly able to suckle if placed on the nipple. Kittens whose lips have been anesthetized lose the ability to find the nipple but if only the tongue is anesthetized, the kitten is able to find the nipple and grasp it but cannot suckle (Anokhin and Shuleikina, 1977).

Most interesting is the sensory control of milk swallowing in rat pups that has recently been investigated by Hall and Rosenblatt (1977). Small catheters inserted through the lower jaw and tongue were used to eject pulses of milk diet to various regions of the mouth, particularly the upper surface of the tongue. Only those directed to the rear of the mouth elicited swallowing, those directed anteriorly elicited tongue movements that expelled the milk. The mother's nipples, it turns out, are of such length that when the pup is sucking, milk ejected from the tip stimulates the rear of the pup's tongue and elicits swallowing.

Suckling in puppies has been shown to be under fine control by the flow of milk from an artificial nipple (Stanley, Bacon, and Fehr, 1970). Varying the interval between milk deliveries can determine the timing of sucking bouts, and varying the rate of flow, can determine the duration of sucking.

The periodicity of suckling in young animals has been viewed as evidence of an endogenous feeding rhythm that carries over into the adult period. Recent evidence in the rat pup and similar, less extensive evidence in the kitten (Shuleikina, 1977) suggest that this may not be the case at early stages of feeding development. The first evidence of this was the finding by Hall, Cramer, and Blass (1977) that suckling-deprived pups and pups that had recently suckled became attached to nipples equally rapidly and suckled equally long until the age of 10 to 14 days. When artificial feeding by mouth tube was instituted in rat pups, it was found that at 5 days of age pups would continue to swallow milk until they were bulging and milk began to be regurgitated (Hall and Rosenblatt, 1977). Only then did they fail to swallow additional amounts of milk but after they had released the mother's dry nipple they were willing to reattach if put to the nipple. The only thing that seemed to prevent further sucking was sleep, which overcame them. This suggests that they are unable to inhibit suckling directly on the basis of stomach loading but only indirectly on the basis of reduced arousal. The regulation of suckling is therefore not yet based upon "hunger" but is based upon a general central arousal and activation of largely peripheral sensory mechanisms that elicit and sustain suckling until arousal declines and sleep intervenes (Rosenblatt, 1976).

Among kittens and a number of other mammals (i.e., pigs, monkeys, chimpanzees, and human infants) the young exhibit preferences for suckling on particular nipples and each young prefers a different nipple or nipple pair (Ewer, 1959, 1961; Rosenblatt, 1971). In kittens this develops around the second and third day. The establishment of nipple position preferences implies that the sensory basis for nipple grasping undergoes an important change at a very early age. This change is based upon learning but, more important, those features of nipples that initially elicit nipple grasping evidently lose some of their capacity to do so very rapidly and are partially replaced by new stimuli that are different for each of the nipple positions. Woll (unpublished) has shown that subtle tactile and olfactory differences between nipples could provide the basis for nipple position preferences in newborn kittens, and McFarlane (1975) has shown that human infants distinguish the odors of their own mother's breast pads from those of other mothers starting around the 6th day and developing ever further by the 10th day.

The experience of olfactory-based suckling responses to the mother may enable young to approach the mother, on the basis of vision and hearing, when these sensory systems become functional. Ivanitskii (cited in Rosenblatt, 1976) conditioned rabbit young to respond to an artificial odor associated with nipple searching while in close contact with the doe. This was completed at the 5th day; five days later when the odor was presented the young ran to the nestbox entrance where the mother usually entered to feed them for that day. As the feeding response developed, the olfactory stimulus acquired new behavioral responses although it had never been associated with these responses before.

Finally, Moltz and Leon (1973) and Leon (1975, 1977) have discovered an olfactory attractant emitted by the mother rat, starting around the end of the second week and continuing through the second month to which young respond by approaching her and, presumably, initiating suckling if given the opportunity. The odor source is a volatile component of the feces that the young ingest but it has been shown that simple exposure to the odor is sufficient without ingestion or suckling for it to become an attractant (Leon, 1977). An interesting aspect of this phenomenon is that young can learn to identify their own mother by the distinctive nature of this volatile component when mothers are fed different diets and under these conditions they approach the odor of their own mother but not that of another mother.

3. *Organization of Reproductive Behavior*

3.1. *Organization of Reproductive Cycles and Behavior*

Reproduction requires the coordination of physiological and behavioral processes in each of the partners and between the two partners. In addition, the pair as a unit must be coordinated with their ecological environment so that they breed at a time when nest or home sites are available, the weather is appropriate, and food and nesting material are available in sufficient supply. Moreover, when the young are born, the female and often the male must coordinate their behavior (and physiology, in the case of the lactating female) with the needs of the young to promote their care and survival. All of these coordinations are based upon stimulus interactions between the female and male and between the pair and their environment at the different stages of the reproductive cycle (Lehrman, 1961).

The discovery, in the late 1940s and early 1950s, of a vascular connection between the hypothalamus of the brain and the anterior pituitary gland, that portion that secretes the gonadal stimulating hormones and prolactin, the lactogenic hormone, largely through the work of Geoffrey Harris and Charles H. Sawyer (see Lehrman, 1959), opened up the possibility of explaining how social and environmental stimuli could influence the reproductive functioning of animals. It was known that many birds and mammals were responsive to seasonal changes in daylength and that they became reproductive as daylength increased during the spring. Moreover, it has been shown that lactation in many mammals was dependent upon suckling stimulation for the production of milk and its release from the mammary glands (Selye, 1934; Ingelbrecht, 1935; see reviews of Grosvenor and Mena, 1974). The discover of the hypothalamic-anterior pituitary connection enables us to understand how external stimuli of various kinds (Hinde, 1965; Lehrman, 1959, 1961, 1965) cause the release of pituitary hormones, which in turn stimulate the secretion of hormones from the gonads and many other endocrine glands (i.e., adrenal glands, thyroid glands, etc.).

Several investigators, among them Daniel S. Lehrman and Robert A. Hinde, were quick to realize the significance of these findings for the analysis of reproductive cycles among birds. The outcome of long series of studies on the ring dove by Lehrman (1965) and on the canary by Hinde (1965), and their colleagues and students, are summarized in Figures 2* and 3. They portray that in both species increasing daylength, as well as diurnal cyclicity of light and dark, initiate the reproductive cycles of both male and female by action on the gonads via the release of the pituitary gonadotrophic hormones (follicle stimulating hormone= FHS and luteinizing hormone= LH). The release of gonadal hormones initiates sexual behavior in the females and males of both species and starts the sequence of physiological changes that eventuates in maturation of ovarian follicles, ovulation, and egg-lay-

*This figure was made in collaboration with Dr. Mei-Fang Cheng.

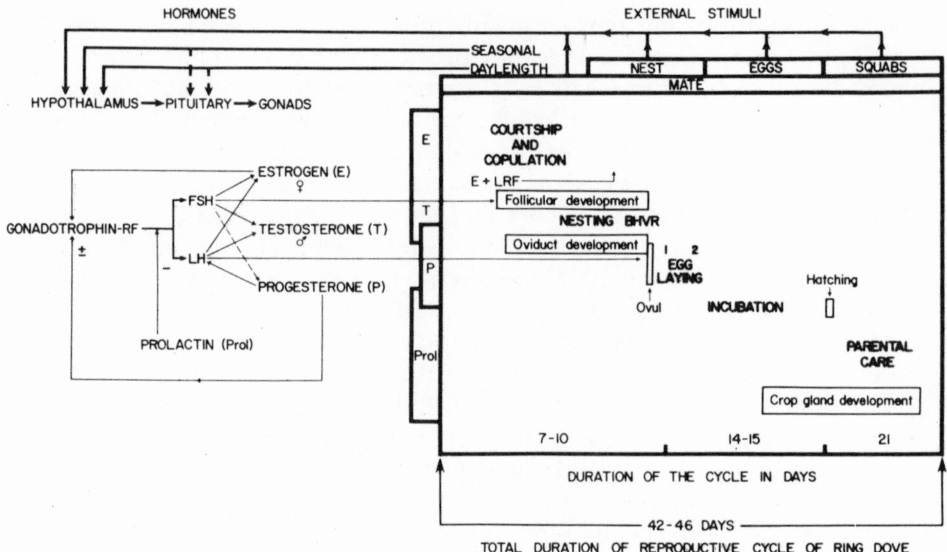

FIGURE 2. Reproductive cycle of the ring dove. The principal behavioral phases are shown chronologically in the center along with the main physiological changes during the cycle. External stimuli associated with each behavioral phase are shown along the top. Hormonal secretions associated with behavioral and physiological changes are shown on the left for males and females. The role of external stimuli in eliciting release of pituitary hormones via the hypothalamus and directly is shown along the top of the figure. Plus and minus indicate stimulatory and inhibitory relationships; unmarked arrows indicate stimulatory relationships.

ing. Associated with these ovarian hormones are various other effects on the reproductive tract (oviduct) and, in the canary, on the ventral skin surface that develops into the richly vascularized, defeathered brood patch, highly sensitive to tactile stimuli from the nest and later the eggs (Fig. 3). Lack of a brood patch in the ring dove does not preclude similar changes in vascularity and sensitivity that play an important role in incubation.

In addition to potentiating courtship and sexual behavior (Cheng, 1973; Cheng and Lehrman, 1975) the gonadal hormones also stimulate nestbuilding in both species although the participation of male and female in nestbuilding and nestbuilding itself is different in the two species. These behavioral interactions between the male and female play an important role in advancing their hormonal conditions to the next stage of the cycle. They include the song of the male in the canary and male calls in the ring dove. In the budgerigar Brockway (1965, 1969) and Steele, Gosney, and Hinde (1977) have shown that the soft

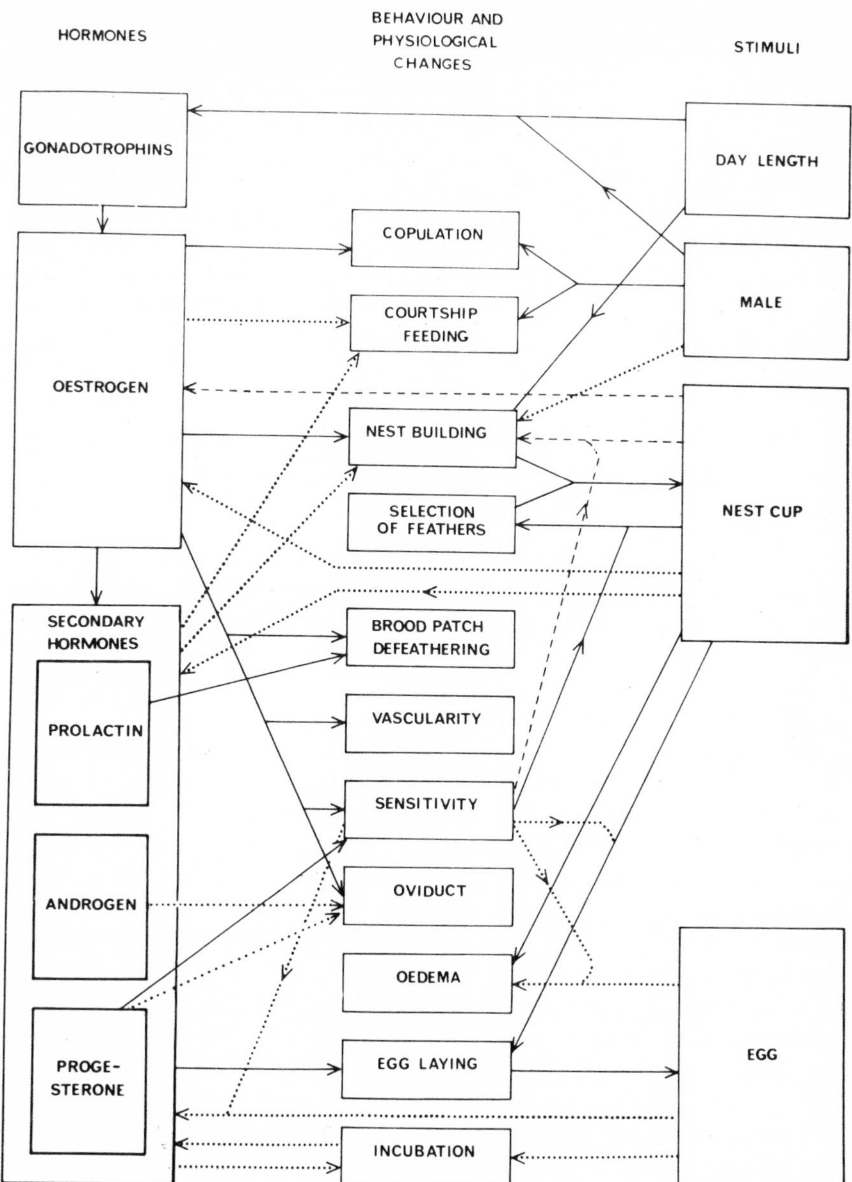

FIGURE 3. Reproductive cycle in the canary. Behavioral and physiological changes are shown in the center, external stimuli associated with these changes are shown on the right, and hormonal secretions are shown on the left. Continuous lines indicate positive effects; discontinuous lines indicate negative effects; dotted lines indicate probable positive relationships not yet certainly established. (Modified from R. A. Hinde, Interaction of internal and external factors in integration of canary reproduction. In F. A. Beach (Ed.), *Sex and behavior.* New York. Wiley, 1965. Reprinted with permission.)

warble of the male is necessary to advance the female through the phases of the reproductive cycle and in the ring dove male calls play a role, though a minor one, in advancing the female to ovulation and egg-laying (Friedman, 1972; Lott and Brody, 1966; Lott, Scholz, and Lehrman, 1967).

Lehrman proposed that courtship played an important role in stimulating ovarian development and the associated physiological and behavioral changes (Cheng, 1974). Friedman (1977) has recently determined the contribution of various aspects of the male's courtship behavior to the female's physiological changes. Using follicular development and oviduct growth as endpoints of hormonal changes, Friedman caged females with a male such that some females received only visual stimulation of courtship while others received only auditory stimulation. Still others received both but not from a male that was actively courting them. Finally, some females were directly courted by the male, and other females viewed the male's courtship behavior at the same time.

Only the female that was directly courted by the male underwent full ovarian development and ovulation; those receiving visual, auditory, or visual and auditory (indirect) stimulation underwent various degrees of development short of complete development. Non-stimulated females remained in quiescent condition. Friedman suggests that an important aspect of courtship, in addition to the particular visual and auditory displays, is the synchrony of interaction between the male and female: When the female performs a courtship behavior the male responds within a short time, a condition that pertained only to those females that were directly courted by males (Lambe and Erickson, 1973). Morris and Erickson (1971) have shown in addition that there is individual recognition of the male by the female, developed during one cycle that is retained during the next cycle, and reproduction is more efficient as a consequence. Gerlach, Heinrich, and Lehrman (1975) and Silver and Wallman (personal communication) have shown how the initial male–female synchrony established during courtship is carried into the incubation phase and may form the basis for pattern of sharing incubation that develops when the eggs are laid.

In the ring dove, where analysis of the reproductive cycle has been extended into the phase of incubation and parental care, the role of the eggs and young as stimuli causing the release of hormones has been explored more than in the canary (Fig. 2). Incubation of the eggs, initiated by the combined actions of estrogen and progesterone (Cheng and Silver, 1975), appears to turn to stimulate the release of progesterone and eventually to initiate the release of prolactin, the hormone that is involved in crop gland development, crop milk production, and parental care. Both sexes share in incubation but what is remarkable is that the male need only participate in actual sitting on the eggs at the beginning of incubation (during laying of the first and second eggs), then he can be removed to a neighboring cage where he can see the female sitting on the eggs and he will remain in incubating conditon with full growth of the crop gland (Friedman and Lehrman, 1968).

The crop gland develops up to a certain size during incubation but cannot be made to grow larger by artificially extending the period of incubation either in the male or in the female (Buntin, 1977). For further development and milk-production, stimuli from squabs are necessary and normally they hatch at this time. Buntin (1977) investigated the aspects of squab stimulation that promote crop development, via the release of prolactin, and found that there are very special conditions under which the squabs have this effect and that these differ slightly in the male and female. Both require the presence of the squabs nearby; that is, the squabs must be in the nest occupied by the parent but the male requires actual contact with the squabs in addition to visual and auditory stimulation while the female requires only auditory stimulation and the visual presence of the squabs.

Of course, not all of the stimulus-induced behavioral changes during the reproductive cycles of the ring dove and canary are a direct consequence of hormones acting on the nervous system to elicit these behaviors. Some are based on peripherally induced changes, which in turn make the animal susceptible to external stimuli in a new way. The canary brood patch mentioned above is a good example of this: at a certain stage in nestbuilding, correlated with the full development of the brood patch, the canary begins to use feathers to line the nest interior in contrast to its previous use of twigs to construct the nest. Hinde, Bell, and Steel (1963) have shown that the brood patch becomes very sensitive at this time, and it may be that the shift from the use of a coarse, possibly irritating nest material to a soft material is governed by this change in brood patch sensitivity (Fig. 3).

Hinde and his co-workers have provided strong evidence that in addition to stimulating the release of hormones via the hypothalamic-pituitary-gonadal axis, external stimuli may affect behavioral responsiveness of female canaries to these hormones. In particular, certain photoperiod schedules result in a greater action of estrogen on nestbuilding (Steel and Hinde, 1976); the same effect can be produced by male song played to female canaries during certain photoperiod schedules (Hinde and Steel, 1976).

Another example is the attachment of the ring dove to its nest and eggs during incubation. This would seem to be caused directly by hormonal stimulation (i.e., progesterone) since not until prolactin has been secreted for some time at the end of incubation do the parents shift their attention to the squabs when they hatch (Fig. 2). Moore (1976) tested females during the first and second breeding cycles for their readiness to choose squabs over nest and eggs at various times during incubation. During the first cycle, nest and eggs were chosen predominantly until shortly before hatching but during the second cycle, after the previous breeding experience of making the transition from nest and eggs to squabs, and after engaging in parental care of the squabs, the squabs were chosen in preference to nest and eggs during early incubation. The hormonal state of the parents does not dictate directly the nature of the choice but during the first breeding cycle this state—in conjunction with the previous attachment to the nest alone, then the nest and eggs during earlier phases of the first breeding cycle—favors the nest and eggs over the new stimulus of the squabs.

In the lizard *Anolis carolinensis* courtship stimulation is essential for follicular maturation and ovulation in the female. While seasonal thermal and photoperiodic stimuli can initiate ovarian maturation, the female depends upon the male's courtship bobbing for the release of the ovulation-promoting hormone LH (Crews, Rosenblatt, and Lehrman, 1974; Crews, 1975). Thus, the dependence of reproductive cycles in the female (and in the male, also) found in many birds and in several mammals has its evolutionary history among reptiles so far as they have been studied.

There is another stimulus-based reproductive phenomenon among these lizards that is perhaps of greater significance since in no other species has this been demonstrated so convincingly. If females in seasonal breeding condition are exposed to males that have not yet established territories and dominance relationships and therefore are still engaged in territorial disputes, their ovaries are actively inhibited from further development and many regress to an earlier maturational phase (Crews, 1975). This is not based simply upon lack of courtship stimulation since castrated males that do not exhibit courtship also do not produce this effect. It is an effect of the aggressive behavior among the males that is occasionally directed at the nearby females. In nature, interestingly enough, females avoid male aggression by not emerging from winter hibernation until the males have become established in their territories and dominance relationships among them have been settled.

3.2. Reproductive Behavior in the Rat

The reproductive cycle in the rat represents only one kind of reproductive strategy that has evolved among mammals but it has characteristics that are common to many species. In discussing this species we shall be able to illustrate the many ways in which external stimuli govern reproduction among mammals. A complete review of even this aspect of the reproductive cycle in the rat is beyond the scope of this article; therefore, we will restrict ourselves to a few selected examples that have received the attention of investigators. These will include the role of copulatory stimuli in the onset of pregnancy in the female, the role of self-licking in mammary gland development during pregnancy, the role of external stimuli in maternal behavior and physiology, and the role of pup stimulation in lactation.

3.2.1. Copulation and Onset of Pregnancy. The mating pattern of the male rat consists of multiple intromissions followed by a single ejaculation. Usually there are 10 intromissions before ejaculation during the first mating and 7 during the next, which may be initiated between 5 and 10 minutes after the first (Sachs and Barfield, 1976). By experimentally limiting the number of intromissions received by a female prior to ejaculation, Adler and his co-workers (see review by Adler, 1974) have shown that a minimum of four intromissions before ejaculation is required for the female to become pregnant. Fewer than 3 intromissions fails to initiate pregnancy but the fault does not lie with the ejaculate. The male's behavior is normal, he has completed the full series of intromissions, but the female has not received the full number of intromissions. Four or more intromissions are required to stimulate the vaginal region sufficiently to cause the release of prolactin from the pituitary gland. This hormone, in turn, stimulates progesterone secretion and the formation of corpora lutea, which are essential for initiating and maintaining pregnancy.

Intromission also plays a role in fertilization by affecting the transport of sperm to the ova via the opening between the cervix and the uterus. The mechanical stimulation of vaginal and cervical sensory receptors by the penis during intromission and ejaculation relaxes cervical-utero sphincter muscles and this is aided by neural and neurohumoral effects that accompany this stimulation. For sperm to enter the uterus in sufficient numbers, however, it is necessary that a vaginal plug be fitted in the opening of the cervix to effect transcervical transport to the uterus. The male and female provide the conditions for the formation of this plug and its positioning in the cervical opening by their behavior during ejaculation: both remain immobile for several seconds after the male expels the ejaculate with a force sufficient to fit it into the opening and to seal it tightly against loss of sperm (Matthews and Adler, 1977). One factor aiding in this process of immobilization may be the induced anesthesia to painful tactile stimulation that cervical stimulation produces as shown by Komisaruk (1974).

The male mating pattern is well suited to its function of impregnating the female and ensuring that the sperm reach the ova to fertilize them. It also creates the hormonal conditions for subsequent implantation of the blastocyst and onset of pregnancy. Even the male's refractory period after ejaculation is adapted to the female's reproductive processes: If he were to remount and copulate again too soon after the previous ejaculation and the female were to receive several intromissions within 2 or 3 minutes after ejaculation, the vaginal plug would be dislodged and only a relatively small number of sperm would reach the uterus to fertilize the ova. The female requires about 4 minutes after receiving the first ejaculate for her to be immune to the effects of a single additional intromission. After 8–10 minutes, however, even 3 intromissions do not reduce the number of sperm entering the uterus. Males tend to recover from postejaculatory refractoriness and they begin mounting and achieving intromission again after 6–7 minutes and their third intromission does not occur until close to 8 minutes afterward. By the time they resume mating, sperm from the previous ejaculation have had the opportunity to fertilize the ova (Matthews and Adler, 1977).

Estrous cycling in the female rat and in many mammalian species is a seemingly smoothly running endocrine pattern from the beginning of follicle development to ovulation and recycling. In certain species, such as the rabbit, cat, and ferret, follicular development stops short of ovulation and the stimulus of mating is required for ovulation and postovulatory neuroendocrine changes to occur. These changes have been studied in great detail in the rabbit and involve copulatory stimulus-induced release of pituitary hormone (luteinizing hormone-LH), which induces ovulation and formation of corpora leutea (Everett, 1961; Rosenblatt, 1967). This should alert us to the possibility that sensory stimuli are involved in the estrous cycle of the female. This has been found to be true at every phase of the estrous cycle (Rosenblatt, 1967).

Females maintained in constant light fail to exhibit estrous cycling and instead they enter what is called constant estrus; they remain at the preovulatory stage, secreting large amounts of estrogen. Under normal circumstances, therefore, light advances follicular development to the point of ovulation but daily alternation of dark/light is required to release LH. Other stimuli may also be effective in releasing LH and for inducing ovulation and the accompanying sexual behavior in females that have been maintained in constant estrus (Brown-Grant, Davidson, and Grieg, 1973).

M. Johns in our laboratory, has shown that not only copulation but also mounting by males and male odor or the odor of bedding soiled by male urine can be effective in stimulating ovulation in 50 to

100% of females. Any stressful stimulus (e.g., ether, new cage, etc.) can also have this effect.

That females are susceptible to external stimulus control of their estrous cycling has been shown in studies in which females that have been housed together develop synchronized patterns of estrous cycling (McClintock, unpublished). A similar phenomenon has been reported among college women sharing dormitory rooms and spending many hours together. At the beginning of the college year menstrual cycles were unsynchronized and essentially randomly distributed among all the women but after several months of living in pairs or small groups, the synchrony of menstrual cycling was greater with pairs or groups than among women living individually. A related finding was that the length of menstrual cycles was shorter by a few days, at most, among women who had two or more contacts with males, even of a nonsexual character, than those who did not (McClintock, 1971).

3.2.2. Self-Licking and Mammary Gland Development during Pregnancy. Pregnancy is behaviorally a rather quiescent period, considering the enormous physiological changes and the period of intense maternal activity that is to follow after the young are born. Among the rather subtle changes that occur is the pattern of self-licking as the female's pregnancy advances. Birch (1956) had noted that self-licking of the genital region increases before parturition but Roth and Rosenblatt (1967) found that more prominent was the increase in self-licking of the nipple regions. After midpregnancy there is an increase in licking of the nipple regions and genital area (i.e., what we have labeled "critical areas" because they are undergoing physiological changes during pregnancy (see Fig. 4), and a corresponding decrease in licking of anterior, noncritical body regions.

This raised the possibility that self-licking is an early form of stimulation required to promote mammary gland function since it has been known for some time that after parturition suckling stimulation is required to maintain the mammary glands. To test this possibility Roth and Rosenblatt (1968) reared pregnant females with wide rubber collars to prevent self-licking during pregnancy. They found that the mammary glands of such females were retarded in development by more than 50%, in terms of the amount of secretory tissue and milk production that was normally present at 22 days, shortly before parturition. Stress was ruled out as a factor since formalin-stressed females showed greater development of the mammary glands, not less.

Herrenkohl (formerly Roth) and Campbell (1976) have done the study that was required to confirm the effect of stimulation of the mammary region on mammary gland development. Pregnant collared

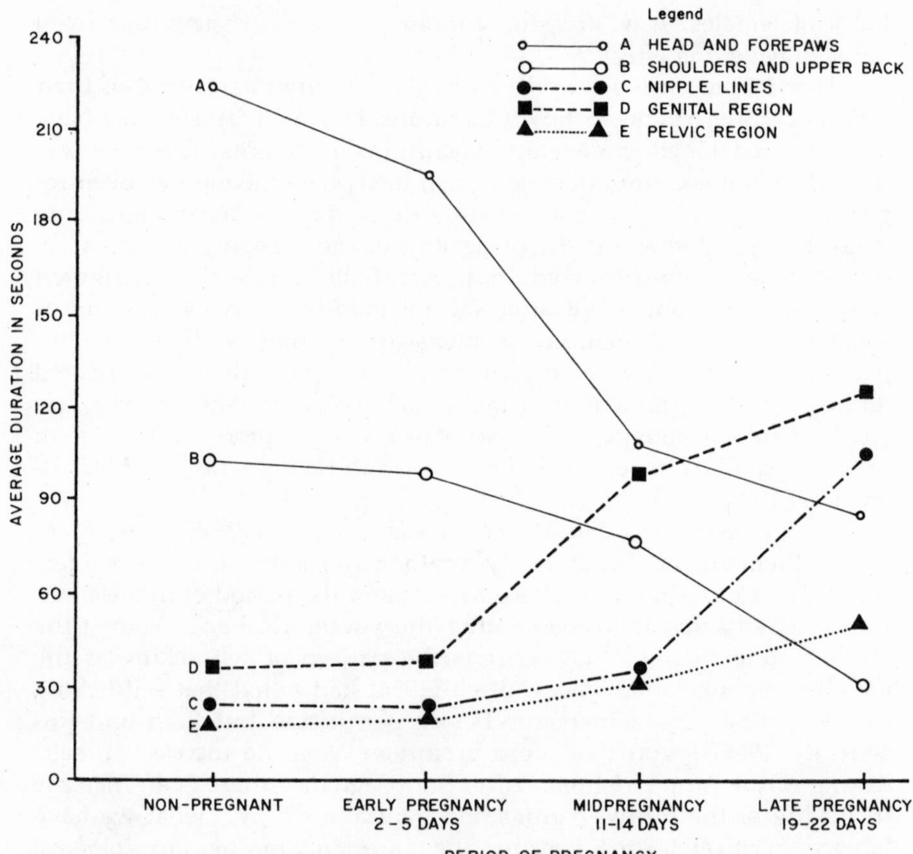

FIGURE 4. Self-licking by females during pregnancy and while nonpregnant. Noncritical body regions (*A* and *B*) and critical body regions (*C, D,* and *E*) are indicated. (From L.L. Roth and J.S. Rosenblatt, Changes in self-licking during pregnancy in the rat, *Journal of Comparative and Physiological Psychology*, *63*, 397–400, copyright 1967 by the American Psychological Association, reprinted by permission.)

females, unable to lick their mammary regions, were stimulated mechanically by means of a machine-driven brush for 30 minutes each day during 22 days of pregnancy. At the end of this period their mammary glands were fully developed, equal to those of noncollared females but various control groups employed to determine the effects of stress, motor sounds, etc. were severely retarded in gland development. Interestingly, virgins stimulated in this way also exhibited considerable mammary gland development.

The implication of all of these findings is that self-licking causes the release of hormones that stimulate mammary gland development and milk formation, toward the end of pregnancy. An alternative explanation was proposed by McMurtry and Anderson (1971), who were able to confirm the above findings using a more refined biochemical method for measuring mammary gland activity in collared and noncollared pregnant females. They proposed that self-licking has a local effect on the mammary glands that enables lactogenic hormones (i.e., prolactin, growth hormone, and adrenocorticotrophic hormone) to have a greater effect on mammary gland development, rather than that the secretion of these hormones is directly affected by the self-licking.

The findings of Whitworth (1972) tend to support the hormone release hypothesis. By using a narrow collar that prevented pregnant females from licking their anterior nipples but allowed them to lick their genital region, and removing the posterior set of nipples and mammary glands, he was able to show that the remaining mammary glands were not retarded in development but had normal amounts of secretory tissue and milk. The converse experiment, surgically desensitizing the genital area and allowing females to lick their nipples and mammary region, also produced normal mammary gland development. It would be difficult to see how licking the genital region can affect the local condition of the anterior mammary glands; a more reasonable hypothesis is that the effect of licking is systemic and is based upon the release of lactogenic hormones (Kolodny, Jacobs, and Daughaday, 1972).

3.2.3. The Role of External Stimuli in Maternal Behavior and Reproductive Physiology. The onset of maternal behavior in the rat is closely associated with the hormonal changes that take place around parturition. Terkel and Rosenblatt (1968, 1971) were able to stimulate maternal behavior in nonpregnant females by injecting them intravenously with small amounts of blood from postpartum mothers and by cross transfusing blood from mothers within 6 hours of parturition. On the basis of these and additional studies on pregnant females that were hysterectomized (i.e., uterus, placentas and fetuses removed) at various times during pregnancy (Rosenblatt and Siegel, 1975), Siegel and Rosenblatt (1975a,b) were able to isolate estrogen as the hormone that most likely stimulates the onset of maternal behavior—not at parturition, as was believed, but before parturition, during the last 24 hours (Rosenblatt and Siegel, 1975; Slotnick, Carpenter, and Fusco, 1973).

After parturition there is a rapid change in the pattern of hormonal secretion as the female, her estrous cycling suspended throughout pregnancy, now undergoes a single estrous cycle, the postpartum estrus. If a male is present she mates with him about eight hours after parturition and she can become pregnant as a result of this mating. At the same time she begins to lactate and exhibit maternal care toward her current litter (Rosenblatt and Lehrman, 1963). The hormonal conditions that gave rise to maternal behavior before parturition are no longer present yet the female continues to exhibit maternal behavior.

These facts, and others yet to be described, have led to the idea that once maternal behavior is initiated on the basis of the hormonal secretions of late pregnancy, it is no longer maintained by these hormones but is dependent solely upon pup stimulation, except of course for the hormones required to maintain lactation and milk let-down. Thus, one can remove the ovaries, the pituitary gland, and adrenal glands immediately after parturition without affecting maternal behavior (although lactation may suffer) and one can inject various hormones, also without effect (see review by Rosenblatt, 1970).

On the other hand, if the pups are removed during parturition and are not returned to the mother until four days later, then the mothers shows no evidence of maternal behavior (Rosenblatt, 1970, 1975; Rosenblatt and Lehrman, 1963). She is dependent upon pup stimulation to maintain the maternal condition that was initially established hormonally. Bridges (1977) has shown that as little as a few minutes contact with pups during parturition (i.e., handling and cleaning every other pup delivered by the mother) is sufficient to enable females to respond to pups fairly rapidly five weeks later. The maintenance of maternal behavior is therefore nonhormonal and based upon external stimulation from the pups.

It is possible to stimulate maternal behavior in estrous cycling females directly by exposing them to pups continuously for several days (Cosnier and Couturier, 1966; Rosenblatt, 1967). Once established, this behavior resembles both quantitatively and qualitatively the behavior of lactating mothers rearing progressively older pups (Fleming and Rosenblatt, 1974a; Reisbick, Rosenblatt, and Mayer, 1975), including the decline of maternal behavior during the third week "postpartum." These facts suggest that there is a strongly developed nonhormonal mechanism for maternal behavior and that it is this mechanism that is called into play by the pups after hormones have triggered the onset of maternal behavior.

The research cited above leads us to suggest that the regulation of maternal behavior undergoes a shift from the hormonal to the nonhormonal mechanism during the first few hours after parturition and the nonhormonal basis becomes more firmly established during the first two or three days postpartum. During this transition period the female is particularly vulnerable to disturbances that might interfere with her care of the young. It is significant, we believe, that when rats breed in overly crowded conditions (Calhoun, 1962) abandonment of the young is confined almost entirely to the first three days; if the mother takes care of the young through this transition period it is unlikely that she will subsequently abandon them.

The discovery of pup-induced maternal behavior in nonpregnant females has enabled us to study the stimulus basis of maternal behavior and to speculate about the mechanisms underlying the onset of maternal behavior. Females initially show some hesitation about approaching and remaining in the vicinity of pups and it requires five or six days of continuous exposure before they overcome this aversion. This can be speeded by confining them in a small cage with the pups and then they exhibit maternal behavior much more rapidly (Terkel and Rosenblatt, 1971).

Pup odors seem to be the basis for the female's aversion to the pups. This was first indicated in studies in which anosmic females (i.e., by removal of the olfactory bulbs) in a few cases responded maternally to pups within 24 hours of their first exposure to them. Anosmia or reduced olfaction can also be produced by intranasal infusion of zinc sulfate, a substance that destroys the olfactory sensory cells, and this also has the effect of inducing rapid onset of maternal behavior. Of course, when the lateral olfactory tracts are lesioned, producing anosmia, a similar effect on maternal behavior is observed (Fleming and Rosenblatt, 1974b,c).

The need to overcome the aversive odors of the pups was nicely demonstrated in a study in which females were treated with zinc sulfate and became maternal in less than one day. However, these females had not overcome the aversive effect of pup odors. The anosmia produced by zinc sulfate is reversible and olfactory function returns in three days to two weeks. After it had returned, the females were once again exposed to pups and this time they required more than 2.5 days to exhibit several components of maternal behavior (Mayer and Rosenblatt, 1975).

Females undergoing parturition show little evidence of an aversion for the newly delivered pups and they exhibit maternal behavior almost immediately. Evidently the phenomenon seen in nonpregnant females is not present in these animals. It may be that the hormones of late pregnancy alter the olfactory sensitivity of the female and the odors are not aversive; these kinds of effects of hormones are known. On the other hand, it may also be that the females have become familiar with the odors that they find on the pups during their self-licking while pregnant. This was Birch's (1956) original proposal and it is not outside the realm of possibility since females do lick the birth fluids that are present on the genital region and these are also present on the young when they are born.

Stimulation by the pups has a number of additional effects upon the mother other than those associated with the maintenance and the decline of maternal behavior. These include the regulation of lactation and control over the entire reproductive physiology of the female. It is beyond the scope of this article to present a full discussion of these topics but a short review of the major points will highlight the degree to which external stimuli regulate the reproductive physiology of the female in a way that is adaptive to both the female's reproductive potential and the needs of the young.

Although mothers may mate successfully during postpartum estrus, implantation of the blastocysts and therefore the start of gestation is under the control of the pups. Their suckling causes an inhibition of FSH (follicles stimulating hormone) and LH release (Rothchild, 1960; Lu, Chen, Grandison, Huang, and Meites, 1976), thereby preventing the secretion of estrogen necessary for implantation at this time when progesterone secretion is already adequate for implantation. The length of the inhibition varies from a few days to up to thirteen days, depending upon the number of suckling pups. Typical litters range from 9 to 12 pups and this is sufficient to produce the maximal duration of delayed implantation. By delaying the implantation of new embryos for 13 days, the suckling pups are assured completion of their own weaning before the new litter appears, about 35 days after their own birth (Mayer, 1963; Nutting and Meyer, 1963; Shelesnyak and Kraicer, 1963).

3.2.4. Lactation and Pup Stimulation. Two of the earliest endocrine responses found to be under the regulation of external stimuli are suckling-induced release of prolactin and oxytocin (Cowie and Folley, 1961; Grosvenor and Mena, 1974). Both of these pup-stimulated endocrine responses on the part of the mother are essential for lactation: prolactin (along with ACTH and other hormones that form the lactogenic complex) is responsible for milk production, and oxytocin for milk let-down or the emptying of milk from the alveoli into the mammary ducts where it can be expressed by the young during sucking.

Although both endocrine responses are based upon suckling stimulation they function in different ways: suckling induces an immediate release of prolactin that continues for the duration of the feeding (Grosvenor and Whitworth, 1976). The prolactin released during one suckling bout is responsible for the milk produced eight hours later and plays no role in production of the milk that is obtained during the suckling bout. Oxytocin, on the other hand, plays an immediate role in suckling and without it pups receive no milk: it is released at intervals, in spurts that, in turn, causes a stream of milk to be expelled into the pups' mouths and throats (Vorheer, Kleeman, and Lehman, 1967).

The reflex release of prolactin and oxytocin can be conditioned to stimuli associated with suckling in advance of the actual stimulation of suckling itself. Grosvenor (1965) and Grosvenor, Maiweg, and Mena (1970) found that after the seventh day, in primiparous mothers, the presence of pups nearby was sufficient to elicit the release of prolactin without the need for actual suckling (i.e., exteroceptive stimuli). Zarrow, Schlein, Denenberg, and Cohen (1972) subsequently found that ACTH, another hormone of the lactogenic complex, was also released by exteroceptive stimuli associated with the pups. Milk let-down, the response to oxytocin, has been conditioned to stimuli associated with nursing in a number of animals and is often seen in human mothers in response to the crying of their infants (Vuorenkoski, Wasz-Höckert, Koivisto, and Lind, 1969).

In view of the fact that young need not suckle in order to cause the release of prolactin and therefore continued milk production, even the decline in suckling in rat pups around three weeks of age would not explain why lactation comes to an end during the fourth week. Grosvenor and his co-workers (Grosvenor and Mena, 1974) have discovered an ingenious mechanism: when pups reach the age of 21 days, in addition to prolactin release, their behavior stimulates the release of some other hormone, presumably an adrenocortical hormone, which blocks the action of prolactin on the mammary glands. Behaviorally it can be observed that the female begins to reject the suckling attempts of the young and to avoid the pups (Reisbick *et al.*, 1975). The corresponding endocrine response is apparently related to stress produced by the activity of the young at this later age. Its effect, however, is to reduce and eventually terminate milk production by the mother.

4. Summary and Overview

Our review has shown that in behavioral development and reproductive behavior and physiology among birds and mammals external stimuli play an important role. The avian embryo exposed to calls by the parent, to sibling and self-produced vocalizations and sounds, learns to respond to these calls posthatching or is synchronized in hatching with its siblings. The mammalian newborn suckles from the mother on the basis of the stimuli she provides first to guide it to her nipples and second to enable it to grasp the nipple and suck. At each stage in its suckling development external stimuli, eventually in the form of social stimuli, contribute to the development of the pattern of feeding. The reproductive cycles of the ring dove and canary provide excellent examples of the role of external stimuli in the organization of behavior. External stimuli elicit behavior from the mate as immediate effects and as long-term effects, cause the release of hormones that in turn affect the behavior of the partners. The maternal behavior of the rat is largely dependent upon external stimulation from the pups after birth and lactation is stimulated by these sensory stimuli both before and after delivery.

External stimuli are effective during development and during reproduction in an ultimate sense because all behavior must be adaptive to the ecological and social environment in which an animal lives. This adaptation is based upon stimuli that the environment provides that signal information vital to the animal's survival. A sharp dichotomy between external and internal determinants of behavior is therefore inaccurate since the effectiveness of external stimuli depends upon their ability to affect internal processes and in all cases that have been studied, internal processes are susceptible to influence as an inherent characteristic of their functioning.

References

Adler, N.T. The behavioral control of reproductive physiology. In W. Montagna, and W.H. Sadler (Eds.), *Reproductive behavior.* New York: Academic Press, 1974.

Alcock, J. *Animal behavior, an evolutionary approach.* Sunderland, Mass.: Sinauer Associated Publishers, 1975.

Anokhin, P.K. and Shuleikina, K. V. System organization of alimentary behavior in the newborn and the developing cat. *Developmental Psychobiology,* 1977, *10,* 385–419.

Beach, F.A. *Hormones and behavior.* New York: Hoeber, 1948.

Becker, R.F., Windle, W.F., Barth, E.E., and Schulz, M.D. Fetal swallowing, gastro-intestinal activity and defecation in amino. *Surgery, Gynecology, and Obstetrics,* 1940, *70,* 603–614.

Beer, C.G. On the responses of laughing gull chicks (Larus atricilla) to the calls of adults. I. Recognition of the voices of parents. *Animal Behaviour,* 1970a, *18,* 652–660.

Beer, C.G. On the responses of laughing gull chicks (Larus atricilla) to the calls of the adults. II. Age changes and responses to different types of call. *Animal Behaviour,* 1970b, *18,* 661–677.

Beer, C.G. Individual recognition of voice and its development in birds. *Proceedings of the 15th international ornithological congress,* 1972, pp. 339–356.

Birch, H.G. Sources of order in the maternal behavior of animals. *American Journal of Orthopsychiatry,* 1956, *26,* 279–284.

Bradley, R.M., and Mistretta, C.M. Investigations of taste function and swallowing in fetal sheep. In J.F. Bosma (Ed.), *Fourth symposium on oral sensation and perception: Development in the fetus and infant,* 1973.

Brazelton, T.B., Koslowski, B., and Main, M. The origins of reciprocity: The early mother–infant interaction. In M. Lewis and L.A. Rosenblum (Eds.), *The effect of the infant on its caregiver.* New York: Wiley, 1974, pp. 49–76.

Bridges, R.S. Long-term effects of pregnancy and parturition upon maternal responsiveness in the rat. *Physiology and Behavior,* 1975, *14,* 245–249.

Bridges, R.S. Parturition: Its role in the long term retention of maternal behavior in the rat. *Physiology and Behavior,* 1977, *18,* 487–490.

Brockway, B.F. Stimulation of ovarian development and egg laying by male courtship vocalization in budgerigars (Melopsittacus undulatus). *Animal Behaviour,* 1965, *13,* 575–578.

Brockway, B.F. Roles of budgerigar vocalization in the integration of breeding behavior. In R.A. Hinde (Ed.), *Bird vocalizations.* Cambridge, England: Cambridge University Press, 1969, pp. 131–158.

Brown-Grant, K., Davidson, J.M. and Grieg, F. Induced ovulation in albino rats exposed to constant light. *Journal of Endocrinology,* 1973, *57,* 7–22.

Buntin, J. Stimulus factors involved in squab induced crop sac growth and nest occupation in ring doves (Streptopelia risoria). *Journal of Comparative and Physiological Psychology,* 1977, *91,* 17–28.

Calhoun, J.B. A "behavioral sink." In E.L. Bliss (Ed.), *Roots of behavior.* New York: Harper, 1962.

Cheng, M.F. Effect of ovariectomy on the reproductive behavior of female ring doves (Streptopelia risoria). *Journal of Comparative and Physiological Psychology,* 1973, *83,* 221–223.

Cheng, M.F. Ovarian development in the female ring dove in response to stimulation by intact and castrated male ring doves. *Journal of Endocrinology,* 1974, *63,* 43–53.

Cheng, M.F., and Lehrman, D.S. Gonadal hormone specificity in the sexual behavior of ring doves. *Psychoneuroendocrinology,* 1975, *1,* 95–102.

Cheng, M.F., and Silver, R. Estrogen-progesterone regulation of nest building and incubation behavior in ovariectomized ring doves (Streptopelia risoria). *Journal of Comparative and Physiological Psychology,* 1975, *88,* 256–263.

Clements, M. and Lien, J. Paired rotation and auditory stimulation of common murre (Uria aalge aalge) embryos and its posthatch effect. *Behavioral Biology,* 1976, *17,* 417–423.

Cosnier, J., and Couturier, C. Comportement maternel provoqué chez les rattes adultes castrées. *Comptes Rendus des Séances de la Société de Biologie, Paris,* 1966, *160,* 789–791.

Cowie, A.T., and Folley, S.J. The mammary gland and lactation. In W.C. Young (Ed.), *Sex and internal secretions* (Vol. 1). Baltimore: Williams & Wilkins, 1961.

Crews, D., Rosenblatt, J.S., and Lehrman, D.S. Effects of unseasonal environmental regime, group presence, group composition, and male's physiological state on ovarian recrudescence in the lizard, Anolis carolinensis. *Endocrinology,* 1974, *94,* 541–547.

Crews, D. Psychobiology of reptilian reproduction. *Science,* 1975, *189,* 1059–1065.

Crook, J.H. Social organization and the environment: Aspects of contemporary social ethology. *Animal Behaviour,* 1970, *18,* 197–209.

Crook, J.H., and Gartlan, J.S. Evolution of primate societies. *Nature,* 1966, *210,* 1200–1203.

Diakow, C. Male–female interactions and the organization of mammalian mating patterns. In D.S. Lehrman, R.A. Hinde, J.S. Rosenblatt, and E. Shaw (Eds.), *Advances in the study of behavior* (Vol. 5). New York: Academic Press, 1974.

Everett, J.W. The mammalian female reproductive cycle and its controlling mechanisms. In W. C. Young (Ed.), *Sex and internal secretions* (Vol. 1). Baltimore: Williams & Wilkins, 1961.

Ewer, R.F. Sucking behavior in kittens. *Behaviour*, 1959, *15*, 146–162.

Ewer, R.F. Further observations on suckling behavior in kittens together with some general consideration of the interrelations of innate and acquired responses. *Behaviour*, 1961, *17*, 247–260.

Fleming, A.S., and Rosenblatt, J.S. Maternal behavior in the virgin and lactating rat. *Journal of Compartive and Physiological Psychology*, 1974a, *86*, 957–972.

Fleming, A.S., and Rosenblatt, J.S. Olfactory regulation of maternal behavior in rats. I. Effects of olfactory bulb removal in experienced and inexperienced lactating and cycling females. *Journal of Comparative and Physiological Psychology*, 1974b, *86*, 233–246.

Fleming, A.S., and Rosenblatt, J.S. Olfactory regulation of maternal behavior in rats: II. Effects of peripherally induced anosmia and lesions of the lateral olfactory tract in pup-induced virgins. *Journal of Comparative and Physiological Psychology*, 1974c, *86*, 233–246.

Freeman, B.M., and Vince, M.A. Development of the avian embryo. Part I. In B.M. Freeman and M.A. Vince (Eds.), *Development of the avian embryo, a behavioral and physiological study*. London: Chapman and Hall, 1974.

Freeman, N.C.G., and Rosenblatt, J.S. The interrelationship between thermal and olfactory stimulation in the development of home orientation in newborn kittens. *Developmental Psychobiology*, 1978a.

Freeman, N.C.G., and Rosenblatt, J.S. Specificity of litter odors in the control of home orientation among kittens. *Developmental Psychobiology*, 1978b.

Friedman, M., and Lehrman, D.S. Physiological conditions for the stimulation of prolactin secretion by external stimuli in the male ring dove. *Animal Behaviour*, 1968, *16*, 233–237.

Friedman, M.B. *Auditory influences on the reproductive system of the ring dove*. Ann Arbor: University of Michigan Microfilms, 1972.

Friedman, M.B. Interactions between visual and vocal courtship stimuli in the neuroendocrine response of female doves. *Journal of Comparative and Physiological Psychology*, 1977, *91*, 1408–1416.

Gerlach, J.L., Heinrich, W., and Lehrman, D.S. Quantitative observations of the diurnal rhythm of courting, incubation and brooding behavior in the ring dove (Streptopelia risoria). *Verhandlungsbericht der Deutschen Zoologischen Gesellschaft*, 1975, *67*, 351–357.

Gottlieb, G. *Development of species identification of birds: An inquiry into the prenatal determinants of perception*. Chicago: University of Chicago Press, 1971.

Gottlieb, G. Development of species identification in ducklings. I. Nature of perceptual deficit caused by embryonic auditory deprivation. *Journal of Comparative and Physiological Psychology*, 1975a, *89*, 387–399.

Gottlieb, G. Development of species identification in ducklings. II. Experiential prevention of perceptual deficit caused by embryonic auditory deprivation. *Journal of Comparative and Physiological Psychology*, 1975b, *89*, 675–684.

Gottlieb, G. Development of species identification in ducklings. III. "Maturational rectification of perceptual deficit caused by auditory deprivation." *Journal of Comparative and Physiological Psychology*, 1975c, *89*, 899–912.

Gottlieb, G. and Vandenbergh, J.G. Ontogeny of vocalization in duck and chick embryos. *Journal of Experimental Zoology*, 1968, *168*, 307–326.

Grier, J.B., Counter, A.S., and Shearer, W.M. Prenatal auditory imprinting in chickens. *Science*, 1967, 1692–1693.

Grosvenor, C.E. Evidence that exteroceptive stimuli can release prolactin from the pituitary gland of the lactating rat. *Endocrinology*, 1965, *76*, 340–342.

Grosvenor, C.E., Maiweg, H., and Mena, F.A. A study of factors involved in the development of the exteroceptive release of prolactin in the lactating rat. *Hormones and Behavior*, 1970, *1*, 111–120.

Grosvenor, C.E., and Mena, F.A. Neural and hormonal control of milk secretion and milk ejection. In B.L. Larson (Ed.), *Lactation* (Vol. 1). New York: Academic Press, 1974.

Grosvenor, C.E., and Whitworth, N. Evidence for a steady rate of secretion of prolactin following suckling in the rat. *Journal of Dairy Science*, 1976, *57*, 900–904.

Hailman, J.P. Comments on the coding of releasing stimuli. In L.R. Aronson, E. Tobach, D.S. Lehrman, and J.S. Rosenblatt (Eds.), *Development and evolution of behavior*. San Francisco: W.H. Freeman and Company, 1970.

Hall, W.G. Weaning and growth of artifically reared pups. *Science*, 1975, *190*, 1313–1315.

Hall, W.G., Cramer, C.P., and Blass, E.M. The ontogeny of suckling in rats. *Journal of Comparative and Physiological Psychology*, 1977, *91*, 1141–1155.

Hall, W.G. and Rosenblatt, J.S. Suckling behavior and intake control in the developing rat pup. *Journal of Comparative and Physiological Psychology*, 1977, *91*, 1232–1246.

Herrenkohl, L.R., and Campbell, C. Mechanical stimulation of mammary gland development in virgin and pregnant rats. *Hormones and Behavior*, 1976, *7*, 183–198.

Hinde, R.A. Interaction of internal and external factors in integration of canary reproduction. In F.A. Beach (Ed.), *Sex and behavior*. New York: Wiley, 1965.

Hinde, R.A., Bell, R.Q., and Steel, E. Changes in sensitivity of the canary brood patch during the natural breeding season. *Animal Behaviour*, 1963, *11*, 553–569.

Hinde, R.A., and Steel, E. The effect of male song on an estrogen-dependent behavior pattern in the female canary (Serinus canarius). *Hormones and Behavior*, 1976, *7*, 293–304.

Hofer, M.A., Shair, H., and Singh, P. Evidence that maternal ventral skin substances promote suckling in infant rats. *Physiology and Behavior*, 1976, *17*, 131–136.

Hubel, D.H. and Wiesel, T.N. Receptive fields of single neurons in the cat's striate cortex. *Journal of Physiology*, 1959, *148*, 574–591.

Hubel, D.H., and Wiesel, T.N. Receptive fields, binocular interaction and functional architecture in the cat visual cortex. *Journal of Physiology*, 1962, *160*, 106–154.

Impekoven, M. Prenatal experience of parental calls and pecking in the laughing gull chick (Larus atricilla). *Animal Behaviour*, 1971, *19*, 471–476.

Impekoven, M. Response-contingent prenatal experience of maternal calls in the Peking duck (Anas platyrhynchos). *Animal Behaviour*, 1973, *21*, 164–168.

Impekoven, M. Responses of laughing gull chicks (Larus atricilla) to parental attraction and alarm calls, and effects of prenatal auditory experience on the response to such calls *Behaviour*, 1976, *56*, 250–278.

Ingelbrecht, P. Influence du système nerveux central sur la mammelle lactante chez le rat blanc. *Comptes Rendus Société de Biologie*, 1935, *120*, 1369–1371.

Ivanitskii, A.M. The morphophysiological investigation of development of conditioned alimentary reaction in rabbits during ontogenesis. *Works Higher Nervous Activity, Physiology Series*, (n.d.), *4*, 126–141.

Kolodny, R.C., Jacobs, L.S., and Daughaday, W.H. Mammary stimulation causes prolactin secretion in non-lactating women. *Nature*, 1972, *238*, 284–285.

Komisaruk, B.R. Neural and hormonal intereactions in the reproductive behavior of female rats. In W. Montagna and W.A. Sadler (Eds.), *Advances in behavioral biology. Vol. II: Reproductive behavior*. New York: Plenum, 1974.

Konishi, M. Development of auditory neuronal responses in avian embryos. *Proceedings of the National Academy of Sciences, U.S.*, 1973, *70*, 1795–1798.

Lack, D. *Ecological adaptations for breeding in birds*. London: Methuen, 1968.

Lambe, D.R., and Erickson, C.J. Ovarian activity of female ring doves (Streptopelia risoria) exposed to marginal stimuli from males. *Physiological Psychology*, 1973, *1*, 281–283.

Langworthy, O.R. A correlated study of the development of reflex activity in foetal and young kittens and the myelinization of tracts of the nervous system. *Contribution to Embryology, Carnegie Institute, Washington*, 1929, *20*, 127–171.

Larsson, K. Sexual behavior: the result of an interaction. In J. Zubin and J. Money (Eds.), *Contemporary sexual behavior: Critical issues in the 1970s*. Baltimore: Johns Hopkins University Press, 1973.

Lehrman, D.S. Hormonal responses to external stimuli in birds. *Ibis*, 1959, *101*, 478–496.

Lehrman, D.S. Hormonal regulation of parental behavior in birds and infrahuman mammals. In C.W. Young (Ed.), *Sex and internal secretions* (Vol. 2). Baltimore: Williams and Williams, 1961.

Lehrman, D.S. Interaction between internal and external environments in the regulation of the reproductive cycle of the ring dove. In F.A. Beach (Ed.), *Sex and behavior*. New York: Wiley, 1965.

Leon, M. Dietary control of maternal pheromone in the lactating rat. *Physiology and Behavior*, 1975, *14*, 311–319.

Leon, M. Filial responsiveness to olfactory cues in Rattus norvegicus. In J.S. Rosenblatt, R.A. Hinde, C.G. Beer, and M.C. Busnel (Eds.), *Advances in the study of behavior* (vol. 8). New York: Academic Press, 1977.

Lettvin, J.Y., Maturana, H.R., McCullough, W.S., and Pitts, W.H. What the frog's eye tells the forg's brain. *Proceedings of the Institution of Radio and Electronics Engineers of Australia*, 1959, *47*, 1940–1951.

Lewis, M., and Rosenblum, L.A. (Eds.), *The effect of the infant on its caregiver*. New York: Wiley, 1974.

Lien, J. Auditory stimulation of coturnix embryos (Coturnix coturnix japonica) and its later effect on auditory preferences. *Behavioral Biology*, 1976, *17*, 231–235.

Lincoln, D.W., Hill, A., and Wakerly, J.B. The milk-ejection reflex of the rat: An intermittent function not abolished by surgical levels of anaesthesia. *Journal of Endocrinology*, 1973, *57*, 459–476.

Lott, D.F., and Brody, P.N. Support of ovulation in the ring dove by auditory and visual stimuli. *Journal of Comparative and Physiological Psychology*, 1966, *62*, 311–313.

Lott, D.F., Scholz, S.D., and Lehrman, D.S. Exteroceptive stimulation of the reproductive system of the female ring dove (Streptopelia risoria) by the mate and by the colony milieu. *Animal Behaviour*, 1967, *15*, 431–435.

Lu, K.H., Chen, H.T., Grandison, L., Huang, H.H., and Meites, J. Reduced luteinizing hormone release by synthetic luteinizing hormone-releasing hormone (LHRH) in postpartum lactating rats. *Endocrinology*, 1976, *98*, 1235–1240.

McClintock, M.K. Menstrual synchrony and suppression. *Nature*, 1971, *229*, 244–245.

McFarlane, J.A. Olfaction in the development of social preferences in the human neonate. In CIBA Foundation, *Parent-infant interaction*. New York: Elsevier, 1975.

McMurtry, J.P., and Anderson, R.R. Prevention of self-licking on mammary gland development in pregnant rats. *Proceedings of the Society for Experimental Biology and Medicine*, 1971, *137*, 354–356.

Matthews, M., and Adler, N.T. Facilitatory and inhibitory influences of reproductive behavior in sperm transport in rats. *Journal of Comparative and Physiological Psychology*, 1977, *91*, 727–741.

Mayer, A.D., and Rosenblatt, J.S. Olfactory basis for the delayed onset of maternal behavior in virgin female rates: Experiential effects. *Journal of Comparative and Physiological Psychology*, 1975, *89*, 701–710.

Mayer, G. Delayed nidation in rats: A method of exploring the mechanisms of ovo-implantation. In A.C. Enders (Ed.), *Delayed implantation.* Chicago: University of Chicago Press, 1963.

Moltz, H., and Leon, M. Stimulus control of the maternal pheromone in the lactating rat. *Physiology and Behavior*, 1973, *10*, 69–71.

Morris, R.L., and Erickson, C.J. Pair-bond maintenance in the ring dove (Streptopelia risoria). *Animal Behaviour*, 1971, *19*, 398–406.

Moore, C. Experiential and hormonal conditions affect squab-egg choice in ring doves (Streptopelia risoria). *Journal of Comparative and Physiological Psychology*, 1976, *90*, 583–589.

Nissen, H.W. Phylogenetic comparison. In S.S. Stevens (Ed.), *Handbook of experimental psychology*. New York: Wiley, 1951.

Noirot, E. The onset of maternal behavior in rats, hamsters and mice. In D.S. Lehrman, R.A. Hinde, and E. Shaw (Eds.), *Advances in the study of behavior.* Vol. 4. New York: Academic Press, 1972.

Nutting, E.F., and Meyer, R.K. Implantation delay, nidation, and embryonal survival in rats treated with ovarian hormones. In A.C. Enders (Ed.), *Delayed implantation*. Chicago: University of Chicago Press, 1963.

Prechtl, H.F.R. Angeborene Bewegungsweisen junger Katzen. *Experientia*, 1952, *8*, 220–221.

Reisbick, S., Rosenblatt, J.S., and Mayer, A.B. Decline of maternal behavior in the virgin and lactating rat. *Journal of Comparative and Physiological Psychology*, 1975, *89*, 722–732.

Rosenblatt, J.S. Social–environmental factors affecting reproduction and offspring in infrahuman mammals. In S.A. Richardson and A.F. Guttmacher (Eds.), *Childbearing-its social and psychological aspects.* Baltimore: Williams and Wilkins, 1967.

Rosenblatt, J.S. Views on the onset and maintenance of maternal behavior in the rat. In L.R. Aronson, E. Tobach, D.S. Lehrman, and J.S. Rosenblatt (Eds.), *Development and evolution of behavior, essays in memory of T.C. Schneirla.* San Francisco: Freeman, 1970, pp. 489–515.

Rosenblatt, J.S. Suckling and home orientation in the kitten: A comparative developmental study. In E. Tobach, L.R. Aronson, and E. Shaw (Eds.), *The biopsychology of development.* New York: Academic Press, 1971.

Rosenblatt, J.S. Selective retrieval by maternal and nonmaternal female rats. *Journal of Comparative and Physiological Psychology*, 1975, *88*, 678–686.

Rosenblatt, J.S. Stages in the early behavioural development of altricial young of selected species of non-primate mammals. In P.P.G. Bateson and R.A. Hinde (Eds.), *Growing points in ethology.* Cambridge, England: Cambridge University Press, 1976.

Rosenblatt, J.S., and Lehrman, D.S. Maternal behavior of the laboratory rat. In H.L. Rheingold (Ed.), *Maternal behavior in mammals.* New York: Wiley, 1963.

Rosenblatt, J.S., and Siegel, H.I. Hysterectomy-induced maternal behavior during pregnancy in the rat. *Journal of Comparative and Physiological Psychology*, 1975, *89*, 685–700.

Rosenblatt, J.S. Turkewitz, G., and Schneirla, T.C. Development of home orientation in newly born kittens. *Transactions of the New York Academy of Sciences*, 1969, *31*, 231–250.

Rosenblum, L.A. The ontogeny of mother–infant relations in Macaques. In H. Moltz (Ed.), *The ontogeny of vertebrate behavior*. New York: Academic Press, 1971.

Rosenblum, L.A., and Kaufman, I.C. Laboratory observations of early mother–infant relations in pigtail and bonnet Macaques. In S.A. Altman (Ed.), *Social communication among primates*. Chicago: University of Chicago Press, 1967.

Roth, L., and Rosenblatt, J.S. Changes in self-licking during pregnancy in the rat. *Journal of Comparative and Physiological Psychology*, 1967, *63*, 397–400.

Roth, L., and Rosenblatt, J.S. Self-licking and mammary development during pregnancy in the rat. *Journal of Endocrinology*, 1968, *42*, 363–378.

Rothchild, I. The corpus luteum-pituitary relationship: The association between the cause of luteotrophin secretion and the cause of follicular quiescence during lactation; the basis for a tentative theory of the corpus luteum-pituitary relationship in the rat. *Endocrinology*, 1960, *67*, 9–41.

Sachs, B.D., and Barfield, R.J. Functional analysis of masculine copulatory behavior in the rat. In J.S. Rosenblatt, R.A. Hinde, E. Shaw, and C. Beer (Eds.), *Advances in the study of behavior* (Vol. 7). New York: Academic Press, 1976.

Schneirla, T.C. Levels in the psychological capacities of animals. In R.W. Sellars, V.J. McGill, and M. Faber (Eds.), *Philosophy for the future*. New York: Macmillan Co., 1949.

Schneirla, T.C. Psychology, comparative. *Encyclopedia Brittanica*, 1962.

Schneirla, T.C. Aspects of stimulation and organization in approach/withdrawal processes underlying vertebrate behavioral development. In D.S. Lehrman, R.A. Hinde, and E. Shaw (Eds.), *Advances in the study of behavior* (Vol. 1). New York: Academic Press, 1965.

Schneirla, T.C., Rosenblatt, J.S., and Tobach, E. Maternal behavior in the cat. In H.L. Rheingold (Ed.), *Maternal behavior in mammals*. New York: Wiley, 1963.

Selye, H. On the nervous control of lactation. *American Journal of Physiology*, 1934, *107*, 535–538.

Shelesnyak, M.C., and Kraicer, P.F. The role of estrogen in nidation. In A.C. Enders (Ed.), *Delayed implantation*. Chicago: University of Chicago Press, 1963.

Siegel, H.I. and Rosenblatt, J.S. Hormonal basis of hysterectomy-induced maternal behavior during pregnancy in the rat. *Hormones and Behavior*, 1975a, *6*, 211–222.

Siegel, H.I., and Rosenblatt, J.S. Latency and duration of estrogen induction of maternal behavior in hysterectomized-ovariectomized virgin rats: Effects of pup stimulation. *Physiology and Behavior*, 1975b, *14*, 473–476.

Slotnick, B.M., Carpenter, M.L., and Fusco, R. Initiation of maternal behaviour in pregnant nulliparous rats. *Hormones and Behavior*, 1973, *4*, 53—59.

Stanley, W.C., Bacon, W.E., and Fehr, C. Discriminated instrumental learning in neonatal dogs. *Journal of Comparative and Physiological Psychology*, 1970, *70*, 335–343.

Steel, E., and Hinde, R.A. Effect of a skeleton protoperiod on the daylength-dependent response to oestrogen in canaries (Sirenus canarius). *Journal of Endocrinology*, 1976, *70*, 247–254.

Steele, E., Gosney, S., and Hinde, R.A. Effect of male vocalizations on the nest-occupation response of female budgerigars to oestrogen and prolactin. *Journal of Reproduction and Fertility*, 1977, *49*, 123–125.

Teicher, M.H. and Blass, E.M. First suckling response of the newborn albino roat: The roles of olfaction and amniotic fluid. *Science*, 1977, *198*, 635–636.

Teicher, M.T. and Blass, E.M. Suckling in newborn rats. Eliminated by nipple lavage reinstated by pup saliva. *Science*, 1976, *193*, 422–425.

Terkel, J., and Rosenblatt, J.S. Maternal behavior induced by maternal blood plasma injected into virgin rats. *Journal of Comparative and Physiological Psychology*, 1968, *65*, 479–482.

Terkel, J., and Rosenblatt, J.S. Aspects of nonhormonal maternal behavior in the rat. *Hormones and Behavior*, 1971, *2*, 161–171.

Tilney, F., and Casamajor, L. Myolenogeny as applied to the study of behaviour. Archives of Neurological Psychiatry, 1924, *12*, 1–66.

Trivers, R.L. The evolution of reciprocal altruism. *Quarterly Review of Biology*, 1971, *46*, 35–57.

Trivers, R.L. Parent-offspring conflict. *American Zoologist*, 1974, *14*, 249–264.

Tschantz, B. Zur Brutbiologie der Trottellumme (Uria aalge). *Behaviour*, 1959, *14*, 2–100.

Tschantz, B. Trottellummen: Die Entstehung der persönlichen Beziehung zwischen Jungvogel und Eltern. *Zeitschrift für Tierpsychologie*, Supplement, 1968, *4*, 1–103.

Tschantz, B., and Hirsbrunner-Scharf, M. Adaptations to colony life on cliff-ledges: A comparative study of guillemot and razorbill chicks. In G.P. Baerends, C.G. Beer, and A. Manning (Eds.), *Evolution in behavior*. New York: Oxford University Press, 1975.

Vince, M.A. Social facilitation of hatching in the bobwhite quail. *Animal Behaviour*, 1964, *12*, 531–534.

Vince, M.A. Artificial acceleration of hatching in quail embryos. *Animal Behaviour*, 1966, *14*, 389–394.

Vince, M.A. Effect of rate of stimulation on hatching time in Japanese quail. *British Poultry Science*, 1968, *9*, 87–91.

Vince, M.A. Embryonic communication, respiration and the synchronization of hatching. In R.A. Hinde (Ed.), *Bird vocalizations*. Cambridge, England: Cambridge University Press, 1969.

Vince, M.A. Some environmental effects on the activity and development of the avian embryo. In G. Gottlieb (Ed.), *Studies on the development of behavior and the nervous system*. Vol. 1. *Behavioral embryology*. New York: Academic Press, 1973.

Vorheer, H., Kleeman, C.R., and Lehman, E. Oxytocin induced stretch reaction in suckling mice and rats: A semi-quantitative bio-assay for oxytocin. *Endocrinology*, 1967, *81*, 711–715.

Vuorenkoski, V., Wasz-Höckert, O., Koivisto, E., and Lind, J. The effect of cry stimulus on the temperature of the lactating breast of primipara. A thermographic study. *Experientia*, 1969, *25*, 1286–1287.

Welker, W.J. Analysis of sniffing of the albino rat. *Behaviour*, 1964, *22*, 223–244.

Wheeler, W.M. *The social insects*. New York: Harcourt, Brace, 1928.

Whitworth, N. *Relationship between patterns of grooming, endocrine function and mammary gland development in the pregnant rat*. Unpublished doctoral dissertation, Rutgers University, N.J.: University Microfilms 1972, 72-27609.

Wilson, E.O. *Sociobiology, the new synthesis*. Cambridge, Mass.: Harvard University Press, 1975.

Windle, W.F. Normal behavioral reactions of kittens correlated with postnatal development of nerve-fibre density in the spinal grey matter. *Journal of Comparative Neurology*, 1930, *50*, 479–503.

Zarrow, M.X., Johnson, N.P., Denenberg, V.H., and Bryant, L.P. Maintenance of lactational diestrus in the postpartum rat through tactile stimulation in the absence of suckling. *Neuroendocrinology*, 1973, *11*, 150–155.

Zarrow, M.X., Schlein, P.A., Denenberg, V.H., and Cohen, H.A. Sustained corticosterone release in lactating rats following olfactory stimulation from the pups. *Endocrinology*, 1972, *91*, 191–196.

Aptitude-Treatment Interactions in Educational Research

Richard E. Snow

In education, the study of person–situation interaction translates into research on individual differences in student aptitudes for learning under differing instructional conditions. An old and vast literature in educational psychology attests to the fact that individual differences in learner aptitudes predict learning outcomes. But a substantial new body of literature also now demonstrates that aptitude variables often interact with instructional treatment variables in these predictions. These so-called aptitude-treatment interactions (ATI) have important implications for the development of instructional theory and research and for instructional improvement. They provide a powerful new means of testing the construct validity of aptitude constructs and of focusing task analyses of instructional situations. They suggest a systematic approach to the individualization of instruction. More than this, they signal that theories in educational research require constructs woven from an understanding of individual differences in psychological processes as these are influenced by differing situational demands; they prove the need for the unified psychological science envisioned by Cronbach (1957). At the same time, they demonstrate that the subject matter of this science is exceedingly complex, so complex in fact that the traditional aim of establishing scientific laws in the form of a few broad and stable generalizations across time and space now seems hopeless (Cronbach, 1975).

Two recent reviews together span the 20 years or so of literature during which ATI research has come of age. The first (Cronbach and Snow, 1977) was a book-length summary and reanalysis of most of the

---

Richard E. Snow • School of Education, Stanford University, Stanford, California 94305. The preparation of this chapter was supported in part by Contract No. N00014–75–C–0882, Office of Naval Research. The views and conclusions contained in this chapter are those of the author and should not be interpreted as necessarily representing the official policies, either expressed or implied, of the Office of Naval Research, the Advanced Research Projects Office, or the U.S. Government.

extant literature, to establish that

> Aptitude × Treatment interactions exist. To assert the opposite is to assert that whichever educational procedure is best for Johnny is best for everyone else in Johnny's school. Even the most commonplace adaptation of instruction, such as choosing different books for more and less capable readers of a given age, rests on an assumption of ATI that it seems foolish to challenge. . . . [Yet] no Aptitude × Treatment interactions are so well confirmed that they can be used directly as guides to instruction. (p. 492)
>
> The substantive problem before us is to learn which characteristics of the person interact dependably with which features of instructional methods. This is a question of awesome breadth. In principle, it calls for a survey of all the ways in which people differ. It requires that individuality be abstracted into categories or dimensions. Likewise, it calls for abstractions that describe instructional events in one classroom after another. The constructs descriptive of persons and instructional treatments pair up to form literally innumerable ATI hypotheses. It is impossible to search systematically for ATI when the swarm of hypotheses is without order. (p. 493)

While the Cronbach–Snow book produced an initial organization of ATI hypotheses, the second review (Snow, 1977) sought to carry this process further, updating the organization with respect to two broad aptitude "complexes" that seemed particularly worthy of further attention. It urged a three-fold attack for future research, consisting of:

> 1. *The examination of the most plausible ATI hypotheses in large scale, long-duration, real-school studies.* This would allow a consolidation of efforts to establish a few ATI hypotheses in settings where they might actually be used. The emphasis in the design of such research would be on representativeness (Snow, 1974) and description (Cronbach, 1975), rather than on laboratory-like control.
>
> 2. *The development of methodology capable of handling the complexities of such research.* This effort would deemphasize the familiar significance testing habits of researchers in favor of the description and analysis of complex relationships. . . .
>
> 3. *The development of a laboratory science for the analysis of aptitude tests and learning tasks, and the ATI constructs based on them. . . .* This would complement the instructional studies with process analyses to provide ideas about possible underlying mechanisms. Embodied in newly understood and/or newly designed aptitude measures, these ideas might then be conveyed to research in the real instructional settings where probable, practically useful ATI can be examined and used. (p. 51)

The present chapter, then, need not attempt a further survey of ATI literature. Rather, it will present only a few selected examples to demonstrate the main features of ATI research, and then give an overview of the sort of theory to be sought in further research on aptitude and learning processes. Methodological points are scattered throughout. A first section deals with definitional matters. Then the example studies are chosen to display current thinking about the interpretation of several of the aptitude constructs of prime interest in educational research, and to cover the range of research approaches from analytic experiments in the laboratory to broad field investigations of a more descriptive nature. The prospectus of theory and methodology outlines a combination of experimental and differential psychological approaches that will hopefully produce a unified cognitive psychology of aptitude and learning in instruction.

1. *Definitions*

1.1. *Aptitude*

An aptitude is an individual difference construct, with its associated measures, that bears a hypothesized or demonstrated relation to individual differences in learning in some particular situation. In education, aptitudes are student characteristics that predict response to instruction under a given instructional treatment. In educational research, then, the defining characteristic of aptitude is *relation to learning*. Measures of "intelligence" or "scholastic ability" identify aptitude because they predict achievement in conventional schooling. Through decades of demonstrations of this prediction, "ability" and "aptitude" came to be thought of as synonyms. But any special ability, cognitive style, personality, motivation, or interest variable that shows relation to learning ought also to be considered as identifying aptitude. There is, then, no traditional domain of differential psychology that should be called aptitudes *a priori*. By adopting this broader definition, the field is left open to the study of new and old constructs alike and to hypotheses about combinations of constructs from different traditional domains.

Within this broad definition, it is nonetheless true that most research on aptitude for learning has concentrated on cognitive ability, and this chapter reflects that emphasis. The concept of general mental ability will be a first cornerstone for any theory of aptitude. The central hypothesis of this chapter and the research program it advocates, is that individual differences in performance on ability tests and learning tasks are manifestations of cognitive processes common to each. Despite historical arguments to the contrary, notably by Woodrow (1946), intelligence is still often defined as the ability to learn. This definition persists because it is parsimonious and intuitively appealing, and because it makes psychological sense. There are theoretical reasons to believe that individual differences in ability and learning derive from the same psychological phenomena whether one takes an environmentalist (e.g., Ferguson, 1954, 1956; J. McV. Hunt, 1961) or hereditarian (e.g., Garrett, 1946; Jensen, 1972) view. And the research often cited in denying the connection is not convincing (Cronbach and Snow, 1977). The two disciplines of differential and experimental psychology, focusing on different aspects of the whole, devised different representation systems and terminology for their points of view—one based on static quantities and vectors in personal mental space, the other on situation—specified mechanistic functions and group acquisition curves. Progress will now best be served by relegating this division of labor and all that it implies to the historical closet, and by avoiding where possible the limitations of discipline-specific terminology.

1.2. Treatment

Treatment variables can also be defined broadly to cover any manipulable situation variable. All experimental variables, whether manipulated within- or between-subjects, are treatment variables. Educational treatments may vary in pace, methods, media, and/or styles of instruction. Classroom or college environments and teacher or counselor characteristics are also treatment variables of interest; while these are not technically manipulable, the student's learning experience is in effect manipulated by assignment or self-selection policies.

1.3. Aptitude × Treatment Interaction (ATI)

Statistically, ATI is defined by the demonstration that different treatments yield nonparallel regression slopes, when one or more learning outcome measures is regressed onto one or more aptitude variables under each of two or more treatment conditions. There are analysis-of-variance approximations to this regression formulation, but these are typically weaker statistically and not to be preferred. (See Cronbach and Snow, 1977, chaps. 2–4, for discussion of various technical details and complications.)

Psychologically, ATI signifies that some person variable is more strongly associated with learning processes or activities in one instructional situation than in another. If the person characteristic represents variance in a performance capability (e.g., an ability test score), a treatment showing a steep aptitude-outcome regression slope may be said to capitalize on, or demand, that performance capability in students, to the detriment of those without that capability. A treatment showing a shallow or negative regression slope may be described as somehow compensating for inaptitude in students, perhaps to the detriment of those showing high performance on the aptitude variable in question. Person variables representing personality or motivational characteristics can also be described in capitalization–compensation terms, but often are interpreted as displaying the "fit" or "match," or lack thereof, between personal and treatment styles. Person characteristics such as sex or socioeconomic status can be thought of as proxies for psychological aptitude variables.

The goal of psychological research on ATI is to understand how and why external treatment conditions influence the network of internal processes represented by aptitude and learning measures so as to facilitate learning in some individuals while at the same time interfering with learning in others. The educational goal is to design situations that promote optimal learning in each kind of person.

2. *ATI Hypotheses and Example Studies*

2.1. *An Ability Complex*

One of the aptitude "complexes" identified previously (Snow, 1977), rests on the concept of general mental ability (G) and its division into crystallized (G_c), fluid-analytic (G_f) and visualization (G_v) abilities. In sheer numbers, measures of G have shown more ATI in instructional studies than any other aptitude. The weight of this evidence suggests that G relates more strongly to learning outcomes when instruction is described as using elaborate or unusual explanations, including discovery or inquiry methods, encouraging learner self-direction, relying heavily on verbiage, or as relatively unstructured, permissive, or rapidly paced. In general, it seems that when instruction places the burdens of information organization and processing more on the learner, high ability students do well while low ability students do poorly. On the other hand, the relation of G to learning tends to be reduced when instructional conditions relieve the learner of some information processing burdens by simplifying or breaking down the task, focusing on essentials, giving redundant text or simplified demonstrations and models, or substituting other media for verbiage. In these latter environments, then, high ability students often do less well than otherwise, while learning is enhanced for low ability students.

Though many studies have obtained this kind of result, there are exceptions, and even the strongest results are not really well understood. Different studies use different measures of G; the majority of measures used seem more nearly to represent G_c, but others would have to be called G_f. No study has adequately distinguished these prime constituents of G, so interpretation is unclear on this point. Descriptions of instructional treatments are also gross.

2.1.1. The Sharps Study. One study that gave this kind of result and also attempted to distinguish G_c and G_f was a dissertation by Sharps (1973). He conducted a large-scale field study as an evaluation of Individually Prescribed Instruction (IPI), using fifth grade classes in four schools. There were 134 students who had experienced IPI programs throughout their school years, and 139 control students who had not experienced IPI. Instructional treatments spanned the year. At the start of the year, six aptitude measures from the *Cattell Culture Fair Intelligence Scales* and the *SRA Primary Mental Abilities* tests were administered in each classroom. These yielded two composites, one for G_c, the other for G_f. Four of the *Iowa Tests of Basic Skills* served as the achievement measure at the end of the year. These were: vocabulary, reading comprehension, arithmetic concepts, and arithmetic problem-solving.

ATI was clear for G_c, not for G_f, on all outcome measures. Figure 1 shows the regression results for the reading comprehension outcome; a similar pattern was observed on other achievement measures. IPI reduced the relation of G_c to outcome. In so doing, it became a superior treatment for low G_c students but inferior for high G_c students. Treatment main effects were slight. G_f gave little or no interaction. But Sharps's analysis did not go far enough to rule out an interpretation based on G. Correlations among aptitudes were not reported and the two composite aptitudes were not defined statistically. A multivariate analysis using a general factor $(G_c + G_f)$ and a contrast factor $(G_c - G_f)$ as aptitudes would test whether G, or G_c alone, accounted for ATI.

But the ATI findings stand and G_c, at least, is implicated. The results replicate those of Crist-Whitzel and Hawley-Winne (1976), who found ATI with G_c in another year-long evaluation of IPI in sixth grade mathematics. In their multiple regression analysis, incidentally, G_f produced a similar interaction after the G_c interaction had been removed statistically. (See Snow, 1977, for further discussion.)

IPI is a system of individually paced instruction relying on specific pretests, geared to carefully specified objectives and sequenced content, with frequent checkpoints as guides and feedback on learner progress, plus mastery tests for each unit. As such it combines many features of the kinds of treatments found in past research to help lower ability learners. The ATI interpretation seems to be that IPI structures the learner's experience in some detail, doing for lower ability stu-

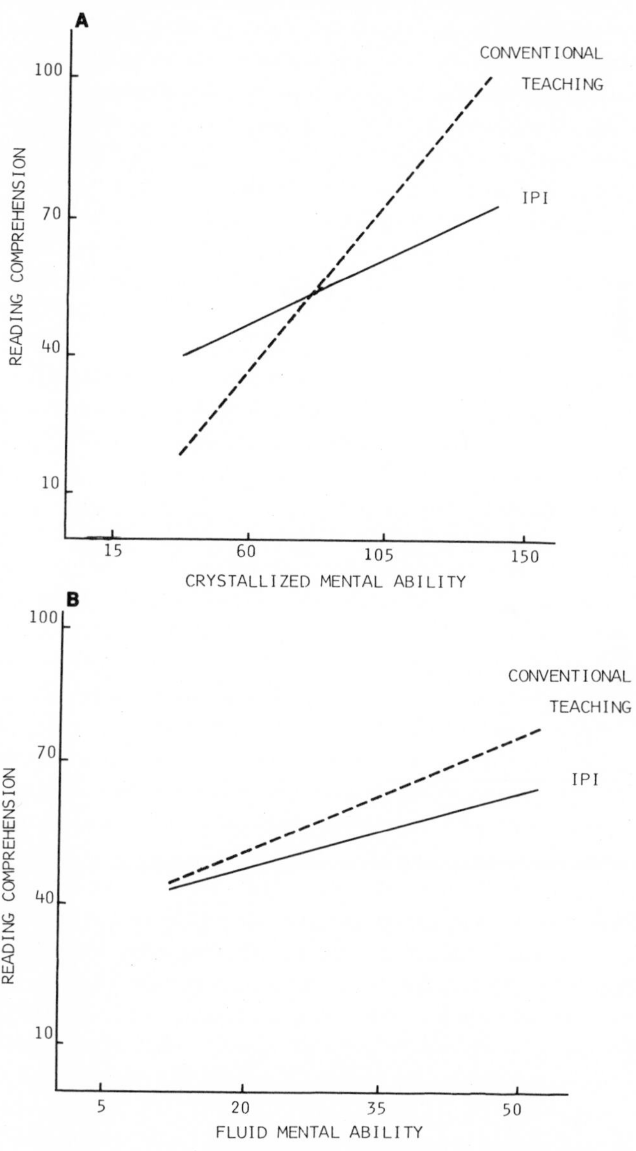

Figure 1. Interaction of crystallized ability (A) and fluid ability (B) with two instructional treatments using reading comprehension as outcome measure (after Sharps, 1973).

dents what they may not be able to do for themselves (i.e., compensating for an inaptitude by removing excess organizational and attentional complexity). In so doing, however, IPI may be dysfunctional for able students, who can organize their own learning; they seem better off with conventional teaching. Whether this dysfunction should be attributed to cognitive interference, or motivational "turn-off," or both, or other factors is unclear. In any event, ATI analysis demonstrates once again that no one instructional treatment is best for everyone, even one that purports to be individualized.

IPI is a fairly well-specified instructional treatment. But what is G_c? It has been interpreted as generalized scholastic achievement, verbal-educational ability, acquired knowledge, informed judgment, awareness of applicable and previously "crystallized" skills and concepts, etc. Lacking a process theory of aptitude, it is difficult to get beyond these traditional traitlike quantitative descriptions. To understand ATI here, we need to understand by what aptitude processes in learning, under each kind of instruction, do strengths and weaknesses in G_c manifest themselves.

2.1.2. The Loftus and Loftus Study. An experiment by Loftus and Loftus (1974) concerned retrieval of information from semantic memory, but it shows, at least by analogy, something of the processes that may be represented by G_c aptitude. Subjects were graduate students in psychology who differed in degree of learning experience in graduate school. They were asked to recall the name of a psychologist, given one of six areas of psychology and the first letter of the psychologist's last name. Reaction time was measured for each student under two conditions: letter first, followed by area designation; area first, followed by letter. It was expected that advanced graduate students would show a pattern of results like that often obtained previously with any well-learned categories: reaction time should be faster when the letter follows the area designation, rather than vice versa, because the learner can find the location in his semantic memory structure where the area designation is stored while the restrictive letter is being presented, thereby saving overall time in the two-step retrieval process. Retrieving the name "Piaget," for example, should be faster in response to the stimulus order "Developmental-P" than with the order "P-Developmental."

Figure 2 is redrawn from that given by Loftus and Loftus, since by convention in ATI research aptitude variables are always assigned to the abscissa. The results show a clear ATI pattern. With advanced graduate students the area-letter order of presentation requires less retrieval time than does the letter-area presentation order. With beginning students the difference between conditions is small and actually

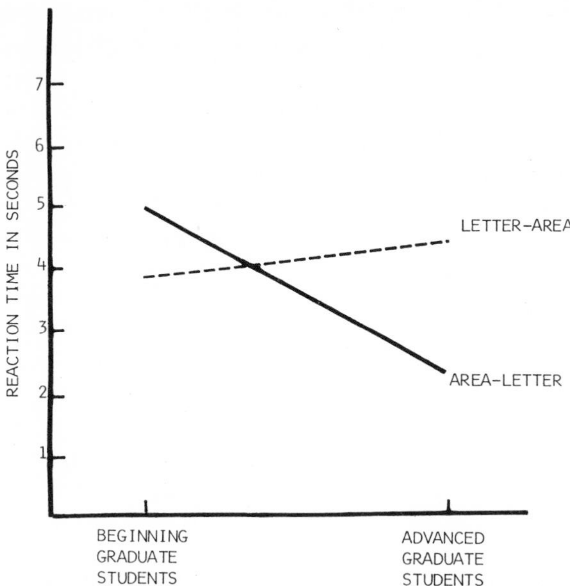

FIGURE 2. Reaction time for beginning and advanced students to produce a psychologist's name under two orders of stimulus presentation (letter-area; area-letter) (data from Loftus and Loftus, 1974, 1976).

reversed! Relatively inexperienced students—lower in crystallized knowledge of psychology—seem not to possess the kind of organized memory structure held by advanced students.

> The implication is that when a student "learns about" psychology, this learning consists of changing the semantic organization of his knowledge about psychology and/or the process of retrieving information about psychology.
>
> [This] suggests a substantial departure from traditional notions about "what is learned" and "what should be tested." In typical educational settings, the student is viewed as learning *facts*. . . . It seems reasonable, however, on intuitive, theoretical, and empirical grounds that "what is learned" goes considerably beyond fact acquisition. Indeed, it is the case that the process of learning involves a reorganization of semantic information and implementation of new retrieval schemes. (Loftus and Loftus, 1976, p. 152)

The reversal for novice graduate students may also make sense. One might speculate that such students learn names first before gaining a well-organized conception of disciplinary subdivisions. Thus, the letter-first condition allows them to start running through their list of associations early; the area designation then helps them to reduce the list or select from it.

These views seem consistent with those of other cognitive theorists. Rumelhart and Norman (1976), for example, speak of "accretion," "restructuring," and "fine tuning" as three distinguishable stages of the sort of complex learning found in educational settings. There is a stage of fact accumulation, which may produce masses of loosely and simply connected knowledge. At some point these masses must be reorganized into more integrated and formalized (crystallized?) structures, and ultimately sharpened into smoothly usable tools of thought. What is important for the purposes of this chapter, however, is the possibility that the sort of semantic structure and retrieval differences demonstrated by Loftus and Loftus may be similar to those discernible throughout years of educational development and captured by general scholastic ability and achievement tests, i.e., by measures of G_c.

2.2. *An Ability–Anxiety–Motivation Complex**

The other aptitude complex suggested for further research (Snow, 1977) concerns two interactional patterns that have appeared fairly frequently but have not been subjected to concerted analysis. One pattern implies that ability and trait-anxiety (A_x) work jointly to yield ATI. Instructional treatments characterized as student-centered and not highly structured by a teacher or other external source, have been found to serve high ability-low anxious students, but also lower ability-high anxious students, better than a teacher-structured treatment; the latter seems better for students showing a high-high or low-low aptitude pattern. The other ATI suggests that more teacher structure helps students higher on achievement via conformity (A_c) while less teacher structure is best for students higher on achievement via independence (A_i). The two measures for these motivational orientations are scales from the *California Psychological Inventory*.

These two interactions are complicated and probably interwoven. There is evidence of correlation between G and A_i, and between A_x and A_c. There is also some indication that each construct relates to differences in study habits among college students. Measurement and data analysis problems need attention here. And there are a variety of other personality constructs that appear to bear conceptual and/or empirical relation to one or more of the constructs in this cluster.

2.2.1. The Daniels and Stevens Study. While new studies of this aptitude complex have not been located, some recent ATI research has looked at "locus of control" as an aptitude interacting with teacher-

*The author is indebted to Andrea Lash for the literature review supporting this section.

controlled versus student self-directed learning. A dimension of internal versus external control might well also reflect student differences in ability, anxiety, and orientation toward independent versus conforming achievement motivation. Daniels and Stevens (1976) administered Rotter's *Internal-External Locus of Control Scale* to 146 college psychology students and divided internal and external strata between a traditional lecture-text-test and an individualized contract-for-grade treatment. After eight weeks of instruction, a multiple-choice achievement test showed marked ATI. Learning outcome was higher for more internal students under the contract plan, while traditional instruction was better for the more external students. This is consistent with the result to be expected if A_i and A_c were used as aptitudes instead of locus-of-control.

However, a composite of grade-point-average, SAT verbal and quantitative scores, and pretest scores was used as covariate in the analysis, and we can think of it as G_c. Means for this composite show the same interaction; traditional instruction served higher G_c students best while the individualized contract treatment was best for lower G_c students. The ATI is similar to the pattern of Sharps' results for G_c. But it was not studied in more detail here, nor were relations between G_c and internal versus external control reported. Clearly, the network of aptitude relations needs to be described and studied directly, not muddled by the uncertainties of analysis of covariance. (On this point, see Cronbach, Rogosa, Price, and Floden, 1976.) Further work might be able to fashion an aptitude construct in which G_c, A_i–A_c, and internal versus external control could be combined psychologically.

Another study (Parent, Forward, Canter, and Mohling, 1975) has obtained a similar interaction, crossing internal versus external control with high and low teacher structuring, but it involved only two hours of instruction in computer programming and included no G measures.

2.2.2. Field Correlational Studies. Some field studies have used an exploratory correlational approach to identify clusters of students, teachers, treatments, etc., that seem appropriately or inappropriately matched for educational purposes. The technique is to measure many characteristics of students and teachers (or other treatments), reduce each of the resulting matrices to fewer workable dimensions, use these to cluster persons into type categories, and then to test interactions between the student and teacher types on one or more outcomes. The approach is methodologically difficult, with many uncertainties yet to be cleared up, and it has not progressed far enough to date to yield clear results. But the approach has the potential of identifying an aptitude complex comparable to that discussed above in a new and different way. Two example studies bear on this possibility but with methodological complications. We can concentrate on selected findings and the methodological problems without attempting to fathom all the details of each study.

Solomon and Kendall (1976) clustered 92 fourth graders using factor scores obtained from a battery of cognitive and motivational premeasures. Six clusters of students resulted. These were then compared on each of five outcome measures. Since some members of each cluster came from "traditional" classrooms while others came from "open" classrooms, it was possible to test ATI. Observation measures were used to characterize the traditional classrooms as involving more closely monitored, systematic group activities, with more formal lecturing to the class as a whole, and open classrooms as involving more variety in individual and small group activities, more informality, fewer rules, and more individual student–teacher interaction. Considering only the achievement outcome, four of the six types of students appeared to do better in traditional classrooms; three of these differences were statistically significant. For two types of students, open classrooms were slightly better than traditional classrooms. This implies ATI.

Cunningham (1975) studied 715 kindergarten children and 108 teachers in a special program for urban, low income areas. Using a battery of premeasures, teachers and children were clustered separately into four types. ATI was then tested in the resulting 4×4 typology. Outcomes were residual scores reflecting posttest achievement and task orientation variance that could not be predicted from the premeasures. Again, ATI were manifest. Different student types showed markedly different achievement with a given teacher type, and each teacher type differed in their success with different student types.

> For example, Type A students earned the highest level of success with the same type of teacher (Type 3) who yielded the lowest level of success for Type C students; and vice-versa, Type C students earned the highest level of success with the same type of teacher (Type 1) who yielded the lowest level of success for Type A students. (Cunningham, 1975, p. 186)

Both of these studies are pioneering exploratory efforts. Yet, neither seems well geared to illuminate ATI, or to connect their findings psychologically to previous ATI research. More experience is needed with this kind of data, and its analysis must face two methodological issues. First, *G* aptitude information ought not simply to be mixed into type descriptions along with myriad other characteristics, considering its apparently central role in learning from instruction. Nor should attempts be made to erase the effects of prior ability from the data so that "other" effects can be isolated. G interacts with other characteristics in ATI, and attempts at statistical control are often ineffective, anyway. Second, typologies merge and submerge the continuous character of individual differences, and promote use of absolute labels, such as "introverted, high ability," when relative–normative information is needed to make cross-type and cross-investigation comparisons. The investigator is never sure where to draw the limits of heterogeneity in defining clusters, and the reader is never sure where they have been drawn. We can illustrate these problems in an attempt to connect the Solomon-Kendall and Cunningham findings to one another, and to prior work.

G can be used as a major organizing variable in each analysis. Figure 3 shows the Solomon-Kendall outcome; each of the six student types is plotted as a vertical "barbell" showing the average achievement difference between treatments for that type on the ordinate, and its position on the prior achievement continuum (assumed to approximate G_c) on the abscissa. Note that the relation of average G_c to average achievement outcome is perfect–positive across type groups in the traditional treatment (solid slope), but strangely jagged in the "open" treatment. Within high and low G_c strata, the G_c-outcome relations appear actually to be zero or negative (dashed slopes) with open instruction, at least when only these few group means are seen.

Other distinguishing characteristics of the student clusters included dimensions called by Solomon and Kendall "compliant, conforming," "personal control," and "autonomous achievement motivation." The first of these seems superficially similar to the A_c construct previously discussed (and perhaps to external locus-of-control). The other two may be combined to approximate A_i (and perhaps also internal control). Thus, an $A_i + A_c$ dimension may be defined to represent general achievement motivation, and $A_i - A_c$ can represent relative status of each group on independent versus conforming orientation. Figure 3 has been labeled to show whether each student type averaged among the highest, lowest, or middle two student clusters on these dimensions in the Solomon-Kendall data.

It is not clear whether the pattern of results is to be judged consistent or inconsistent with previous findings. To the extent that the open treatment is similar to IPI, the G_c relations here appear consistent with those of Sharps, for example. But if open instruction is interpreted as "student-centered," allowing independent student activities and autonomous responsibilities, previous findings would lead us to expect such a treatment to suit high G students better. A clear distinction between G_c and G_f here might have clarified this. Also the trend of Figure 3 suggests negative correlation between $A_i - A_c$ and

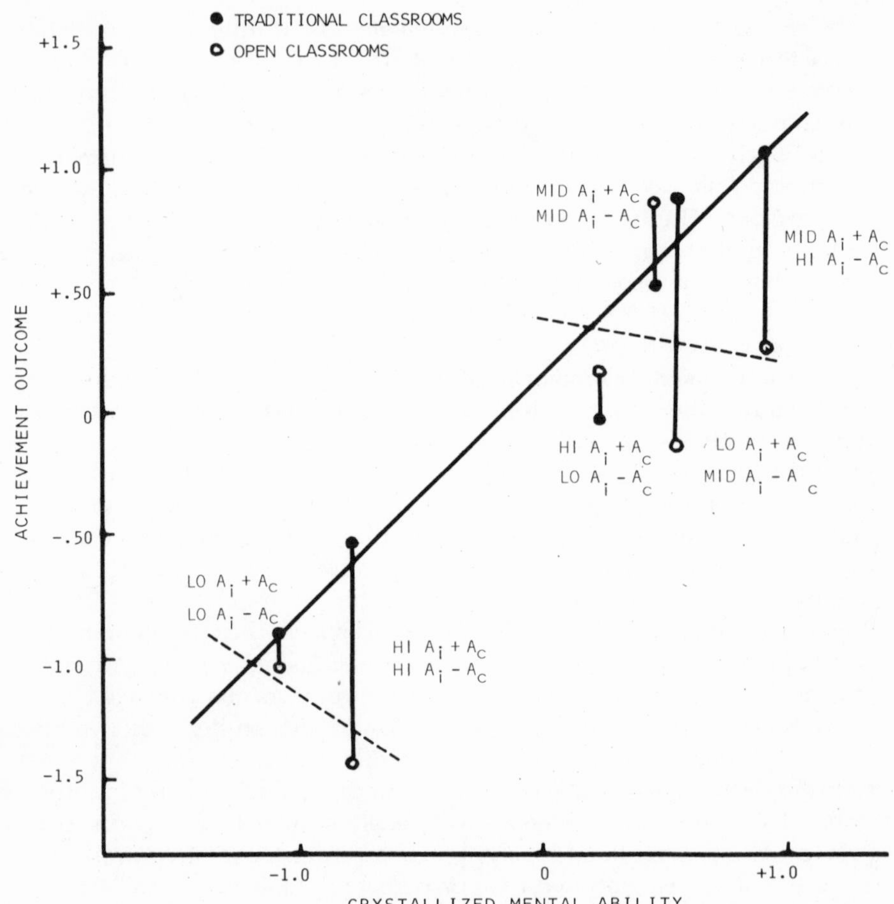

FIGURE 3. Average achievement for each of six student types (vertical barbells) in open and traditional classrooms as a function of average crystallized ability, achievement motivation ($A_i + A_c$), and independence versus conformity ($A_i - A_c$) of each student type (data from Solomon and Kendall, 1976).

achievement outcome, at least within levels of G_c, for the open treatment. This is also contrary to previous results.

The Cunningham data are shown in Figure 4, along with the labels he assigned to student and teacher types. Despite the covariance analysis, the four student types (A, B, C, and D) differ on G and this appears to affect the results. Also, since both prior achievement scores and an estimate of IQ from the *Draw-A-Man Test* were used by Cunningham, we can approximate the distinction between G_c and G_f. While student Types A and B each show similar averages on G_c and

G_f, student Types C and D have contrasting profiles on these two dimensions. Type C is higher on G_f than G_c; Type D is higher on G_c than G_f. There are thus two kinds of ATI patterns apparent in the figures. One is the contrast between C and D. The other concerns either of these and the effects for student Types A and B.

The teachers differed on variables other than those used to form type labels, and some of these seem more suggestive of psychological differences operative between types of teachers. Teacher Types 1 and 2 scored high on teacher direction and subject-matter integration, and teacher Type 1 was lowest on student direction and empathy. Teacher Type 3 was highest on student direction and empathy. Both teacher Types 3 and 4 scored low on teacher direction and subject-matter integration, but high on student-centering and subject-matter emphasis. Thus, the data suggest that Type C students are served best by teacher-centered instruction and worst by student-centered instruction, while the reverse is the case for Type D students, as well as Type A students. For student Type B, teacher Types 2 and 3 are best; these teachers score highest on empathy and student direction, even though teacher Type 2 is also similar to teacher Type 1 on teacher-centered variables. The trends are similar for both language and mathematics achievement outcomes.

Apparently, then, contrasting high ability student groups (Type A and possibly Type B) with some low ability groups (Type C, with $G_f > G_c$, and described as introverted, disadvantaged, white, and female), student-centered situations are better for Highs and teacher-centered situations are better for Lows. This is consistent with previous results, though not with one interpretation of the Solomon-Kendall data. However, for other low ability students (Type D with $G_c > G_f$ and described as slow, alienated, and male), the teaching styles do not differ much and student-centering actually seems to have the edge.

The data of both studies are complicated and the attempt to unravel the analyses here, without recomputation, may be crude, even misleading. It should be clear at least that comparison across studies is not straightforward. We cannot be sure how ability levels or treatments compare because normative continua are absent or obscured by artificial type boundaries. There may be no base of comparison, anyway, since Cunningham's students, especially, differ from those of other studies in age; aptitude constructs may not deserve similar interpretations at drastically different ages. Even so, all these studies seem to be homing in on a common set of aptitude and treatment variations and the ATI patterns found among them may become orderly as methods of analysis are sharpened and coordinated.

Even with orderly ATI patterns available from instructional stud-

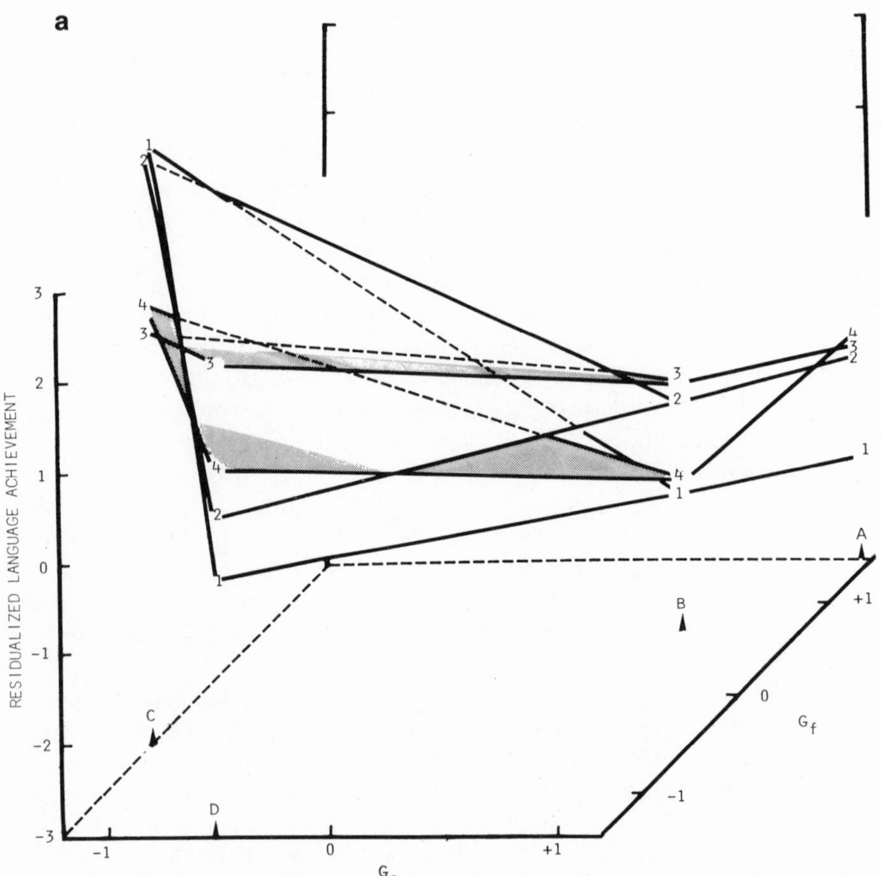

FIGURE 4. Average residualized (a) language and (b) mathematics achievement for each of four student types under each of four teacher types as a function of average student crystallized ability (G_c) and fluid-analytic ability (G_f) (data from Cunningham, 1975, who described each type as follows: Teacher type 1: white, subject integration; Teacher type 2: black, experienced; Teacher type 3: inexperienced, student centered, empathetic; Teacher type 4: white, experienced, student centered; Student type A: young, advantaged; Student type B: extroverted, black, female; Student type C: introverted, disadvantaged, white, female; Student type D: slow, alienated, male).

ies, theoretical work will still be hampered by the absence of detailed descriptions of aptitude and learning constructs in process terms. Given that aptitude complexes involving G_f, G_c, A_i, A_c, and such other variables as A_x or locus-of-control yield consistent ATI results, the question remains: How can we reach a psychological understanding of

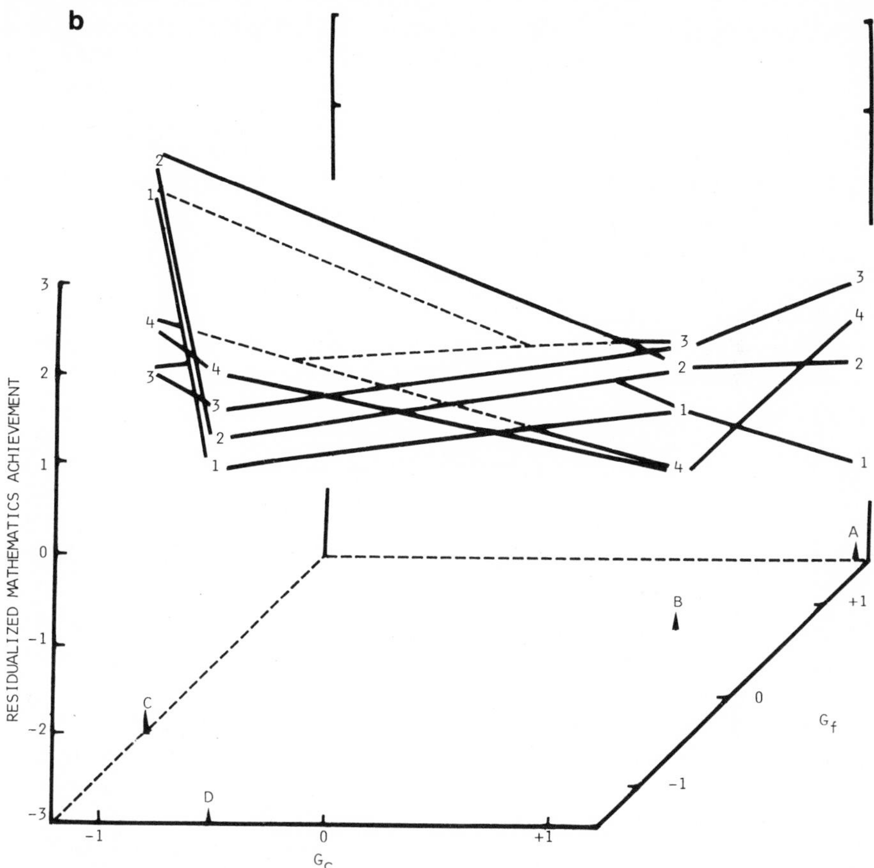

how this mixture of individual differences works in this or that instructional situation?

2.3. *The Question of Cognitive Style*

One kind of aptitude construct that has been pushed toward process description falls under the general heading of "cognitive style." Style constructs also seem convenient in discussing the mixtures of ability and personality variables referred to above as aptitude complexes. But the concept of style is deceptive. Cognitive style measures are usually interpreted as identifying a form of individual differences distinctly new and different from the traditional ability and personality trait constructs. Yet, these measures can often show strong correlation with ability tests; the relation of Witkin's field independence measures to several Wechsler performance IQ subtests is a prime example, suggesting that "fluid-analytic ability" and "field independence" are close to synonymous (Cronbach and Snow, 1977). And the style conception of a measure is questionable whenever a person is unable to attain a higher score than he or she actually does. Further research will need to distinguish between the ability and preference components of such constructs for interpretative purposes. One step in this direction will be to include G_c and G_f reference tests along with style measures in any ATI study.

Aside from the interpretation problem, however, research conducted under this aegis has begun turning up some interesting findings. One example comes from a line of studies by McLeod (see McLeod, Carpenter, McCornack, and Skvarcius, 1976). College students (N = 116) in a teacher-training program were randomly divided among four instructional treatments on arithmetic operations in bases other than ten. Treatments differed in the degree of structured guidance provided by printed materials and instructors and also in the use of manipulative versus symbolic presentation. The *Hidden Figures Test* served as aptitude and produced ATI on several outcome measures. The results seemed due mainly to the guidance variable; able students did best with minimum guidance, while less able students were better off with maximum guidance. With aptitude interpreted as G_f or G, the finding is consistent with many other ATI studies showing that aptitude-outcome regression slopes become steeper as instruction provides less direct structure to guide learning activities. An interpretation based on the field-independence concept need not be inconsistent with this; guidance helps field dependent students distinguish the key stimuli to be learned. Other ATI studies using the *Hidden Figures Test* (See, e.g., Koran, Snow, and McDonald, 1971) have suggested similar interpretations. What is needed now is a more detailed process description of the learning-related activities implied by such aptitude and treatment differences.

2.4. *Learning in Individual and Small Group Settings*

One last example opens up a whole new side to the study of person–environment interaction in education. Most instructional research, whether concerned with ATI or not, has interpreted treatment effects on learning as an individual psychological event. Yet, learning in school is also a social process; it occurs in part through interpersonal transactions. Research on group processes in education, on the other hand, has usually ignored effects at the individual level.

Webb (1977) conducted a unique experiment to compare learning in individual and in small group settings, taking individual differences in aptitude into account as well. She manipulated the grouping of students on *G* to form uniform and mixed ability groups, and also observed group processes to detect the roles different students took in different groups. Subjects were 66 high school students learning to solve several kinds of problems in mathematics. Both immediate and delayed posttests were used.

Effects on learning outcome were found to depend on individual students' ability, on student's ability relative to that of other group members, and on the role each student took in his or her group. The complex results are best quoted in full.

> Types of grouping interacted to some extent with condition of learning. For mixed-ability groups on immediate tests, the group condition was superior to the individual condition. For uniform-ability groups on immediate tests, the two conditions of study were equally effective. On delayed tests, however, average scores were higher after learning in the individual condition than after members learned in interacting groups. The regressions of delayed tests on ability in uniform-ability groups showed evidence of an ATI effect. On delayed tests, groups above the median on abiity performed better after learning in the group condition than after learning in the individual condition. Groups below the median showed better delayed performance after learning in the individual condition than after learning in the group condition.
>
> On immediate tests, higher-ability males performed better than higher-ability females, whereas lower-ability females performed better than lower-ability males. An ATI effect was found among males: the group setting was advantageous for higher-ability males and detrimental to lower-ability males. . . .
>
> Ability level within groups interacted with type of grouping. Judging especially by delayed tests, high-ability students performed equally well after learning in mixed-ability groups or individually, and less well after learning in uniform-ability groups. For medium-ability students the order from best to worst conditions was uniform-ability grouping, individual learning, mixed-ability grouping. For low-ability students the order was mixed-ability grouping, individual learning, uniform-ability grouping.
>
> These results were in part explained by the roles students played in group process. Whether a high-ability student assumed a teaching role in the group was associated with better retention. High-ability students in mixed-ability groups often explained to less-able members, whereas highs in uniform-ability groups rarely did so. Highs who actively taught in mixed-ability or in uniform-high-ability groups showed excellent delayed performance; those who did not teach were comparatively weak on delayed tests.
>
> Low-ability students who received coherent explanations, as happened often in mixed-ability groups, performed better than those who did not. In a uniform-low-ability group, however, explanations did not appear to help the student who was the target. Explanations given by low-ability

> members were unclear and often incorrect. Indeed, low-ability students often confused each other. Hence, low-ability students in uniform-low-ability groups were better off working singly.
>
> Medium-ability students who actively interacted in solving problems benefited from group learning. In uniform-medium-ability groups all members worked through computations, explained, and received explanations. No member was more active than another, and no member assumed a particular role. In these groups, medium-ability students showed excellent performance, particularly on immediate tests. In mixed-ability groups those medium-ability students who did not play active teaching roles or aggressively ask for explanations were ignored. Subsequently, they performed worse than after individual learning. Those who actively taught did well on all tests. Those who received explanations did less well, but better than after individual learning. (pp. 81–83)

Thus, it seems clear that the environment for school learning is both an instructional and a social treatment, in interaction with individual ability. Educational research will thus need to examine individual × group or class interactions within instructional treatments as well as individual × instructional treatment interactions. (See also Cronbach and Webb, 1975). This magnifies our view of the complexity of interactions in education considerably.

3. *A Theoretical and Methodological Projection*

The examples provided above, along with those reviewed elsewhere, should be sufficient to show that ATI often occurs and often in complex patterns, but that findings from different studies do occasionally show patterns similar enough to support more general hypotheses. These studies also suggest that the methodology of ATI experiments, and perhaps of educational research more generally, is too often insufficient to sustain clear interpretations about person–situation interactions.

One might look forward to the day when educational experiments would be conducted on precise and elaborated operational definitions of aptitudinal and situational constructs, with their data analyzed in full multivariate regalia. Certainly there are many suggestions for improving research methodology along these lines that should be put into effect (Cronbach and Snow, 1977; Kerlinger and Pedhazur, 1973). But the economics of educational research, if not the varied predilections of educational researchers, argues against such a prediction ever coming to full fruition. More likely, advances will be attained by laboratory theoretical analysis of aptitude constructs in information processing terms, by rich description of aptitudinal and situational variations observable in different, real school settings, and by deep thought about the meaning of aptitude-situation interaction in such settings. Two aspects of ATI phenomena need particularly to be pursued to deeper theoretical understanding: one concerns the construct validity of major interacting aptitudes, the other the processes through which these strengths and weaknesses are capitalized upon or compensated for by situational characteristics.

3.1. Construct Validity of Aptitudes

There are literally thousands of potential individual difference variables relevant to cognition, learning, and instruction. At a relatively molar level stand dozens of ability constructs that have been demonstrated over and over again in differential psychology for decades. Verbal or crystallized ability is one such construct. Fluid-analytic ability and spatial ability are also examples. Each of these might be related at another level to a variety of information processing parameters such as those studied by Hunt (1977). At this level, however, there are hundreds of other individual differences detectable in the details of information processing in particular situations. And individuals probably differ not only in parameter measures associated with particular steps in a processing model, but also in the sequence in which several steps are taken, in the inclusion–exclusion of certain steps, and in the structural and strategic character of the whole performance. We are not likely to find one-to-one correspondences between such process differences and molar ability constructs. Process differences probably combine in complex ways to account for ability test differences. Hunt demonstrated this point; it was also nicely expressed by Herbert Simon (1976) in describing the kinds of complex performance differences observed in computer simulations that may combine to account for general intelligence differences. Simon noted that the varieties of differences in computer simulation programs might constitute a performance description of general intelligence. But he also speculated that general mental ability might reflect "*individual differences in the efficacy of the learning programs that assemble the performance programs*" (Simon, 1976, p. 96, emphasis added). Also, at a still more molecular level, there is a vast jungle of biochemical and neurophysiological differences, at least some of which seem clearly relevant to psychological differences in learning and cognition.

This vast complexity of individual differences can never be covered comprehensively in theory. To deal with it at all, differential psychologists have adopted some conventions based on the principle of parsimony. Human abilities are conceived to be arranged in a hierarchy with general intelligence at the peak, divisible into more and more specific abilities and skills at successively lower levels. This allows one to choose a level of specificity to fit particular theoretical or practical needs. No one level is "correct" for all purposes. At times a few molar constructs are most useful; in other situations, finely differentiated constructs may be needed. But new constructs or interpretations are accepted only if they are empirically distinguishable from constructs already in the hierarchy. Also, constructs at any level must be demonstrable by more than one independent measure. Individual difference constructs, then, are defined by *between-task-relations,* not by single tasks. Newell (1972) recently decried the fact that cognitive psychology was composed of about 40 different camps, each with its own pet task. The study of individual differences forces upon cognitive psychology the rigors of construct validation. Greeno's (1977) studies of language understanding require the use of relational constructs because language processing is inherently relational. Hunt (1977) has also used multiple measurements of memory processes. But when such work seeks to connect process measures to ability constructs such as verbal ability or spatial ability, the latter constructs must also be measured in more than one way. Otherwise we cannot know whether the reported relations are only specific to one test or refer more generally to the construct. Further, we cannot interpret such findings in the hierarchy of ability organization unless we know whether the relations refer to verbal or spatial ability uniquely, or to the general intellectual component that runs through verbal and nonverbal measures alike. Individual difference variance in all psychological measures, not just in tests, can be divided into at least three kinds of components: common variance, reflecting sources of individual differences also reflected in other measures and thus generalizable beyond any particular measure; specific variance, reflecting sources of individual differences unique to a particular measure; and error variance. Efforts to identify individual differences in psychological processes operating within any measure should center on the common variance component, and must distinguish the three—common, specific, and error—to do this.

In short, research in this area needs to reference the whole network of ability relations in order to interpret particular aptitude–process connections.

The multitrait–multimethod reasoning of Campbell and Fiske (1959) has long been the criterion of construct validity in differential psychology. The ATI formulation has to go beyond this. Aptitude–process constructs for ATI research are validated by demonstrating that aptitude–learning relations can be changed by situational manipulations. One shows thus that the relation of aptitude to learning outcome in a specified situation is understood well enough to be controlled. The consideration of person–situation interaction forces an experimental S–R–R paradigm (see Snow, 1976) on differential psychology for its construct validation, just as it forces the multitrait–multimethod paradigm on experimental psychology.

3.2. *Capitalization and Compensation*

Individual differences among human beings come into play upon situational demand. Individuals seem to meet these demands by capitalizing on their aptitudes, and by compensating for their inaptitudes. Where possible, in effect, they substitute aptitudes they possess for those they lack. In the same sense, situations can be said to capitalize on some individual differences and to compensate for others. The practical problem to which all research on aptitude is ultimately addressed is the design of situations in such a way as to capitalize upon and/or to compensate for the existence of these individual differences. Capitalization and compensation thus seem to be general functions of persons, of situations, and of person–situation interactions. Research on aptitude will need to build a process theory powerful enough to control these functions for practical use.

But how can such functions be conceptualized in more detail to guide research toward such a theory? ATI research to date has shown that relations of aptitudes to learning outcomes can range from strongly positive to strongly negative, across varying situations. This range is schematized in Figure 5.

Considering general ability (*G*) as aptitude, the aptitude-outcome relations typically found in conventional classroom instruction approximate that shown for Treatment A in Figure 5. It appears that conventional instruction has been geared over the years to capitalize on the kinds of cognitive skills represented by *G*. Learners who have these skills are permitted and expected to exercise them in such situations. Learners who cannot bring such skills to bear will do poorly. Presumably the situation represented by Treatment A lacks something needed by such learners. Attempts to provide that something have often centered on organizing the instruction in smaller more manageable chunks, substituting other media for verbiage, directing learner attention to the key stimuli, and allowing slower, self-pacing. The IPI treatment of the Sharps Study, as noted above, is one good example of this approach. But as this compensatory approach improves the situation for low-*G* learners, it seems to reduce learning outcome for high-*G* learners. In the extreme, explicit models that help to channel low-*G* learners into the required performance also seem to disrupt what it is

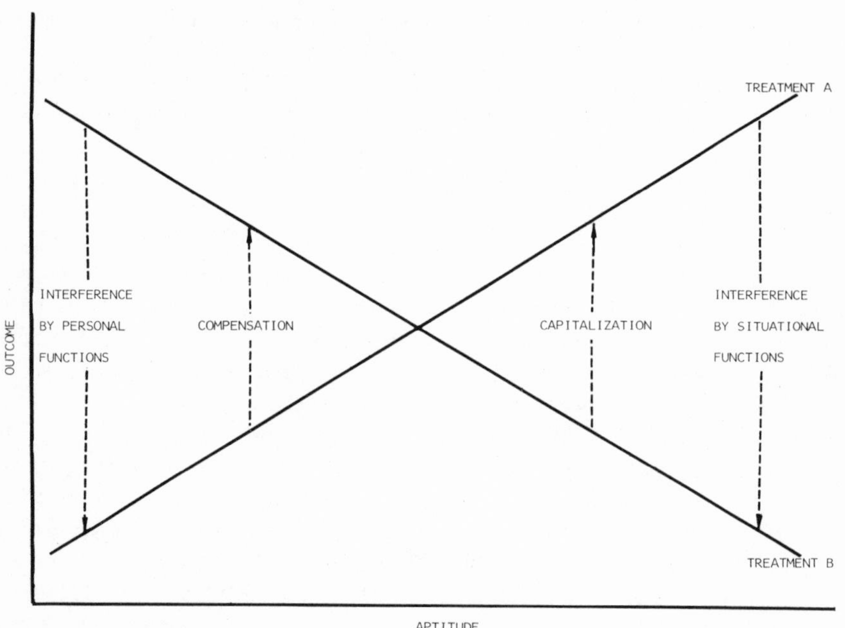

FIGURE 5. Hypothetical effects of capitalization, compensation, and interference functions in aptitude-treatment interaction.

that the high-*G* learners do well on their own. Interference with the able learner's idiosyncratic and personally efficient processes seems to be the most likely hypothesis. As instruction constrains or supplants the personally unproductive activities of less able learners, it does the same for the productive personal activities of the more able learners. One might apply similar interpretations in reverse. As Treatment B is modified by removing compensatory features, interference with learning in low-*G* students comes into play through the increasing action of dysfunctional cognitive activities. More able learners increasingly can bring into play their own effective strategies. The locus of interference shifts from situational determinants to personal determinants. There is thus a kind of see-saw relation between situational and personal characteristics.

This hypothesis can be applied as well to other ATI results, including those involving personality aptitude constructs. The anxious learner's dysfunctional activities can be constrained by Treatment B but these constraints produce dysfunctional activities in nonanxious learners. More independent students can be allowed to exercise this preference in Treatment A, but the situational constraints of Treatment

B produce reaction in such students even while providing the structure to which more conforming students can respond.

This line of reasoning does not go far enough at present. But it does suggest that compensation versus capitalization functions and personal versus situational interference functions need to be the focus of future research. The ultimate goal is demonstration that aptitude measures connect to instructional treatment variations in understandable and predictable ways. Aptitudes and instructional treatments described with common process models should make this possible. But the proof is in the real-school, long-duration, instructional studies. Hopefully, laboratory analyses of aptitude and continuing ATI studies in the field will be conducted as parallel, closely coordinated transactions.

References

Campbell, D.T., and Fiske, D.W. Convergent and discriminant validation by the multitrait–multimethod matrix. *Psychological Bulletin*, 1959, *56*, 81–105.

Crist-Whitzel, J.L., and Hawley-Winne, B.J. Individual differences and mathematics achievement: An investigation of aptitude-treatment interactions in an evaluation of three instructional approaches. Paper presented at the meeting of the American Educational Research Association, San Francisco, April 1976.

Cronbach, L.J. The two disciplines of scientific psychology. *American Psychologist*, 1957, *12*,671–684.

Cronbach, L.J. Beyond the two disciples of scientific psychology. *American Psychologist*, 1975, *30*, 116–127.

Cronbach, L.J., Rogosa, D., Price, G., and Floden, R. Analysis of covariance—Angel of salvation, or temptress and deluder? Occasional paper, Stanford Evaluation Consortium, Stanford University, 1976.

Cronbach, L.J., and Snow, R.E. *Aptitudes and instructional methods: A handbook for research on interactions*. New York: Irvington, 1977.

Cronbach, L.J., and Webb, N. Between-class and within-class effects in a reported aptitude × treatment interaction: Reanalysis of a study by G.L. Anderson. *Journal of Educational Psychology*, 1975, *67*, 717–724.

Cunningham, W.G. Impact of student–teacher pairings on teacher effectiveness. *American Educational Research Journal*, 1975, *12*, 169–189.

Daniels, R.L., and Stevens, J.P. The interaction between the internal–external locus of control and two methods of college instruction. *American Educational Research Journal*, 1976, *13*,103–113.

Ferguson, G.A. On learning and human ability. *Canadian Journal of Psychology*, 1954, *8*, 95–112.

Ferguson, G.A. On transfer and the abilities of man. *Canadian Journal of Psychology*, 1956, *10*, 121–131.

Garrett, H.E. A developmental theory of intelligence. *American Psychologist*, 1946, *1*, 372–378.

Greeno, J.G. Theory of language processing. Paper presented at the Symposium on Individual Differences, Cognition, and Learning, annual meeting of American Association for the Advancement of Science, Denver, February 22, 1977.

Hunt, E.B. Verbal IQ and information processing. Paper presented at the Symposium on Individual Differences, Cognition, and Learning, annual meeting of American Association for the Advancement of Science, Denver, February 22, 1977.

Hunt, J.McV. *Intelligence and experience.* New York: Ronald Press, 1961.

Jensen, A.R. *Genetics and education.* London: Methuen, 1972.

Kerlinger, F.N., and Pedhazur, E.J. *Multiple regression in behavioral research.* New York: Holt, Rinehart and Winston, 1973.

Koran, M.L., Snow, R.E., and McDonald, F.J. Teacher aptitude and observational learning of a teaching skill. *Journal of Educational Psychology,* 1971, *62,* 219–228.

Loftus, E.F., and Loftus, G.R. Changes in memory structure and retrieval over the course of instruction. *Journal of Educational Psychology,* 1974, *66,* 315–318.

Loftus, G.R., and Loftus, E.F. *Human memory: The processing of information.* Hillsdale, N.J.: Erlbaum, 1976.

McLeod, Douglas B., Carpenter, Thomas P., McCornack, Robert L., and Skvarcius, R. Cognitive style and mathematics learning: The interaction of field independence and instructional treatment in numeration systems. Paper presented at the Annual Meeting of the National Council of Teachers of Mathematics, Atlanta, April 1976.

Newell, A. You can't play 20 questions with nature and win. In W.G. Chase (ed.), *Visual information processing.* New York: Academic Press, 1972.

Parent, J., Forward, J., Canter, R., and Mohling, J. Interactive effects of teaching strategy and personal locus of control on student performance and satisfaction. *Journal of Educational Psychology,* 1975, *67,* 764–769.

Rumelhart, D.E., and Norman, D.A. Accretion, tuning, and restructuring: Three modes of learning. Report No. 7602, Center for Human Information Processing, University of California, San Diego, August 1976.

Sharps, R. A study of interactions between fluid and crystallized abilities and two methods of teaching reading and arithmetic. Unpublished doctoral dissertation, The Pennsylvania State University, 1973.

Simon, H.A. Identifying basic abilities underlying intelligent performance of complex tasks. In L.B. Resnick (Ed.), *The nature of human intelligence.* Hillsdale, N.J.: Erlbaum, 1976.

Snow, R.E. Representative and quasi-representative designs for research on teaching. *Review of Educational Research,* 1974, *44,* 265–292.

Snow, R.E. Theory and method for research on aptitude processes. *Technical Report #2, Aptitude Research Project,* School of Education, Stanford University. Stanford, Calif.: 1976.

Snow, R.E. Research on aptitudes: A progress report. In L.S. Shulman (Ed.), *Review of research in education.* Vol. 4. Itasca, Ill.: Peacock, 1977.

Solomon, D., and Kendall, A.J. Individual characteristics and children's performance in "open" and "traditional" classroom settings. *Journal of Educational Psychology,* 1976, *68,* 613–625.

Webb, Noreen M. Learning in individual and small group settings. *Technical Report #7, Aptitude Research Project,* School of Education, Stanford University. Stanford, Calf.: 1977.

Woodrow, H. The ability to learn. *Psychological Review,* 1946, *53,* 147–158.

*Internal and External Determinants of Behavior in Psychodynamic Theories**

Paul L. Wachtel

1. Introduction

The distinction between inner and outer determinants of behavior, or some variant of that distinction, has been common in discourses on human behavior from the time of the Greek philosophers to the most recent A.P.A. journal. Although not identical to the inner-outer question, questions of freedom versus determinism, of responsibility and punishment versus rehabilitation, of environmentalism versus instinctualism or environmentalism versus mentalism, of organismic versus conditioning models, and many other recurrent themes and debates are clearly recognizable as, so to speak, loading on the same factor.

The inner-outer distinction is common because it is in many respects a useful one; and whether due to a Kantian imperative or a widespread habit, it seems to present itself almost as a kind of perceptual given. Yet, it is also a very tricky distinction. The terms "inner" and "outer" may have very different meanings for different theorists or in different contexts.

It is easy enough to make a distinction between events "inside the skin" and all others. Often, more "hard-headed" or operationalist writers do just that, and it suits their purposes fairly well, largely because one of their purposes is to minimize the role of "inner" factors, in the pursuit of a psychology predominantly concerned with the impact of environmental events. To a growing number of psychologists, however, the distinction between internal and external determinants is not a prelude to the separation of the internal chaff from the external wheat, but a serious effort to include in their theorizing all of the events and processes that are important in determining who

*Part of the form and focus of the present chapter was a function of the originally proposed title of this volume: Internal and External Determinants of Behavior.

Paul L. Wachtel • Department of Psychology, City College of the City University of New York, New York 10031.

we are and what we do. Once such a course is undertaken, deciding what is meant by inner and outer becomes much more difficult. For a concern with what is inner that is not a dismissive concern introduces the investigator to a host of complexities.

Consider a stomach pain, for example. In one sense, this seems to be an event "inside the skin." Yet, in seeking to determine why a person left the room at a particular point in the conversation, the occurrence of the pain seems an explanation more extrinsic* to his personality than would be an explanation stressing his discomfort about the topic being discussed. If he "really" left because his stomach hurt rather than because the topic made him uncomfortable, this seems to tell us less about "him."

Were we to be told, however, that his stomach pain should be understood not as a purely physical complaint but rather as something "psychosomatic" or (even more so) as something "hysterical," then the locus of our understanding seems to shift, especially if we learn that he tends to get such pains (and "therefore" to have to leave) primarily when certain topics come up in conversation. The pain occurs in the same "place" in either event (or perhaps—we don't really know how to talk about such matters—in the stomach in one case and "in the head" in the other, but clearly "within the skin" as that term is used in its simplest version). Yet, the locus of our explanation and our understanding has shifted considerably.

The concepts of internal and external determinants of behavior, therefore, do not, in much of the psychological literature, refer necessarily to inside and outside of the body. What, then, do they refer to? Inside and outside of what? Schafer (1972), in examining the use of such concepts in psychoanalytic theorizing, asks a similar question. He concludes that there is no really satisfactory answer. To locate the events inside or outside of the body, or organism, or even brain, will miss the point of the distinction the theorist is concerned with (cf. the above example of the stomach pain). "Mind" or "ego" are somewhat closer, but to place events "within" them is to treat them as places or things, whereas they are more appropriately viewed as concepts designating "classes of events" (p. 411). Schafer argues that terms such as "inner" and "outer" in psychoanalytic theorizing are not merely harmless metaphors but rather habits of thought with rather serious consequences: They are confusing, unnecessary, and lead to concreteness of thinking and reification of abstract concepts; they in-

*The distinction between *intrinsic* and *extrinsic* factors may be a more useful one than that between *internal* and *external* factors, especially in light of the important role that the person himself plays in bringing about what can seem to be an "external" event (see below and Wachtel, 1973; 1977a).

troduce extra assumptions that complicate theorizing and require the elaborate pursuit of irrelevant questions; they confuse theory and observation, and lead to theorizing that has the primitive, pimary-process qualities of the archaic fantasies that are being theorized about, and thus they represent "more a repetition or continuation of the problem than a clarification or explanation of it" (p. 423).

Schafer in no way minimizes the distinctions and experiences that the concepts of inner and outer are designed to approach. Rather, he contends that this particular way of talking about the issue is inelegant and mischievous. Schafer, the author of an entire book on "internalization" (1968), is very much concerned with notions of "inner" and "outer" as categories of human thought, and in his view it makes an enormous difference for how people act and feel whether they experience something as "within" them or not. But he views much of this kind of thinking by all of us as a residue of early, primitive forms of mental activity, and hence hardly a basis for mature theorizing. Thus, for Schafer, it is important that theories take into account that people will think of things as inside or outside, as taken in, swallowed up, spit out, etc. But in theorizing about such primary-process events one must use the secondary-process modes of thought that are essential to rational understanding (even of the irrational).

The linguistic reforms in psychoanalytic theorizing that Schafer advocates seem potentially of considerable value, and may well help to clarify the empirical referents of psychoanalytic propositions and thereby to aid in the evaluation of which propositions are of lasting value and which should be relinquished as false leads or hunches. This would be a valuable outcome not just for psychanalytic theory but for psychology as a whole. For the serious flaws in psychoanalytic theory-making, and the tendency of many analysts to persist in advocating improbable propositions with little reliable empirical support, has led many academic psychologists to over-react, rejecting all concepts of unconscious motivation, motivational conflict, or (in some cases) even conceptions such as fantasy, expectancy, etc. This has led to an impoverishment of psychological theorizing and to an academic psychology that is precise about trivial matters but that, when it turns to such realms as psychotherapy, must smuggle in contraband clinical concepts in the dark of night (not a condition that leads to close or effective scrutiny; see Wachtel, 1977a (especially chaps. 6 and 7).

But a close re-examination of psychoanalytic theory will, I think, suggest that the prevalence of theorizing in terms of inner and outer worlds is due not only to the unfortunate influence of Freud's "metapsychology" (that aspect of Freud's theorizing that writers such as Schafer and Klein (e.g., 1974) view as an effort to put a natural-science cloak over a discipline more akin to the humanities, an effort strongly criticized by Schafer and by Klein). It is due, as well, to a substantive feature of Freudian theorizing that minimizes the role of things presently happening in the person's life as determinants of the psychological processes that are the central concern of psychoanalytic theory.

2. *A Historical Glimpse at Psychoanalytic Thought*

Closer examination of the role of concepts of inner and outer in psychoanalysis requires a brief historical look at the evolution of psychoanalytic ideas.

Freud's initial psychological theorizing was organized around the conception that "hysterics suffer from reminiscences" (Breuer and Freud, 1895). This was a conception that derived rather directly from empirical observations, and made a great deal of sense in terms of what Freud observed. His patients came to him with a variety of distressing symptoms, which disappeared only when, after much effort, they came to remember certain important childhood events that they were first unable to recall.

As is well known, the hypothesis that behind the patient's symptoms lay inaccessible memories of real events did not stand up to further scrutiny, and was shortly revised by Freud. Before it was, however, a distinct cast was given to psychoanalytic thought, a mode of thinking still persistent in much psychoanalytic writing and in large measure responsible for the gulf between psychoanalytic thought about personality change and other points of view on these matters dominant in academic circles. The specific aspect of psychoanalytic thought to which I am referring is its emphasis on the continuing effect of the past upon the present (and the implicit, if not absolutely logically necessary, corollary, of a relative lack of importance attributed to current events in the patient's life).

Freud's initial observations led him to seek historically earlier for the real explanation of the patient's problems and for their cure. When he reconceptualized his patient's reports as fantasies derived from childhood wishes, Freud retained his conceptual and methodological strategy of seeking for understanding in the patient's history rather than in current factors. In some ways this had highly salutary consequences. For one, it shed a good deal of light on childhood, pointing us to notice things that had been overlooked theretofore (and even providing some interesting perspectives on why such dramatic and obvious things should have been so largely overlooked for so long). I for one believe that Freud's insights, especially as modified and elaborated by Erikson (e.g., 1963), and as developed by child-observation work, provide a crucial foundation for any understanding of childhood; my conviction on this score has increased greatly since being a father of two small children.

But if Freud's emphasis on his adult patients' pasts had some very positive consequences, his particular way of conceptualizing how the past was influential was more questionable. It was, I believe, one of the important, and poorly understood, factors responsible for the unnecessary and counterproductive hostility of many academic psychologists to the idea of unconscious motivation. For Freud in many important respects retained the model of the traumatic memories period almost unchanged into the theory of conflict over infantile wishes, and even into the ego psychology that emerged in 1923 and has been increasingly dominant in psychoanalytic thought over the past half century.

In the hysteria period, Freud postulated that certain memories that were unacceptable to the patient's conscious sense of himself were intentionally repressed. Importantly, this did not just make them unconscious. It also somehow separated the psychological processes associated with such memories from the rest of everyday psychological functioning, so that they were not subject to the constraining and modifying effects of the organized nature of psychological processes. Whereas ordinary memories are subject to modification and reduction in intensity in a variety of ways (e.g., by comparison with other memories and/or with new perceptual input, by the application of logic, the placing of things into perspective, the reduction in importance of something once action is taken or it is "cried out," or by whatever is involved in simply "forgetting"), these memories did not seem to be. Their hypothesized effects (i.e., the symptoms that observation and theory suggested were linked to them) persisted powerfully so long as they remained in this split-off state, and when the memories were finally recovered, they appeared with an intensity and clarity quite different from what one might expect from everyday remembering. Elsewhere (Wachtel, 1977a), in a more extended discussion of the implications of the history of psychoanalytic thought, I have likened this picture of the preservation of memories in their original form (keeping them fresh and like new) to the discovery by arctic explorers of woolly mammoths frozen in the ice, whose meat was almost as fresh and edible as the day millennia before when they were frozen; I have therefore referred to this early model of preservation of memories in their original form as the "woolly mammoth" model.

Now, it is important to recognize that when Freud revised his view of what it was that was repressed, he did more than just salvage his theory. He also expanded its range so that for the first time it had the possibility of being a general psychology. The traumatic-memories theory has a necessarily limited application. It was relevant only to those unfortunates who happened to have particular unusual things happen to them in childhood, and it was of necessity a theory of neurosis only, not a general theory of personality. The new theory, in contrast, dealt with the child's way of dealing with aspects of his own development. The wishes and fantasies Freud felt he detected in the histories and in the dreams of his neurotic patients he found evident as well in the behavior and the creative products of mankind in general. Had Freud's first theory been correct, had neurotic symptoms in fact been due to the repression of real childhood traumas, Freud would have been a great name in the history of medicine, but would have had little impact upon our conception of human nature, our views of human development, or our social mores and child-rearing practices (other than to make us more careful in hiring governesses or nursery school teachers). The untenability of his initial theory led him to develop a conceptual framework whose legitimate scope was the entire range of cultural and psychological phenomena.

In one crucial way, however, Freud's theorizing did not change after the rejection of the traumatic-memories theory: he retained the essential features of the "woolly mammoth" model; only now, *impulses* were seen as preserved in their original state instead of veridical memories. Childhood wishes, which under ideal circumstances would evolve, change with new experiences, be integrated into, modified by, and coordinated with the evolving structure of aims and adaptive efforts, were, if repressed, preserved in their original form, to exert a continuing and unmodified influence and demand upon psychological functioning.

As in the earlier model, it was not just their unconsciousness that was viewed as important. Perhaps even more important was their unmodifiability, their persistence in primitive form and lack of accommodation to everything else that the person felt, wanted, and believed. Freud saw his patients as showing signs of continuing to strive for and long for things that were quite incompatible not only with their moral codes but with their realistic picture of what is possible or even desirable (e.g., what they had observed since the age of four might lead them to be much more interested in other women than in their mothers, but in an isolated, unacknowledged, yet crucially important, way they continued to exhibit the old yearnings). Such considerations led Freud to refer to unconscious processes, in perhaps too colorful or potentially reifiable language, as "timeless," allowing of contradictory impulses side by side, etc.

The final, and most sophisticated, development of the "woolly mammoth" model, and its logical outcome, appeared when Freud recast his theory in 1923 in terms of the ego, id, and superego. Now it was made explicit that adaptation to reality was accomplished by a coordinated, organized system of psychological processes (the ego), grounded in perception, including, but not limited to, the experience of self-feeling, and from which certain psychological processes (e.g., repressed wishes) were excluded. Being excluded, they did not (like those wishes that were part of the organized ego system) get modified and coordinated with the rest of what we saw, felt, and wanted, but persisted instead as (to use an earlier metaphor of Freud's) a foreign body. To make very clear that it was this cut-off, uncoordinated aspect of repressed wishes that was most crucial, Freud revised his slogan for the goal of the psychoanalytic process from that of "making the unconscious conscious" to "where id was, let ego be." Thus, while consciousness was still important in the theory, what was more important than consciousness *per se* was the reintegration of psychological functioning, the resolution of the split in our functioning that enabled certain of our activities to go on in opposition to, rather than in coordination with, other of our activities [I have discussed these issues, and their clinical implications, at greater length elsewhere (Wachtel, 1977a)].

This reconceptualization called the attention of analysts to the ego, that is, to coordinated adaptational efforts and to their link to (in fact their organization around) perception of environmental (as well as organismic) events. And analysts have indeed since then studied adaptation and perception in meaningful ways. But these have to a large degree been studied as aspects that modify the great core issues posed by repression, intrapsychic conflict, and the demands of the id. Psychoanalytic technique still aims to foster a regressive transference neurosis, in which the original childhood longings and fantasies can emerge and be reintegrated with the rest of the personality. Despite some recognition by modern analysts that transference manifestations usually are linked to some actual characteristic or action of the analyst, transferences are still seen as essentially occurring despite the current reality rather than because of it. This feature of the psychoanalytic view, and its link to the early "woolly mammoth" model, is particularly clear in the following quotation from Stone (1961), which is especially noteworthy since his monograph was a particularly well-regarded effort to modernize the psychoanalytic relationship and bring it closer to what would be implied by modern ego psychology. Stone writes that

> true transference . . . retains unmistakably its infantile character. However much the given early relationship may have contributed to the genuinely adult pattern of relationships (via identification, limitation, acceptance of teaching; for example), its transference derivative differs from the latter,

> *approximately in the sense which Breuer and Freud (1895) assigned to the sequelae of the pathogenic traumatic experience, which was neither abreacted as such, nor associatively absorbed in the personality*. (p. 67, italics added)

This stress on the locked-in, persistent, and unchanging remnant of the past is, I believe, the major and perhaps only substantive obstacle to the integration of the psychoanalytic approach with the approaches to psychological phenomena dominant in the academic world. Not only does the "woolly mammoth" model deemphasize environmental control, and hence clash with the observations that have most influenced academic psychologists, it also influences what analysts observe and look for, and thus perpetuates itself. Classical analysts, guided by this model, emphasize free association and attempts to discern the inner dynamics of the patient. The patient's behavior is of interest primarily as a reflection of what is going on within him. With such a method and focus, it is difficult to discern the subtle influence of interpersonal cues, not only upon the patient's actions, but upon his motives and fantasies as well. The analyst's theory sets him to look predominantly for sequences from inside out, so to speak, and his method and viewpoint lead him to see just that (just as most experimentally grounded conceptions lead one to see primarily the outside-in sequences—see Wachtel, 1973; 1977a).

Moreover, this kind of theorizing unnecessarily sharpens the distinction between "inner" and "outer" and seems to imply that these are two entirely separate realms. The radical linguistic surgery that Schafer proposes would perhaps not seem so essential were this not the case. Although metaphors can, as Schafer indicates, be a source of considerable confusion and mischief, they can also spur creative thought; indeed, we can hardly do without them. Notions of internal and external have reached such a problematic state in psychoanalysis at least in part because of the considerations just discussed. I will try to indicate below some of the ways in which psychodynamic concepts may be employed in a somewhat different theoretical context, in which some of these difficulties may be less prevalent.

3. *Wishes as Cause and Effect**

Traditionally, psychoanalysts have sought to understand unconscious fantasies or wishes essentially as independent variables. They have been concerned with the effects produced by such phenomena far more than with understanding what leads to their occurrence, at

*Portions of this section are drawn from Wachtel (1977a).

least when trying to understand phenomena of adult behavior and personality. Although there has been a good deal of interest in what causes such wishes and fantasies to develop in childhood, and in what conditions at that time make them likely to remain of persisting importance, there has been little effort to account for the adult's unconscious fantasies and wishes as a function of the way the person is currently living his life. These wishes and fantasies are treated essentially as a given, something within the person that accounts for the behavior he manifests.

In modern psychoanalytic theorizing, the internal givens are not just wishes and fantasies, but a variety of ego processes, of both a defensive and adaptive nature. It is recognized far more explicitly that perception of environmental events will play a role in how the individual behaves and feels. But the emphasis is largely on these events as triggers for releasing or evoking particular impulses or conflicts that are structural features of the personality. There is little consideration of how these structures may themselves be a function of the manifest events of the patient's life at present (see Wachtel, 1977a).

It has been my experience, however, that closer scrutiny of the conditions under which a particularly troublesome impulse tends to be triggered suggests that the situation that evokes the impulse can be understood as a self-created situation. The relations among the person's manifest behavior, the situations it leads to, the desires that are aroused, and the fantasies that guide and interpret experience are interlocking ones in which no aspect is more basic or causal than any other. A cycle of events can usually be discerned as a common pattern in the person's life such that the situation that tends to evoke an impulse tends to be the situation that the arousal of that impulse tends to lead to (see Wachtel, 1977a). Similarly, the defense that may commonly be employed to ward off a frightening wish or feeling is likely to be, ironically enough, one of the major causal factors in keeping that wish or feeling a prominent (if not necessarily conscious) feature of the person's psychological life.

Consider, for example, the kind of individual who appears to the classical Freudian as someone who has developed a strong reaction-formation against deep-seated feelings of rage. From the classical perspective, the rage is viewed as "deeper" and "earlier"; it is more the cause of the reaction-formation than vice versa (though, of course, it doesn't cause it directly. The arousal of anxiety and appraisal of danger, for example, are intermediate events). Inquiry is thus directed toward elucidating the historical origins of the rage, which is seen as having been there for a long time for reasons that have to go do with the patient's childhood rather than primarily with what is currently going on. And, indeed, one can often discover events and situations in the person's childhood that do seem to be intimately related to the life pattern that still characterizes the person. Perhaps we can reconstruct that at a young age he harbored frightening violent urges toward his father, and that he desperately struggled to cover up. The struggle in which he is engaged today may be sufficiently similar that it does not seem unreasonable to suggest that he is still defending against the same childhood wishes. Indeed, his dreams may suggest that the object of at least some of the hostile feelings with which he struggles may continue to be his father (even though such an idea is abhorrent to him), and other indications as well may point to warded-off rage involving his father.*

If one looks closely, however, at how he lives his life from day to day, one begins to entertain a rather different idea about why the pattern of excessive meekness and frightening, warded-off hostile urges characterizes his life. One sees that, however the pattern got started, it tends to keep itself going by the consequences it generates. The person's excessively unaggressive, cooperative, self-denying way of living is likely to lead him to continually accrue experiences in which he is taken advantage of, ignored, or overridden. He may manage to be well liked and positively regarded, but probably at the cost of subordinating his own real desires and interests to those with whom he ingratiates himself. Thus, he is likely to be continually confronted with the kinds of limitations and frustrations that tend to make people angry, and indeed if one looks closely at the dreams, fantasies, and private thoughts of such persons they frequently evidence signs of anger quite at odds with their manifest life-style and image.

One can see this excessively unassertive and self-abnegating behavior as motivated by the need to cover up his strong aggressive urges, and this would be correct as far as it goes. But it is equally the case that such a life-style generates rage. Disavowed anger may be a continuing feature of his life from childhood, but the angry thoughts that disturb his dreams tonight can be understood by what he let happen to himself today.

Such a person is caught in a vicious circle. Having learned early to fear his angry feelings, he has built up overt patterns of behavior designed to squelch and hide them. Even the smallest assertion seems dangerous because he senses† an enormous reservoir of violence be-

*See page 279 for a different perspective from the "woolly mammoth" view of why people remain preoccupied with parental figures.

†Here, as elsewhere in our discussion, the use of terms such as sense, believe, fear, etc. does not necessarily imply a conscious experience. See Schafer's (1972) discussion of the false issue raised when such terms are taken to mean a concern only with what is conscious.

hind it. Yet, it is in just such excessive restriction upon his assertiveness that the conditions for further violent urges are created.

In one sense, he guards against his anger for good reason: as he is at any given moment, he *is* potentially explosive, he *is* resentful and full of hatred, he *would* be nasty and vindictive if he were not trying so hard to be otherwise. Ironically, if he were not so frequently bending over backward, if he could act with reasonable assertiveness and demand a fair return from others, he would discover that the underlying rage would diminish. But because at any given moment real aggressive inclinations and fantasies have accrued from his way of living, he is afraid to act assertively. So he once more squelches himself, thereby arousing the fierce resentment that will in turn motivate his further self-abnegation and lead once again to strong, if unacknowledged, resentment. In such fashion he perpetuates his personal myth that there resides within him an untouchable kernel of rage that is part of the essence of who he is. And to a substantial degree this myth may be subscribed to by his analyst as well, in the analyst's view that the anger is "in" the patient from the past, rather than a response to his life circumstances.

4. *Perspectives on Personality Development*

The perspective just described shares a good deal with traditional psychoanalytic theorizing. It attributes a substantial role to unconscious motives and fantasies, emphasizes conflict and defense, and stresses the strong hold that irrational anxieties can have on the person's view of what is possible and desirable. It differs largely in that it assigns a far greater role to perceptual input in maintaining the seemingly irrational and inappropriate unconscious fears, wishes, and fantasies—and thereby a correspondingly diminished role in their maintenance to the effect of repression in cutting off aspects of the personality from further influence by such input (the "woolly mammoth" model).

In principle, there is nothing incompatible about examining the present feedback processes that maintain patterned sets of motives, expectations, and strategies of living and looking as well at the effects of repression and the dissociation of psychological systems in doing the same. (In fact, in my own clinical practice, I do look at both to some extent.) But, as I have discussed in detail elsewhere (Wachtel, 1977), the two perspectives on psychological development point to different therapeutic strategies and lead the therapist to act in ways that will inevitably limit data relevant to evaluating and articulating one or the other view of the patient's dilemma. In emphasizing the interpersonal feedback perspective, I am making a heuristic choice, one based on an evaluation that the implications and potentials of the intrapsychic model have been more thoroughly examined and that new insights and new kinds of observations are more likely to be generated by the less thoroughly mined lode; and based, as well, on an analysis that suggests that the interpersonal version of psychodynamic thought lends itself more readily to an integration with such active-intervention approaches as behavior therapy and family therapy, an integration I believe to hold the brightest prospects for an advance in the field of psychotherapy as well as for advances in personality theory (see Wachtel, 1977a, and below).

In holding that the unconscious motives and fantasies and the debilitating conflicts that therapists can discern in their patients are not primarily a result of locked-in residues from the past, but rather are a function of how the person continues to live his life, one's view of the role of history in the therapeutic enterprise is likely to be modified. The painstaking unraveling of early experience does not seem as critical as it does from a classical Freudian perspective. In its place is likely to be an increased concern, as described below, with various active-intervention techniques that can break into the vicious circles that keep going both the maladaptive behavior and the motives, fantasies, and conflicts that can seem to underlie it.

Such a shift in therapeutic strategy may seem to some readers to imply an antidevelopmental point of view. For several reasons, however, this is not the case. First of all, there remain times when, even from the perspective offered here, it is useful for people to gain some insight into the events that have shaped their behavior patterns, both to facilitate discrimination between past and present contingencies (see Dollard and Miller, 1950) and to enable the patient to be relieved of guilt feelings stemming from an excessive sense of responsibility for his dilemma. Secondly, the therapist can often be helped by a knowledge of the patient's history to understand aspects of the patient's present difficulties and to be alerted to noticing subtle features of interaction that might otherwise pass him by (see Wachtel, 1977a, chap. 7). Finally, as a theory of personality, the particular psychodynamic perspective described here must account for how various personality patterns develop, as well as how they are perpetuated. The model is primarily one of progressive or cumulative development, based on cyclical reconfirmation of anticipated experiences, rather than one emphasizing hierarchical structuring and the persisting effects of locked-in early tendencies—unlike Freudian theory, these early tendencies are seen as continuing not despite what actually goes on in the person's daily adult living, but precisely because of what is going on (and is largely brought about by those very same tendencies)—but the theory is indeed concerned with understanding development. While seeing such understanding as less relevant for bringing about change in the psychological problems of adults than does Freudian theory, the perspective offered here does concern itself with developmental issues for other reasons: e.g., for purposes of prevention of disorder or facilitation of personality growth; for purposes of guiding therapeutic work with children; and for providing a perspective on "human nature" that can guide efforts at social change and philosophical inquiry into value issues.

From the present point of view, then, understanding how adaptive and maladaptive personality patterns develop is of substantial concern. Indeed, even the critical role that psychoanalysis attributes to the very early years of life in determining later patterns does not distinguish it from an interpersonal or transactional psychodynamic perspective.* From the latter perspective, too, those early years are likely to be critical. The first few years of life are far more different from the rest of the life span for human beings than for any other creature. Humans have their view of the world and its possibilities shaped at a time when they are practically different organisms from what they will be later. In many respects, the caterpillar is far more like the butterfly than is the human toddler (much less infant) like the fully developed adult; and our ability to fulfill the potential that our later development should promise is often limited by our continuing, in important aspects of our living, to hold a world view that reflects that "previous existence." We start life in a position of extreme helplessness, largely at the mercy of giants whom we can barely comprehend and whom we love and hate with intensities that reflect both our intense neediness and our primitive cognitive development.

In those early years there is indeed reason to strive to be acceptable to those upon whom our very lives literally depend, as there is also good reason to fear that a fleeting idea or impulse will lead to action—and action whose consequences we hardly know how to comprehend or predict. The world is a dangerous and confusing place in the early years, and even if childhood can be a time of considerable joy and happiness, too—which I believe it can be and often is—it is a

*Providing a name for the present point of view is difficult. The terms "interpersonal" or "transactional" seem most descriptive but it is not identical to Sullivan's interpersonal approach, and is quite unlike the transactional analysis of Berne. The reader will see obvious debts to the writings of Horney, Sullivan, and Erikson in particular, but especially as elaborated in Wachtel (1977a), it goes in directions rather distinct from any of these writers. Elsewhere (Wachtel, 1977b), I have used the term "cyclical psychodynamics."

time when we necessarily learn a wide range of precautions and restrictions that we must subsequently unlearn or modify if we are not to be sadly limited adults. We must drastically modify those early precautions, or more generally the early view we have of what the world is and how it works, because in later years we are not (or need not be) such helpless creatures; we can afford to dare to chart our own course, to risk displeasing others, and to judge for ourselves what we want and what we can do. Moreover, we must make those changes because not only were our earlier views appropriate to a far different kind of organism than after 15 or 20 years we have become, but also they were formed by a mind that is only a pale shadow of that we now possess. Even as adults, we only approximate "reality" in our constructions of it, but those constructions exceed our early effort in both complexity and accuracy to such a degree that, as adults, we are amazed and fascinated when we observe the actual cognitive operations of the child's mind.

Yet, in many ways, or in many aspects of our living, we do not advance much beyond those early glimpses of what life holds. We continue to long for things that our present life circumstances would seem to largely render obsolete. We continue to fear saying, doing, or thinking things that perhaps were problematic for us as two-year-olds or four-year-olds but that are the key to full, rich living as adults. We continue to implicitly hold beliefs (say, about what happens when a penis enters a vagina, or when one says "no" or "I don't like that," or when one tries to be strong or tries to be weak) that if we examined with our full powers of logic would appear absurd to us. And we do all of this, in many instances, without really being aware that we do so, often being aware instead of having headaches, or feeling depressed, or not feeling comfortable outside the house alone, or not staying very long with any one intimate partner.

It is such observations—or in many instances, inferences from observations—that have impressed psychoanalysts with the persistence of childishness in almost all adults. The interpersonal psychodynamic theorist (whose views are also shaped very largely by sympathetic listening to the intimate secrets of people desperate enough to try to stop hiding) similarly sees childishness implicit in much of adult living, and sees striking continuities between the feelings and fantasies of the early years and those (not necessarily conscious) of the adult. But his view of how the observed continuities are mediated is likely to be very different. Instead of stressing hierarchical layering of preserved residues, he instead examines how the early motives and fantasies are cyclically perpetuated by the kinds of behaviors they lead to and the responses that are then evoked in others, responses that, as illustrated below, are likely to create just the kind of experience that makes the original wish and the original view of the world still seem salient.

For example, the two-year-old who has developed an engaging and playful manner is far more likely to evoke friendly interest and attention on the part of adults than is the child who is rather quiet and withdrawn. The latter will typically encounter a less rich interpersonal environment that will further decrease the likelihood that he will drastically change. Similarly, the former is likely to continually learn that other people are fun and are eager to interact with him, and his pattern too is likely to become more firmly fixed as he grows. Further, not only will the two children tend to evoke different behavior from others, they will also interpret differently the same reaction from another person. Thus, the playful child may experience a silent or grumpy response from another as a kind of game and may continue to interact until perhaps he does elicit an appreciative response. The quieter child, not used to much interaction, will readily accept the initial response as a signal to back off.

*4.1. The Role of "Accomplices" in Development**

If we look at the two children as adults, we may perhaps find the difference between them still evident, one outgoing, cheerful, and expecting the best of people, the other rather shy and unsure anyone is interested. A childhood pattern has persisted into adulthood. Yet, we really don't understand the developmental process unless we see how, successively, teachers, playmates, girl friends, and colleagues have been drawn in as "accomplices" in maintaining the persistent pattern. And, I would suggest, we don't understand the possibilities for change unless we realize that even now there are such "accomplices" and that if they stopped playing their role in the process, it would be likely to eventually alter.

It is important to recognize, however, that it is not that easy to get the accomplices to change. The signals we emit to other people constitute a powerful force field. The shy person does many sometimes almost invisible things to make it difficult for another person to stay open to him very long. Even a well-intentioned person is likely to eventually help confirm his view that others aren't really very interested.

Thus, from this perspective, the early pattern persists not despite changing conditions, but because the person's pattern of experiencing and interacting with others tends to continually recreate the old condi-

*Portions of the next few sections are drawn from Wachtel (1977a).

tions again and again. In many cases, the effects are subtle and not readily apparent without careful scrutiny. But on close inspection, each person may be seen to rather regularly produce a particular skewing of responses from others that defines his idiosyncratic interpersonal world. Even in seemingly similar situations, we are each likely to encounter slightly different interpersonal cues, which may render the texture of the experience critically different. We then act (again) in a way that seems appropriate to this particular state of affairs, and create the conditions for others to again and again set the stage for the pattern to be repeated. Rather than having been locked in in the past by an intrapsychic structuring, then, the pattern seems from this perspective to be continually being formed, but generally in a way that keeps it quite consistent through the years. It may appear inappropriate because it is not well correlated with the adult's "average expectable environment," but it is quite a bit more closely attuned to the person's idiosyncratically skewed version of that environment.

5. *Transference and Schemata*

Emphasis on such a cyclical recreation of interpersonal events, and on the real behavior of "accomplices" in perpetuating characterological patterns, does not imply that the person is perceiving every situation "objectively." Most clinicians have seen abundant examples of patients' distortions of what is going on, particularly in transference phenomena. Such aspects of psychological functioning must be included in any viable account of how neurotic patterns are perpetuated. But rather than relying on the metaphors that analysts have traditionally employed in conceptualizing such phenomena, I prefer to think in terms of the Piagetian notion of schema; for such a notion implies that not only do we assimilate new experiences to older, more familiar ways of viewing things (as is implicit in the concept of transference), we also do eventually accommodate to what is actually going on.

Thus, as in transference phenomena, new people and new relationships tend to be approached in terms of their similarity to earlier ones; and frequently, particularly in the special conditions of the psychoanalytic situation, one sees what appear to be quite arbitrary assumptions and perceptions occurring. But in principle, I would suggest, accommodation is always proceeding apace and would, with nonreactive sources of stimulation, eventually lead to a fairly accurate picture of what one is encountering. The problem is that other people are not nonreactive. How they behave toward us is very much influenced by how we behave toward them, and hence by how we initially perceive them. Thus, our initial (in a sense distorted) picture of another person can end up being a fairly accurate predictor of how he will act toward us, because based on our expectation that he will be hostile, or accepting, or sexual, we are likely to act in such a way as to eventually draw such behavior from the person and thus have our (initially inaccurate) perception "confirmed." Our tendency to enter the next relationship with the same assumption and perceptual bias is then strengthened and the whole process likely to be repeated again.

Such a perspective enables us to understand both continuity and change in the same terms. In a large number of cases, this process of "distorted" perception leading to a skewing of responses from others, and hence to a "confirmation" of the problematic way of experiencing, continues for years, and produces the phenomena so familiar to analytic observers. At times, however, a figure appears who, by virtue of his interpersonal history and personal force field, serves (with good or ill effect) to intervene in the developmental process rather than simply confirm present directions.* The patient's behavior may make this an unlikely process to persist, but if it does, it can be expected that he will eventually accommodate to this new input and show substantial change in an important aspect of his life. It is likely that many of the "spontaneous" cures that make the controls in psychotherapy research so tricky are the result of such accommodative processes.†

6. *Ties to "Early Objects"*

In describing this view of development, there is one more issue it is important for us to consider at this point. Frequently psychoanalytic exploration reveals that, without awareness, the person remains tied in his fantasy life and in his secret striving to figures from his early past. Typically, discovery of such a tie is viewed as accounting for the inhibitions and symptoms of the adult. The pull from the past is regarded as the causal influence. We shall now consider an alternative way of understanding this common observation.

As but one example, let us consider still another set of interlocked influences our two-year-old might encounter and then perpetuate.

*Less dramatic instances of this sort in which each person changes a bit are common. Usually, however, the change is small, because each participant is free to leave rather than change. The more constrained to be together, the more each can alter the other.

†It is also a good part of the professional therapist's skill to be able to be a source of change in this way. As Wolf (1966) has described, however, this is often rather difficult for the therapist to do.

Suppose that he is not encouraged by his family to develop the skills that can help him gain greater independence from them. This need not take the form of outright prohibition or interference. Indeed, often the knot is tighter when not readily visible, as when an ambivalent parent gives explicit encouragement to the child's budding independence but in subtle ways undermines it. Perhaps mother, without noticing it, is more frequently warm and attentive when the child sweetly says, "I love you, mommy," than when he shows her something he has put together; or cuddles him when he stands apart from the other children ("to make him feel better, so he won't be afraid to play") instead of helping him to initiate play or joining in with the group of children until her child is comfortable there. There are many ways in which, through ignorance or unacknowledged intent, a mother or father can bind and cripple a child while thinking he is encouraging independence.

When such is the case there is likely to be a point where the child's fearful clinging is recognized as distinguishing him from his age-mates, and not infrequently the parental reaction is likely to be a nagging, complaining, or insulting one, motivated by parental anxiety, embarrassment, guilt, or desperation. Even if the parent does not come out with "What's wrong with you? Why can't you be like the other kids?" or some similar assault, simply continuing to encourage participation in age-appropriate activities, when not accompanied by effective efforts to help the child accomplish the transition, can be experienced as punishing and cause the child considerable pain.

A child caught in such a developmental tangle is likely to remain more tied to his parents than most children his age. Having fewer alternative sources of gratification and security, he is likely to feel more than most the need to be mommy or daddy's little boy. Not only is this likely to further impede the exploration and assertion needed to develop the skills that would get him out of this dilemma; it is also likely to make him quite fearful of expressing anger or disagreement toward his parents—and this in circumstances more likely than usual to arouse anger. So we see an unhappy little child, afraid to venture forth, clinging to mother in a way that angers her (even as it also may gratify), feeling frustrated and irritated and perhaps even, if it is the case, sensing the grasping intent in the mother's harmful cloistering, yet desperately trying to be loyal and a good boy to at least have *mother* securely; and in so doing, preventing himself from developing the independence and expansiveness that are necessary for him to be able to loosen his hold on mother or to feel able to cope with the complexity of his feeling toward her.

If the dilemma confronting this child is in the "neurotic" range, then he will continue to grow despite all these inhibitions. There are enough countervailing forces in innate developmental processes, as well as in the expectations and reward structure of the larger social order, and even in other aspects of their own parents' behavior, that millions of children with such a history grow up to become taxpayers, spouses, and parents and thus in a very general way functioning adults. It takes a rather extraordinary effort to inhibit cognitive and personality growth so completely that these rather minimal criteria of "normality" are not achieved.*

But the situation I have described takes its toll. He does not "make it" without pain and struggle, and usually he does not make it without a price. In many respects he may advance along the way more slowly than his age-mates, getting there eventually but always feeling a little bit behind or a little out of it, venturing less, mastering less, so again venturing less, etc. By gross criteria, he may function well, yet in the more private, subtle, and intimate aspects of his life he will show the scars of his early years. He may, for example, evidence reasonable social ease and competence in general, but be inhibited in making sexual advances. Or, he may be able to initiate sexual activity quite easily, and "perform" adequately, but may not experience complete sexual release and satisfaction. Or, perhaps the sexual aspect of sexual relationships is fully satisfying but does not seem linked to an intimate sharing of personal feelings.

Any of these limitations in living could, if found to occur in conjunction with evidence for disavowed ties to parental figures, be attributed to the effects of those ties. That has traditionally been the understanding of such observations by analysts; and the implication drawn has been that one must work on untangling those ties in order to increase the patient's freedom in living. But again, it makes equal sense to consider, for example, how longings for the ideal caretaker–beauty (mother) of childhood might be fostered by a current life style that excludes fully satisfying experiences of intimacy and sensual satisfaction.

The lure of the Oedipal imagery is strengthened each time the person has an encounter that proves to be frustrating or disappointing. Whatever role the vicissitudes of feeling for mother may have played in starting the person on a life course that is in some important respects restricted in freedom, concrete interactions with later figures

*These criteria are meant simply to point to the *kind* of general achievements that tend to distinguish neurotic difficulties from more severe ones. It is in no sense meant to imply that individuals who do not marry, or do not have children, suffer from any personality disorder. My judgment on this would tend to be different, however, were the person completely lacking in human relationships.

tend to be significant in perpetuating it. If one is anxious or hesitant about sexuality or intimacy, one teaches one's partners to be similarly inclined. Satisfying sexuality and the experience of intimacy require a mutual trust and understanding. If an individual enters a new relationship in a hesitant way, the partner cannot long continue to be open with him, and he will find confirmed again and again throughout his life that his defensiveness in such situations is "justified," since he is inevitably disappointed and finds his partners tensing up or closing off in ways that hurt (and lead him to again be hesitant the next time and again evoke a complementary response from his partner).*

7. Therapeutic Implications

The differences between the above version of psychodynamic thought and that of Freudian psychoanalysis have important bearing on how one approaches the conduct of psychotherapy.† The present perspective, with its emphasis on self-perpetuating, cyclical processes (see also Wachtel, 1977b), points to a far more active role for the therapist, who must use his psychodynamic understanding not only to empathize with the patient and help him achieve insight, but also to help the patient to break into the vicious circles that have characterized his life. Intervention becomes a key focus of the therapist's efforts.

In much traditional psychodynamic writing on therapy, explicit interventions by the therapist are discouraged both on ethical grounds (see Wachtel, 1977a, chap. 12) and on the assumption that such intervention, or any "high profile" activity by the therapist, makes it harder for the patient to recognize how much of his reactions really have little to do with the current reality and reflect instead the continuing influence of his past. The view that the residues of past interactions have been internalized, and will remain frozen (though active) in their original form unless a process of uncovering reveals them and their inappropriateness to the critical scrutiny of the patient's ego, has led to a deemphasis on directly intervening in troubling life patterns. A time-consuming, indirect course appears, in this light, to be

*It should be clear that I am here describing something that does not necessarily go on consciously. Far from explicitly justifying a limited sex life on the basis of his partner's responses, the person may well extol both his partner's and his sex life for quite a while. Only careful scrutiny may reveal the particular dissatisfaction or lack of freedom in the person's life.

†See Wachtel (1977a) for futher detailed examination and illustration of the implications for psychotherapy.

the only way to overcome the effects of the past in any relatively thorough and extensive way (see Wachtel, 1977a, chap. 3).

From the present perspective, however, the effects of the past are a result not of some primarily internal set of influences but of an interlocking series of influences, both organismic and environmental in nature, which can continue to bring about, in the present, conditions and reaction-patterns that have characterized the person's life for many years. Given such a view, the therapist is likely to be far less hesitant to try to intervene in the patient's daily life patterns. He will feel less of a need to do "nothing" in order to demonstrate that the patient's reaction has little to do with him, both because he recognizes that he cannot do "nothing" (that, for example, silence from someone to whom one turns for help is striking and provocative, not neutral) and because he views the patient as always responsive to something, and wants to help the patient to understand the total situation he tends to create (including both the responses he evokes in others, including the therapist, and his idiosyncratic way of interpreting what transpires) and not just how he sees what isn't there.

The therapist operating from the perspective described here will view the work of interpretation and elucidating unconscious processes as facilitated rather than impaired by providing aid in dealing with life circumstances. If the intensity of unconscious desires or fantasies can be diminished by helping to change exacerbating life patterns, then those desires and fantasies can become less threatening and can be more readily recognized and controlled. Often, understanding or insight may be impeded by a pattern of behavior that intensifies frightening impulses to such a degree that only desperate defensive efforts seem permissible to the patient. Interpretive efforts are then bound to prove ineffective in helping the patient come to recognize the feelings and wishes that frighten him. Probably much failure of interpretive therapy is due to insufficient consideration of how the patient's neurotic behavior leads to intensification of forbidden impulses. We are too used to overemphasizing the other direction.

It has long been recognized that a particularly bad home situation can limit the effectiveness of analytic therapy, that the person's environment may undermine the gains of the analytic sessions. But the view of the neurotic process discussed above would suggest that in an important sense almost *all* patients live in growth-impeding environments. For one thing, the important figures in the person's life are usually engaged in a relationship with the patient in which the characterological features of the patient's neurosis are assumed. They have learned to come to terms with and have a stake in the old patterns of interchange, and frequently will exert considerable pressure to keep things as they were, even if mutually self-defeating. Resistance, then, is evident not only in the patient but also in his partners in important relationships. These figures have been chosen by the patient at least in part because they are willing and able to participate in the kinds of interaction that his character leads him to continually seek. Transference is manifested not only in perceptual distortions, that is, in seeing the past in the present when the present really is different. It also is manifested in creating old situations again, in really living with and relating to people who resemble figures from our past. Furthermore, not only do we choose people who fit our old categories and expectations, we also evoke a particular side of whomever we meet, and tend to elicit from others behavior that confirms old expectations.

Much of this goes on outside of awareness. The training that dynamically oriented therapists of all schools receive in discerning disavowed wishes and unacknowledged fantasies is critical in enabling the therapist to develop a full understanding of the life patterns that trouble the patient. The therapist must be sensitive to such unacknowledged organizing processes, and to the feelings evoked in him by being with the patient. But it is important to recognize that often understanding alone is not sufficient to help the patient change and grow in the face of the many conservative forces tending to keep things the same.

Frequently, for example, patients will report that in one situation or another they don't know what to say. Part of this "not knowing" is usually due to anxiety and defensive inhibition, and ceases to be a problem when the patient is less afraid of particular feelings or inclinations. But part is also frequently a result of a lifetime of cheating oneself out of opportunities to learn the effective behavior that most of us take for granted by the time we are adults. Children must go through a long process of learning how to effectively channel and express their feelings. Their initial efforts are quite crude, and would be readily discouraged were adults' standards of moderation and articulate expression applied to them. Fortunately, expectations are usually geared to the person's developmental stage and in most respects we gradually learn how to express ourselves in ways that bring us satisfying interactions with other people.

But where neurotic inhibitions have prevented this gradual learning process the adult who is perhaps almost for the first time expressing a need rather than inhibiting it is likely to do so in rather ineffective or inappropriate fashion. As therapists, we are set to be sympathetic toward these initial expressions of honest feeling, and we respond empathically and encouragingly to behavior in our patients that we often would not tolerate in our friends. But I believe that when the poignant struggle we observe in our sessions does not lead to the kind of progress in the patient's way of living that we hope for, it is often because other figures in the patient's life are not nearly as encouraging of these first crude efforts as we are. In addition to having a stake in old ways, as discussed above, these figures also employ different standards in reacting to the patient's behavior, and in their reactions they again teach the patient that honesty is dangerous.

When one views the patient's problem not as something "in" him, but as a self-perpetuating pattern of transactions, maintained in the present by the way in which interpersonal consequences and (often unconscious) motives and fantasies generate each other, one sees a need both for interpretation and active intervention.

8. The Relation between Psychoanalysis and Other Approaches

As I have elaborated elsewhere (Wachtel, 1977a; 1977b), the cyclical psychodynamic conception described here can be integrated with the perspectives dominant in academic personality research far more readily than can the more predominantly intrapsychic model of Freudian theory. As a psychodynamic model, it points to a great many process and content variables that have been largely ignored in academic research, but that, when framed in this way, are seen as complementary rather than contradictory to the academic conceptions. It is responsive to the influential contemporary critiques of psychodynamic thought that fault psychoanalysis for failing to recognize the degree to which human behavior must be understood as responsive to changing situational cues. Yet, it avoids the trap of "situationism" (Bowers, 1973), and attributes a robust and nonepiphenomenal role to the individual's motives, fantasies, and other organizing processes. Aspects of the perspective described here have contributed to critiques not only of the Freudian emphasis on history and intrapsychic structure, but also of traditional experimental methodology in personality research (Wachtel, 1973) and of much of the research on cognitive style (Wachtel, 1972).

The perspective offered here is "interactional," but can be distinguished from much work that goes under that label by its reluctance to treat "person variables" and "situation variables" as thoroughly independent. In much personality research, the interactionism comes in at the point of statistical analysis, when variables that are originally defined and conceptualized as very separate are combined additively and their statistical interaction viewed with interest. From the present perspective, however, it is hard to distinguish person variables and situation variables (or "internal" and "external" determinants). Aspects of the person and the situation he is in continuously interact. The appropriate mathematical representation for such interaction is not the statistical model of analysis of variance, but rather the model of the integral calculus. In most real-life situations, only for a diminishingly small instant is any person–effect manifested that is independent of the situation or does any situation unfold that is independent of the person who encounters (and changes) it.

References

Bowers, K.S. Situationism in psychology: An analysis and a critique. *Psychological Review*, 1973, *80*, 307–336.

Breuer, J., and Freud, S. (1895) *Studies on hysteria. Standard Edition* (Vol. 2). London: Hogarth, 1955.

Dollard, J., and Miller, N.E. *Personality and psychotherapy*. New York: McGraw-Hill, 1950.

Erikson, E.H. *Childhood and society*, 2nd ed. New York: Norton, 1963.

Klein, G.S. *Psychoanalytic theory: An exploration of essentials*. New York: International Universities Press, 1976.

Schafer, R. *Aspects of internalization*. New York: International Universities Press, 1968.

Schafer, R. Internalization: Process or fantasy? *Psychoanalytic Study of the Child*, 1972, Vol. 27.

Stone, L. *The psychoanalytic situation*. New York: International Universities Press, 1961.

Wachtel, P.L. Cognitive style and style of adaptation. *Perceptual and Motor Skills*, 1972, *35*, 779–785.

Wachtel, P.L. Psychodynamics, behavior therapy, and the implacable experimenter: An inquiry into the consistency of personality. *Journal of Abnormal Psychology*, 1973, *82*, 324–334.

Wachtel, P.L. *Psychoanalysis and behavior therapy: Toward an integration*. New York: Basic Books, 1977a.

Wachtel, P.L. Interaction cycles, unconscious processes, and the person–situation issue. In D. Magnusson and N. Endler (Eds.), *Personality at the crossroads: Issues in interactional psychology*. Hillsdale, N.J.: Lawrence Erlbaum Associates, 1977b.

Wolf, E. Learning theory and psychoanalysis. *British Journal of Medical Psychology*, 1966, *39*, 1–10.

Stress-Related Transactions between Person and Environment

Richard S. Lazarus
and Raymond Launier

Because stress implies a particular kind of commerce between a person (or animal) and environment, it provides an ideal vehicle for addressing the subject matter of this book on internal and external determinants of behavior. We believe this issue is expressed especially well by differentiating between two metatheoretical concepts, transaction and interaction. We have been drawn inexorably toward an emphasis on transaction by the very nature of stress phenomena and the evolving theoretical perspective within which we have worked.

1. *Transaction and Interaction*

In response to Mischel's (1968) challenge that situational rather than personality factors by and large determine behavior, there has been much current debate (cf. Endler and Magnusson, 1976) about what seems to us to be a pseudo-issue that, one might have thought, had already been disposed of long ago. Aside from mobilizing analytic thought and serving as a refresher course on the complexities of human behavior, the debate merely recapitulates extreme ideological positions long ago referred to by Murphy (1947) as the "organism error" and the "situational error." We would have supposed that most personality and social psychologists, regardless of their own particular interests, had by now implicitly or explicitly accepted a multifactorial and interactional view of the determinants of human action and reaction (see also Pervin's discussion of the centralists and peripheralists

Richard S. Lazarus • Department of Psychology, University of California, Berkeley, California 94720. Raymond Launier • Department of Psychology, University of California, Berkeley, California 94720. Fellowship support by Grant No. AG00002, awarded by the National Institute of Aging, is gratefully acknowledged.

of H. A. Murray, this volume). However, one important distinction has typically been overlooked, namely, between transaction and interaction.

1.1. The Transactional Perspective—Pure Description of Process

In our cognitive–phenomenological analysis of psychological stress, several varieties of relationships are said to occur between the personal and the environment, these being mediated by cognitive appraisal processes (cf. Lazarus, Averill, and Opton, 1970). The three key stress-relevant relationships are harm–loss, threat, and challenge. These relationships refer neither to person nor environment as separate sets of variables, but they describe a balance of forces such that environmental demands tax or exceed the resources of the person. A demand is such that if it is not met and neutralized somehow, there will be harmful consequences for the person. We are aware that demands can also arise internally and be in conflict intrapsychically; however, here we want to emphasize environmental demands as they relate to person characteristics.

Harm–loss, threat, and challenge are relational concepts that subtly transcend the separate sets of person and environment variables of which they are comprised. That is, when we are describing such relationships and the processes underlying them, the separate variables of person and environment are combined into a new concept (e.g., threat) at a higher level of analysis. Threat cannot be described in terms of person or environment alone, but must be defined by both. For example, a person may be threatened because the external demand seems very taxing and the resources for managing it weak, or the threat may arise from a weak demand that nevertheless appears stronger than the available resources for managing it. Both sides of the equation are necessary to the appraised relationship, meaning that threat depends on the "balance of power between the demands and the resources" (cf. Lazarus, 1966).

In speaking of harm–loss or threat, for example, we are only attempting to describe the hypothetical psychological relationship that underlies the observed pattern of reaction, not explain or predict it. Although such description is very important, theory can and should go much further by forming the speculative basis of choosing observable antecedent or causal variables of which the particular relationship is a function. Correctly applied, descriptive analysis in a cognitive-phenomenological theory need only be temporarily circular as long as it is followed by the necessary empirical research on determinants (Kaplan, 1964). The history of the once rejected concept of instinct points this up very well, especially as researchers began to find ways of identifying the external and internal stimuli that account for the unfolding pattern of species behavior (cf. Lehrman, 1964).

To make possible such cause and effect research we must embed the various relational categories of our description in antecedent person and environment variables and study their interplay in affecting stress and coping reactions. With respect to personality variables we might look to patterns of motivation for clues about situations that will be damaging or threatening, or to beliefs about the environment (i.e., as being hostile) and about one's own resources for mastering it (see, for example, Lazarus's 1966 discussion of beliefs underlying chronic threat and anxiety). With respect to situational variables, imminence of harm, probability of harm, and ambiguity might be considered as causal variables (also Lazarus, 1966). However, attention to causal variables leads us rapidly away from transaction and description to the more familiar and comfortable concept of interaction.

1.2. The Interactional Perspective—The Search for Determinants

Once we start to look for determinants of hypothetical transactions or relationships, our analytic model follows the logic of analysis of variance in which one partitions the person and environment antecedent variables in accordance with the proportion of outcome variation they account for separately and by interaction. The separate variables contributing to transactions or relationships are now, in effect, restored to the system, making the analysis deterministic. However, there are serious difficulties with a hasty and slavish use of this traditional interactional research model, debates about the relative importance of personality and situational variables notwithstanding.

For example, some of the research that focuses on partitioning of causal variables has not studied antecedent personality variables directly, but their role has been inferred from variations in reaction. Examples include the research of Endler, Hunt, and Rosenstein (1962), Endler and Hunt (1966; 1968), Nelson, Gridder, and Mutterer (1969), Bishop and Witt (1970), and Ekehammer, Magnusson, and Ricklander (1974), all of whom have used a situation–response (S–R) type of inventory to analyze the components of variance of stress reactions such as anxiety and anger (or aggression). In an S–R inventory the respondent rates his or her likely reaction on a number of scales for each of several situations. This yields a three-dimensional data matrix, situations by reactions by persons, which can be analyzed for main effects and interactions. However, in an S–R type of inventory there are situational inputs and response inputs (subjectively rated) from which personality characteristics might be inferred, but no personality inputs. There is no effort to specify and measure personality traits that might be entered into the data matrix. Strictly speaking, research of this type is not capable of identifying personality traits (e.g., patterns of commitment, belief systems) as determinants of stress reaction to various types of situations, although this could be done (as, for example, in the research of Glickstein, Chevalier, Korchin, Basowitz, Sabshin, Hamburg, and Grinker, 1957).

Another difficulty with traditional research strategies seeking to document the interactions between persons and environment as determinants of stress reactions is, we think, even more serious: Because such research is usually strictly deterministic rather than descriptive and process-oriented, it deals with static or structural variables; that is, it uses some single measure of a presumably stable property of persons (traits) or environment. When a statistical interaction is found, the presumption is usually made—without benefit of direct observation—that this is tantamount to an actual interactive process.

For example, evidence has been found that, compared with a vigilant style of coping, an avoidant style (as measured by a personality test) leads to a weaker stress response prior to upcoming surgery and a stronger one following surgery (cf. research summarized in Goldstein, 1973). From this it is then assumed that under the threat of surgery, differences in the coping process must account for the divergent reaction patterns. However, no attempt is made in such research to examine the processes so-called avoidant and vigilant persons actually use in coping with the threat. In other words, the actual description of process is absent; it is simply assumed that the trait of vigilance or avoidance would be manifest as process, though research instances occur in which no relationship is found between a trait measure of coping and the actual process of coping during a threat situation (cf. Cohen and Lazarus, 1973).

Although researchers often speak of a statistical interaction between person and environment as an interactive process, they are really looking at static fractions of variance rather than an actual interactive process. Is the one necessarily equivalent or analogous to the other? Thus, a personality trait such as avoidance may be shown to interact with a situational variable, say, degree of imposed threat, but without further observation it can only be speculated that when "avoiders" confront a high threat situation, they are actually in the process of avoiding thinking about the threat. Everything rests on whether the supposed trait is really being acted out in the research situation, and what little we know about the construct validity and predictive significance of personality trait measurement argues against such an assumption being true in any given instance.

Another serious defect of the analysis of variance logic of interaction is that it tends to imply a linear or one-way cause and effect model going generally from environment or situation, via person (mediation), to response (cf. Overton and Reese, 1973; Altman, 1976; Lazarus and Cohen, 1978). Indeed, for a long time psychology has thought mainly in terms of S–R, or S–O–R causal sequences. Yet one of the important but often forgotten premises of personality psychology has been the principle of multiple causation and overdetermination in which the same act or reaction is fed by many rather than a single antecedent event. An alternative premise is that causation also goes in the other direction, often originating in the person as an active agent in the person–environment transaction, and resulting in changes in that environment (cf. White, 1959). In short, there is *reciprocity of causation*: the person thinks and acts and thereby changes the person–environment relationship; information about this is fed back to the person through cognitive activity. Moreover, the environment often actively resists our efforts to cope by changing it.

This reciprocity of causation is especially evident if one studies psychological stress and coping over time, as in disabling illness or bereavement. In bereavement, for example, the nature of the stress changes over time, as do the coping tasks that the person must perform. As described by clinical researchers, there is first apt to be shock and disbelief at the loss, along with behaviors and fantasies that can be interpreted as efforts to preserve or restore the lost loved one. However, feedback from the environment makes it increasingly clear to the bereaved person that the loved one is physically gone and will never return. The individual is in the coffin, there is a tombstone (in Jewish mourning this is typically revealed or visited within a year after death), the house or apartment no longer contains the living presence or voice, and the multiple daily activities and relationships that used to include the loved one no longer do. As the initial shock and numbness wear off, depression, anger, guilt, anxiety, and other affects come in their place. The coping task is now to accept the loss, and ultimately to reinvest in new love objects, commitments, and activities. This changes the psychological environment. Clearly, grieving is a long and complex sequence of processes involving many self-induced changes in the person–environment relationship, and in the cognitive and coping processes that are often referred to as "grief work" (Lindemann, 1944).

The continuous flow of such person–environment relationships in stress, emotion, and coping cannot comfortably be encompassed within the traditional S–O–R, linear causation models, or within the statistical concept of interaction. Such a flow, and the changing relationships involved in it, need to be examined in purely descriptive terms before one asks the more analytic questions about the respective causal roles of variables of person and environment. One must remember that these variables, and their salience, are constantly changing with the flow of adaptive commerce as the person acts on the environment and in accordance with feedback from it. The relationship may change, say, from harm–loss to restitution or mastery, or from threat to a benign-positive appraisal, or remain refractory to change. Decompensation and growth are also taking place at various stages of the adaptational commerce.

Coping changes the person–environment relationship, and strong emotions do not usually last for long, but ebb and flow, or change over time as the relationship changes. There are, of course, regularities or stabilities in the relationship and its course, too, and these must be first described before they can be analyzed for their determinants. One determining factor in such stability may be that the person often remains basically in the same environment over time (living in the same house, having the same spouse, working in the same shop, etc.). Another factor is that the person carries around stable tendencies (e.g., beliefs about vulnerabilities or about the outside world, commitments, and coping styles) so that he or she is led to appraise certain events in the same or similar ways.

In any event, we need to be as much concerned with such relationships and processes as we are with their determinants. Both frames and reference—the descriptive, transactional, and the deterministic, interactional—must be incorporated into the same framework of understanding. In fact, most explanations of the natural world are presented in terms of both structures and processes, and the senior author (Lazarus, 1971b) has previously used a geological analogy to point up their differences and interrelations. For example, the area in which we live is comprised of hills, valleys, riverbeds, trees, and brush, etc., which are relatively stable and familiar fixtures of the landscape. The hills, valleys and rivers came into being through processes involving upheavals of the earth's surface. Once formed, this topography has, in turn, influenced the direction of wind striking the ground, storm patterns, the direction and rate of water flow, etc. Further, the flow of water and wind is, in turn, continually changing the geological structures themselves, for example, wearing down the hillsides, depositing and eroding organic matter, and so on. Thus, we see a constant interplay between the more or less stable structures and the moving, changing forces or processes. Our knowledge of any geological phenomenon would be incomplete unless we looked at both structure and process and their interplay. Similarly, personality psychology needs to be concerned with both structure or stability and change or process (also termed dynamics). It has seemed to us that lately we have been overly concerned with the former at the expense of the latter.

2. *The Concept of Stress*

Throughout the history of its usage the concept of stress has meant different things to different persons.* There seem to have been three main variations. (1) Perhaps most commonly, stress is regarded as a stimulus, i.e., a condition that generates turbulence or reactive change of some sort. (2) Stress has often meant the turbulent reaction itself, i.e., the response. One must also note that whether as a stimulus or response, stress is treated, often unwittingly, at each of the three different scientific levels of analysis: the social, psychological, and physiological or tissue (see Lazarus, 1966; Lazarus, 1971b; Lazarus and Cohen, 1976). (3) Stress, has, of course, also been treated as a relational or transactional concept describing certain kinds of adaptive commerce between any system (e.g., a person) and an environment. The latter is the view adopted here. The key issue now becomes that of specifying the relational rules involving the stimulus and response that govern the emergence of stress phenomena.

The question of what type of stimulus provokes the stress response now becomes the first basic and substantive issue of stress theory and research. There are two logical candidates: On the one hand, we might look to a situational or environmental event; on the other hand, we can ascribe causal significance to biological and psychological characteristics of the person or animal. Thus, the issue of the sufficient and necessary condition of the stress response devolves into the fruitless, perennial debate between environmentalists and organismicists, or situationalists and personologists. We say fruitless because to us the answer is clearly that both are crucial causal elements in a complex, multivariate system.

For example, the Holmes and Rahe type of research on stress and illness has focused on external provokers of the stress reaction such as

*The reader may wish to consult other treatments of the history and character of the stress concept, for example, those of Lazarus, 1966; Appley and Trumbull, 1976; Scott and Howard, 1970; Hinkle, 1974; and Mason, 1975; to mention some of the best known.

loss of a loved one, divorce, loss of a job, etc. Aside from Rahe, who appears to have moved away from an extreme environmentalist position (see Rahe, 1974), no attention is paid to the contribution of the person to the stressful commerce with the environment. It is as if the person were merely the passive victim of adventitious events. The other extreme alternative is to say that by virtue of certain psychobiological characteristics, it is the person who creates the stress events or carries responsibility for the type and severity of the stress reaction. We see here an instance of "the situation error" in the former alternative while the latter remains an instance of "the organism error" (Murphy, 1947).

The situational or stimulus approach bears the crucial defect that there are always individual differences in the quality, intensity, and duration of reaction to the same environmental event. We learn, for example (Glass and Singer, 1972), that the effects of noise depend on the way it is evaluated by the person and to what extent the person believes it can be controlled. Whether high population density is responded to subjectively as stressful crowding turns out to depend on the meaning given to such a condition—meaning that in turn arises in considerable degree from culture and personality—and the tasks that must be performed (Altman, 1975; Stokols, 1976). A situation will be reacted to as a threat by one person, a challenge by another, and mostly irrelevant by a third. Even in military combat some persons will develop severe psychopathological reactions while others will seem little affected (Grinker and Spiegel, 1945). As Allport (1937, p. 325) put it epigrammatically, "The same fire that melts the butter, hardens the egg."

On the other hand, it would be equally irrational to suggest that the personality is the sole or even primary agent of the stress reaction. Highly troubling and demanding events do happen to some and not to others at any given time of life, there being great variation in their frequency, type, and patterning. We are usually not responsible for natural and social disasters such as earthquakes, economic depressions, or whatever, although in some instances we may contribute to them or cope with them with different effectiveness (see, for example, Sims and Baumann, 1972, on tornado deaths). Many personal disasters too occur adventitiously. Thus, although personality and organismic factors play an important role as antecedents of the stress response, they cannot be regarded as the sole agent, and their causal role remains difficult to tease out from the other, environmentally based factors.

Be that as it may, one way personality probably operates as a factor in the stress response is by having an impact on the individual's vulnerability in any given situation, whether or not one is aware of this vulnerability. Vulnerability in the psychological sense is not the emotional or distress response itself, which is the way Weisman and Worden (1976) use the term, but an appraisal of the capability of being harmed or in danger; in short, it is a psychological liability derived from one's personality and/or one's circumstances. Such vulnerability affects whether one anticipates harm or benefit. For example, deep personal commitments to achievement and success may leave an individual threatened by the prospect of poor performance or failure in an evaluative situation, while lack of such commitment makes threat less likely or weaker (Vogel, Raymond, and Lazarus, 1959). An individual with the conviction that the setting is hostile or dangerous, and who feels generally inadequate, is far more likely to feel threatened and react with anxiety than one who has high confidence in the available resources for mastery, or who believes the environment is usually benign or nurturant. Vulnerability probably has a wide variety of developmental and situational causes. The classic studies of Grinker and Spiegel (1945) of members of air combat crews who developed stress disorders point strongly to the role of pre-existing "neuroses" (i.e., before the airmen entered military service) in generating vulnerability to "breakdown" during combat. Other research (e.g., Merbaum and Hefez, 1976) has occasionally failed to confirm this possibility, however.

Another way personality might operate to affect stress reaction is by determining choices throughout the life cycle, thus determining the environmental areas of, say, work, play, and intimacy within which an individual operates. Some arenas may be avoided because the individual construes them as dangerous or overpowering, and others are sought because they permit or are necessary to growth of long-range competencies and self-realization. It has been shown, for example, that persons with low confidence in their competencies are likely to seek relatively secure and undemanding occupations, while those with high self-confidence are more apt to reach for demanding and challenging occupational roles (Liberty, Burnstein, and Moulton, 1966). It is likely that some type of self-selective process operates in most of the choices people make at each stage of the life cycle, including career, changing jobs, love and marriage, having children, deciding on divorce, voluntary relocation, and so on, each decision or choice having significance for the vulnerability of the person to certain kinds of stressful experiences. In sum, we cannot sensibly consider the stress response as solely dependent on events external to the person, since humans are not passive responders to whatever happens. Rather, they perceive, evaluate, and therefore select and shape their environments to some extent, thus contributing to or preventing certain kinds of stress from ever happening (Lazarus, 1975).

Nowhere is confusion about this more evident than in the list of life events employed by Holmes and Rahe (Holmes and Masuda, 1974). Many of the items in their scale seriously confound adventitious happenings in the environment with the contribution to the life change made by the person. Death of a spouse (one of the items in their list) might be relatively free of this confounding. On the other hand, marriage and divorce can be quite another story, as are loss of job, job promotion, pregnancy, and so on. In each of these latter instances the person usually contributes something, often much, to making the life event happen. In some cases a person may be merely the passive object of rejection by the marital partner in a divorce action, but in others the movement toward divorce may be a mode of coping by one or both partners involved in a poor relationship.

As we suggested, the meaning sphere encompassed by the term "stress" is any event in which environmental or internal demands (or both) *tax or exceed the adaptive resources* of an individual, social system, or tissue system. This makes stress a very broad concept, encompassing as it does a social system, an individual system (psychological), or a tissue system (physiological). The senior author (Lazarus, 1966; 1971b) has previously provided arguments for viewing stress as a very general rubric rather than a precisely defined single process. Nevertheless, at all levels of analysis the operative phrase in the above definition is "tax or exceed." To tax is to levy a charge or exact a tribute, burden, or cost, whether this cost is great or small, and whatever its form. Thus, stress involves a transaction in which resources must be mobilized; the more the mobilization, the greater the cost and the more likely is outcome in doubt. In stress, mobilization occurs because adequate automatic responses are not available with which to manage the demand (White, 1974).

In psychological terms, stress requires a judgment that the transaction involves jeopardy (threat), harm–loss, or an opportunity to overcome hardship and grow (challenge) by drawing upon more than routine resources. When a demand exceeds resources, the individual is psychologically overwhelmed (trauma) and defeated, as it were. Its seriousness depends on the stakes involved (e.g., the commitment). The outcome could well be exhaustion, collapse, regression, or decompensation (to use some of the terms of clinical psychology).

The two basic components of such a general relational definition, demands and resources, have a commonsense ring and so are often not further defined. Environmental demands are external events that impose adaptive requirements that, in the event of failure of suitable action, will lead to negative consequences. Internal demands refer to goals, values, commitments, programs, or tasks acquired by an individual (or social system or tissue system) whose thwarting or postponement would have negative consequences or implications. Adaptive resources consist of any properties of the system that have the potential capacity to help meet demands and hence to prevent the negative consequences that failure of suitable action would entail. As we said, whether or not transactions are stressful always depends on the balance of power, so to speak, between the two opposing forces, demands and resources (Lazarus, 1966; see also Klausner, 1971).

The traditional engineering use of the term "stress" is also relational, load being the environmental force exerted on a substance, strain being its resultant deformation, and stress being the relationship between the dimensions of load and the characteristics of the objects. However, the analogy of physical objects to biological systems, and to sensate and thinking organisms, has a potential weakness. In the engineering usage, what is usually omitted are the processes by which social systems, tissue systems, and psychological systems maintain themselves, thereby constantly altering their relationship with the environment while retaining viability and a degree of constancy. At the psychological level this transformational activity, which includes cognitive as well as coping processes (see White, 1974 and Murphy, 1974) characteristic of a phylogenetically advanced psychological system, very significantly alters the manner in which stress dynamics must be viewed.

3. *Early Theoretical Research Efforts of the Lazarus Group*

In the late 1940s and 1950s, much research on stress took place in the laboratory. It was focused mainly on investigation of two problems, namely, ego-defensive processes in memory and perception presumably generated by anxiety, and the effects of stress conditions, such as electric shock or failure, on skilled performance and learning. During that period, the laboratory experiment was highly venerated as the best means to test notions about psychodynamic processes.

In the early 1960s Lazarus and his associates sought a more naturalistic way of creating and studying stress processes in the laboratory. Motion picture films appeared ideal because they did not depend on deception but relied on the natural tendency of people to react emotionally while watching others have damaging experiences (Lazarus, Speisman, Mordkoff, and Davison, 1962). It was a comparatively simple matter to assess a subject's reported distress repeatedly during a film showing, and to record autonomic nervous system and organ reactions continuously as these ebbed and flowed with the reaction to the filmed events. The naturalism of the film paradigm did not require sacrifice of the experimental control and fairly precise measurement of the laboratory. Further, many antecedent variables could be manipulated; since the theoretical emphasis was always on psychological mediators of the stress reaction, the research centered on cognitive appraisal and intrapsychic modes of coping.

3.1. Research on Cognitive Appraisal and Intrapsychic Coping

From the outset, the guiding outlook was that stress could not be defined at the stimulus level alone, but depended on the ways environmental events were construed by the individual, that is, their appraised significance for well-being, and on the coping resources and options available and used (Lazarus, 1966). An obvious step in the laboratory study of film-induced stress reaction was to evaluate the meditating role of cognitive appraisals by manipulating such appraisals experimentally. There followed a series of studies (Speisman, Lazarus, Mordkoff, and Davison, 1964; Lazarus and Alfert, 1964; Lazarus, Opton, Nomikos, and Rankin, 1965; Nomikos, Opton, Averill, and Lazarus 1968; Folkins, Lawson, and Opton, 1968; Folkins, 1970; Monat, Averill, and Lazarus, 1972; and Koriat, Melkman, Averill, and Lazarus, 1972) showing that variations in appraisal were indeed associated with concomitant degrees and kinds of stress reaction.

It is unnecessary here to describe in detail the above studies since they have already been reviewed elsewhere (e.g., Lazarus, 1968; Lazarus, Averill, and Opton, 1970). The line of thought represented in this research can be sufficiently well illustrated by summarizing one of the most important early experiments (Speisman *et al.*, 1964) in which ego-defense theory provided the conceptual basis for the appraisal manipulation. A silent film showing a rite of passage among Australian aborigines in which there was presented a series of crude operations on the penis and scrotum of adolescent boys was used to generate stress reactions. Three sound tracks, employed like travelogue narratives, were created for the film: (1) a trauma passage that focused on the main sources of threat (e.g., pain, disease, sadism, castration) in the film; (2) a denial/reaction-formation passage that characterized the procedures as harmless, undistressing to the boys, and even a source of joy; (3) an intellectualization passage communicating emotional detachment from the film events.

The trauma sound track was found to enhance stress reactions (both subjective and autonomic) compared with a control condition, while both denial and intellectualization sound tracks reduced it. The magnitude of the ameliorative effects appeared to depend on personality characteristics: subjects disposed to denial as a form of coping showed less stress-reduction in response to the intellectualization passage than to denial, and vice versa for intellectualizers. In sum, we had influenced the appraisal process and in so doing had also altered the level of stress response; however, the magnitude of this effect depended on personality characteristics of the subjects, being greater when the content of the manipulation was compatible with coping or thinking predispositions. The latter finding is a fine example of interaction between causal determinants, in this case an environmental condition (i.e., the experimental treatment) and a personality disposition.

The experiment summarized above had studied mediating appraisals in two ways, namely, by external manipulation or influence (sound tracks), and by the selection of subjects differing in the disposition to appraise or cope in a given way. Later studies using similar research strategies (e.g., Lazarus and Alfert, 1964; Lazarus *et al.*, 1965) shifted the manipulation from sound tracks to orientation passages played prior to the film, and used other types of stressful films. Still others (e.g., Nomikos *et al.*, 1968) added new strategies, for example, manipulation of appraisal indirectly by varying the time period a subject awaited a stressful confrontation, and directly assessing appraisal processes (Folkins, 1970). Still other experiments used direct rather than vicarious or film-induced threats, e.g., electric shock (Monat *et al.*, 1972; Monat, 1976), and varied degree and kind of uncertainty about whether a harmful event would occur and when it would occur. One study instructed subjects to use self-generated intrapsychic devices to enhance or reduce the stress response (Koriat *et al.*, 1972) and examined some of the cognitive strategies used in each case.

This program of empirical research confirmed the powerful role played by the mediating processes of cognitive appraisal, and by intrapsychic modes of coping (e.g., denial, intellectualization, etc.) in determining the stress response degree and kind. Given the subjects' commitment to participate and the mild nature of the threats, direct actions designed to alter the situation (such as leaving the experiment) were not realistically available, and so the above program of research emphasized intrapsychic modes of coping and did not address large classes of coping activities operative in life stress. It also implicated personality dispositions (Opton and Lazarus, 1967; Averill, Olbrich, and Lazarus, 1972) as factors in appraisal and coping. Finally, the above research encouraged the further and continuing elaboration of psychological stress theory—in fact, the theory of emotions in general—from a cognitive point of view (Lazarus, 1966; Lazarus, 1968; Lazarus, Averill, and Opton, 1970; Lazarus and Averill, 1972; Lazarus, 1975).

It is worth noting in passing that other laboratories have also successfully employed variants of the above theoretical and research paradigm in the study of stress and coping (e.g., Holmes and Houston, 1974; Bennett and Holmes, 1975; Geen, Stonner, and Kelley, 1974; Neufeld, 1970, 1975, 1976; Neufeld and Davidson, 1971; Shean, Faia, and Schmaltz, 1974; Shiomi, 1974; Baker, Sandman, and Pepinsky, 1975; Rogers and Mewborn, 1976; and probably others). This perspective has also been used in a cognitively oriented treatment program for alcohol abuse (Sanchez-Craig and Walker, personal communication). Such research has provided a substantial data base for the proposition that how a person appraises and copes with an environmental stressor has important bearing on the emotional and adaptive outcomes. However, the emerging conceptual framework and the research cited above has also highlighted for us the limitations of a strictly laboratory approach to the study of stress and coping, since the most central theoretical issues turn out to be somewhat refractory to laboratory-generated data.

3.2. *Limitations of the Laboratory*

At this stage of our knowledge the laboratory experiment seems not to be the ideal research strategy with which to study stress, coping, and their adaptational outcomes. We feel increasingly that these topics must be studied in the life setting where they occur. Five main limitations of the laboratory stand out:

First, laboratory experiments do not readily provide descriptive ecological information on the sources of stress response in the daily lives of ordinary persons, for example, the major life changes that they face, their chronic daily hassles, the patterns of emotional reaction such persons experience, or the patterns of coping they utilize (cf. Lazarus and Cohen, 1976).

Second, laboratory experiments provide no information about the role of stress and coping in various processes that lead to adaptational outcomes such as somatic illness, social functioning, and morale. These outcomes emerge slowly over time, and stress in the laboratory experiment is normally a time-limited event. It is not enough to examine momentary hormonal or autonomic nervous system changes, i.e., what Kagan and Levi (1974) have called "precursors of disease," because we have no way of knowing which of these changes will lead to actual disease unless we study the onset of such disease concurrently (cf. Luborsky, Docherty, and Penick, 1973), nor have researchers been able to predict disease dependably through prior assessments. Moreover, coping processes emerge and change over time following a severe loss and in other threat situations. The laboratory is ill equipped to examine such time-linked or stage-oriented transactional processes, especially mechanisms that are multifactorial and involve complex feedback.

Third, practical and ethical considerations make it impossible to generate stress reactions of the type and severity found in real life, or to study a suitable range of coping processes even modestly representative of what happens in nature. Though mild threats and harms (such as pain) are less subject to restriction on ethical grounds, there is reason to doubt that valid rules about stress and coping could be generated from such pale shadows of real-life stresses.

Fourth, although laboratory experimentation is prized for the precise control it supposedly offers, and the ability to isolate variables and to manipulate them to get at cause-and-effect relationships, this control is often quite illusory, especially in research on psychodynamic and social processes. The experimenter often incorrectly defines what is going on in terms of the particular stimulus conditions he has manipulated, while in reality, much of central importance is occurring in the transaction between experimenter and subject, between subject and the laboratory context, and within the subject, that goes unacknowledged (cf. Orne, 1962; Rosenthal, 1966). To the extent that the desired laboratory control can actually be achieved, it is often bought at the expense of meaningful analogues between the laboratory and real life that are, after all, the former's only justification.

Finally, most experiments on stress and coping, despite claims to the contrary, are fishing expeditions rather than precise tests of carefully delineated hypotheses stemming from sharply articulated and systematic theoretical propositions. We are not yet ready to capitalize on the special virtues of the laboratory to evaluate stress theory because it is premature to search for elegant, reductive principles to test. Our greatest need now is to try to describe what is happening in everyday life with respect to stress and coping processes, and to try to relate these processes to various outcomes of interest such as morale, social functioning, and health/illness. We need to expand our set of concepts about mediating psychological processes such as appraisal and coping, and to develop a technology for measuring them in life settings. Some of the implications of such a view for actual nonlaboratory research have been spelled out elsewhere (Lazarus and Cohen, 1976).

4. *Current Transactional Formulations*

The linchpins of our theoretical formulations have been and still are two-fold, namely, cognitive appraisal and coping. The concept of appraisal remains pretty much as it was defined earlier (Lazarus, 1966) with a few additions and elaborations; however, we have been emphasizing coping increasingly as a crucial determining factor in emotion and adaptive outcome.

4.1. *Cognitive Appraisal Processes*

That which distinguishes ordinary "cold" perception (see Arnold, 1960) from cognitive appraisal is that the latter is evaluative in a personal sense. Appraisal consists of a continuously changing set of judgments about the significance of the flow of events for the person's well-being. Such judgments are always taking place—adaptive commerce with the environment is continual and ever-changing—though appraisals may also have certain stabilities or repetitious features, too, as we noted earlier.

Cognitive appraisal can be simply understood as the mental process of placing any event in one of a series of evaluative categories related either to its significance for the person's well-being (primary appraisal) or to the available coping resources and options (secondary appraisal). As a concept, it is related to, but not the same as, information processing (Mandler, 1975).

4.1.1. Primary Appraisals. It seems useful to identify three basic categories of primary appraisal of *well being*: A person may consider a given event to be either (1) irrelevant, (2) benign–positive, or (3) harmful.

Appraisal of an event as *irrelevant* means that the person does not consider it as having any implication whatsoever for well-being in its present form (although this appraisal could quickly change as the stimulus configuration changes, or upon reflection), Such an appraisal is probably analogous to the ultimate habituation of the "orienting response" in animals (some writers speak of this as the "what is it?" response). For example, a dog that suddenly becomes alert, turning toward a noise, sniffing at and listening to it, ultimately ceases to respond to it after it has been repeatedly experienced to be adaptively irrelevant, that is, as signaling neither danger nor reward.

A *benign–positive* appraisal means that the person regards an event as signifying a positive state of affairs; all is well, and if no threat to such a state impends, one may relax and attend to whatever else is on the agenda. No adaptive or coping effort related to the event is required, but in addition, the person feels comfortable, or the immediate experience may be that of joy, love, exhilaration, depending on the flow of events and their interpretation. General experience, or the presence of certain cues, may suggest to the person that this condition is time limited, or that effort may be needed to retain or enhance it. In such an instance, a benign–positive appraisal may combine with, or shade off into, mild threat over the possibility of its loss. Such complex appraisals are probably quite common, and in light of the normally complex patterns of emotion humans experience, they may be the rule rather than the exception. Some persons may, for example, never experience joy uncontaminated by apprehension (things can't possibly remain this good) or guilt that implies an appraisal process that is a mixture of benign–positive and threatening.

It should be evident from the above discussion of benign–positive appraisals that we are concerned with a cognitive theory of emotion in general, as well as of psychological stress. The two topics are closely linked. The latter is somewhat more limited in scope, applying only to negatively toned emotions such as fear, anxiety, guilt, sadness–depression, envy, jealousy, anger, and so on, and leaving out such positively toned emotions as joy, love, exhilaration, and the like. Although our emphasis in this chapter is on the psychodynamics of the stress emotions, a subset of emotions, as it was in Lazarus (1966), the concept of mediating cognitive appraisals and most of what we have to say here also has relevance to the larger rubric of emotions in general.

Our emphasis on the causal influence of cognitive processes on stress and emotion does not mean that stress and emotion, in turn, do not affect cognition. We are convinced, in fact, that the relations among cognition, emotion (or affect), and motivation are exceedingly complex two-way streets, with emotion often disrupting or interfering with cognitive activity, motivation (we prefer the term "commitment" to suggest long-term, stable goals and values) influencing the appraisal of harm or threat, emotion helping developmentally to shape motivation and cognition, and so on. However, the theoretical route from cognitive activity to emotion as a reaction has been underemphasized, indeed de-emphasized, in psychology for many decades. In our view, this leaves out the most important factor shaping the intensity and quality of a given emotional response and, therefore, our emphasis here on the role of cognition in emotion is long overdue.

Stressful appraisals, as we have said, are of three types, namely, harm–loss, threat, and challenge, all three involving some negative evaluation of one's present or future state of well-being, but challenge providing the least negative and the most positive feeling tone.

Harm–loss refers to damage that has already occurred, for example, a door permanently closed on a short- or long-term commitment, a central conception about oneself and the world that has been overturned, damage to one's self or one's social esteem, an interpersonal loss or an incapacitating injury. *Threat* concerns harm or loss that has not yet happened but is anticipated. As has been well documented in field studies of serious illness, harm and threat are apt to be mixed as when, for example, severely burned (Hamburg, Hamburg, and DeGoza, 1953) or otherwise incapacitated patients (Visotsky, Hamburg, Gross, and Lebovits, 1961), have to face the present loss of their normal function, financial status, and careers—that is, harm–loss that has already happened—but also must cope with the implications of their condition for the future. In bereavement, not only must the person who has lost a loved one somehow have to accept the damage already done, but a variety of future (anticipatory) demands such a loss entails must also be considered. Anticipatory coping involves a different set of rules than coping with harm that has already happened.

One of the most interesting and obscure issues in the field of stress, coping, health, and illness, concerns the distinction between threat and challenge. The difference seems to be a matter of positive versus negative tone, that is, whether one emphasizes in the appraisal the potential harm in a transaction (threat), or the difficult-to-attain, possibly risky, but positive mastery or gain (challenge). Whether one or the other appraisal occurs probably depends in part on the configuration of the environmental events themselves. It probably also depends on the person's beliefs about the potential for mastery, a hypothesis that could be tested empirically. Some persons seem characterized by a style of thinking that disposes to challenge rather than threat. Moreover, people commonly value, and make an effort to "put a good face on things," to exercise the "power of positive thinking," to "keep a stiff upper lip" in the face of adversity, etc. The implicit assumption here is that challenge is a better state of mind than threat, a more effective way to live and function, and possibly a way to achieve better somatic health.

To what extent challenge in the above sense overlaps with denial defense is unclear. Denial is so loosely defined in practice, varying from merely seeing things in a positive light to actual self-deception in the face of threatening information, or merely a social presentation of self, that without more careful specification and assessment it would be difficult to distinguish between these diverse appraisal processes. Thus, it is called denial when persons appear to deny that they are ill even when they have never been clearly informed that they are, when they accept that they are ill but appear inattentive or oblivious to the life-threatening implications of that illness, and even when they realize they are soon to die but seem to believe their psychological identity will never be lost (as in reincarnation, life after death, resurrection, or living on in others' minds). Weisman (1972) refers to this latter kind as stage 3 denial. And Becker (1973) treats the whole of life as one coordinated effort at denial of death. Few concepts have been more casually used, both clinically and in research, as that of denial. In a larger sense, the technology of assessment of cognitive appraisal and intrapsychic coping processes in general is very poorly developed at the present time.

Another unsettled issue concerning challenge is whether or not it has different adaptive consequences than threat. Presumably, challenged persons have better morale and are more cheerful, at least superficially, in the face of adversity than threatened persons. More difficult to evaluate is whether this advantage extends also to the adequacy of social functioning, and to somatic health and disease. As we noted earlier, the initial assumption in the life events scaling of Holmes and Rahe was that any kind of stressful life change has damaging consequences for health regardless of how it is appraised, depending on how much adaptive effort it requires. Recently, however, Selye (1974) has seemed to abandon his extreme generality position by distinguishing between harmful and constructive stress, though he has not said whether or not the bodily reaction in each case (i.e., the General Adaptation Syndrome) is the same. If the same somatic reaction occurs to threat and to challenge, then the distinction is merely a matter of attitude or behavior rather than of tissue damage; however, if challenge results in less disease than threat, there is reason to believe the somatic reaction (GAS) could also be different in each. The issue is only researchable if threat and challenge can be reliably distinguished and the complex profile of hormonal and tissue response delineated (see Mason, 1974).

Harm–loss, threat, and challenge are broad categories of primary appraisal and each could be further broken down into a variety of subtypes. Thus, one can speak of loss of or damage to social or self-esteem, beliefs, or some other function or aspect of self (e.g., loss of commitments, social status, integrity, or career opportunities). Similarly, there can be threat to one's physical integrity. Challenge too can take equally diverse forms depending on the functions, values, motives, or commitments at stake. It is possible that such distinctions have relevance to the person's stress reaction. For instance, Spielberger (1972) has reported evidence that some people, especially those with weak self-esteem, are vulnerable to anxiety primarily when facing ego-related threats as opposed to physical harm. Therefore, it may ultimately be useful to differentiate further among the broad appraisal categories we have been discussing, especially if we are to understand the relations between appraisal and complex emotional states.

4.1.2. Secondary Appraisals. The essential difference between secondary appraisal and primary appraisal lies in what is being evaluated. Secondary appraisal deals with coping resources and options. The word secondary does not mean that it necessarily follows primary appraisal in time or is less important. Perhaps, therefore, it would have been better at the outset to have used different terms, such as "appraisal of coping resources" and "appraisal of well-being," but so much has already been written that it is now best left alone. In any case, cognitions about coping options and resources can arise and be stored in memory well before the primary appraisals of threat or harm–loss occur. For example, we may notice ways of escaping a theater, or about how to prepare for examinations, without necessarily having any sense of immediate danger. We can use this knowledge, however, when signs of danger are noted. The two forms of appraisal also influence each other. The knowledge that one can overcome a potential danger may make that danger moot; and the knowledge that one is in danger typically mobilizes a search for information about, or an evaluation of, what can and cannot be done (Janis, 1974, refers to this as vigilance). The important point, however, is that secondary appraisal is important in shaping the coping activities of the person under psychological stress, as well as in shaping the primary appraisal process itself.

Past discussion of secondary appraisal (Lazarus, 1966) has been quite incomplete, and it still remains to spell out various types of secondary appraisal, how they feed back to primary appraisal (in shaping degree of threat), and how they shape the coping process. We cannot carry such an analysis very far here, but we can illustrate the kind of analysis that needs to be made. We might imagine a person anticipating an upcoming job interview and who appraises the transaction as threatening, that is, there is a high likelihood of being rejected for the job. A number of alternative secondary appraisals about this are possible, each having different implications for threat and coping. A few examples can be offered below:

1. "As things stand now, I will probably be rejected. This is a very damaging outcome because I have no other job opportunities. If I had the ability to deal effectively with the interview, I could be hired, but I don't have the ability. Moreover, there is no one to help me. The situation is hopeless."

2. "As things stand now, I will probably be rejected. This is a very damaging outcome because I have no other job opportunities. If I had the ability to deal effectively with the interview, I could be hired. I believe I do have such ability and I must think out what would make me an attractive candidate, rehearse, and take a tranquilizer two hours before the interview to control my nervousness."

3. "As things stand now, I will probably be rejected. This is a very damaging outcome because I have no other job opportunities. If I

had the ability to deal effectively with the interview I could be hired, but I don't. However, I have a good friend who knows the personnel manager, and I think he will help me."

4. "As things stand now, I will probably be rejected. This would be too bad because I need a job and this one looks very attractive. However, there are other possibilities, so if I am not hired I can try those."

5. "As things stand now, I will probably be rejected. This is a very damaging outcome because I have no other job opportunities. I never get a fair shake in life because I am (black, a Jew, a foreigner, ugly, a woman, etc.), or because of the policy of affirmative action, which puts me at a disadvantage. It is a corrupt world."

Clearly, the secondary appraisal in (1) not only reinforces the threat, but it pictures things as quite hopeless. A person in this transaction might well feel depressed and decide not to bother with the interview at all.

The individual in (2) is at first threatened and anxious, but in the secondary appraisal process finds grounds for considerable hope, the primary appraisal shifting in the direction of challenge as opposed to threat. This individual is also taking whatever steps can be figured out to cope with the threat, a process that increases the chances of mastery, and in all likelihood decreases the distress at this stage of the coping process.

In (3) the individual goes through a similar process, but instead of relying on personal coping resources, believes there is a well-placed and favorably oriented friend. If internal and external constraints against this are minimal, the coping response will be to contact that friend to seek help.

In (4) we have an individual who judges the potential harm of rejection as mild, since there are other options. There is, therefore, little threat, nor will there be much preparatory mobilization of effort.

Finally, in (5) the blame for the situation is viewed as external, and although the threat seems as great and the outcome as damaging as in (1), the central emotion experienced is likely to be anger rather than depression or anxiety. Moreover, the person with this kind of secondary appraisal may cope actively by voting for a racist, joining a dissident group, bringing suit against the unfair practices of the employer, or engaging in any other of a variety of forms of coping described by Merton (1949) as applying to groups under conditions of social unrest. The important point is that secondary appraisal, oriented as it is to possible coping resources and options, not only influences the primary appraisal process itself, mitigating or enhancing threat or the sense of harm, but it also shapes coping activity.

The appraisal processes being considered here are not necessarily conscious or deliberate; they can occur without awareness, though we often do think consciously and deliberately about coping options, especially in anticipatory situations that emerge slowly and allow reflection.

The central reason why secondary appraisal has so much to do with the primary appraisal of harm–loss, threat, and challenge is to be found in the definition of psychological stress itself. A potential harm is not a harm if the person can master it easily, and if it is appraised as such there is little or no threat. The resources a person believes are available are arrayed psychologically against the dangers and harms being faced, and are a crucial cognitive factor in the generation of the psychological stress response.

4.1.3. Reappraisals. The feedback system pointed to above has been formalized (Lazarus, 1966) by expanding the concept of appraisal to include information from one's own reactions and from the environment, as well as further reflection that, in turn, could lead to reappraisal. Stress emotions, and emotional states in general, ebb and flow, and change in quality with changing transactions with the environment (Lazarus, 1975). Such a process requires a cognitive appraisal mechanism that is constantly in flux as a result of new input. Situationism emphasizes mainly input from the environment, and of course, to be adaptive, behavior must be to some degree in tune with such input. On the other hand, while not denying the above, our perspective also implies that such input is filtered through a cognitive system with relatively stable characteristics (personality traits, if one prefers).

In addition to reappraisal as a result of feedback, there is another kind of reappraisal that can be called *defensive* (Lazarus, 1966). The individual who is threatened, say, by a given transaction, may cope with the appraised threat by denying, detaching psychologically from it (intellectualization), or whatever, thus producing a largely self-generated and self-deceptive reappraisal. In effect, that which was originally appraised as threatening is now reappraised defensively as nonthreatening, or even desirable (as in reaction-formation). But we have begun to cross the line into the topic of coping, which is our next concern.

4.2. Coping Processes

There are intuitive and empirical grounds for believing that the ways people cope with stress are even more important to overall morale, social functioning, and health/illness than the frequency and severity of episodes of stress themselves. Yet, despite widespread conviction about the great clinical and theoretical importance of coping, there exists only a spotty though growing literature on this topic. It might be useful to begin our discussion of coping by pointing up some of the inadequacies of existing thought since these suggest directions in which we must go to produce a viable psychology of coping.

4.2.1. Inadequacies of Existing Thought. First, because much of the research on coping has been done by personality psychologists interested in consistency or stability, it has typically focused on the structural factor of coping style or disposition and not on coping processes as they actually occur in life stress (cf. Cohen and Lazarus, 1973). Therefore, we have many measures of coping traits (Moos, 1974), but few that are descriptive of how the person actually handles a particular harm, threat, or challenge (Lazarus *et al.*, 1974).

At best, stability can only be a limited part of coping for a number of reasons: (1) One must be prepared for change if adaptation is to be effective; (2) Variability in the coping response makes growth possible, whereas stability implies a static, inflexible person; (3) Even when a particular coping process works reasonably well and is therefore worth keeping, there may well be other alternatives that have advantages or even a better solution than has been tried. This means that in ontogenetic coping, as in phylogenesis, it may be best to keep trying alternatives, thus increasing the variability of one's potential responses. (4) Finally, that which seems stable is not really as fixed as might be assumed, except perhaps in severe psychopathology (see Shapiro, 1965). Psychologically speaking, one's environment constantly changes because the person changes. A frequent theme of this chapter is that we have been too readily seduced into looking for stability or consistency when, from certain functional perspectives, change and flux may well be more important.*

Second, describing and measuring coping processes is by no means a simple task. Coping with a given life crisis usually involves a complex amalgam of many specific acts, behavioral, intrapsychic, preventive, and restitutive. Since the important sources of psychological stress in life are often temporally extended and changing, coping also involves sequences (or stages) and patternings of many acts and thoughts over time and across a wide range of adaptive contexts. Moreover, each of the stages and contexts shapes and constrains somewhat what can be and is done by the person. Thus, although we can concentrate on avoidance as a single act, in most life crises such as ter-

*We are indebted to Professor Shlomo Breznitz of Haifa University for pointing out to us some of these reasons.

minal illness, the process of avoidance involves a whole concatenation of thoughts and acts in many different contexts and at many different moments as the illness progresses. A person may choose to deny or avoid the thought of the terminal nature of his illness, but then face subtle or direct contrary evidence from a doctor, nurse, friend, or family member. How does an individual react to the countervailing evidence? Is the avoidance maintained and if so, how? Does the person get angry, frightened, leave the scene, become confused, refuse to listen, change the subject, misinterpret the information, and proceed to maintain the avoidance in every context? Or, is the avoidance utilized only in situations where it is well supported by the evidence and the manifest attitudes of others, or at the very least under ambiguous input, dropping it in favor of other intrapsychic devices under other circumstances? Moreover, while a person is manifestly denying some fact or its implication, simultaneously there may exist what Weisman (1972; see also Hackett and Weisman, 1964) has called "middle knowledge" in which below the surface there is a more accurate sense of what is really happening. Reliably describing and quantifying complex coping patterns over time and circumstances and identifying their determinants is a major technical challenge.

The descriptive task is made more difficult in the absence of an agreed-upon theory of coping. Although the term, coping, is widely used, only a very few systematic works have been published on the subject. These include one by Menninger (1963), a book by the senior author (Lazarus, 1966), a book edited by Coelho, Hamburg, and Adams (1974), and an important article by Haan (1969). A new work by the latter author (Haan, 1977) has just appeared that is an elaborate analysis of coping. In addition, spotty efforts have been made to study coping in stress research (e.g., Folkins, 1970; Murphy and Moriarty, 1976; Lazarus, 1975; and Weisman and Worden, 1976). The systematic study of coping processes has only just begun to burgeon. To date we have mostly anecdotal clinical observation. One reason for this is the lack of available measures of coping processes (as opposed to coping styles). Theory and taxonomy can only develop when systematic research on how people cope in a variety of stressful transactions goes hand in hand with attempts to examine theoretically the nature and correlates of coping. We are still a long way from having an analysis that both covers the ground and simultaneously provides a concrete, detailed set of descriptive categories.

Complicating this descriptive task is ambiguity about the acts that should or should not be classed as coping. Virtually everything we do has adaptive significance and the scope of the concept of coping is often allowed to become coextensive with adaptation itself. For example, Weisman and Worden (1976) define coping as "what one does about a perceived problem in order to bring about relief, reward, quiescence, or equilibrium," in short, almost identical to adaptation, though their research on coping was directed primarily to cancer patients. A few writers, like ourselves, have attempted to narrow the meaning sphere of coping by distinguishing coping from adaptation (e.g., White, 1974; Murphy, 1974). The main distinction drawn seems to be a matter of whether or not the person has a well-established or automatic response readily available (as when we step on the brake when the traffic light turns red) as opposed to being in a situation for which the adequate response is unclear, unavailable, difficult to mobilize, or its adequacy doubtful. Our own definition of coping adopts this distinction: Coping consists of efforts, both action-oriented and intrapsychic, to manage (i.e., master, tolerate, reduce, minimize) environmental and internal demands, and conflicts among them, which tax or exceed a person's resources. Reference to taxing or exceeding resources places coping within the rubric of psychological stress, thus narrowing its scope somewhat to a subset of adaptation (see also Lazarus, 1968). Nevertheless, the concept may still be excessively broad, especially at its outside margins where great ambiguity still exists, though in our view it is still workable if we strive for adequate descriptive categories at its core or center.

Third, we believe that most studies of coping have been too narrowly focused with respect to the range of activities that coping naturally encompasses. For example, we agree with White (1974) that defensive processes have been given an inordinate amount of attention at the expense of other modes. Thus, despite the fact that anticipatory stress (or threat) is one of the most common types of stressful experiences, little attention has been paid to cognitive processes involved in the anticipation of harm (exceptions include Janis, 1962; Withey, 1962; and Breznitz, 1976), to preventive coping, and to efforts to maintain already desirable conditions that are seen as endangered. And relatively little attention has been paid also to social and institutional arrangements facilitating or impairing coping (again, exceptions include Mechanic, 1974; Moos, 1973; Mitchell, 1969; Granovetter, 1973; Caplan, 1975; and others).

Fourth, the heavy preoccupation with defense mechanisms also has the effect of creating an overemphasis on failure of coping and pathology rather than on effectiveness and growth. Yet, in a review of studies of coping with the severe personal crisis of incapacitating and life-threatening illness, Hamburg and Adams (1967) noted how well such persons often do under very damaging circumstances. A few observers have emphasized that people often grow from stressful life

TABLE I
Coping Classification Scheme

Instrumental focus	Temporal orientation			
	Past–present		Future	
	Functions			
Self	1. *Altering the troubled transaction (instrumental)*	2. *Regulating the emotion (palliation)*	1. *Altering the troubled transaction (instrumental)*	2. *Regulating the emotion (palliation)*
	Coping modes			
	a. Information seeking b. Direct action c. Inhibition of action d. Intrapsychic	a. Information seeking b. Direct action c. Inhibition of action d. Intrapsychic	a. Information seeking b. Direct action c. Inhibition of action d. Intrapsychic	a. Information seeking b. Direct action c. Inhibition of action d. Intrapsychic
	Functions			
Environment	1. *Altering the troubled transaction (instrumental)*	2. *Regulating the emotion (palliation)*	1. *Altering the troubled transaction (instrumental)*	2. *Regulating the emotion (palliation)*
	Coping modes			
	a. Information seeking b. Direct action c. Inhibition of action d. Intrapsychic	a. Information seeking b. Direct action c. Inhibition of action d. Intrapsychic	a. Information seeking b. Direct action c. Inhibition of action d. Intrapsychic	a. Information seeking b. Direct action c. Inhibition of action d. Intrapsychic
	Appraisals			
	Harm		Threat or challenge; maintenance	
	Thematic character			
	Overcoming, tolerating, making restitution, reinterpreting past in present		Preventive or growth-oriented processes	

events (cf. Murphy, 1962), as well as decompensating or breaking down (Grinker and Spiegel, 1945; Menninger, 1963). Yet, existing research does not tell us much about effective and ineffective forms of coping, or the developmental conditions under which coping competencies are enhanced or damaged by stress encounters.

4.2.2. Classification of Coping. We have been attempting to deal with some of the existing gaps and inadequacies in coping theory by expanding somewhat on the simple classificatory scheme for coping earlier introduced by Lazarus (1974; 1975), and by changing the ordering of categories. For example, whereas before the main superordinate categories of coping were direct action and palliation (which included intrapsychic modes), now we have placed these and other "coping modes" under two main headings under "Functions," namely, *Altering the Troubled Transaction* (*instrumental*), and *Regulating the Emotion* (*palliation*). This is a distinction that has also been made by others (e.g., Mechanic, 1962), and which we believe is fundamental. The new scheme for coping classification, presented in Table I, also attempts to take into account several other important factors and distinctions to be described below, such as "temporal orientation," "instrumental focus," "relevant appraisals," the "thematic character" of the coping process, and "coping modes." The latter are categories for identifying the specific forms of coping utilized in any stress context.

Let us begin with *temporal orientation.* As indicated in our earlier discussion of primary appraisal, coping with past or present harm–loss usually requires different cognitions and actions than coping with future harm (threat). Such differences are reflected in the row in Table I identified as thematic character. Thus, past harm–loss must be overcome, tolerated, made restitution for, or reinterpreted in the context of the present. On the other hand, future harm (threat) requires attempts at maintaining the status quo or preventing that harm by taking action to head it off or neutralize it. The reader will notice that in the table we have juxtaposed threat and challenge under "appraisals," and preventive and growth-oriented processes under "thematic character." In doing so we are trying to be consistent with our previous position that stress in future perspective need not be dominated by harm-appraisals, but can be appraised in a positive, potential gain sense. When we accept challenges that heavily tax our resources, we are naturally exposing ourselves to potential harm, but with a positive rather than negative mental attitude, and this is precisely what happens when we are growth-oriented. When, for example, a child or adolescent in the course of development moves toward independence from a secure and nurturant parent–child relationship, risks must be taken in the interests of forward movement or growth (see also White, 1974). In any system of thought about coping and adaptation, room must be made for a distinction between threat and challenge, and between efforts at prevention of harm and those directed toward growth.

We would include the term "maintenance" under future time orientation. In the psychology of coping, emphasis is usually placed on change rather than what might be called maintenance of the status quo, though much coping activity has the function of preserving and holding on to a desirable state of affairs. In keeping with our use of the term "coping" only in the context of stress, maintenance forms of coping by definition only arise when the person senses that the status quo has been endangered; in short, a person does not make efforts to preserve or maintain the status quo unless it is threatened.

As can be seen from Table I, coping efforts can have two alternative instrumental foci: They can be directed toward the environment, or toward the self, or both, since either or both can be appraised by the individual as responsible for the troubled person–environment relationship (stress). Moreover, altering either or both could reduce or eliminate stress or make it more tolerable. If one has a noisy neighbor, one can enjoin or threaten in order to change bothersome behavior, or one can try to eliminate the nuisance by a variety of other aggressive means. On the other hand, one can try to modify oneself so as to improve the situation, by trying not to be disturbed by the noise, by enjoying or participating in it, or by leaving the premises. Much coping consists of attempting to change one's own characteristics (e.g., goals, beliefs, habits of reacting) in the face of stress. These two alternatives of changing self or environment bear an analogy of Piaget's (1952) distinction between the adaptive processes of accommodation and assimilation. In accommodation children modify their own cognitive schemata or actions to conform to the characteristics or requirements of the external object, while in assimilation the environment is modified or adapted to internal schemata and needs, as when a pencil is mouthed as a pacifier or used as a hammer. This distinction between the two foci of coping, environment and self, is applicable regardless of whether one is dealing with past–present harm–loss, or with future threat or challenge.

The functions of coping listed in Table I include two main ones, namely, whether its intended effect is to alter a stressful person–environment relationship, or to control the emotional reaction arising from that relationship. A similar distinction has been drawn between the crisis-related functions of social support in adaptation and health (Pinneau, 1976; Kaplan, Cassel, and Gove, 1973; Parsons and Bales, 1955). Some social relationships have value to the person because they provide information or services necessary for coping as, for example, when funeral arrangements are made for a bereaved friend; other social relationships in crisis mainly serve emotional needs, as in reassuring a threatened spouse (faced, say, with loss of job, failure in an examination, etc.) that the spouse is respected, loved, and appreciated whatever happens.

Much coping is directed at the instrumental or problem-solving aspects of a stressful person–environment transaction. If coping as problem-solving is ineffective, the threat will not go away or the challenge remains unmet. A danger must be avoided or protected against; a strong commitment can only be realized by taking steps to do what is necessary to attain it; if one is seriously ill, medical help may have to be sought; if one is injured, the flow of blood needs to be staunched; if someone important to one's well-being has been insulted, that person must be mollified; if one doesn't know what is wrong or what to do, information about the situation must be sought. Much of psychological development consists of gaining information and skills with which to ward off or overcome harm–loss or meet challenge so that one's life plans can be realized in the face of obstacles, dangers, and opportunities.

Efforts to regulate emotions (cf. Lazarus, 1975) are also an extremely important aspect of coping. There are three obvious reasons:

1. Stress emotions such as anxiety, fear, guilt, anger, sadness–*depression,* envy, jealousy, and so on, are painful or distressing. It is this feature of emotion that was first emphasized in tension-reduction psychodynamic theories such as those of Freud and associative-learning reinforcement theory. Their painfulness was viewed as leading to the acquisition of both "healthy" and "pathological" modes of coping (e.g., defense mechanisms).

2. Strong emotions such as anxiety often interfere with adaptive functioning by serving as a distraction or producing selective attention, thereby narrowing the normal range of cue utilization (cf. Easterbrook, 1959). From the latter standpoint, it is often useful for a person to find ways of controlling the emotion, keeping it within bounds, or reducing it where possible, not merely by mastering the impaired transaction (which may be impossible), but by directly regulating the emotional state itself.

3. Psychological stress means that the person (or animal) is in some jeopardy and must mobilize physiologically to cope in the fashion suggested in Cannon's (1963) concept of the emergency reaction or Selye's General Adaptation Syndrome (1946, 1956, 1976). A threatened, challenged or harmed person is an aroused being, which means that the *internal milieu* is disturbed unless this disturbance is short-circuited by a successful defense (cf. Lazarus and Alfert, 1964; Lazarus *et al.*, 1965). If the disturbance is both severe and prolonged or repeti-

tive, somatic illness can be a consequence (cf. Mason, 1970). One of the specific recent versions of this psychosomatic hypothesis can be found in the area of personality and cardiovascular disorder (Rosenman and Friedman, 1970).

To the extent that some or all diseases can be regarded as the price of mobilization to cope, then preservation of stability in the internal environment despite other important requirements of adaptation is essential to bodily health. It would make little sense for the person to act in the interests of psychological survival only to succumb physiologically in the process. Effective coping must strike a reasonable balance between these concerns. Disengagement from the fray from time to time may be an essential requirement for adequate adaptation, providing the opportunity for restoration and the selection of new priorities (cf. Klinger, 1975).

Several additional coping functions, not indicated in Table I, can also be considered in addition to problem-solving and palliation. We could suggest three, namely, maintaining one's options (White, 1974), tolerating or relieving affective distress (Rosenzweig, 1944), and maintaining positive morale (Kubler-Ross, 1969).

The above comments bring us to the final category of coping in Table I, namely *coping modes.* There are four: information seeking, direct action, inhibition of action, and intrapsychic modes. You will note that all four modes are included within the two main functions, the instrumental and the emotion-regulatory, and all four can deal with past–present and future, and self and environment. In effect, one may use each mode of coping either for altering a troubled person–environment relationship or for controlling the emotion, either in a past–present condition of harm or a future threat, and directed either at the self or the environment.

For example, *information seeking* has the obvious instrumental function of providing a basis for action to change the transaction, but it also may be employed to make the person feel better by making the transaction seem more under control. As noted by Janis (1968), a person may bolster a difficult decision and feel better about it by seeking only information that agrees with it and avoiding dissonant information. Similarly, the information sought may be relevant to a past trauma and be designed to help reinterpret it, or be directed at trying to read the future. Or, it may be aimed at finding out what needs to be changed in the environment, or in the self, to manage a stressful transaction.

Various forms of *direct action* are also located within the various coping factors revealed in Table I. Such action can be instrumental as in building a storm shelter to protect against tornadoes, or designed to regulate an emotion as in drinking, taking tranquilizers, or engaging in muscle relaxation or biofeedback. It can be aimed at overcoming a past harm–loss as when a grieving person becomes buried in work or seeks a new love relationship, or at a (future) threat as in the earlier illustration of building a storm shelter. Direct action can also be employed to alter oneself (e.g., stopping smoking, seeking punishment for one's sins), or to change the environment (e.g., seeking revenge against an enemy). Moreover, since in a complex social and intrapsychic world every form of direct action carries reality or moral constraints and dangers, we are also capable of *inhibition of action* to accord with environmental and intrapsychic characteristics, and an analysis could be made for inhibition that is quite similar to the one we have made for direct action.

Finally, *intrapsychic* modes of coping also fall within each of the coping factors listed in the table. Included are all cognitive processes designed to regulate the emotion by making the person feel better, in short, things a person says to himself or herself and forms of attention deployment such as avoidance. Such intrapsychic processes can also have an instrumental value as when a person tries self-reassurance to lower destructive anxiety while taking a critical examination, or they may have the function of regulating the emotion for the sole purpose of reducing pain or distress. Intrapsychic modes can be oriented to past harm–loss as in reinterpretation of a traumatic event in the present, or to a future harm as in the denial of threat. And it can be focused on self ("I am not bad, inept, ugly," or whatever), or on the environment ("There is no danger, I do not have a fatal illness, I am loved").

This list of modes or forms of coping can be further expanded if one wishes to include effective versus ineffective processes (assuming rules for this could be established), successful versus unsuccessful ones (e.g., whether or not a person really is fooled by his efforts at denial [cf. Lazarus, 1966], or whether or not avoidance of thinking about something succeeds [cf. Horowitz, 1975]), legal, illegal, or extralegal forms of coping (as in Merton's, 1949, sociological analysis of collective coping), or coping that is primitive or based on rational, flexible, mature modes of thought (Haan, 1969). We cannot say as yet which if any of these subcategories of coping will prove of value in the description and analysis of coping processes.

4.2.3. Choice of Coping. A theory of coping requires eventual specification of the conditions under which coping processes and modes are selected. We are not now prepared to do this fully, but we can suggest a few principles.

The determinants of coping are probably multiple. Some reside in the environmental context. For example, certain environmental demands strongly shape what the person must do to become extricated from a particular danger or to meet a social requirement. An example is the coal-mining disaster studied by Lucas (1969) in which a number of men were trapped following an explosion. The most obvious requirement in this situation was for the men, operating in the dark and exposed to the danger of further explosion and collapsing walls, to find a way out. After much effort, it became apparent that there was no exit, leaving only the hope that they would be found by search parties. However, this meant that they would have to conserve their water supply, which had dwindled rapidly during their frantic and protracted search for an exit. When this water was ultimately exhausted, they tried to stave off deadly thirst by drinking their urine, an exceedingly difficult and distressing task in which most succeeded.

Although these successive coping decisions were mediated by the trapped miners' secondary appraisal of the situation, including the mistaken but not unreasonable search for an exit during which the problem of water was ignored, the details of the environmental situation served as powerful determinants of the direct coping actions taken. There simply was not much room for variation in secondary appraisal, related to what had to be done, although appraisals concerning grounds for hope or despair showed considerably more variation that, in turn, undoubtedly depended on highly personal life agendas.

The point is that each stress and coping situation has its own unique features shaping the saliency and appropriateness of possible actions, though at a more abstract level of analysis they may share properties in common. When we attempt to assess coping and its effectiveness in various contexts of stress, we must learn to extract the common demands and processes and to ignore the unique details, which teach us little about coping and more about the specific environmental context. What must be done to survive in a freezing mountain environment will obviously be different from that required for survival in the tropics. However, such differences are largely trivial if we are to understand coping, psychologically speaking. Environmental details can obscure the important variations in coping process that have to do with competence, judgment, and other person variables relevant to the coping process. The environmental configuration certainly shapes what is done; however, what is probably of greater interest is that, given the same or similar environmental configurations, different individuals or groups respond in different ways, and given many different environments, we may nonetheless find certain common properties among the coping processes employed.

Individual variation in the choice of coping undoubtedly depends on a number of factors. We would like to illustrate four such factors that might influence whether a person engages in direct action, the inhibition of action, intrapsychic modes, or information seeking. These are: (1) degree of uncertainty, (2) degree of threat, (3) the presence of conflict, and (4) degree of helplessness.

1. High degree of *uncertainty* (or ambiguity) ought to decrease use of direct action and increase information seeking, failure of which should encourage intrapsychic modes of coping. There are, of course, many types of uncertainty. It has been shown experimentally that temporal uncertainty, that is, not knowing when a harmful confrontation will occur, coupled with the conviction that harm is inevitable and fairly imminent, encourages cognitive avoidance (cf. Monat *et al.*, 1972; Monat, 1976). A possible reason for this kind of effect is that when one doesn't know what is going to happen, when it will happen, and what its outcome is likely to be, there is little that can realistically be done without more accurate information. If such information is unavailable, the person is pushed toward intrapsychic processes such as denial, avoidance, intellectualization, or whatever. The alternative is to suffer or tolerate chronic, perhaps mounting anxiety during the period of anticipation.

2. When the degree of *appraised threat* mounts to severe levels, this appears to encourage increasingly desperate and primitive modes of coping, for example, rage, panic, personality disorganization, confused thinking, or defense mechanisms, even when more realistic and flexible modes of coping might help. Such primitivation of coping under increasingly severe threat has been discussed at length by Menninger (1954; 1963), and called ego-failure by Haan (1969). Folkins (1970) has experimentally shown an association between degree of stress and primitivized thought using Haan's method of evaluating the quality of cognitive coping activity.

3. *Conflict* is important because it makes a nondamaging solution impossible, since acting on behalf of one impulse, goal, or commitment requires the thwarting of the other. Under such conditions psychological stress is inevitable, but direct actions are immobilized (or they oscillate between the goals), and the person is pushed to rely on intrapsychic modes. The bodily distress must be regulated somehow and psychic distress tolerated or defended against. The concept of conflict is central to the traditional clinical emphasis on the defense mechanism in neurosis; the neurotic person is said to be unaware of the hidden agenda that blocks direct action. This view of unconscious conflict also led Dollard and Miller (1950) to characterize the neurotic's

adaptive efforts as having the appearance of stupidity to everyone but the victim, because the latter has been unable to relinquish the immobilizing self-deceptions.

4. *Helplessness* is still another potent determinant of coping mode. Harm that has already been incurred, and inevitable future harms, cannot be prevented by action but only accepted, tolerated, or reinterpreted. Direct action is predicated on the secondary appraisal that one can do something to restore a harm–loss or compensate for it, or that there is some way to prevent a threatened harm from happening (see Seligman, 1975). And when helplessness escalates to hopelessness, we approach a condition of total immobilization of action and attendant depression (cf. Beck, 1967, 1976). In passing, the concept of helplessness must also be tied in with its antithesis, the positive sense of control one can have over a transaction (see Lefcourt, 1973; Averill, 1973), and all the recent research on locus of control (see Lefcourt, 1976).

The four factors touched on above are all mediating cognitive appraisals, although the fit between appraisal and reality is usually pretty good for most persons. Nevertheless, the conditions shaping coping include not only characteristics of the objective environment, but also personality characteristics such as hidden neurotic agendas, special premises or belief systems, limitations in intelligence or experience resulting in inappropriately deployed attentional processes and mistaken inferences, etc., that affect how the individual appraises the relationship with that environment.

5. Concluding Summary

We end with the same theme with which we began, namely, that adaptation as a perspective for studying human life, and especially the specific theoretical research arenas of stress and coping, require a relational view of person and environment. To think fruitfully of stress and coping, these must be seen as a special kind of transaction between a person of a particular sort (i.e., with plans, commitments, hidden agendas, and belief systems) and an environment with its own characteristics (e.g., demands, constraints, and resources).

If we take this theme seriously, certain things follow. First, we must treat the person as an active agent of change on the environment as well as a respondent to that environment. Second, we need to give as much attention to describing transactional relationships and the processes involved in them as we do to their causal determinants. These determinants reside in the interaction of the separate sets of variables of person and environment. Third, these relationships are characterized as much by flux and change as by stability and consistency. When stress occurs, and for effective coping with it, either the person changes as emotion ebbs and flows, or the environment must change, or both. This means that it is necessary to observe stress-related transactions as they take place over time, often in sequences or stages. Fourth, we must be prepared to view stress-related transactions with the environment as mediated psychologically. From our point of view, the most important mediational process is cognitive, that is, it involves perception, thought and judgment, which transform the separate variables of person and environment into the appraisal categories of harm–loss, threat, and challenge; cognitive appraisals also direct the person toward various available coping options.

Throughout this chapter we have used our past and current research and theoretical formulations about stress and coping to illustrate the above themes and principles, and to demonstrate what we have meant by the concepts of transaction and interaction. First, we reviewed briefly our older laboratory research and offered a critique of the laboratory paradigm for studying stress and coping. We next reviewed and enlarged on our earlier formulations about cognitive appraisal processes, especially secondary appraisal, by illustrating how during the same threatening confrontation different appraisals result in differing degrees and kinds of stress reaction, and different coping processes. We also reorganized and enlarged upon our earlier schemes for classifying coping processes, and discussed some of the principles for evaluating the effectiveness of coping in the light of its multiple functions, and underlying the choice of coping.

Our purpose, however, has not only been to review and update our theoretical approach, but also to demonstrate in specific details how a cognitive–phenomenological approach to stress and coping forces on us a transactional, mediational, time-oriented, and process-oriented perspective. We are certain that only a radical change in outlook, research paradigm, and conceptual language, will allow us to escape the doldrums into which research and theory on psychodynamics and adaptation have lapsed using the research models and language of the recent past. This chapter represents a current stage of thinking in our own efforts to break with certain past perspectives and evolve a more fruitful way of thinking. Only future research will demonstrate whether or not our present outlook for viewing and studying stress-related person–environment relationships will advance us beyond the point at which we stand now in our knowledge and understanding.

ACKNOWLEDGMENT

Appreciation is expressed to several readers of earlier drafts of this paper, especially to Dr. Frances Cohen of University of California, San Francisco, for their helpful comments and critiques.

References

Allport, G.W. *Personality: A psychological interpretation*. New York: Holt, Rinehart & Winston, 1937.

Altman, I. *Environment and social behavior: Privacy, personal space, territory and crowding*. Monterey, Calif.: Brooks Cole, 1975.

Altman, I. Environmental psychology and social psychology. *Personality and Social Psychology Bulletin*, 1976, *2*, 96–113.

Appley, M.H., and Trumbull, R. *Psychological stress: Issues in research*. New York: Appleton-Century-Crofts, 1967.

Arnold, M.B. *Emotion and personality*. New York: Columbia University Press, 1960 (2 vols.).

Averill, J.R. Personality control over aversive stimuli and its relation to stress. *Psychological Bulletin*, 1973, *80*, 286–303.

Averill, J.R., Olbrich, E., and Lazarus, R.S. Personality correlates of differential responsiveness to direct and vicarious threat: A failure to replicate previous findings. *Journal of Personality and Social Psychology*, 1972, *21*, 25–29.

Baker, W.M., Sandman, C.A., and Pepinsky, H.B. Affectivity of task, rehearsal time, and physiological response. *Journal of Abnormal Psychology*, 1975, *84*, 539–544.

Beck, A.T. *Depression*. New York: Harper & Row, 1967.

Beck, A.T. *Cognitive therapy and the emotional disorders*. New York: International Universities Press, 1976.

Becker, E. *The denial of death*. New York: The Free Press, 1973.

Bennett, D.H., and Holmes, D.S. Influence of denial (situational redefinition) and projection on anxiety associated with threat to self-esteem. *Journal of Personality and Social Psychology*, 1975, *32*, 915–921.

Bishop, D.W., and Witt, P.A. Sources of behavioral variance during leisure time. *Journal of Personality and Social Psychology*, 1970, *16*, 352–360.

Breznitz, S. False alarms: Their effects on fear and adjustment. In I. Sarason and C.D. Spielberger (Eds.), *Stress and anxiety*. Vol. 3. New York: Academic Press, 1976.

Cannon, W.B. *The wisdom of the body*. New York: W.W. Norton, 1963. First published in 1932.

Caplan, G. *Organization of support systems for civilian populations*. Lecture delivered at the International Conference on Psychological Stress and Adjustment in Time of War and Peace, Tel Aviv, Israel, January 6–10, 1975.

Coelho, G.V., Hamburg, D.A., and Adams, J.E. (Eds.). *Coping and adaptation*. New York: Basic Books, 1974.

Cohen, F., and Lazarus, R.S. Active coping processes, coping dispositions, and recovery from surgery. *Psychosomatic Medicine*, 1973, *35*, 375–389.

Dohrenwend, B.S., and Dohrenwend, B.P. (Eds.). *Stressful life events: Their nature and effects*. New York: Wiley, 1974.

Dollard, J., and Miller, N.E. *Personality and psychotherapy*. New York: McGraw-Hill, 1950.

Easterbrook, J.A. The effect of emotion on cue utilization and the organization of behavior. *Psychological Review*, 1959, *66*, 183–201.

Ekehammar, B., Magnusson, D., and Ricklander, L. An interactionist approach to the study of anxiety. *Scandinavian Journal of Psychology*, 1974, *15*, 4–14.

Endler, N.S., and Hunt, J. McV. Sources of behavioral variance as measured by the S–R Inventory of Anxiousness. *Psychological Bulletin*, 1966, *65*, 336–346.

Endler, N.S., and Hunt, J. McV. Inventories of hostility and comparisons of the proportion of variance from persons, responses, and situations for hostility and anxiousness. *Journal of Personality and Social Psychology*, 1968, *9*, 309–315.

Endler, N.S., Hunt, J. McV., and Rosenstein, A.J. An S–R Inventory of Anxiousness. *Psychological Monographs*, 1962, *76* (No. 17), 1–33.

Endler, N.S., and Magnusson, D. (Eds.). *Interactional psychology and personality*. New York: Wiley, 1976.

Folkins, C.H. Temporal factors and the cognitive mediators of stress reaction. *Journal of Personality and Social Psychology*, 1970, *14*, 173–184.

Folkins, C.H., Lawson, K.D., and Opton, E.M., Jr. Desensitization and the experimental reduction of threat. *Journal of Abnormal Psychology*, 1968, *73*, 100–113.

Geen, R.G., Stonner, D., and Kelley, D.R. Aggression anxiety and cognitive appraisal of aggression-threat stimuli. *Journal of Personality and Social Psychology*, 1974, *29*, 196–200.

Glass, D.C., & Singer, J.E. *Urban stress*. New York: Academic Press, 1972.

Glickstein, M., Chevalier, J.A., Korchin, S.J., Basowitz, H., Sabshin, M., Hamburg, D.A., and Grinker, R.R. Temporal heart rate patterns in anxious patients. *AMA Archives of Neurology and Psychiatry*, 1957, *78*, 101–106.

Goldstein, M.J. Individual differences in response to stress. *American Journal of Community Psychology*, 1973, *1*, 113–137.

Granovetter, M.S. The strength of weak ties. *American Journal of Sociology*, 1973, *78*, 1360–1380.

Grinker, R R., & Spiegel, J.P. *Men under stress*. New York: McGraw-Hill, 1945.

Haan, N.A tripartite model of ego functioning values and clinical research applications. *Journal of Nervous and Mental Disease*, 1969, *148*, 14–30.

Haan, N. *Coping and defending: Processes of self-environment organization*. New York: Academic Press, 1977.

Hackett, T.P., and Weisman, A.D. Reactions to the imminence of death. In G.H. Grosser, H. Wechsler, and M. Greenblatt (Eds.), *The threat of impending disaster*. Cambridge, Mass.: The MIT Press, 1964, pp. 300–311.

Hamburg, D.A., and Adams, J.E. A perspective on coping: Seeking and utilizing information in major transitions. *Archives of General Psychiatry*, 1967, *17*, 277–284.

Hamburg, D.A., Hamburg, B., and DeGoza, S. Adaptive problems and mechanisms in severely burned patients. *Psychiatry*, 1953, *16*, 1–20.

Holmes, D.S., and Houston, B.K. Effectiveness of situational redefinition and affective isolation in coping with stress. *Journal of Personality and Social Psychology*, 1974, *29*, 212–218.

Holmes, T.H., and Masuda, M. Life change and illness susceptibility. In B.S. Dohrenwend and B.P. Dohrenwend (Eds.), *Stressful life events: Their nature and effects*. New York: Wiley, 1974, pp. 45–72.

Horowitz, M. Intrusive and repetitive thoughts after experimental stress. *Archives of General Psychiatry*, 1975, *32*, 1457–1463.

Janis, I.L. Psychological effects of warnings. In G.W. Baker and D.W. Chapman (Eds.), *Man and society in disaster*. New York: Basic Books, 1962, pp. 55–92.

Janis, I.L. Stages in the decision-making process. In R. Abelson, E. Aronson, (Eds.), *Theories of cognitive consistency: A sourcebook*. Chicago: Rand McNally, 1968, pp. 577–588.

Janis, I.L. Vigilance and decision making in personal crises. In G.V. Coehlo, D.A. Hamburg, and J.E. Adams (Eds.), *Coping and adaptation*. New York: Basic Books, 1974, pp. 139–175.

Kagan, A., and Levi, L. Adaptation of the psychosocial environment to man's abilities and needs. In L. Levi (Ed.), *Society, stress and disease*. Vol. 1. London: Oxford University Press, 1971, pp. 399–404.

Kaplan, A. *The conduct of inquiry*. San Francisco: Chandler, 1964.

Kaplan, B.H., Cassel, J.C., and Gore, S. *Social support and health*. Paper presented at American Public Health Association Meetings, San Francisco, November 9, 1973.

Klausner, S.Z. *On man in his environment*. San Francisco: Jossey-Bass, 1971.

Klinger, E. Consequences of commitment to and disengagement from incentives. *Psychological Review*, 1975, *82*, 1–25.

Koriat, A., Melkman, R., Averill, J.R., and Lazarus, R.S. The self-control of emotional reactions to a stressful film. *Journal of Personality*, 1972, *21*, 25–29.

Kubler-Ross, E. *On death and dying*. New York: Macmillan, 1969.

Lazarus, R.S. *Psychological stress and the coping process*. New York: McGraw-Hill, 1966.

Lazarus, R.S. Cognitive and personality factors underlying threat and coping. In M.H. Appley and R. Trumbull (Eds.), *Psychological stress: Issues and research*. New York: Appleton-Century-Crofts, 1967.

Lazarus, R.S. Emotions and adaptation: Conceptual and empirical relations. In W.J. Arnold (Ed.), *Nebraska symposium on motivation*. Lincoln: University of Nebraska Press, 1968.

Lazarus, R.S. *Personality*. 2nd Ed. Englewood Cliffs, N.J.: Prentice-Hall, 1971a (paperback).

Lazarus, R.S. The concepts of stress and disease. In L. Levi (Ed.), *Society, stress and disease*. Vol. 1. London: Oxford University Press, 1971b, pp. 53–58.

Lazarus, R.S. The self-regulation of emotions. In L. Levi (Ed.), *Emotions—Their parameters and measurement*. New York: Raven Press, 1975, pp. 47–67.

Lazarus, R.S., and Alfert, E. The short-circuiting of threat. *Journal of Abnormal and Social Psychology*, 1964, *69*, 195–205.

Lazarus, R.S., and Averill, J.R. Emotion and cognition: With special reference to anxiety. In C.D. Spielberger (Ed.), *Anxiety: Current trends in theory and research*. Vol. II. New York: Academic Press, 1972, p. 242.

Lazarus, R.S., Averill, J.R., and Opton, E.M., Jr. Toward a cognitive theory of emotion. In M. Arnold (Ed.), *Feelings and emotions*. New York: Academic Press, 1970, p. 207.

Lazarus, R.S., Averill, J.R., and Opton, E.M., Jr. The psychology of coping: Issues of research and assessment. In G.V. Coelho, D.A. Hamburg, and J.F. Adams (Eds.), *Coping and adaptation*. New York: Basic Books, 1974, pp. 249–315.

Lazarus, R.S., and Cohen, J.B. The study of stress and coping in aging. Paper given at the 5th WHO Conference on Society, Stress and Disease: Aging and old age. Stockholm, Sweden, June 14–19, 1976, L. Levi, Chairman.

Lazarus, R.S., and Cohen, J.B. Environmental stress. In I. Altman and J.F. Wohlwill (Eds.), *Human behavior and the environment: Current theory and research*. New York: Plenum, 1978.

Lazarus, R.S., Opton, E.M., Nomikos, M.S., and Rankin, N.O. The principle of short-circuiting of threat: Further evidence. *Journal of Personality*, 1965, *33*, 622–635.

Lazarus, R.S., Speisman, J.C., Mordkoff, A.M., and Davison, L.A. A laboratory study of psychological stress produced by a motion picture film. *Psychological Monographs*, 1962, *76* (34, Whole No. 553).

Lefcourt, H.M. The function of the illusions of control and freedom. *American Psychologist*, 1973, *28*, 417–425.

Lefcourt, H.M. *Locus of control: Current trends in theory and research*. New York: Halstead Press, 1976.

Lehrman, D.S. The reproductive behavior of ring doves. *Scientific American*, 1964, *211*, 48–54.

Liberty, P.G., Burnstein, E., and Moulton, R.W. Concern with mastery and occupational attraction. *Journal of Personality*, 1966, *34*, 105–117.

Lindemann, E. Symptomatology and management of acute grief. *American Journal of Psychiatry*, 1944, *101*, 141–148.

Luborsky, L., Docherty, J.P., and Penick, S. Onset conditions for psychosomatic symptoms: A comparative review of immediate observation with retrospective research. *Psychosomatic Medicine*, 1973, *35*, 187–204.

Lucas, R.A. *Men in crisis*. New York: Basic Books, 1969.

Mandler, G. *Mind and emotion*. New York: Wiley, 1975.

Mason, J.W. Strategy in psychosomatic research. *Psychosomatic Medicine*, 1970, *32*, 427–439.

Mason, J.W. Specificity in the organization of neuroendocrine response profiles. In P. Seeman and G.M. Brown (Eds.), *Frontiers in neurology and neuroscience research*. First International Symposium of the Neuroscience Institute, University of Toronto, 1974.

Mason, J.W. A historical view of the stress field, Part I. *Journal of Human Stress*, 1975, *1*(1), 6–12.

Mechanic, D. *Students under stress*. New York: The Free Press, 1962.

Menninger, K. Regulatory devices of the ego under major stress. *International Journal of Psychoanalysis*, 1954, *35*, 412–420.

Menninger, K., with Mayman, M., and Pruyser, P. *The vital balance*. New York: Viking Press, 1963.

Merbaum, M., and Hefez, A. Some personality characteristics of soldiers exposed to extreme war stress. *Journal of Consulting and Clinical Psychology*, 1976, *44*, 1–6.

Merton, R.K. *Social theory and social structure*. New York: The Free Press, 1949.

Mischel, W. *Personality and assessment*. New York: Wiley, 1968.

Mitchell, J.C. (ed.). *Social networks in urban situations*. Manchester, England: Manchester University Press, 1969.

Monat, A. Temporal uncertainty, anticipation time, and cognitive coping under threat. *Journal of Human Stress*, 1976, *2*, 32–43.

Monat, A., Averill, J.R., and Lazarus, R.S. Anticipatory stress and coping reactions under various conditions of uncertainty. *Journal of Personality and Social Psychology*, 1972, *24*, 237–253.

Moos, R.H. Conceptualizations of human environments. *American Psychologist*, 1973, *28*, 652–665.

Moos, R.H. Psychological techniques in the assessment of adaptive behavior. In G.V. Coelho, D.A. Hamburg, and J.E. Adams (Eds.), *Coping and adaptation*. New York: Basic Books, 1974, pp. 334–399.

Murphy, G. *Personality*. New York: Harper & Row, 1947.

Murphy, L.B. Coping, vulnerability and resilience in childhood. In C.V. Coelho, D.A. Hamburg, and J.E. Adams (Eds.), *Coping and adaptation*. New York: Basic Books, 1974, pp. 69–100.

Murphy, L.B., and Moriarty, A.E. *Vulnerability, coping, and growth*. New Haven: Yale University Press, 1976.

Murphy, Lois, and Associates. *The widening world of childhood: Paths toward mastery*. New York: Basic Books, 1962.

Nelson, E.A., Gridder, R.F., and Mutterer, M.L. Sources of variance in behavioral measures of honesty in temptation situations: Methodological analyses. *Developmental Psychology*, 1969, *1*, 265–279.

Neufeld, R.W.J. The effect of experimentally altered cognitive appraisal on pain tolerance. *Psychonomic Science*, 1970, *20*, 106–107.

Neufeld, R.W.J., and Davidson, P.O. The effects of vicarious and cognitive rehearsal on pain tolerance. *Journal of Psychosomatic Research*, 1971, *15*, 329–335.

Neufeld, R.W.J. Effect of cognitive appraisal on *d′* and response bias to experimental stress. *Journal of Personality and Social Psychology*, 1975, *31*, 735–743.

Neufeld, R.W.J. Evidence of stress as a function of experimentally altered appraisal of stimulus aversiveness and coping adequacy. *Journal of Personality and Social Psychology*, 1976, *33*, 632–646.

Nomikos, M.S., Opton, E.M., Jr., Averill, J.R., and Lazarus, R.S. Surprise versus suspense in the production of stress reaction. *Journal of Personality and Social Psychology*, 1968, *8*, 204–208.

Opton, E.M., Jr., and Lazarus, R.S. Personality determinants of psychophysiological response to stress: A theoretical analysis and an experiment. *Journal of Personality and Social Psychology*, 1967, *6*, 291–303.

Orne, M.T. On the social psychology of the psychological experiment: With particular reference to demand characteristics and adrenocortical functioning. *American Psychologist*, 1962, *17*, 776–783.

Overton, W.F., and Reese, H.W. Models of development: Methodological implications. In J.R. Nesselroade and H.W. Reese (Eds.), *Life span developmental psychology: Methodological issues*. New York: Academic Press, 1973.

Parsons, T., and Bales, R.F. *The family: Socialization and interaction process*. Glencoe, Ill.: The Free Press, 1955.

Pervin, L.A. Theoretical approaches to the analysis of individual–environment interaction. This volume.

Piaget, J. *The origins of intelligence in chilren*. New York: International Universities Press, 1952.

Pinneau, S.R., Jr. *Effects of social support on occupational stresses and strains*. Paper delivered at American Psychological Association Convention, Washington, D.C., September, 1976.

Rahe, R.H. The pathway between subjects' recent life changes and their near-future illness reports: Representative results and methodological issues. In B.S. Dohrenwend and B.P. Dohrenwend (Eds.), *Stressful life events: Their nature and effects*. New York: Wiley, 1974, pp. 73–86.

Rogers, R.W., and Mewborn, C.R. Fear appeals and attitude change: Effects of a threat's noxiousness, probability of occurrence, and the efficacy of coping responses. *Journal of Personality and Social Psychology*, 1976, *34*, 54–61.

Rosenman, R.H., Friedman, M. Coronary heart disease in the Western Collaborative group study: A follow-up experience of 4½ years. *Journal of Chronic Disease*, 1970, *231*, 173–190.

Rosenthal, R. *Experimenter effects in behavioral research*. New York: Appleton-Century-Crofts, 1966.

Rosenzweig, S. An outlne of frustration theory. In J. McV. Hunt (Ed.), *Personality and the behavior disorders*. New York: Ronald, 1944.

Runyan, W.Mc. *The life course as a theoretical orientation: Sequences of person X situation intraction*. Unpublished paper.

Sanchez-Craig, M., and Walker, K. Teaching alcoholics how to think defensively: A cognitive approach for the treatment of alcohol abuse. Addiction Research Foundation, Toronto, Canada, 1974.

Scott, R., and Howard, A. Models of stress. In S. Levine and N.A. Scotch (Eds.), *Social stress*. Chicago: Aldine, 1970, pp. 259–278.

Seligman, M.E. P. *Helplessness: On depression, development and death*. San Francisco: W.H. Freeman, 1975.

Selye, H. The general adaptation syndrome and disease of adaptation. *Journal of Clinical Endocrinology*, 1946, *6*, 117–230.

Selye, H. *The stress of life*. New York: McGraw-Hill, 1956.

Selye, H. *Stress without distress*. Philadelphia: Lippincott, 1974.

Selye, H. *The stress of life*. (Rev. ed.) New York: McGraw-Hill, 1976.

Shapiro, D. *Neurotic styles*. New York: Basic Books, 1965.

Shean, G., Faia, C., and Schmaltz, E. Cognitive appraisal of stress and schizophrenic subtype. *Journal of Abnormal Psychology*, 1974, *83*, 523–528.

Shiomi, K. The roles of anticipation and defense mechanism in experimentally induced anxiety. *Psychologia*, 1974, *27*, 150–158.

Sims, J.H., and Baumann, D.D. The tornado threat: Coping styles of the North and South. *Science*, 1972, *176*, 1386–1392.

Speisman, J.C., Lazarus, R.S., Mordkoff, A.M., and Davison, L.A. The experimental reduction of stress based on ego-defense theory. *Journal of Abnormal and Social Psychology*, 1964, *68*, 367–380.

Spielberger, C.D. Anxiety as an emotion state. In C.D. Spielberger (Ed.), *Anxiety: Current trends in theory and research*. Vol. 1. New York: Academic Press, 1972, pp. 23–49.

Stokols, D.A typology of crowding experiences. In A. Baum and Y. Epstein (Eds.), *Human response to crowding*. Hillsdale, N.J.: Lawrence Erlbaum Associates, 1976.

Visotsky, H.M., Hamburg, D.A., Gross, M.E., and Lebovits, B.Z. Coping behavior under extreme stress. *Archives of General Psychiatry*, 1961, *5*, 423–448.

Vogel, W., Raymond, S., and Lazarus, R.S. Intrinsic motivation and psychological stress. *Journal of Abnormal and Social Psychology*, 1959, *58*, 225–233.

Weisman, A.D. *On dying and denying*. New York: Behavioral Publications, 1972.

Weisman, A.D., and Worden, J.W. The existential plight in cancer: Significance of the first 100 days. *International Journal of Psychiatry in Medicine*, 1976, *7*, 1–15.

White, R. Strategies of adaptation: An attempt at systematic description. In G.V. Coelho, D.A. Hamburg, and J.E. Adams (Eds.), *Coping and adaptation*. New York: Basic Books, 1974, pp. 47–68.

White, R.W. Motivation reconsidered: The concept of competence. *Psychological Review*, 1959, *66*, 297–333.

Withey, S.B. Reactions to uncertain threat. In G.W. Baker and D.W. Chapman (Eds.), *Man and society in disaster*. New York: Basic Books, 1962, pp. 93–123.

Index

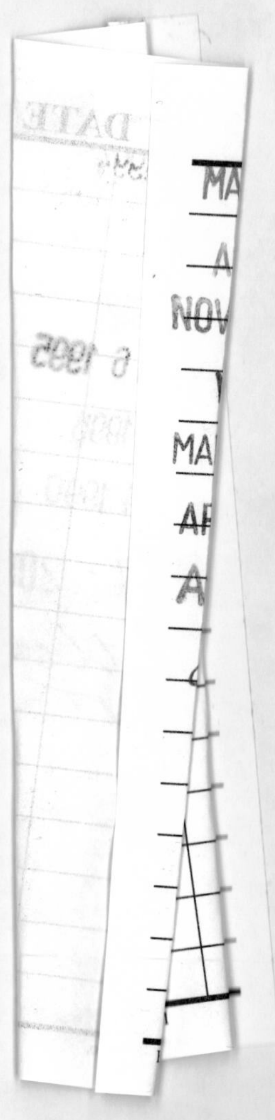